I0818975

ALL OF ME IS ILLUSTRATED

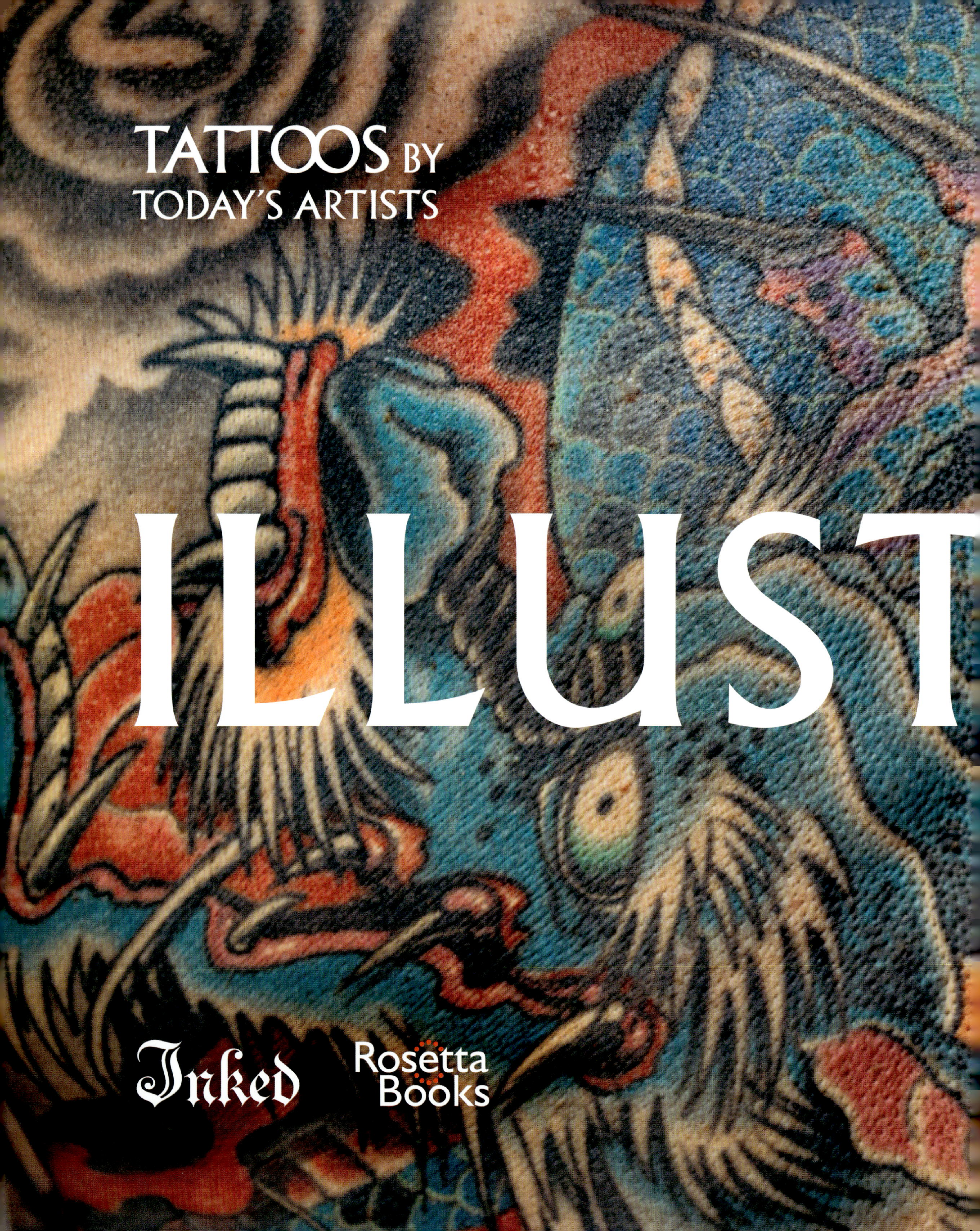
TATTOOS BY
TODAY'S ARTISTS
ILLUST
Inked
Rosetta
Books

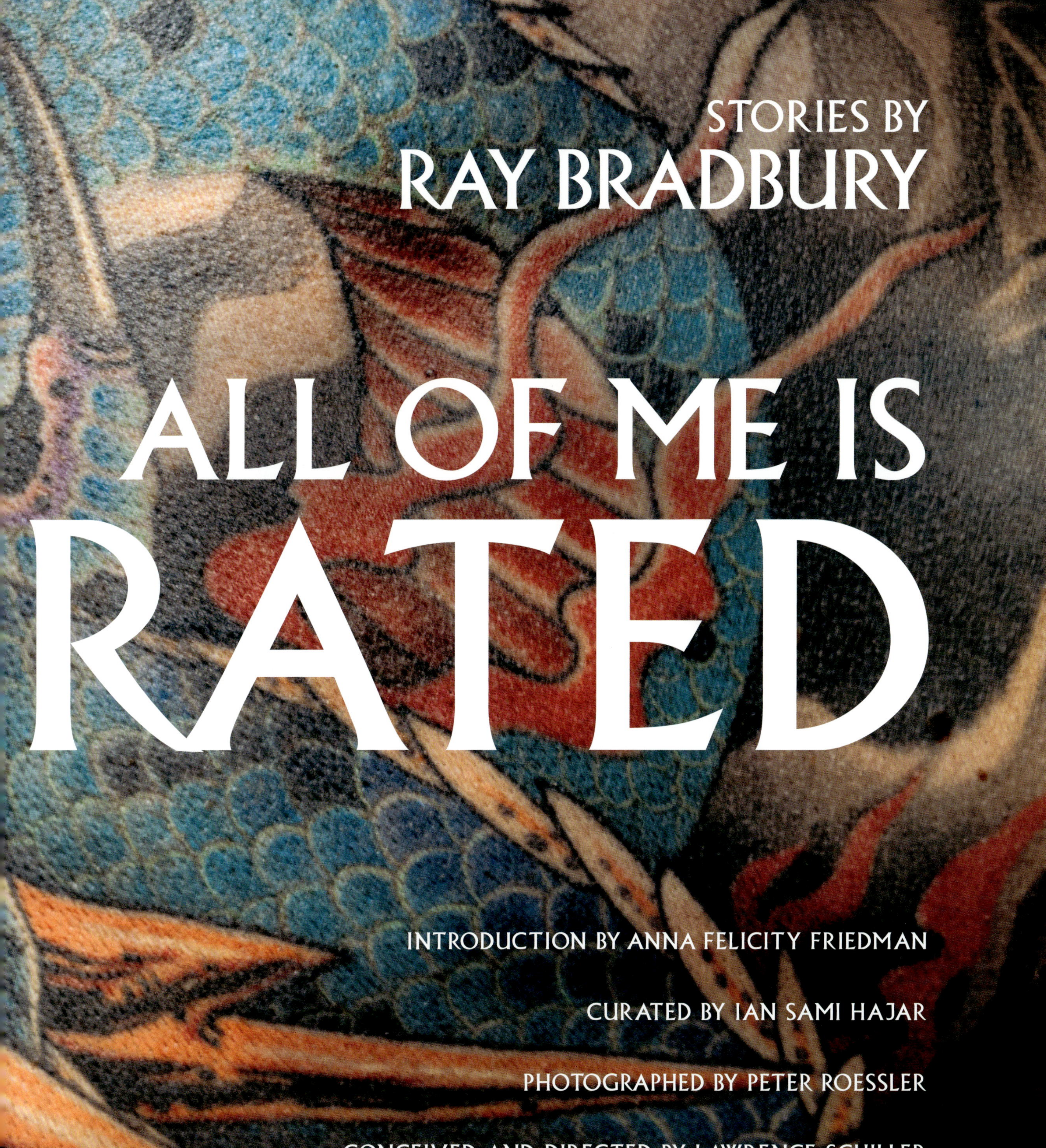
STORIES BY
RAY BRADBURY
ALL OF ME IS
RATED
INTRODUCTION BY ANNA FELICITY FRIEDMAN
CURATED BY IAN SAMI HAJAR
PHOTOGRAPHED BY PETER ROESSLER
CONCEIVED AND DIRECTED BY LAWRENCE SCHILLER

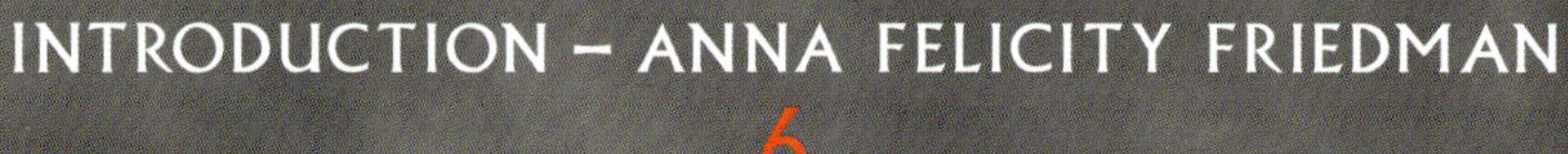

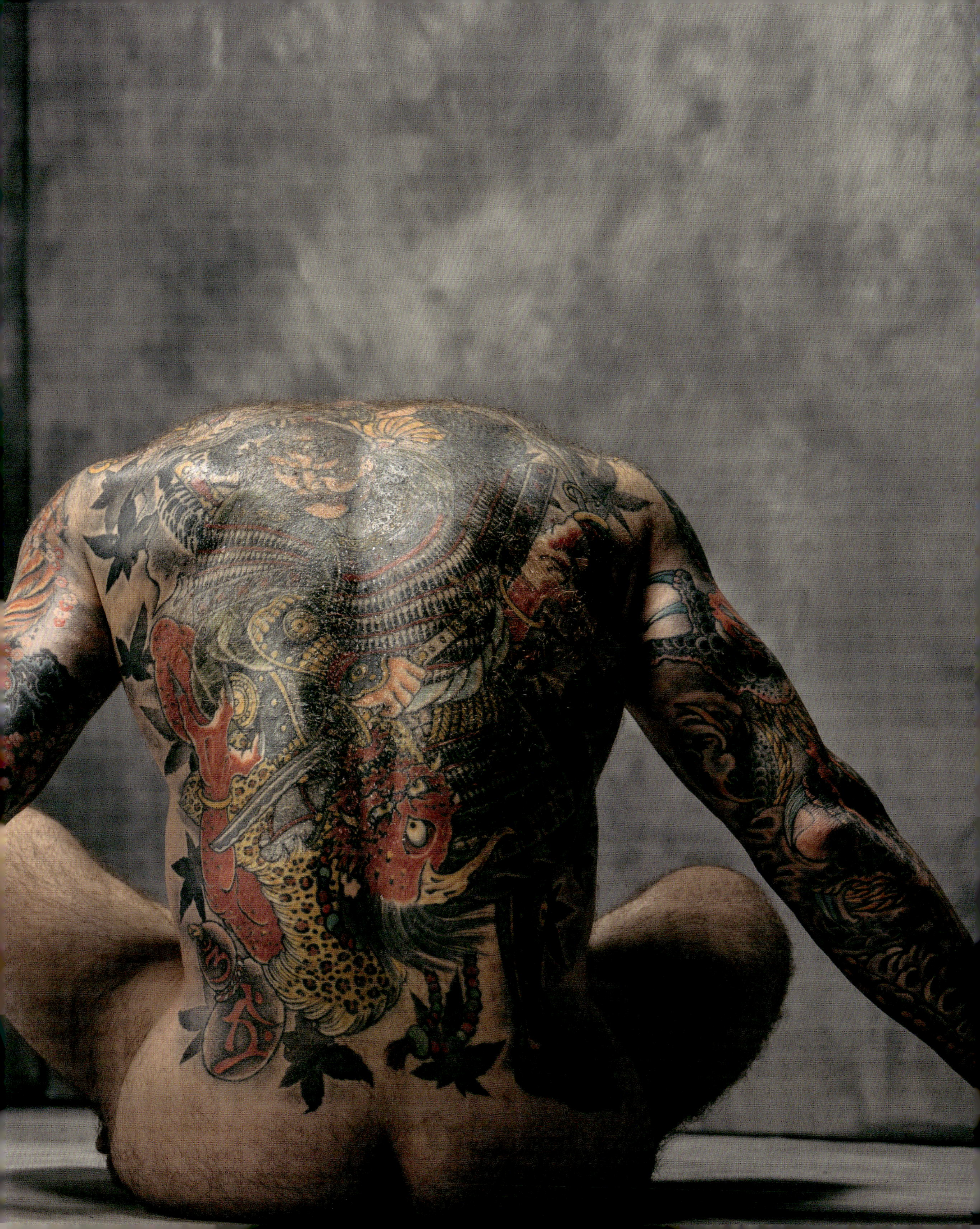

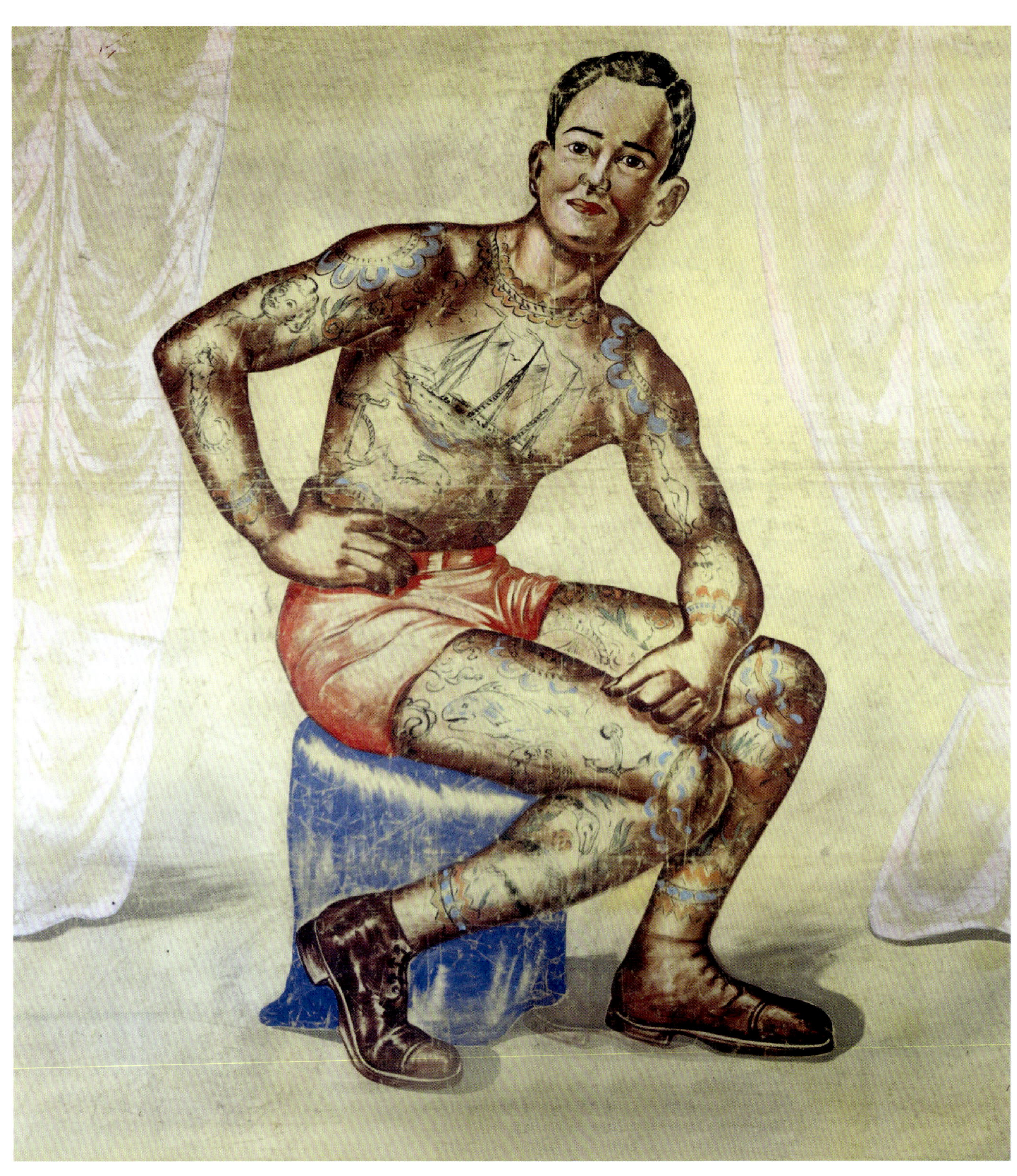

A sideshow banner from the 1920s–30s represents what Ray Bradbury
might have seen when he encountered his first Illustrated Man.

ANNA FELICITY FRIEDMAN

INTRODUCTION

It was a rainy, summer day in the late 1980s, long before smart phones kept us incessantly occupied, when I climbed three flights of stairs to a little-used attic room in the rambling house in which I grew up. This room, paneled floor to ceiling with cozy, pine beadboard, was a catchall of sorts. Among the odds and ends cluttering the floor, usually forgotten bookshelves filled with dusty old paperbacks beckoned me. Bored, and looking for something in which to immerse my mind, I scanned the shelves for a new read.

As a bookwormy teen, I had previously found some gems among overly erudite tomes and stodgy classics: racy novels, thought-provoking poetry, formative philosophy, and on this day... Ray Bradbury's collection of short stories *The Illustrated Man*. I was into punk and weirdness, but tattoos were still unusual when I was in high school. My friends and I would read to tatters copies of the only widely circulated tattoo magazines in production then, *Outlaw Biker Tattoo Revue* and *Tattoo*, which we could only find in the city — not our sleepy suburban bedroom community. In those magazines, I saw a vision of my future heavily tattooed self, permanently positioned on the fringes of society through my bodily adornments. But a magazine can take the imagination only so far. Bradbury's frame story, "The Illustrated Man," offered me a mesmerizing character to ponder. What stories might my future tattoos tell to others?

Tattoos and perceptions of them have transformed enormously from 1950–51. *Esquire* first published Bradbury's short story in July 1950, after which the author used the character again as a frame device for the prologue and epilogue to *The Illustrated Man* collection. Tattooing was mired in a dark time in its history then, perhaps at its lowest point of popularity in modern times. The heyday of the circus sideshow had passed, tattooing was mainly relegated to skid-row areas and the vicinity of military bases, and, aside from macho characters like the soon-to-be-conceived Marlboro Man, tattoos were not for everyday people. By the 1950s, tattooed men held little appeal — especially compared to tattooed ladies — and Bradbury masterfully captured the pathos of being a washed-up tattoo performer, despite still being an extraordinary work of art, in his portrayal of Mr. William Philippus Phelps.

Earlier, in the 1930s, when Bradbury first encountered circus and sideshow performers, tattoos were special. Tattooed attractions, particularly women, enjoyed celebrity. Roaring '20s adventure stories, mysteries, and romance novels with tattooed characters, like Howard Pease's *The Tattooed Man*, which first appeared in 1926 and which Bradbury is known to have read, enjoyed widespread popularity. Albert Parry, author of *Tattoo: Secrets of a Strange Art* (one of the few book-length investigations of tattooing in the early to mid-20th century), estimated that at the time of publication in 1933, there were approximately three hundred "completely tattooed men and women in this country, making, or trying to make, a living by exhibiting themselves." This desire to be a star, countered by how fleeting such fame could be, manifests in Bradbury's short story "The Illustrated Woman" where he unfolds the rationale behind Emma Fleet's tattoo distress — that her husband's love for her will wane if she can't grow more canvas.

While there have always been heavily tattooed men and women, in the pages of this book you will see how far extensive tattooing has evolved in the present day. "Windows looking in upon fiery reality," as Bradbury writes in the prologue, tattoos can communicate compelling narrative, evoke strong emotion, conjure fantasy, or just dazzle with aesthetic wonder. In the 21st century, tattoos may finally have carved themselves a solid niche in human expression that might withstand the ebbs and flows of historical opinion. To read Bradbury's three tattooed-person tales embedded within this glorious parade of contemporary inked bodies breathes new life into his notions about how tattoo meanings can change, how the viewer of a tattoo can see something different from what the owner might have intended, and how psychology intersects with the desire to permanently inscribe one's skin.

I crept back down the stairs, fantasizing about the embellishments I wanted to get. Tattoos were illegal in my home state of Massachusetts, necessitating travel to neighboring New Hampshire to the biker shops that did brisk business serving out-of-towners on weekends. I couldn't wait until I met the age minimum of eighteen to become permanently marked as an outsider, as a creative soul, as an iconoclast. Shortly after that first tattoo pilgrimage, before my twenty-first birthday, I became one of only a few hundred women in America with full tattooed sleeves. Little did I know that only a decade later I'd be trendy, an early adopter of large-scale tattoos that would overtake mainstream culture as a coveted accessory, a mark of prestige, a desired vogue. If I could travel back in time, I might choose different tattoos, given what is possible today. Yet gazing at weathered, inked skin — witness to pain, delight, and everything in between — offers comfort.

Will the future hold Bradbury-esque tattoos that can transform at the whim of their owners? A wistful day might offer a window into nostalgia, a challenging stretch could summon visual armor, a joyful time would explode into vibrant ornamentation…

Pages 10–11: Tattoo artists Jon Mesa (left) and Alisha Gory (right) wear illustrations that together represent the work of more than thirty artists. Mesa's front was tattooed by Seth Wood, and Gory's back was done by Jon Sultana and Zac Scheinbaum.

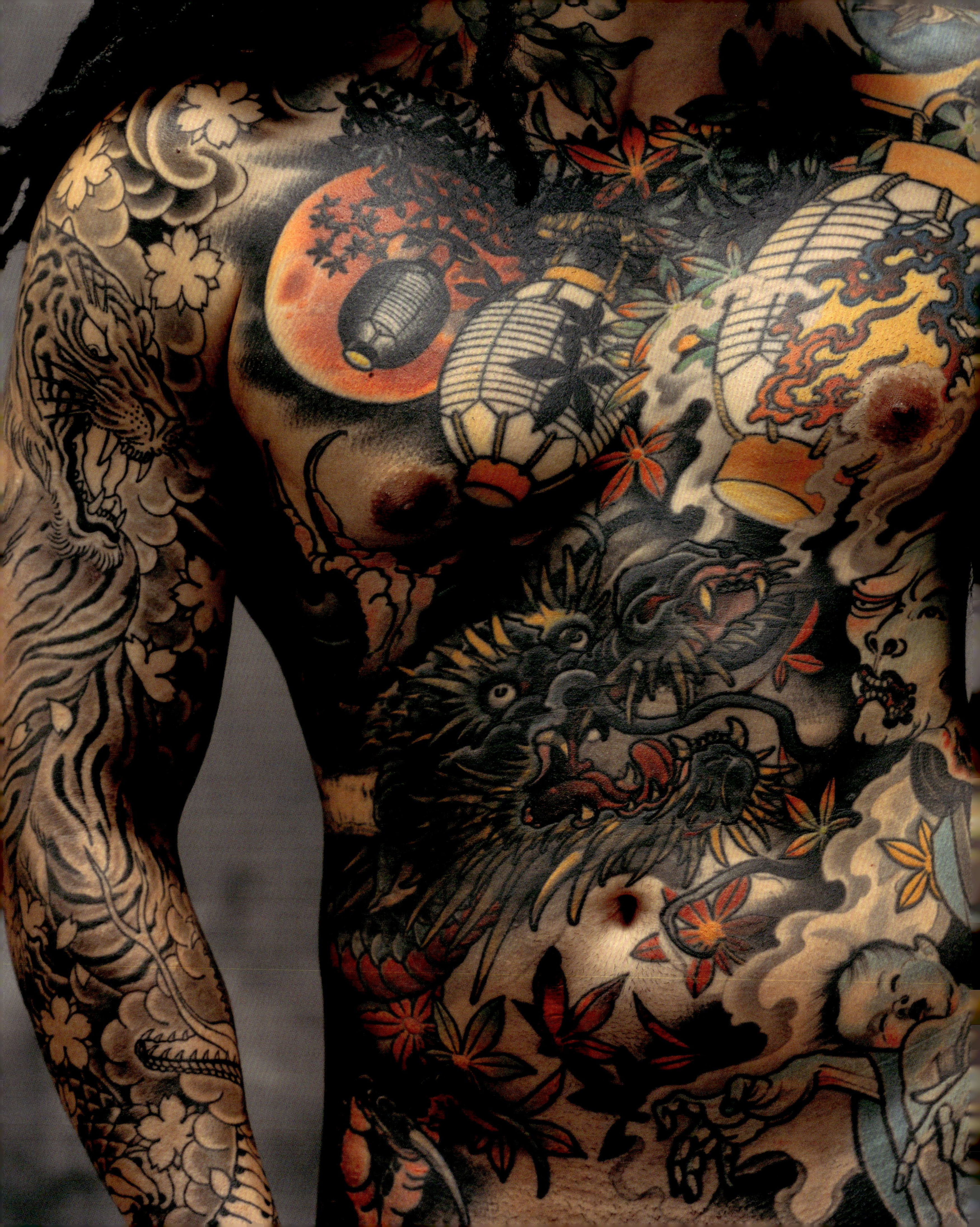

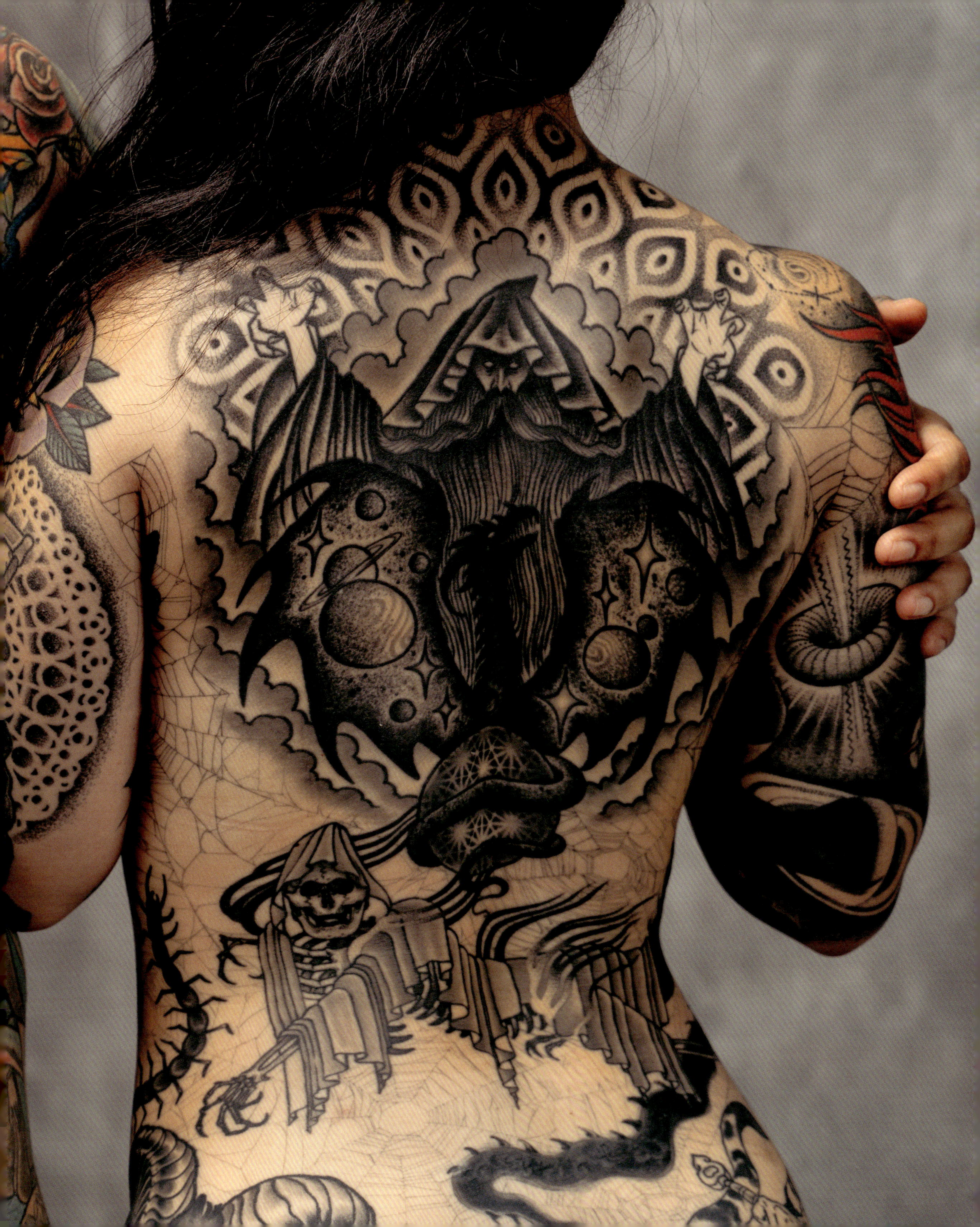

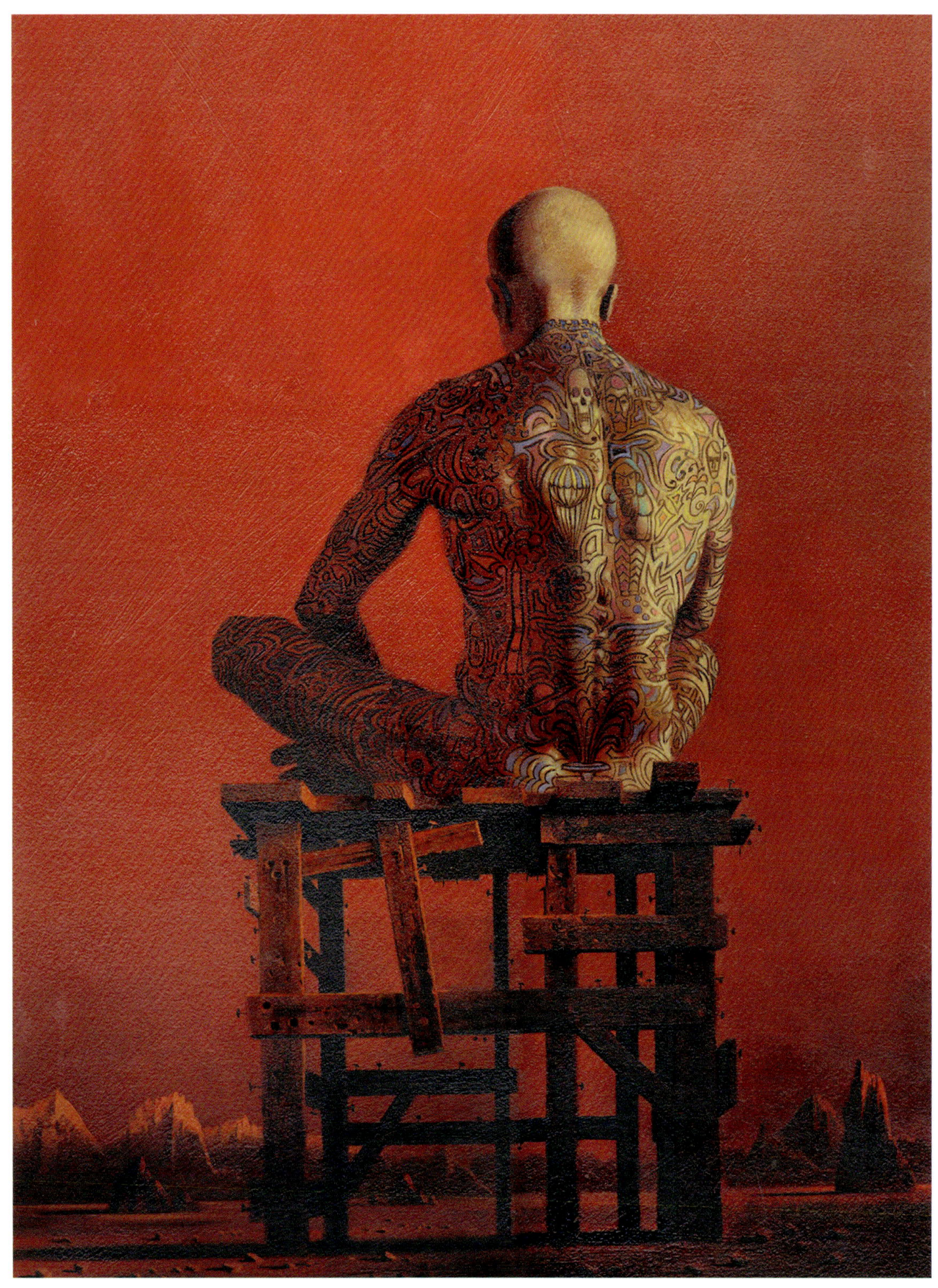

Dean Ellis' cover illustration for the first paperback edition of *The Illustrated Man.*

PROLOGUE

It was a warm afternoon in early September when I first met the Illustrated Man. Walking along an asphalt road, I was on the final leg of a two weeks' walking tour of Wisconsin. Late in the afternoon I stopped, ate some pork, beans, and a doughnut, and was preparing to stretch out and read when the Illustrated Man walked over the hill and stood for a moment against the sky.

I didn't know he was Illustrated then. I only knew that he was tall, once well muscled, but now, for some reason, going to fat. I recall that his arms were long, and the hands thick, but that his face was like a child's, set upon a massive body.

He seemed only to sense my presence, for he didn't look directly at me when he spoke his first words:

"Do you know where I can find a job?"

"I'm afraid not," I said.

"I haven't had a job that's lasted in forty years," he said.

Though it was a hot late afternoon, he wore his wool shirt buttoned tight about his neck. His sleeves were rolled and buttoned down over his thick wrists. Perspiration was streaming from his face, yet he made no move to open his shirt.

"Well," he said at last, "this is as good a place as any to spend the night. Do you mind company?"

"I have some extra food you'd be welcome to," I said.

He sat down heavily, grunting.

"You'll be sorry you asked me to stay," he said. "Everyone always is. That's why I'm walking. Here it is, early September, the cream of the Labor Day carnival season. I should be making money hand over fist at any small town sideshow celebration, but here I am with no prospects."

He took off an immense shoe and peered at it closely. "I usually keep a job about ten days. Then something happens and they fire me. By now every carnival in America won't touch me with a ten-foot pole."

"What seems to be the trouble?" I asked. For answer, he unbuttoned his tight collar, slowly. With his eyes shut, he put a slow hand to the task of unbuttoning his shirt all the way down. He slipped his fingers in to feel his chest.

"Funny," he said, eyes still shut. "You can't feel them but they're there. I always hope that someday I'll look and they'll be gone. I walk in the sun for hours on the hottest days, baking, and hope that my sweat'll wash them off, the sun'll cook them off, but at sundown they're still there."

He turned his head slightly toward me and exposed his chest. "Are they still there now?"

After a long while I exhaled. "Yes," I said. "They're still there."

The Illustrations.

"Another reason I keep my collar buttoned up," he said, opening his eyes, "is the children. They follow me along country roads. Everyone wants to see the pictures, and yet nobody wants to see them."

He took his shirt off and wadded it in his hands. He was covered with Illustrations from the blue tattooed ring about his neck to his belt line.

"It keeps right on going," he said, guessing my thought. "All of me is Illustrated. Look." He opened his hand. On his palm was a rose, freshly cut, with drops of crystal water among the soft pink petals. I put my hand out to touch it, but it was only an Illustration.

As for the rest of him, I cannot say how I sat and stared, for he was a riot of rockets and fountains and people, in such intricate detail and color that you could hear the voices murmuring small and muted, from the crowds that inhabited his body. When his flesh twitched, the tiny mouths flickered, the tiny green-and-gold eyes winked, the tiny pink hands gestured. There were yellow meadows and blue rivers and mountains and stars and suns and planets spread in a Milky Way across his chest. The people themselves were in twenty or more odd groups upon his arms, shoulders, back, sides, and wrists, as well as on the flat of his stomach. You found them in forests of hair, lurking among a constellation of freckles, or peering from armpit caverns, diamond eyes aglitter. Each seemed intent upon his own activity; each was a separate gallery portrait.

"Why, they're beautiful!" I said.

How can I explain about his Illustrations? If El Greco had painted miniatures in his prime, no bigger than your hand, infinitely detailed, with all his sulphurous color, elongation, and anatomy, perhaps he might have used this man's body for his art. The colors burned in three dimensions. They were windows looking in upon fiery reality. Here, gathered on one wall, were all the finest scenes in the universe; the man was a walking treasure gallery. This wasn't the work of a cheap carnival tattoo man with three colors and whisky on his breath. This was the accomplishment of a living genius, vibrant, clear, and beautiful.

"Oh yes," said the Illustrated Man. "I'm so proud of my Illustrations that I'd like to burn them off. I've tried sandpaper, acid, a knife…"

The sun was setting. The moon was already up in the East.

"For, you see," said the Illustrated Man, "these Illustrations predict the future."

I said nothing.

"It's all right in sunlight," he went on. "I could keep a carnival day job. But at night—the pictures move. The pictures change."

I must have smiled. "How long have you been Illustrated?"

"In 1900, when I was twenty years old and working a carnival, I broke my leg. It laid me up; I had to do something to keep my hand in, so I decided to get tattooed."

"But who tattooed you? What happened to the artist?"

"She went back to the future," he said. "I mean it. She was an old woman in a little house in the middle of Wisconsin here somewhere not far from this place. A little old witch who looked a thousand years old one moment and twenty years old the next, but she said she could travel in time. I laughed. Now I know better."

"How did you happen to meet her?"

He told me. He had seen her painted sign by the road: SKIN ILLUSTRATION! Illustration instead of tattoo! Artistic! So he had sat all night while her magic needles stung him wasp stings and delicate bee stings. By morning he looked like a man who had fallen into a twenty-color print press and been squeezed out, all bright and picturesque.

"I've hunted every summer for fifty years," he said, putting his hands out on the air. "When I find that witch I'm going to kill her."

The sun was gone. Now the first stars were shining and the moon had brightened the fields of grass and wheat. Still the Illustrated Man's pictures glowed like charcoals in the half light, like scattered rubies and emeralds, with Rouault colors and Picasso colors and the long, pressed-out El Greco bodies.

"So people fire me when my pictures move. They don't like it when violent things happen in my Illustrations. Each Illustration is a little story. If you watch them, in a few minutes they tell you a tale. In three hours of looking you could see eighteen or twenty stories acted right on my body, you could hear voices and think thoughts. It's all here, just waiting for you to look. But most of all, there's a special spot on my body." He bared his back. "See? There's no special design on my right shoulder blade, just a jumble."

"Yes."

"When I've been around a person long enough, that spot clouds over and fills in. If I'm with a woman, her picture comes there on my back, in an hour, and shows her whole life — how she'll live, how she'll die, what she'll look like when she's sixty. And if it's a man, an hour later his picture's here on my back. It shows him falling off a cliff, or dying under a train. So I'm fired again."

All the time he had been talking his hands had wandered over the Illustrations, as if to adjust their frames, to brush away dust—the motions of a connoisseur, an art patron. Now he lay back, long and full in the moonlight. It was a warm night. There was no breeze and the air was stifling. We both had our shirts off.

"And you've never found the old woman?"

"Never."

"And you think she came from the future?"

"How else could she know these stories she painted on me?"

He shut his eyes tiredly. His voice grew fainter. "Sometimes at night I can feel them, the pictures, like ants, crawling on my skin. Then I know they're doing what they have to do. I never look at them anymore. I just try to rest. I don't sleep much. Don't you look at them either, I warn you. Turn the other way when you sleep."

I lay back a few feet from him. He didn't seem violent and the pictures were beautiful. Otherwise I might have been tempted to get out and away from such babbling. But the Illustrations... I let my eyes fill up on them. Any person would go a little mad with such things upon his body.

The night was serene. I could hear the Illustrated Man's breathing in the moonlight. Crickets were stirring gently in the distant ravines. I lay with my body sidewise so I could watch the Illustrations. Perhaps half an hour passed. Whether the Illustrated Man slept I could not tell, but suddenly I heard him whisper, "They're moving, aren't they?"

I waited a minute.

Then I said, "Yes."

The pictures were moving, each in its turn, each for a brief minute or two. There in the moonlight, with the tiny tinkling thoughts and the distant sea voices, it seemed, each little drama was enacted. Whether it took an hour or three hours for the dramas to finish, it would be hard to say. I only know that I lay fascinated and did not move while the stars wheeled in the sky.

Eighteen Illustrations, eighteen tales. I counted them one by one. Primarily my eyes focused upon a scene, a large house with two people in it.

I saw a flight of vultures on a blazing flesh sky, I saw yellow lions, and I heard voices. The first Illustration quivered and came to life....

COLLECTORS

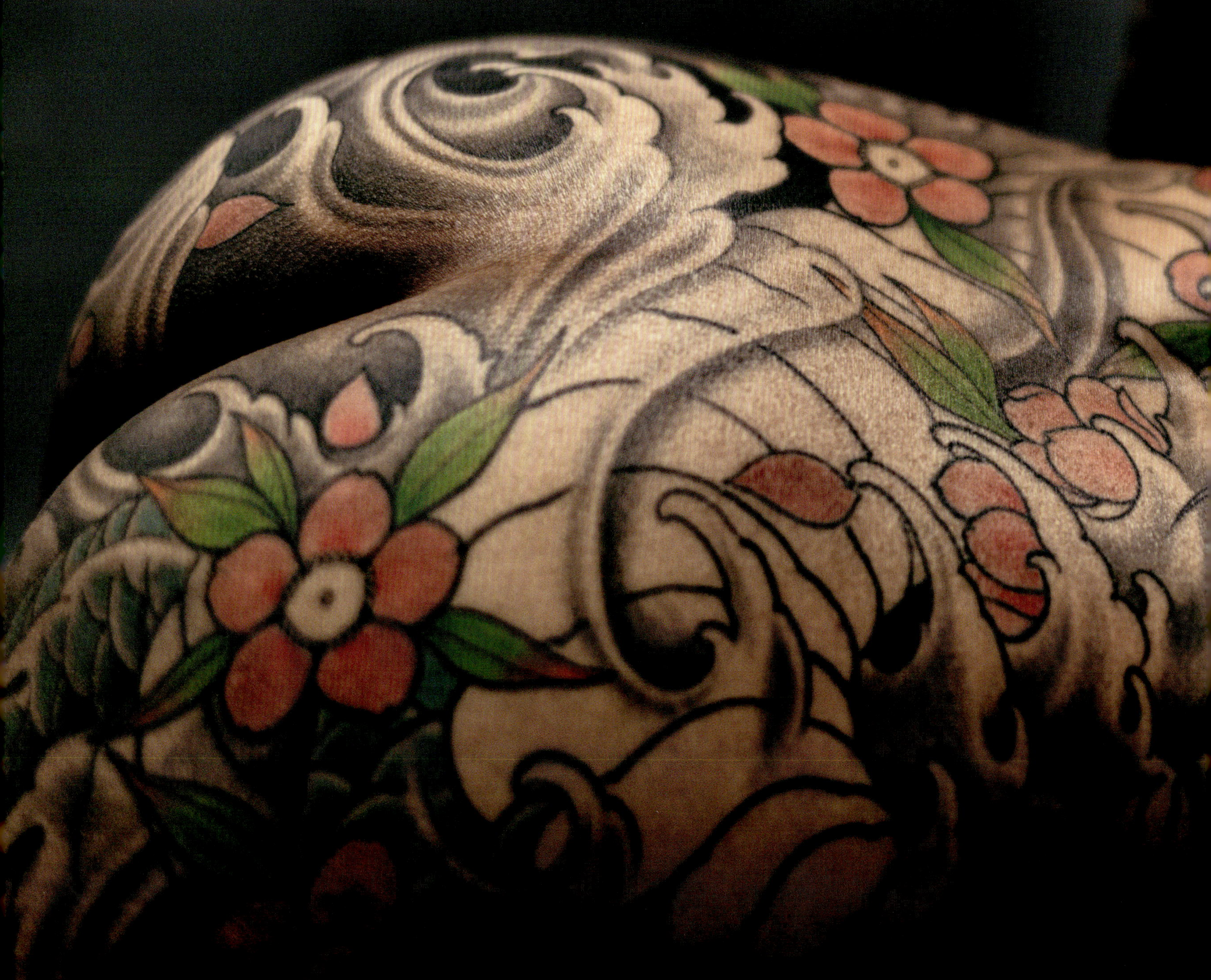

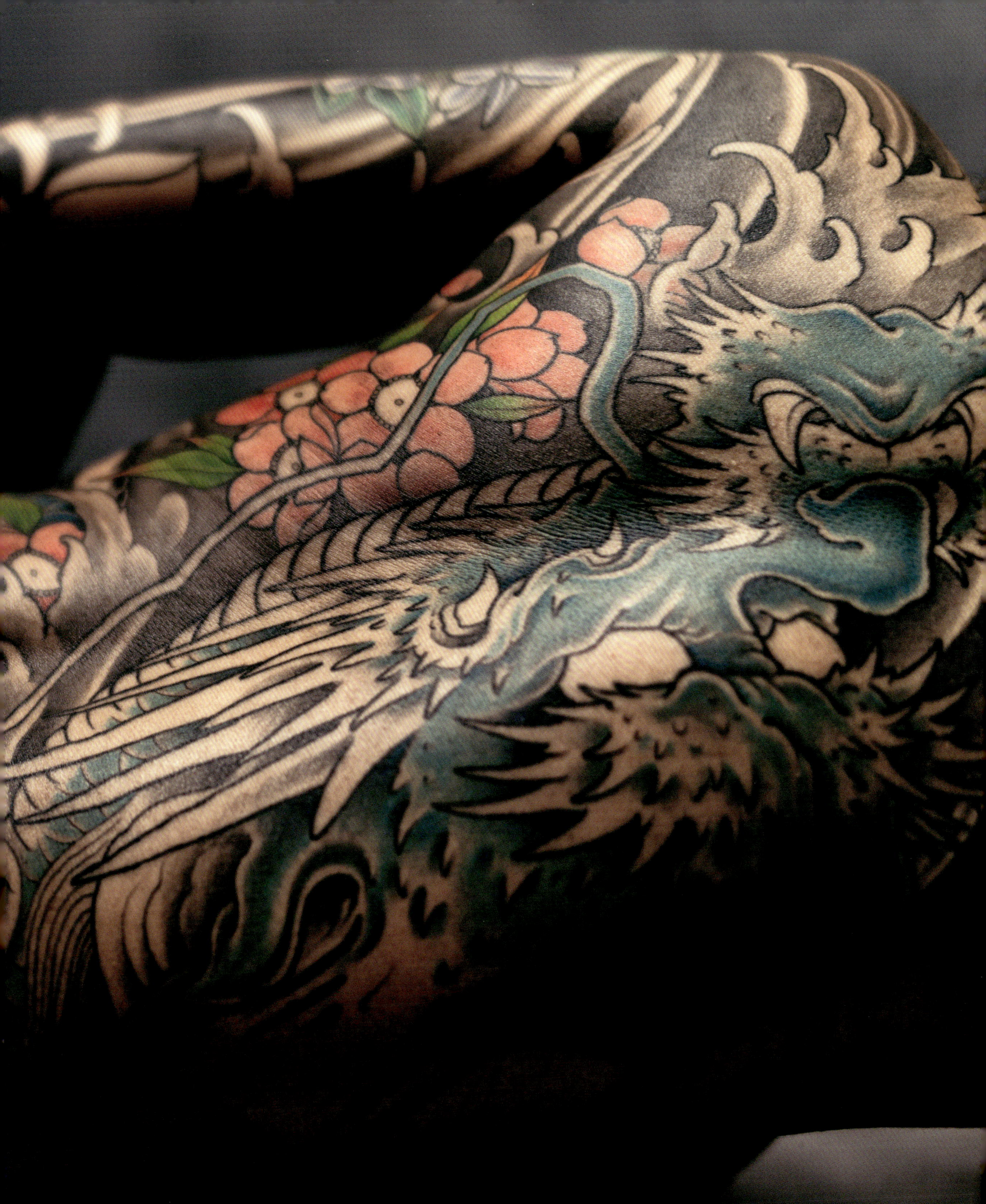

Pages 18–19: Dian Fermin Zielke's dragon bodysuit, tattooed by Kevin Marr Horikema, consists of traditional oriental designs with splashes of modern styles, to serve as a reminder of her own strength.

Opposite: Sedrick Montano, nicknamed Seddy Blasted, is a proud tattooed dad and barber who builds race cars.

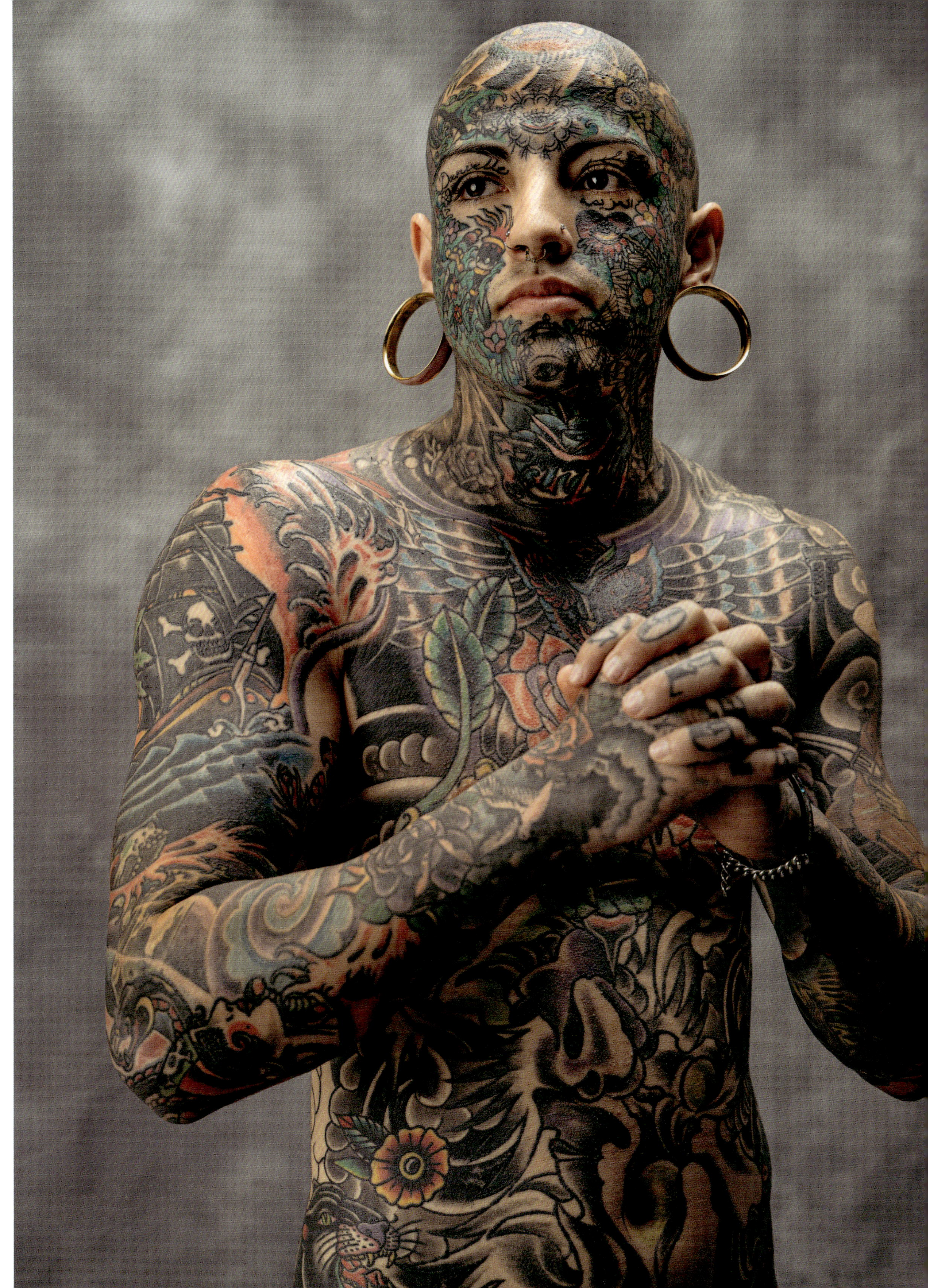

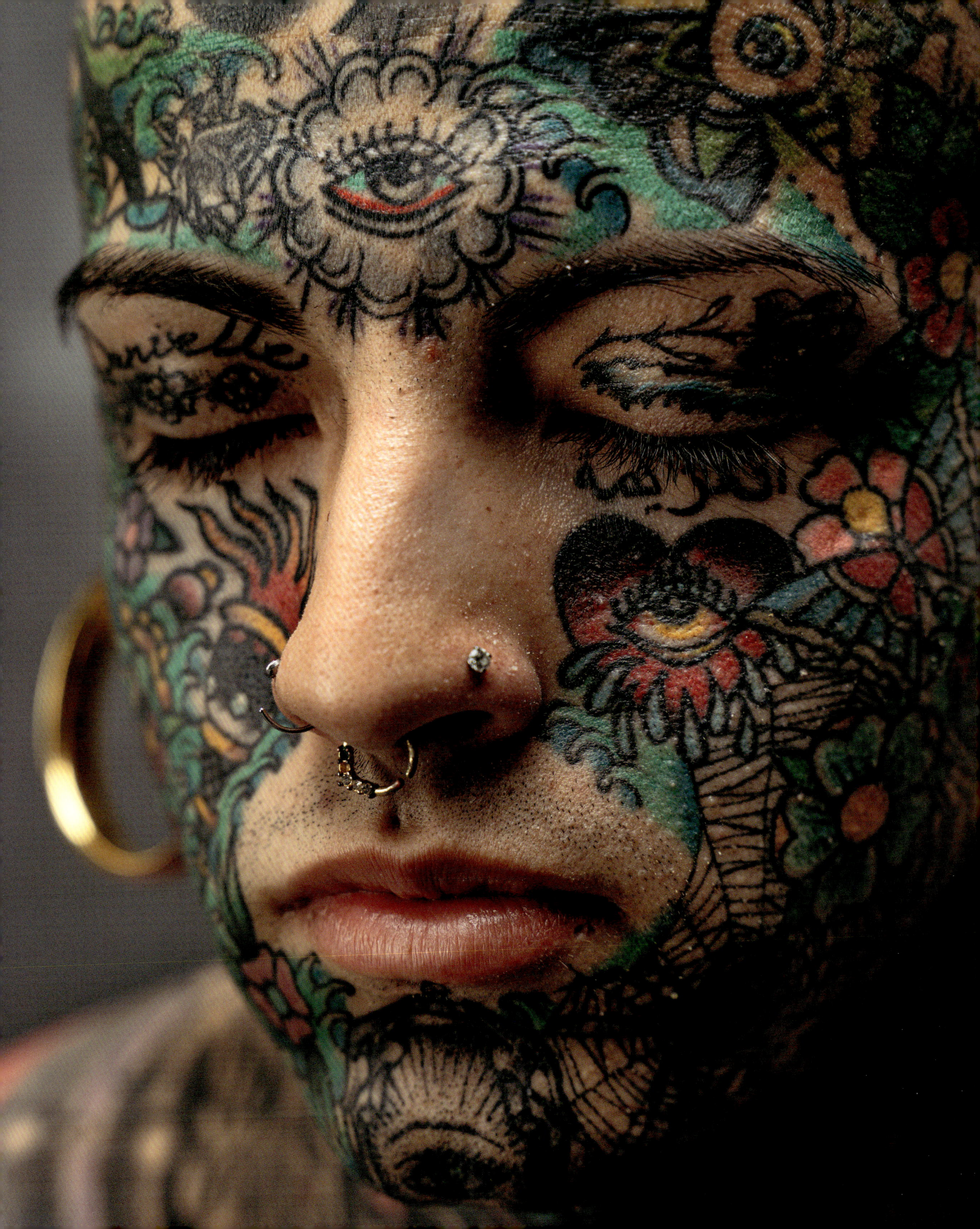

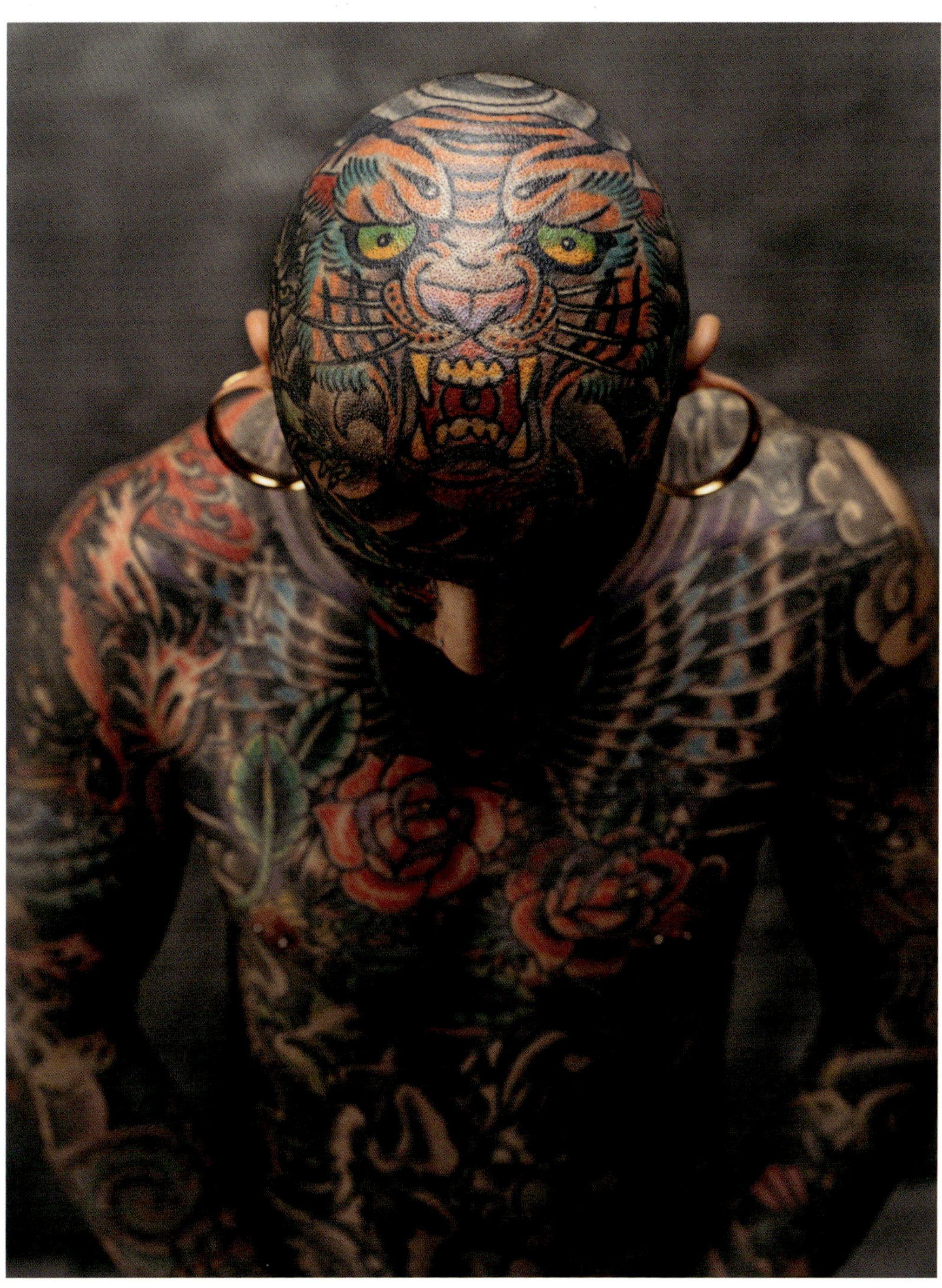

Opposite: Montano's main artist, Alex Atencio, illustrated most of his bodysuit, including his face and head.

Above: His tattoo collection, a mix of Japanese and bright American traditional tattoos, was predominantly done at Por Vida Tattoo in Albuquerque, New Mexico, where Montano resides.

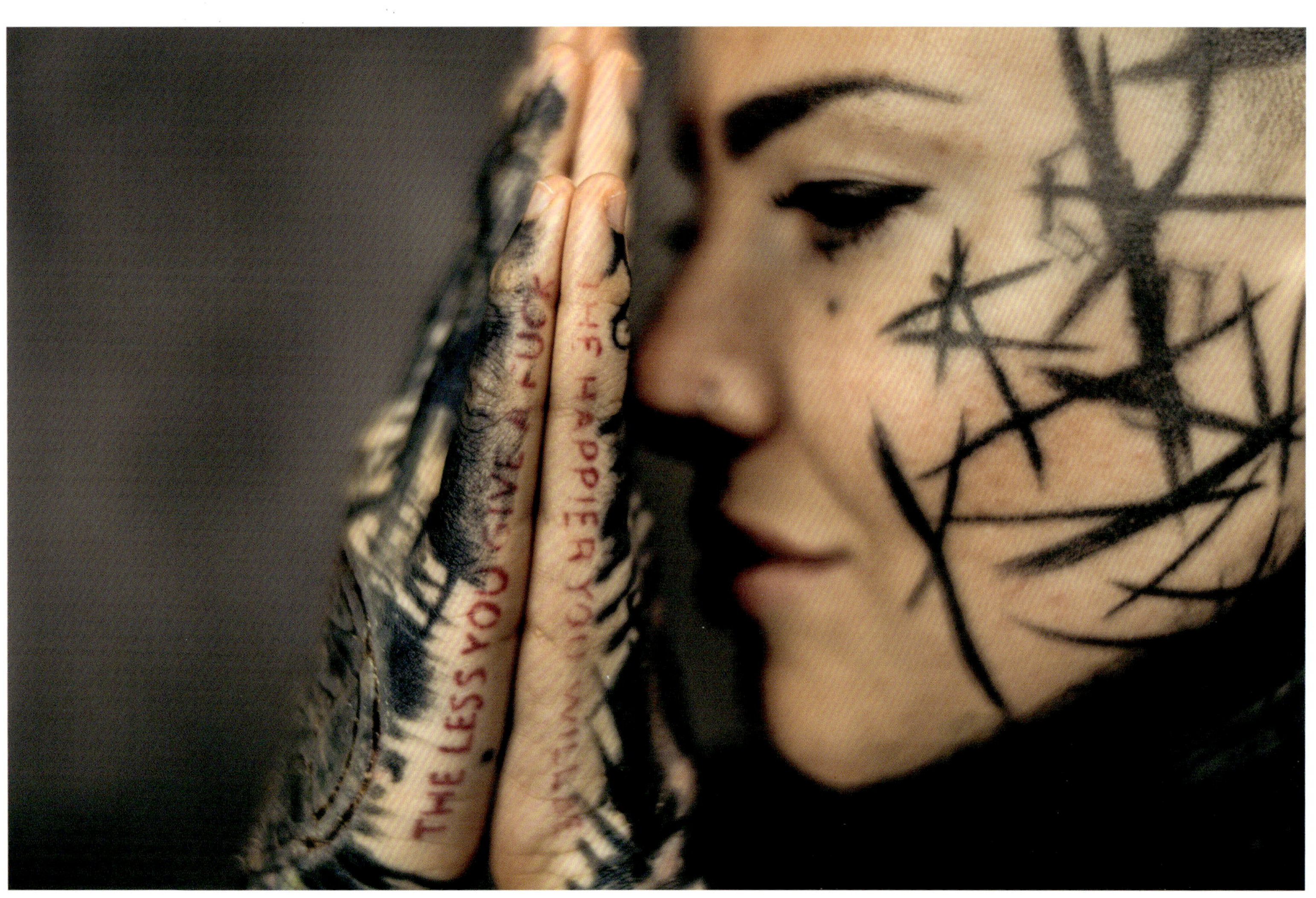

Tattoo artist and collector Michela Bottin wears heavy blackwork by artist Valerio Cancellier.

Opposite: "Tattoos make me feel more comfortable," says Bottin. "It's like having a shield that makes me feel safer inside my own skin."

Pages 26–27: Along with Cancellier's illustrations, Bottin's collection comprises the work of fifteen other artists, including Jason Ackerman, Ruco, Alex Pinna, and Gianluca Artico.

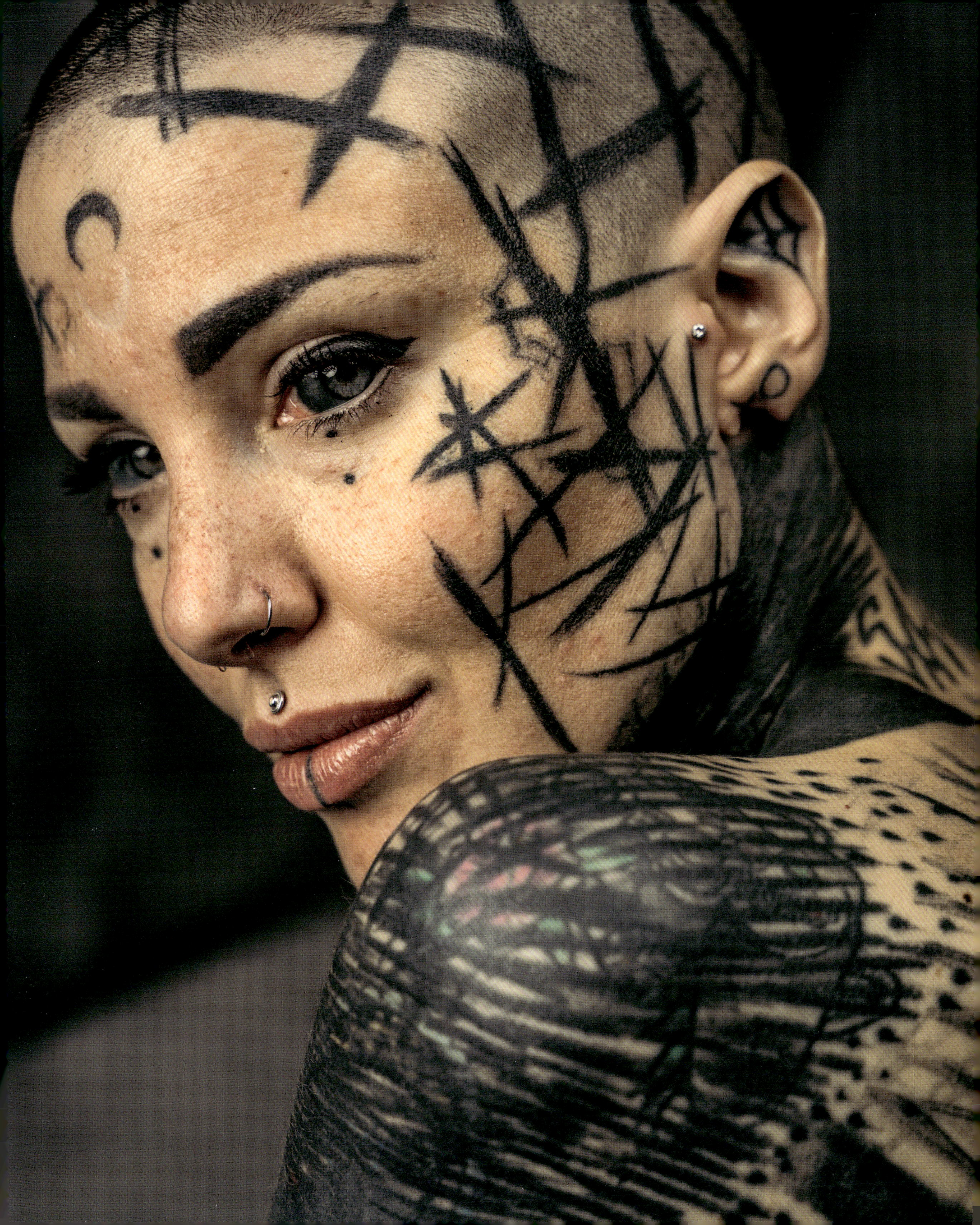

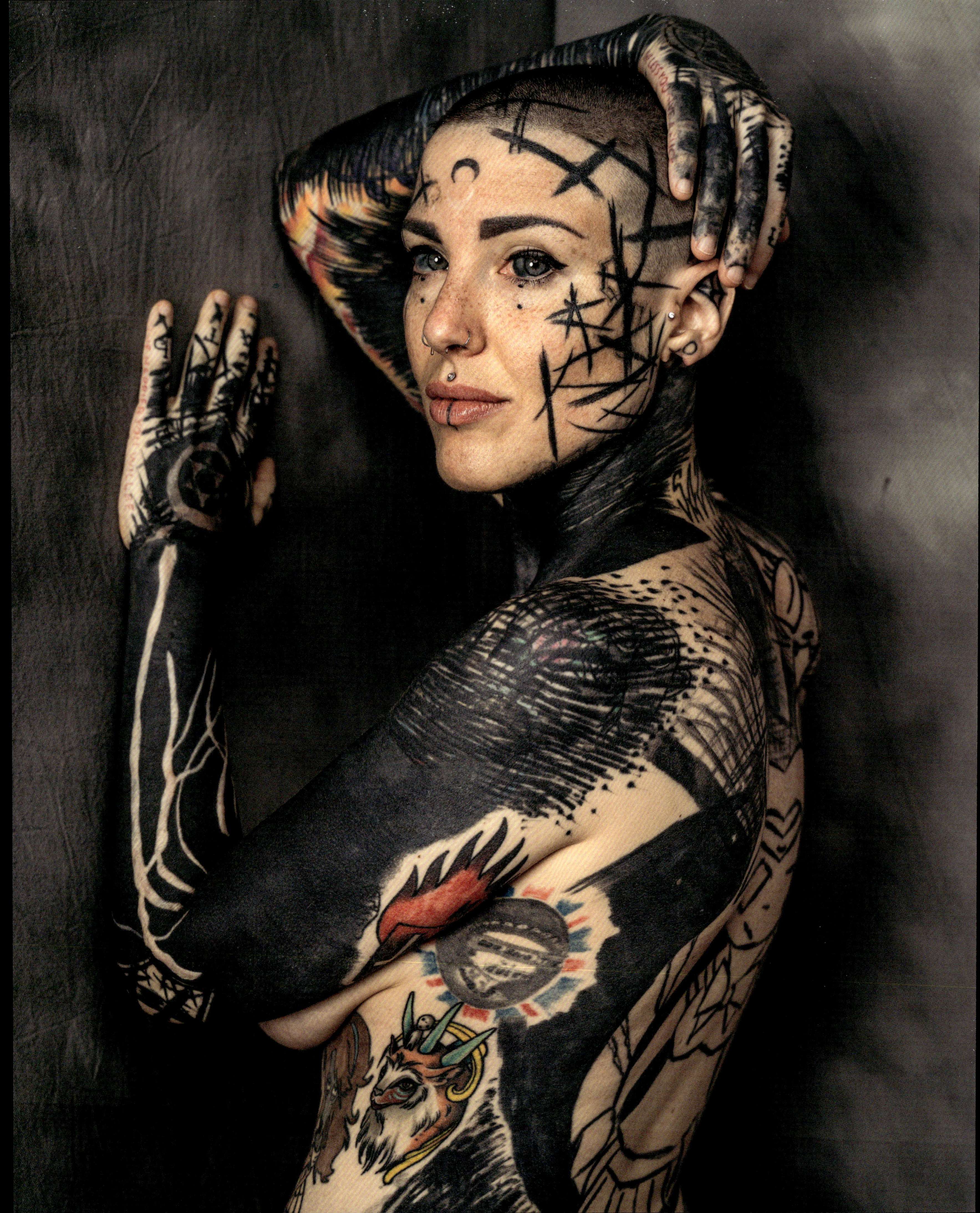

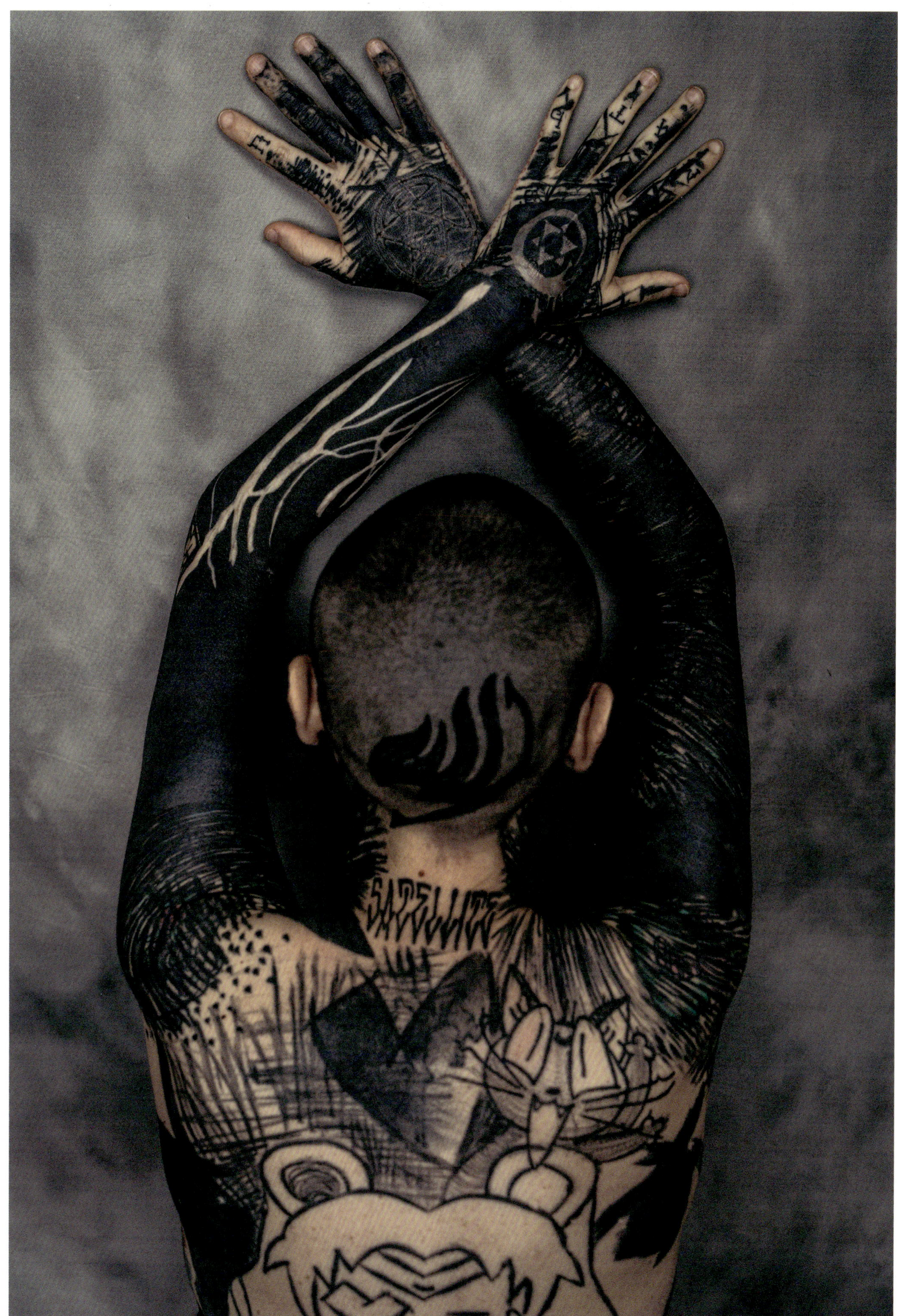
SATELLITE

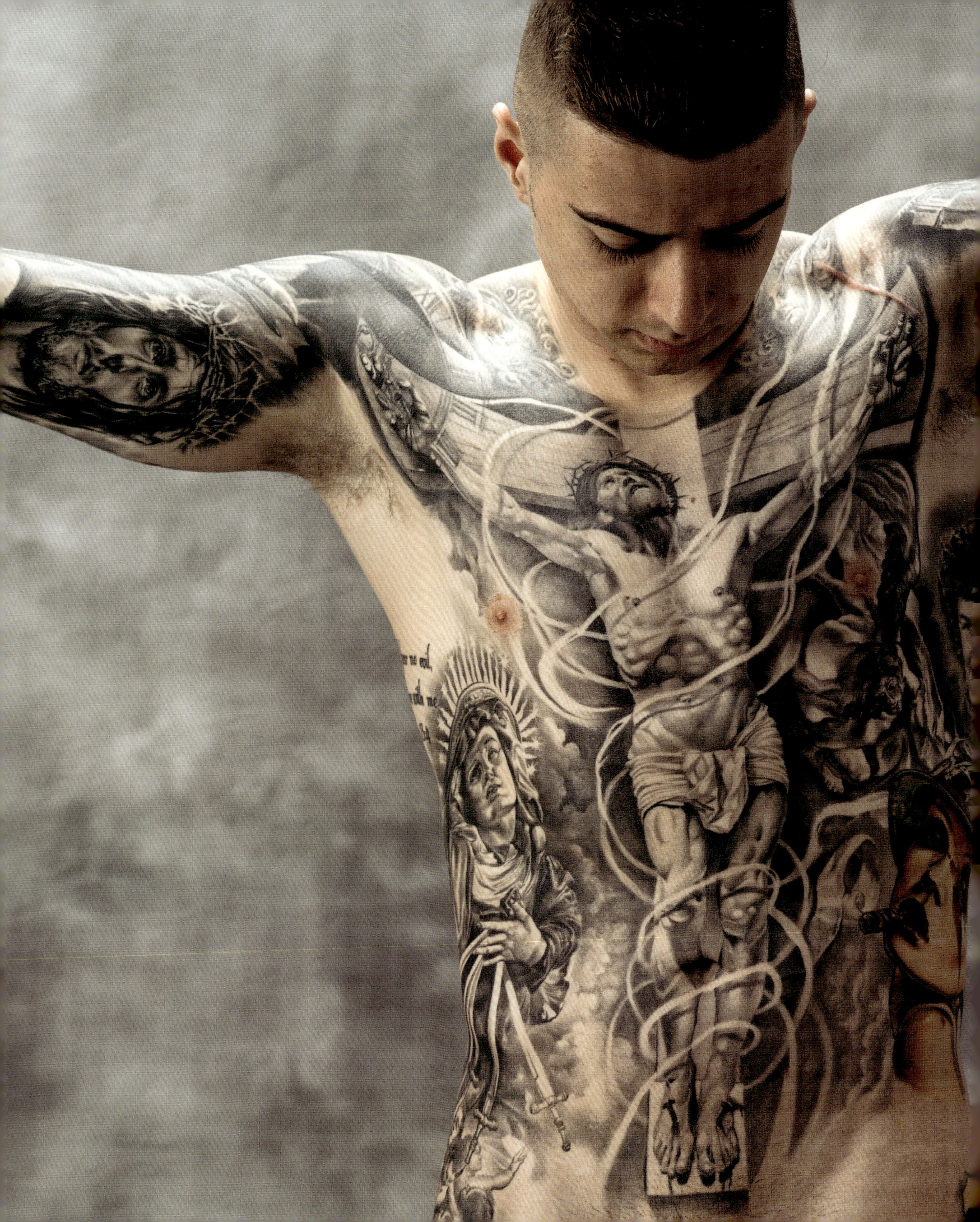

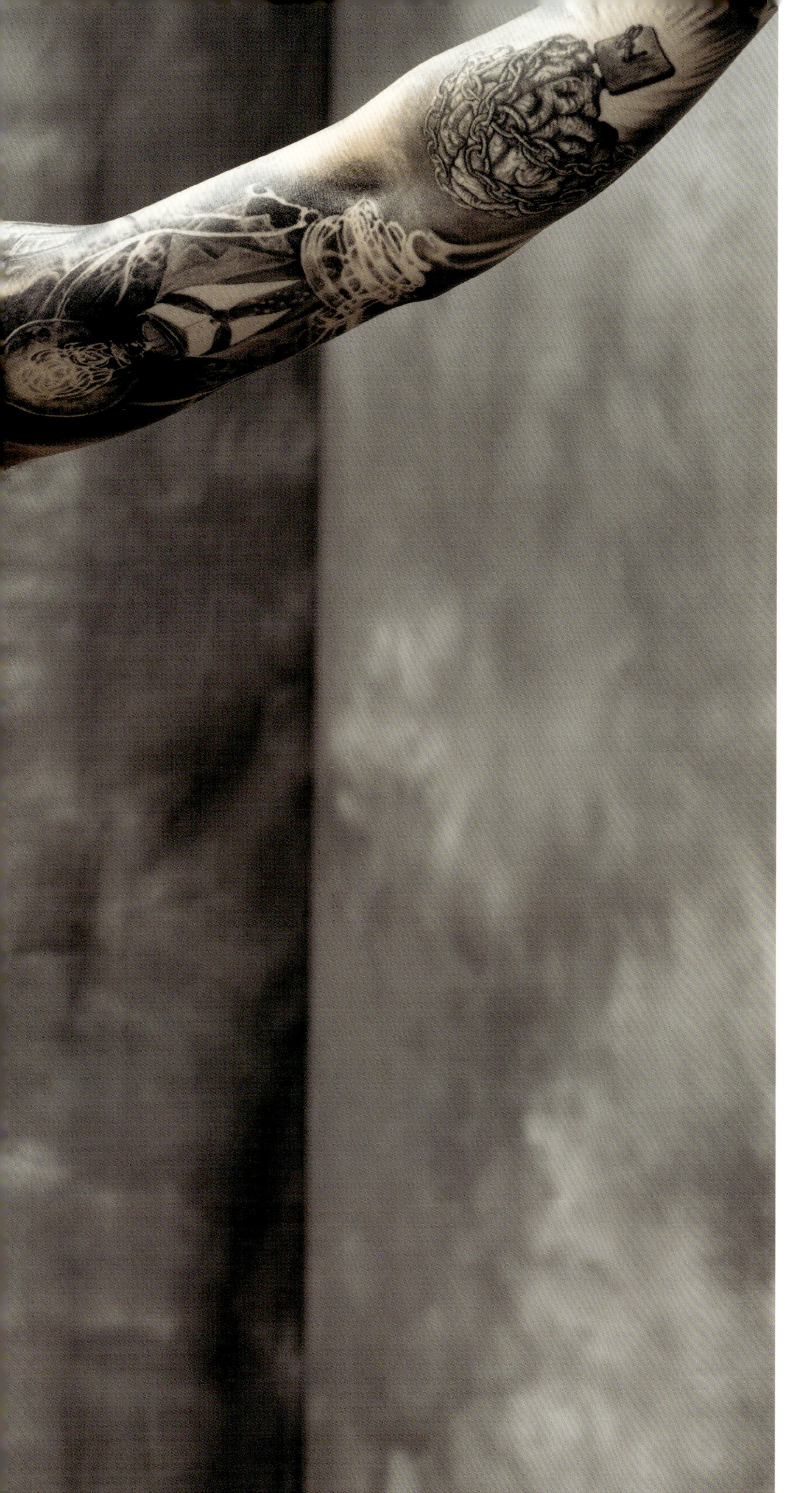

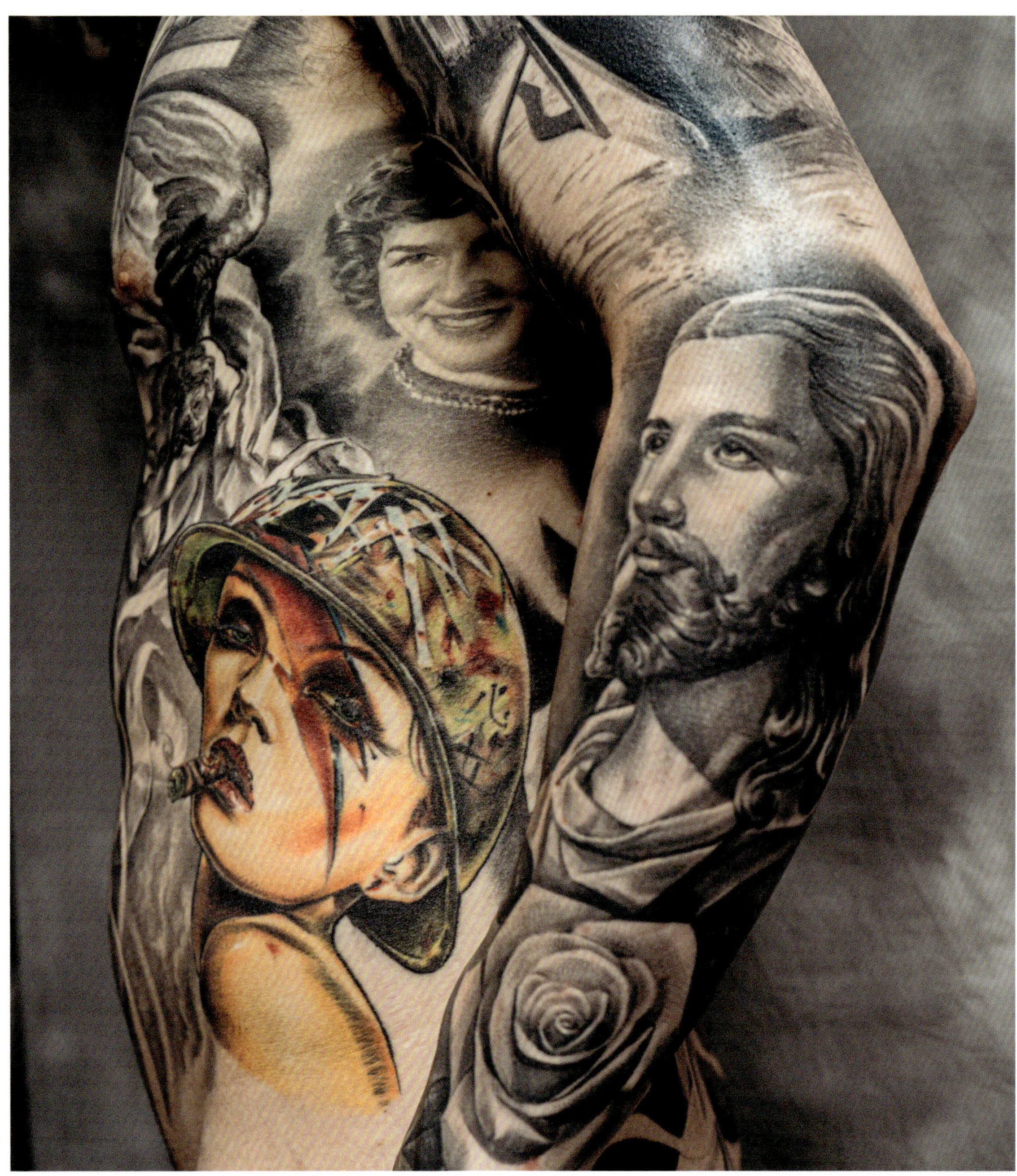

Pages 28–29: Jordan Feno started his largely black-and-grey realism collection with a Jesus piece on his inner right bicep. His chest was tattooed by Matt Jordan.

Above: Feno selects his artists because of their uniqueness, creativity, and signature style.

Opposite: Of Feno's many religious tattoos, his favorite is the weeping Madonna by Nikko Hurtado on his inner left calf.

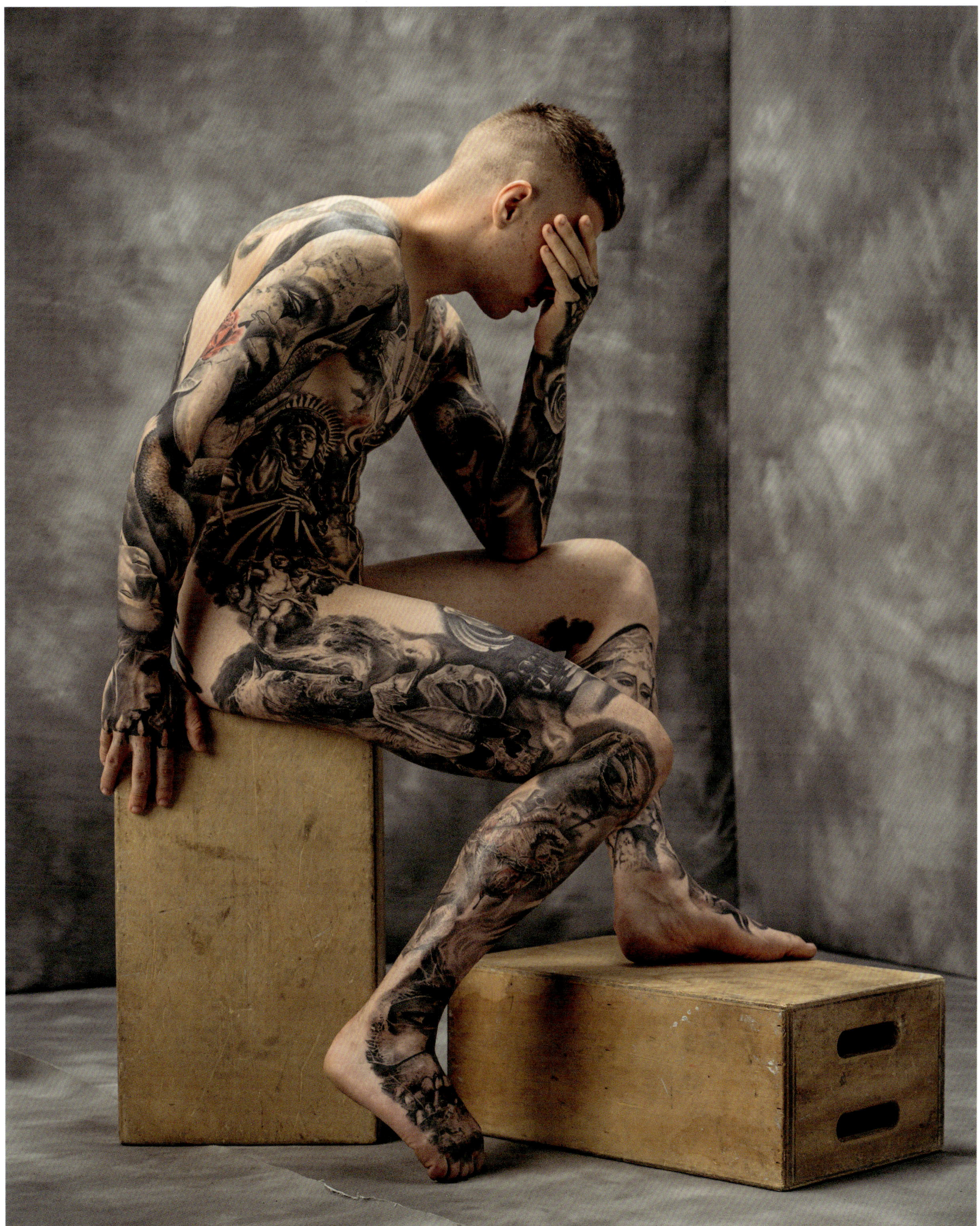

Toomer (left), Crazee (middle), and Mikey Cortez (right) have been collecting tattoos since their teenage years, illustrated by artists like TA2galie, Preach, and Lorenzo Baca.

Pages 34–35: Baca did the majority of work on Cortez (left), including the portraits and his head and face tattoos. Favoring the crude look of prison tattoos, Cortez had Cody Beastly do the "ATR" on his back, standing for his crew, Above the Rest. TA2galie has been working on Toomer's backpiece (middle) for more than a year to cover four old tattoos. Crazee (right) started his tattoo collection at age thirteen and is predominantly covered by the hand of artist Pint Uno.

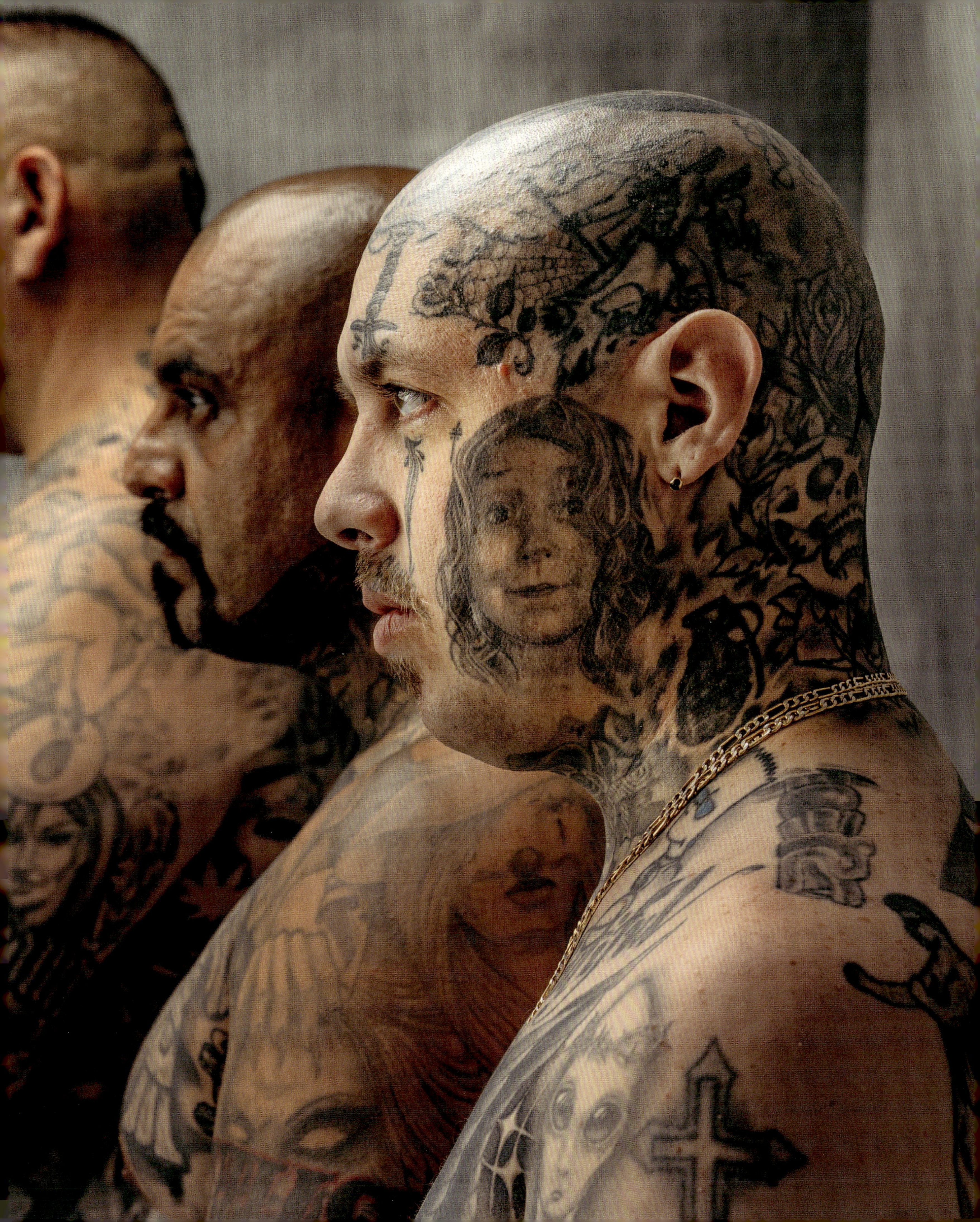

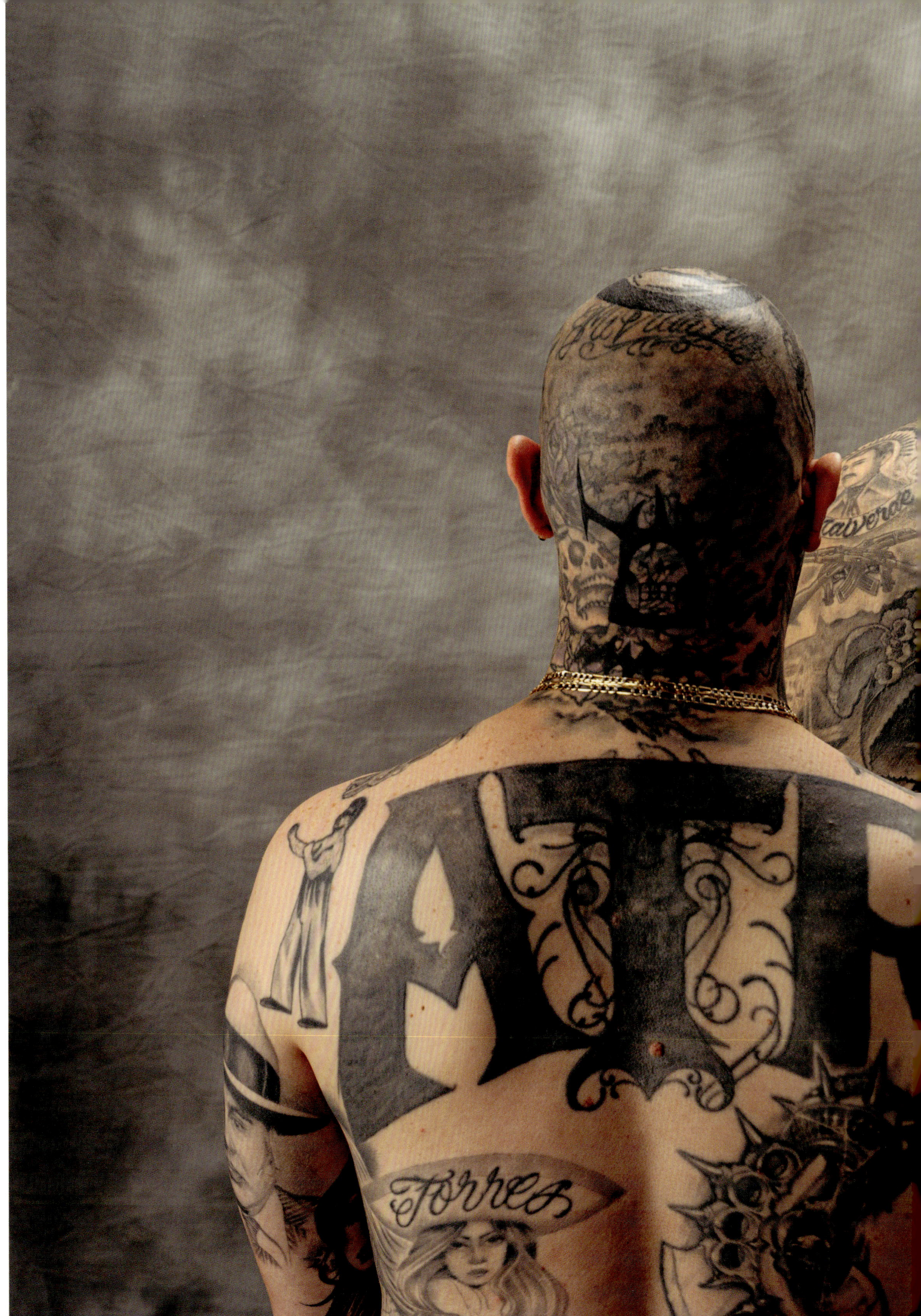
Torres

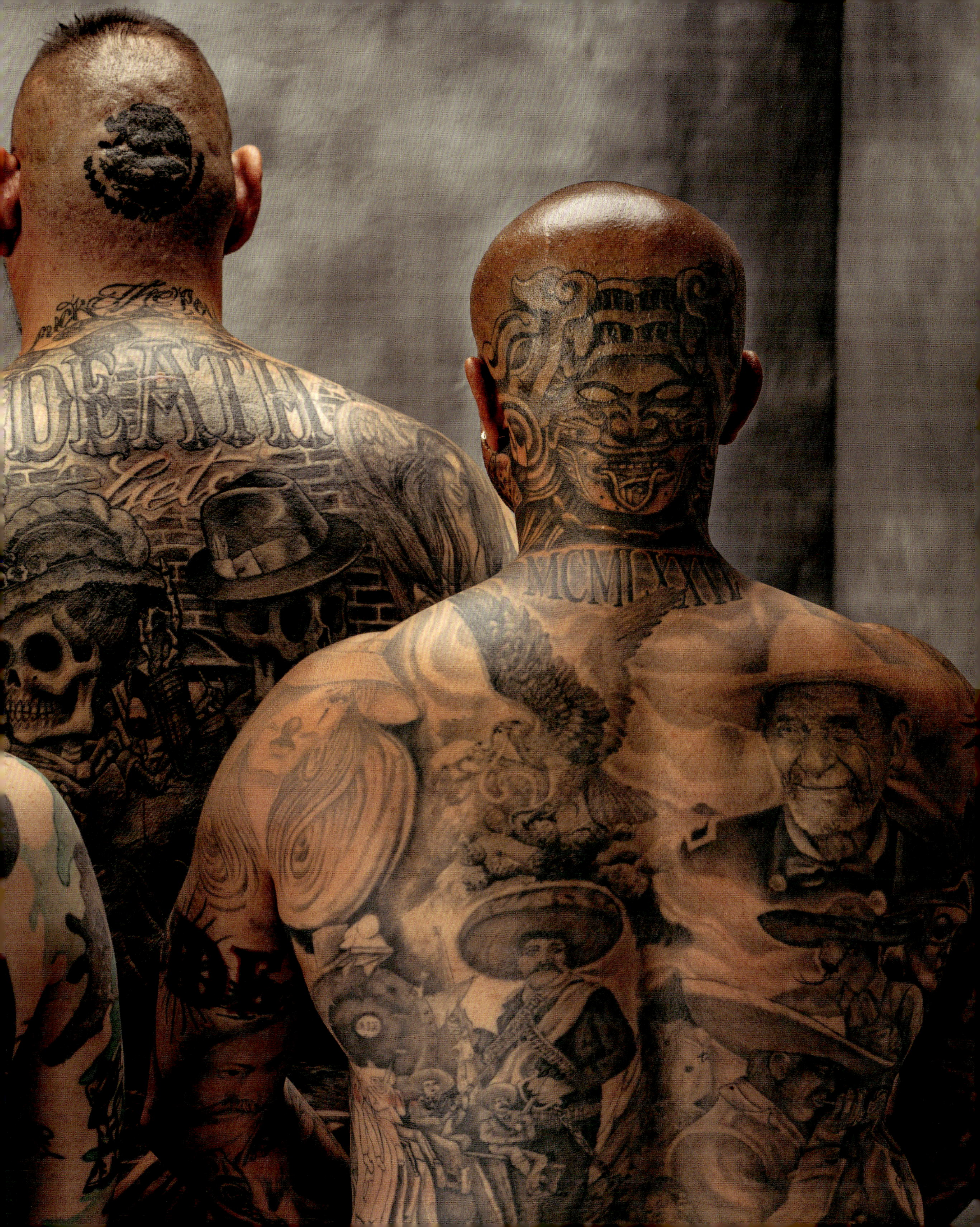
DEATH
MCMLXXII

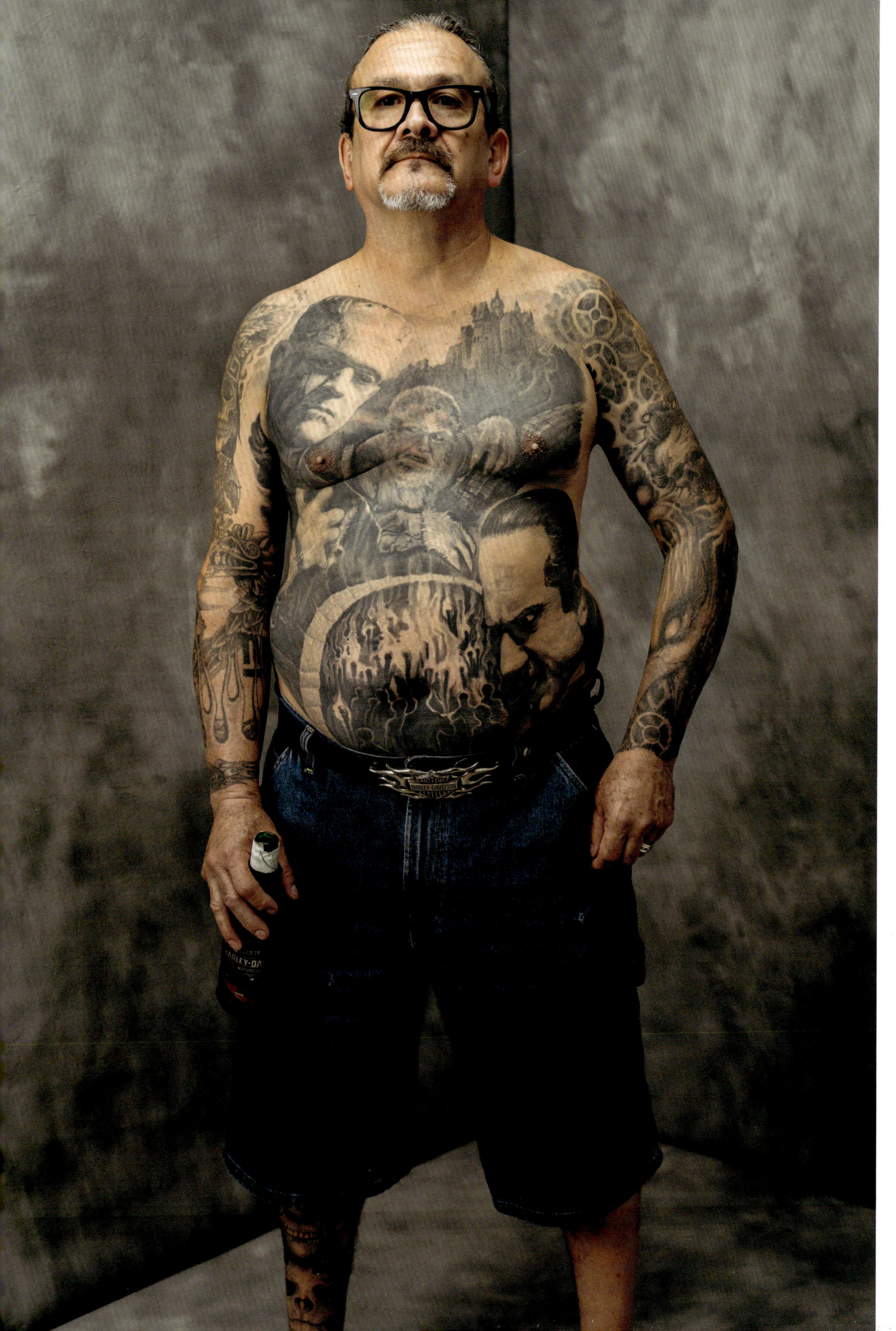
MOTOR
HARLEY-DAVIDSON
CYCLES

Illustrated by Paul Booth, Michael Gallegos says his chest piece “came from a combination of drink and old horror movies.”

Wendy Riley was tattooed by Mikey Sarratt, Jason Goodman, and Christian Carden.
She says each tattoo frees her a little more.

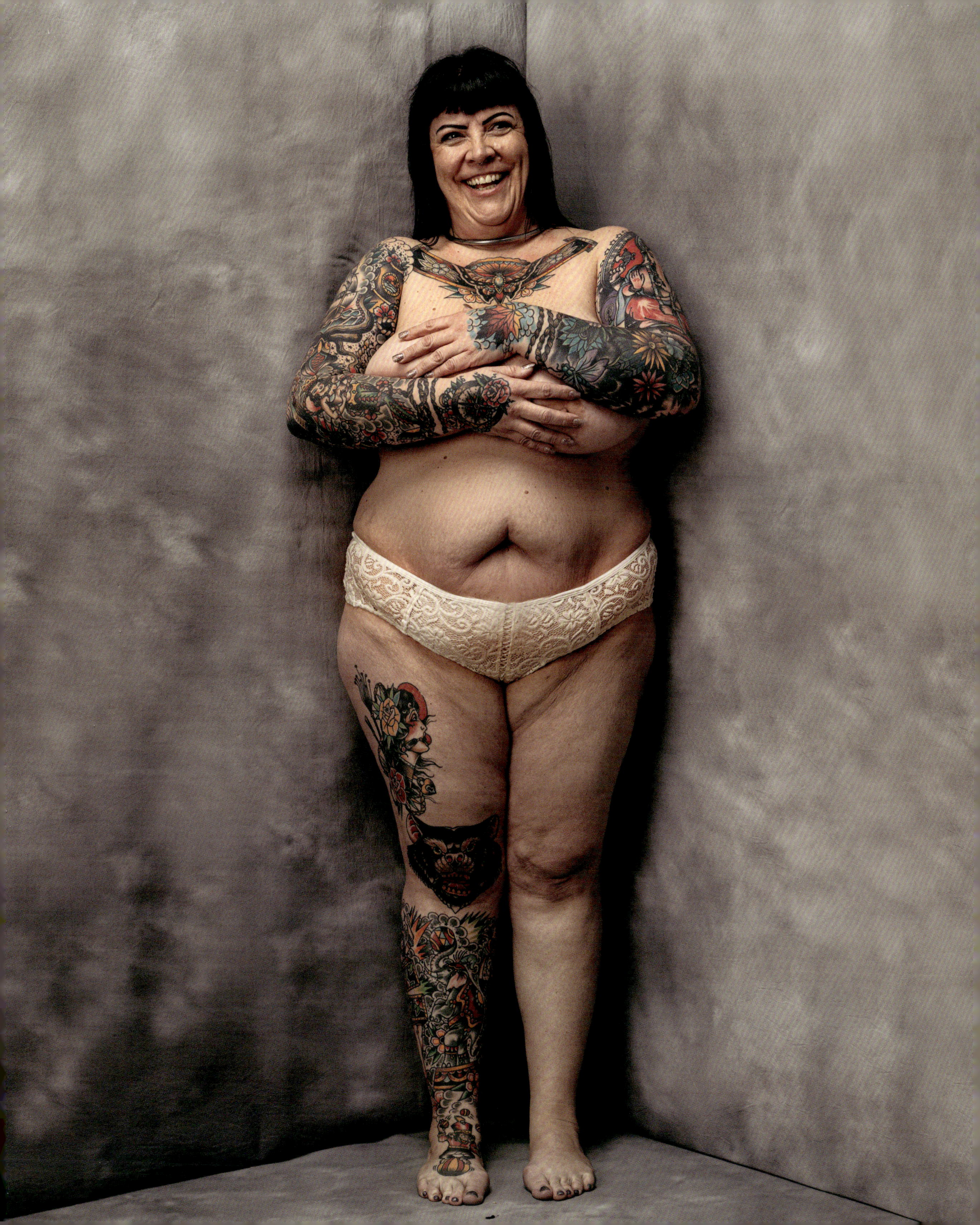

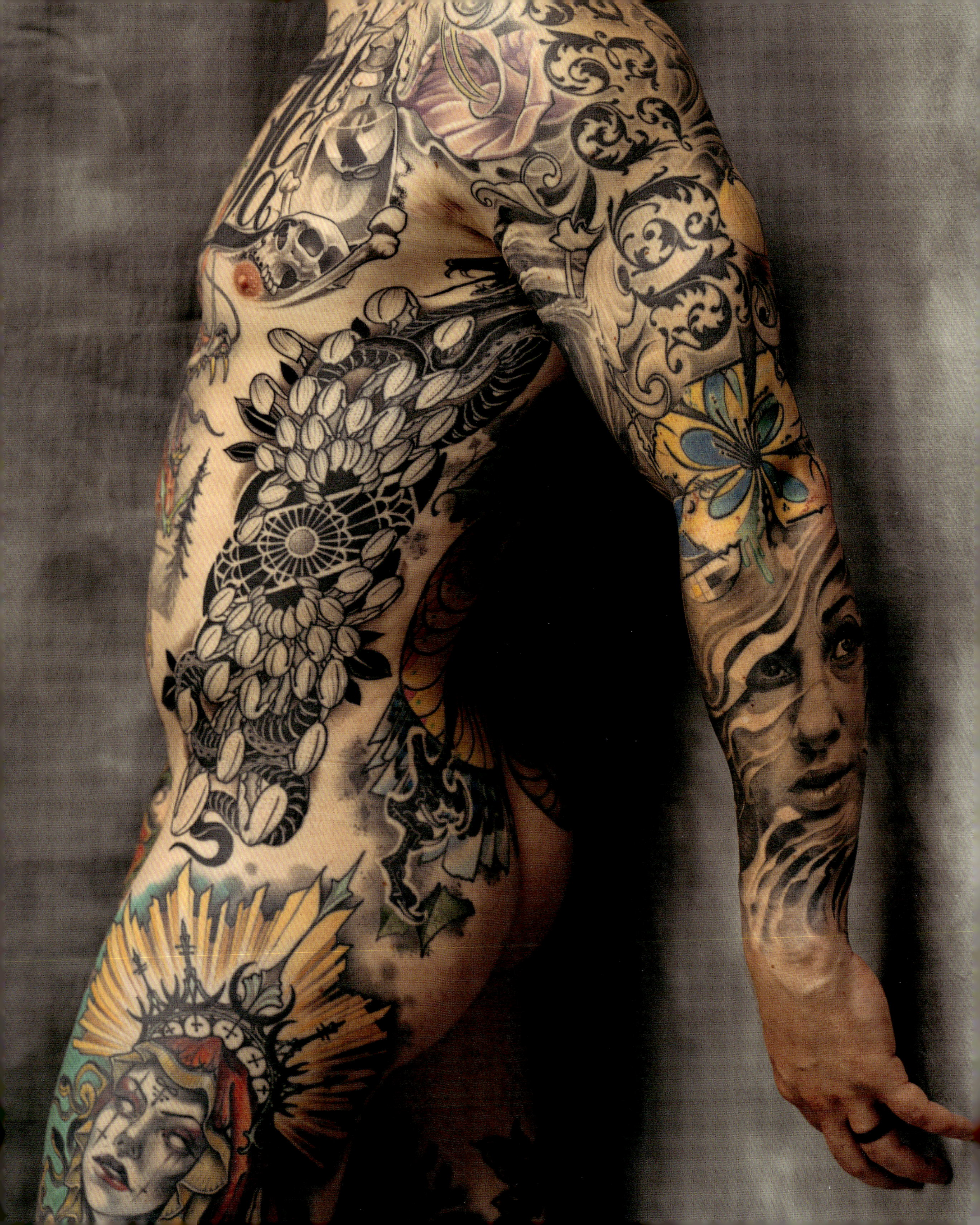

Anthony Rizzuto has over three hundred hours of work, from such artists as Josh Duffy, DJ Tambe, Arlo DiCristina, Steve Wimmer, and Jayce Wallingford.

Chad Best has been collecting tattoos for more than twenty-five years, including work by Keith Duggan, Giovanni Peña, J-Rod, Geo Collins, Ray Spooks Joya, Legion Avegno, Oscar Gomez, and Tom DePriest.

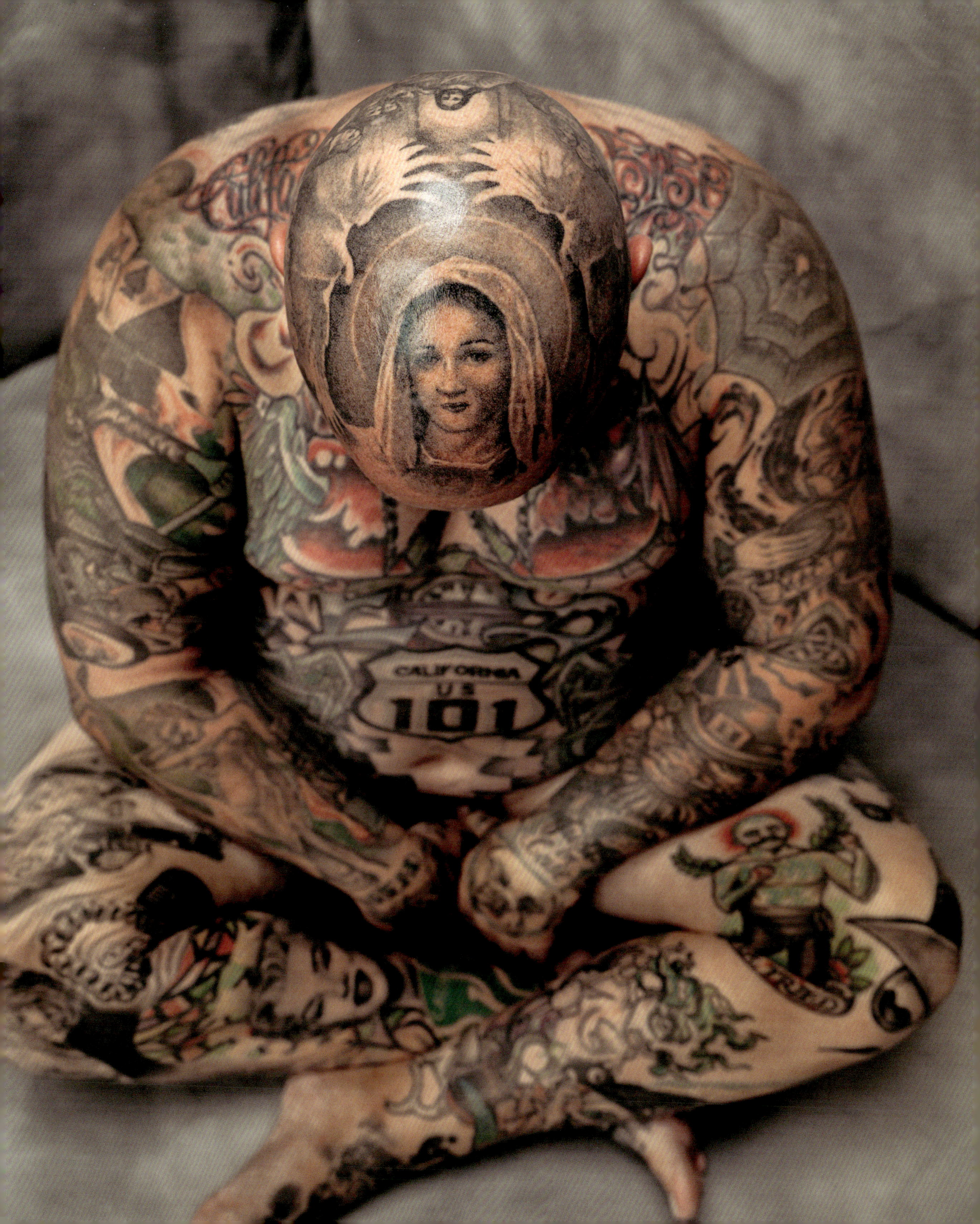
CALIFORNIA
U.S
101

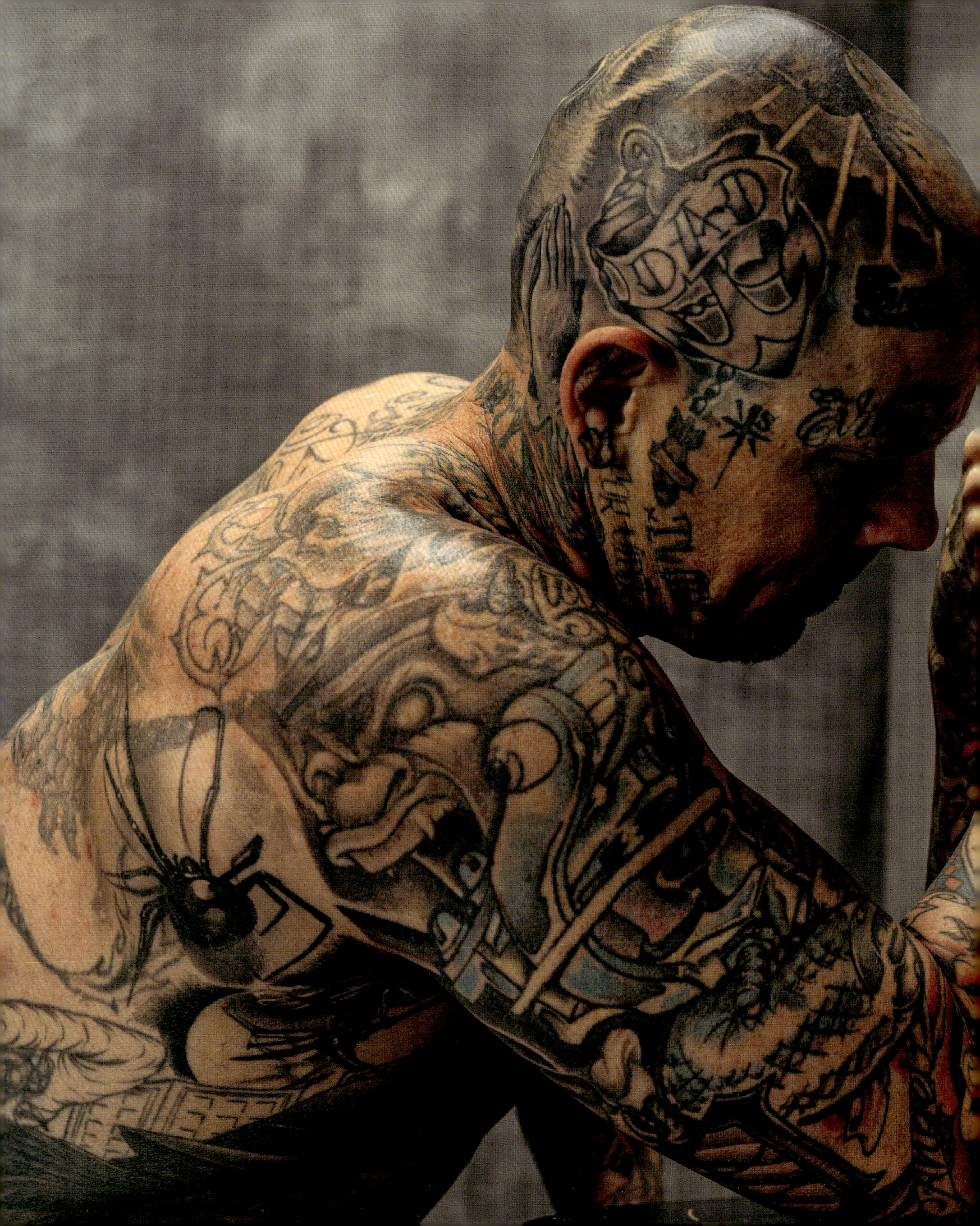

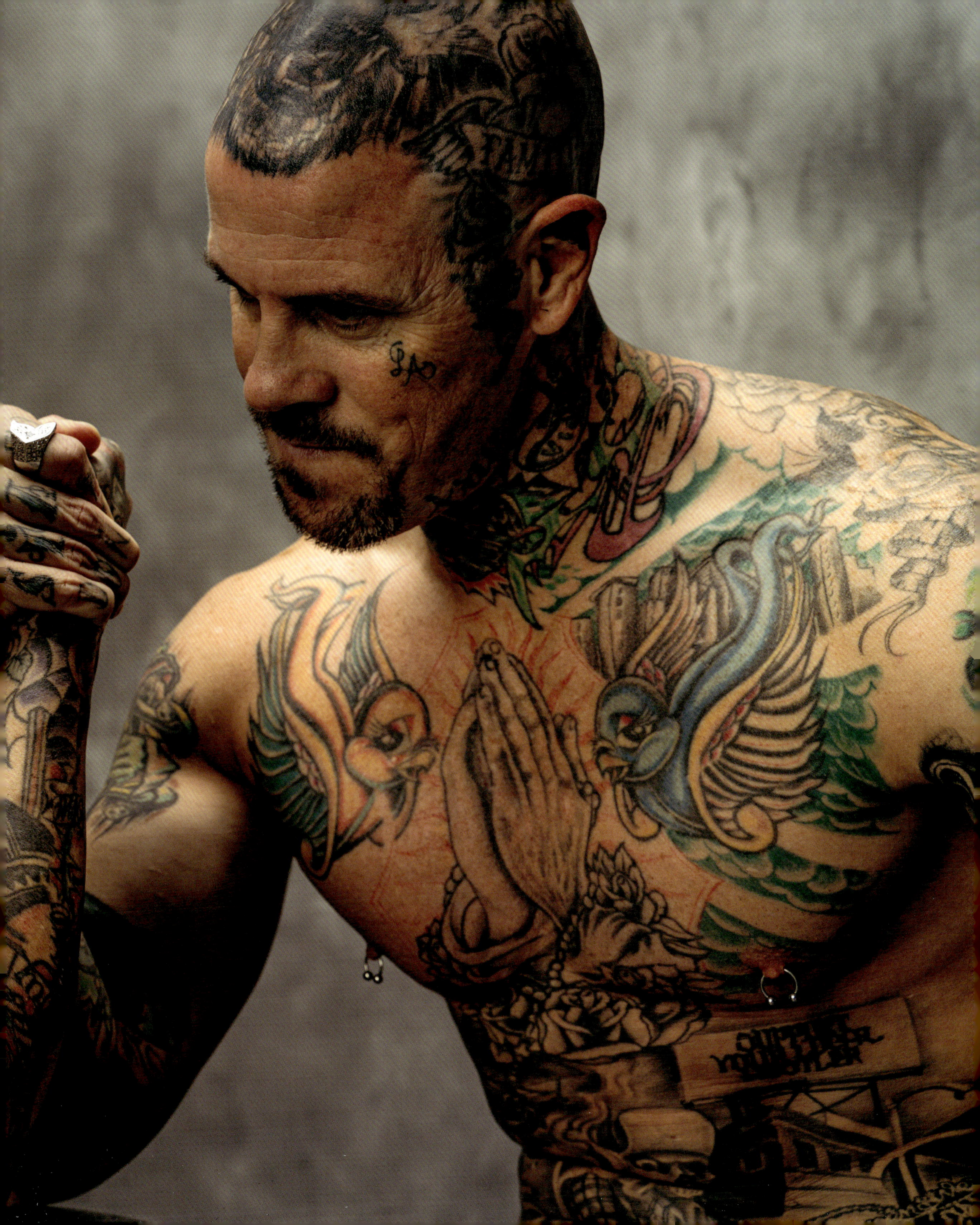

Pages 44–45: While Brian "Evil Twin" Vaillancourt's lettering (left) was done by his twin brother, Mark (right), much of the twins' art was done at Inkslingers in Alhambra, California, including illustrations by Brian Gonzales, Frank Sanchez, Marky Chavez, Kurt Vanderjagt, and Lawrence Fong.

Opposite: Christopher Gray's large-scale, bold, and colorful tattoo collection is especially recognized for his chest piece, completed in over ten sessions, by traditional artist Grez.

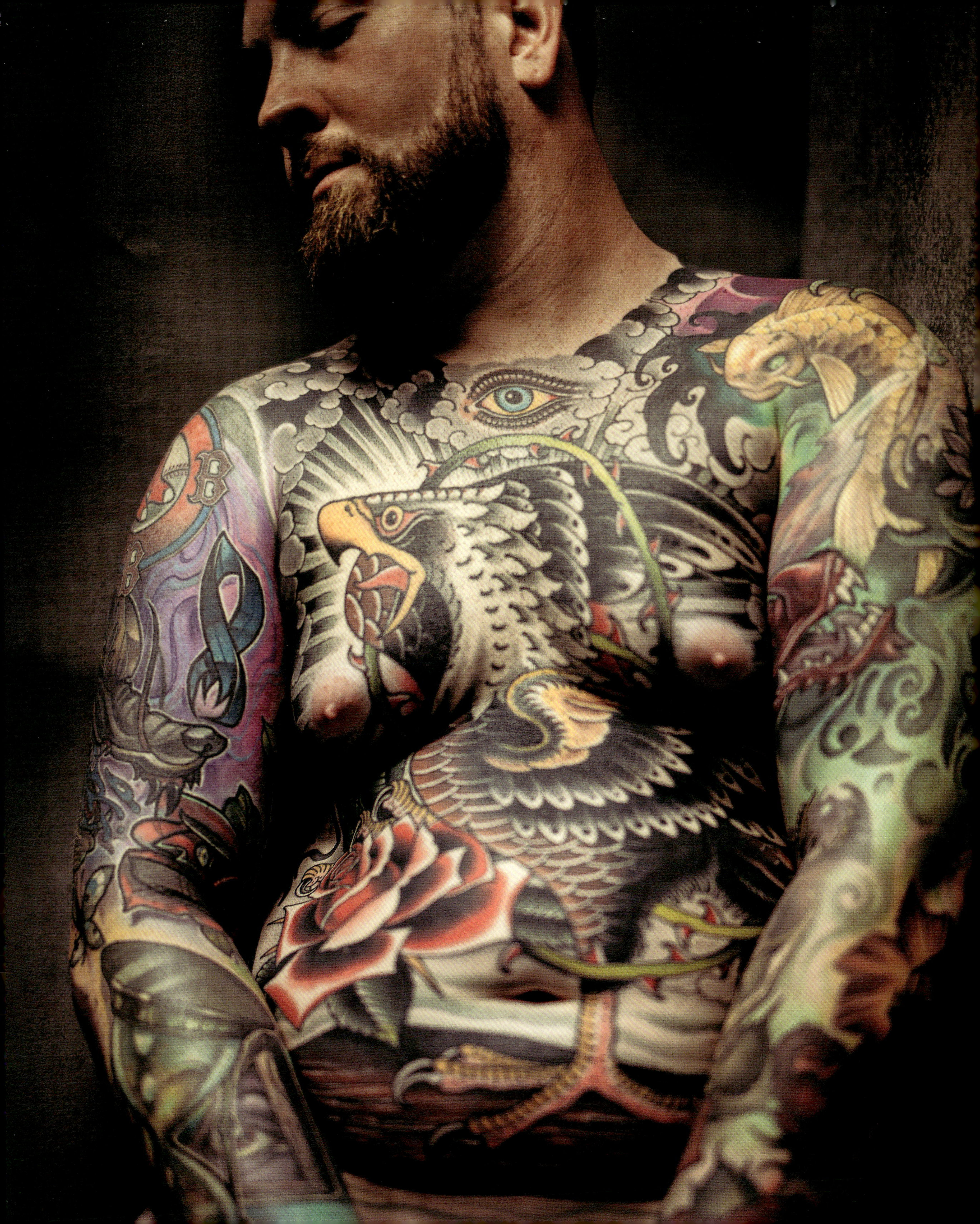

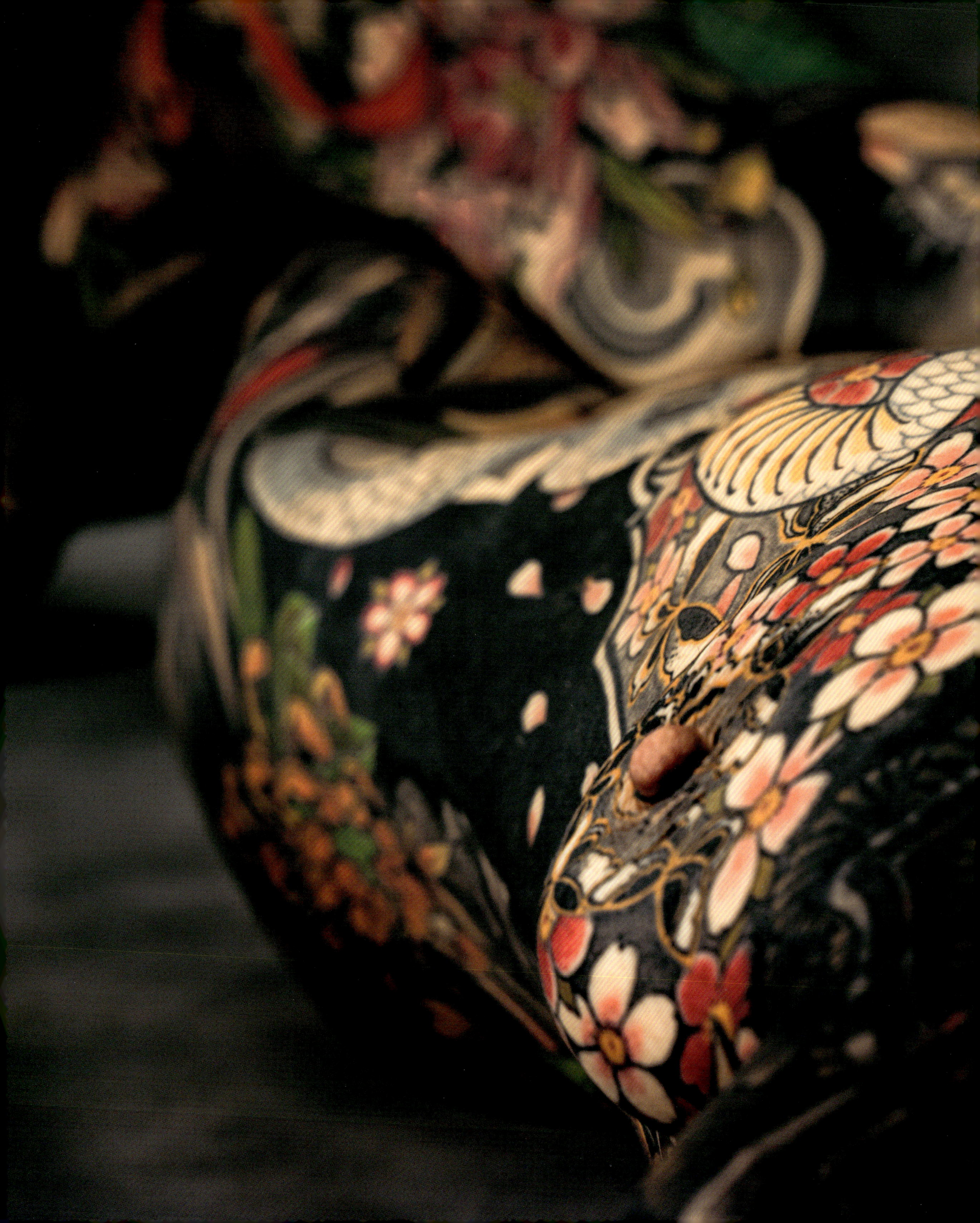

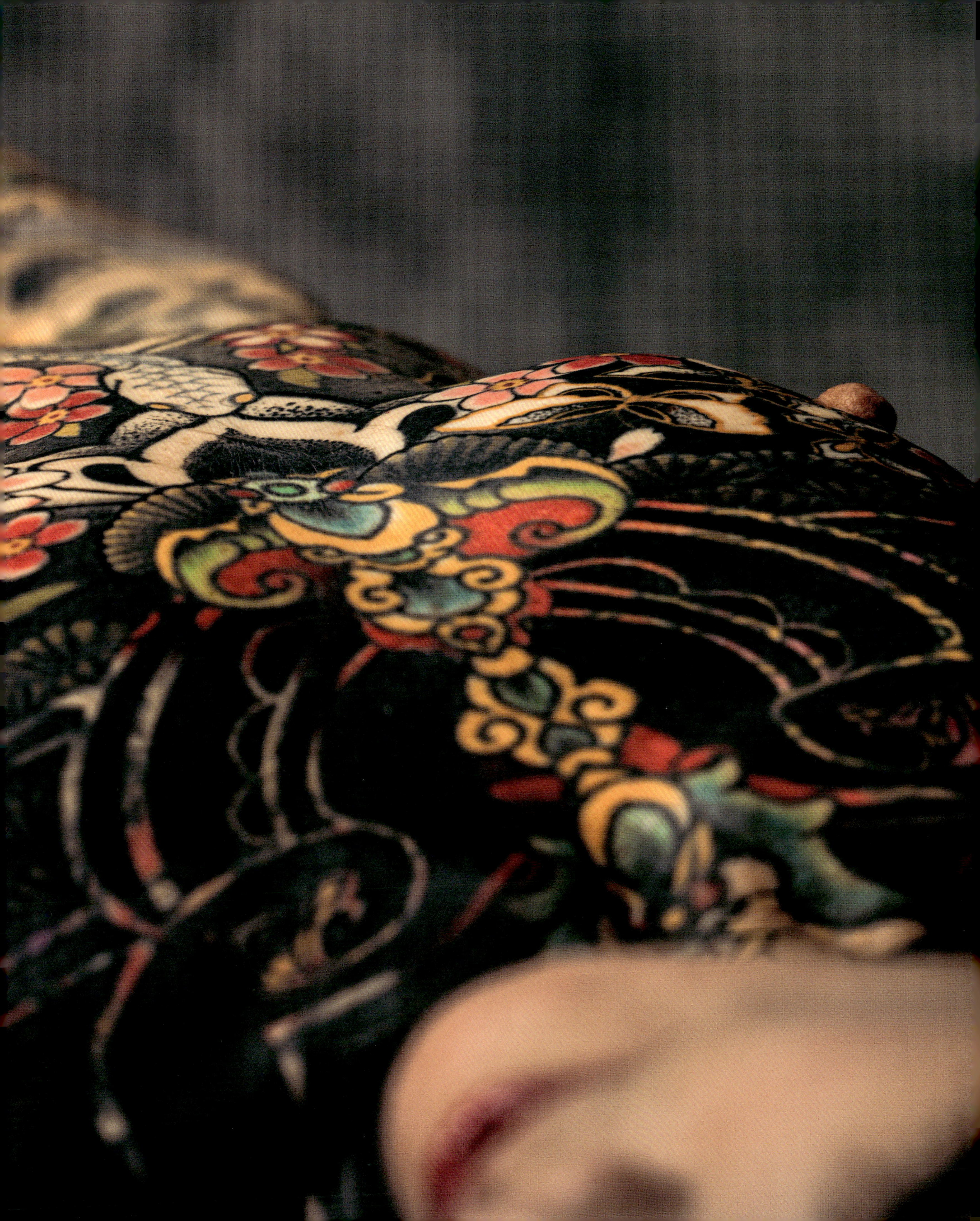

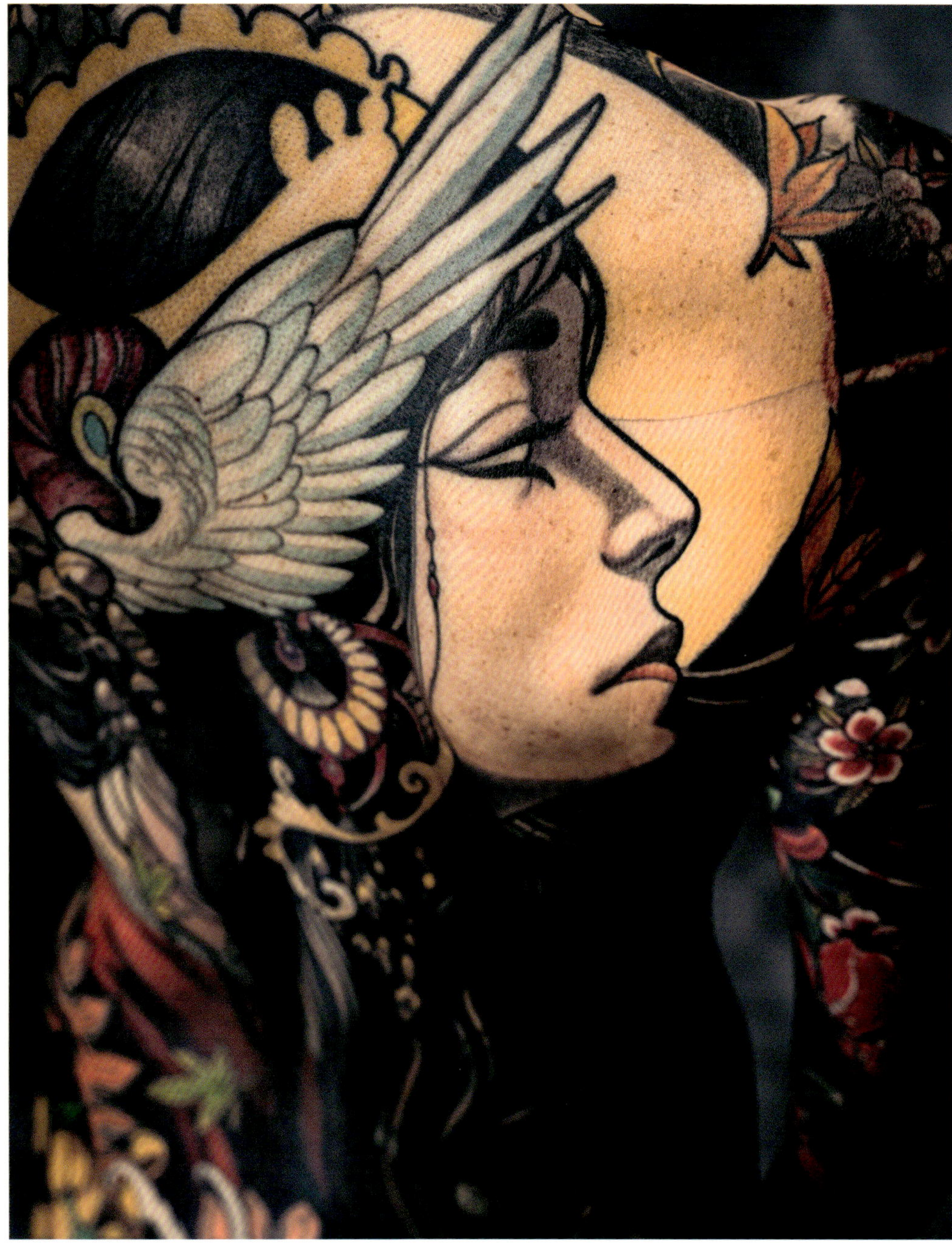

Pages 48–49: The neo-Japanese bodysuit that artist Jayme Goodwin illustrated for KeaLani Lada includes the Art Nouveau style Lada has always gravitated toward.

Above and opposite: Lada's tattoo collection is a physical and visual expression of how she views life: "The triumph of joy over pain."

Pages 52–53: She is drawn to the significance of the art and the existential value of being tattooed, saying, "Just as the inevitability of death is what gives life its meaning, the permanence of tattoos is what gives them great meaning to me."

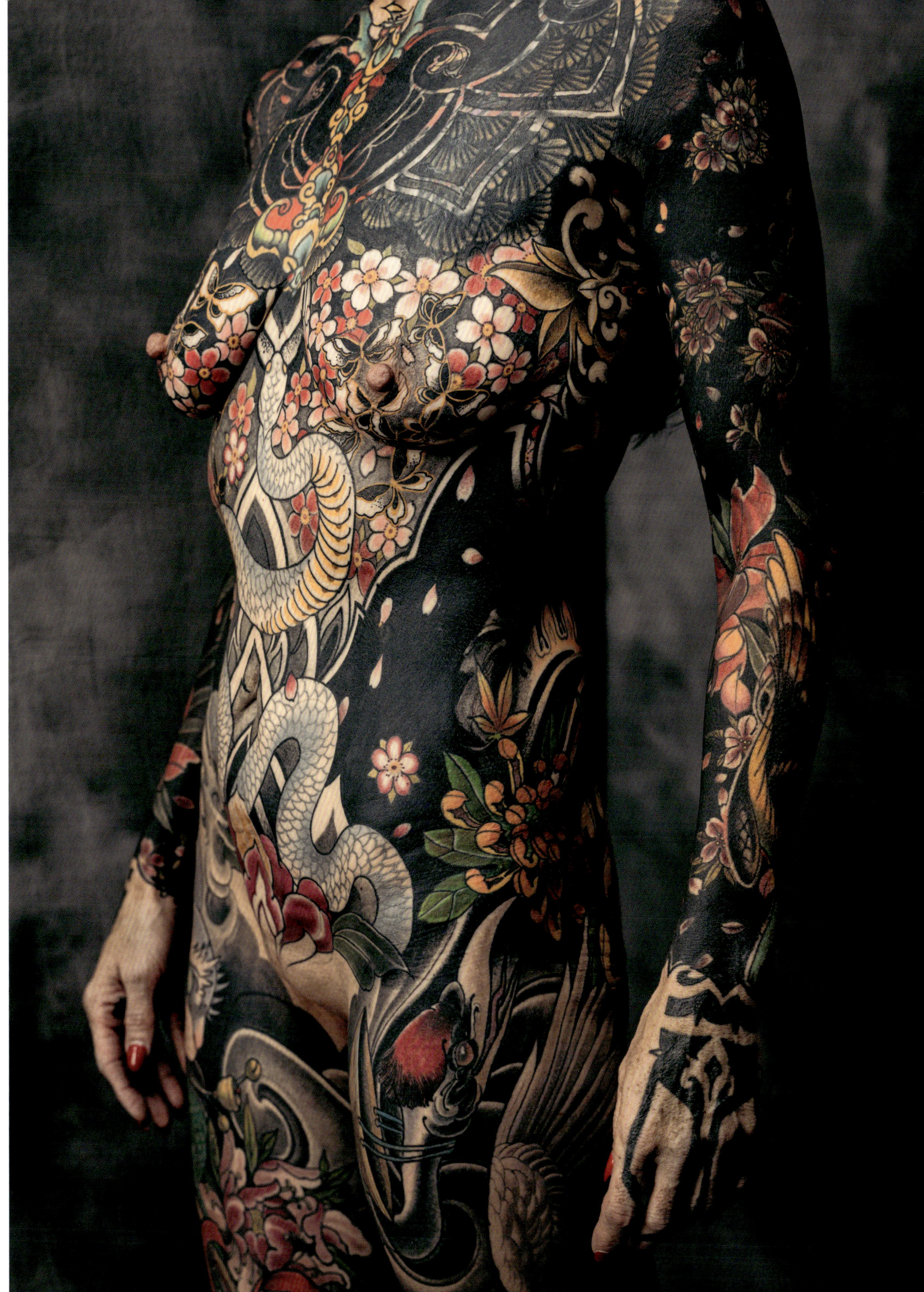

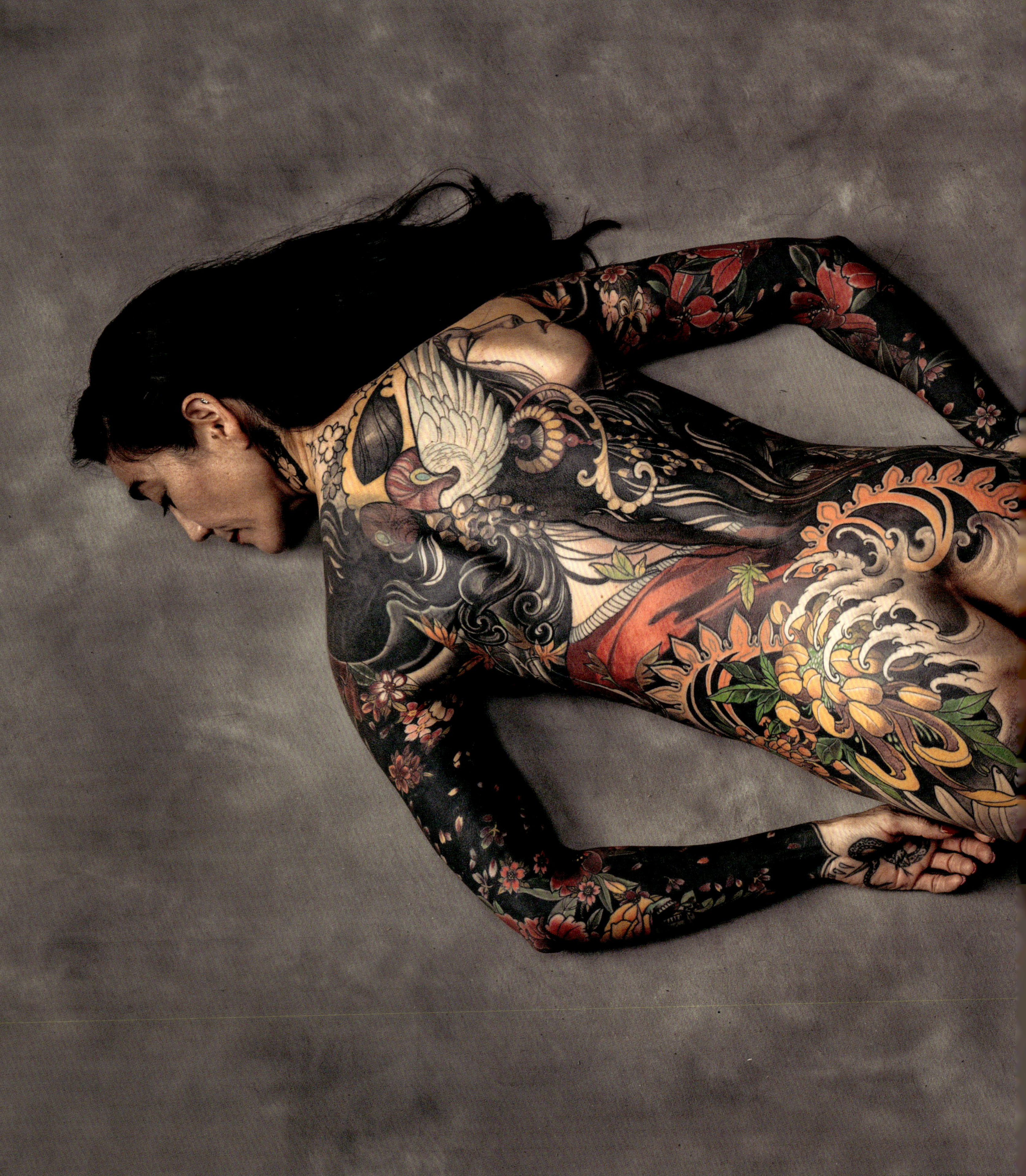

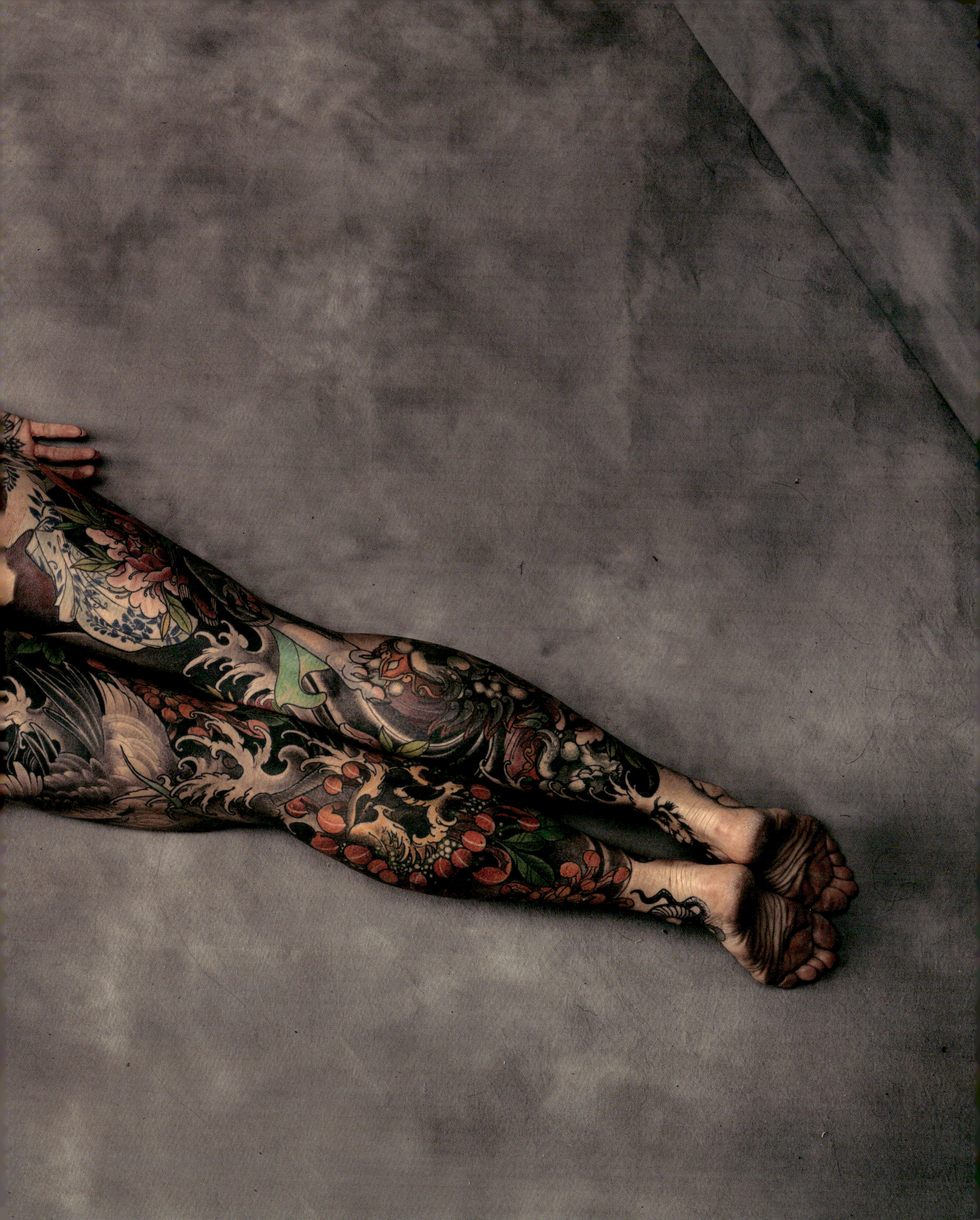

Alongside the pieces Evan Seinfeld has tattooed on himself, he wears work from more than twenty-five artists, including Mike Perfetto, Marcus Pacheco, Mike Rubendall, Mark Mahoney, and Paul Booth.

Pages 56–57: Tattooed in upward of fifty countries around the world, Seinfeld now has been getting inked almost exclusively by Brian Gonzales at Inkslingers in Alhambra, California, the last few years. Gonzales' work includes Seinfeld's head tattoos and blackwork arm.

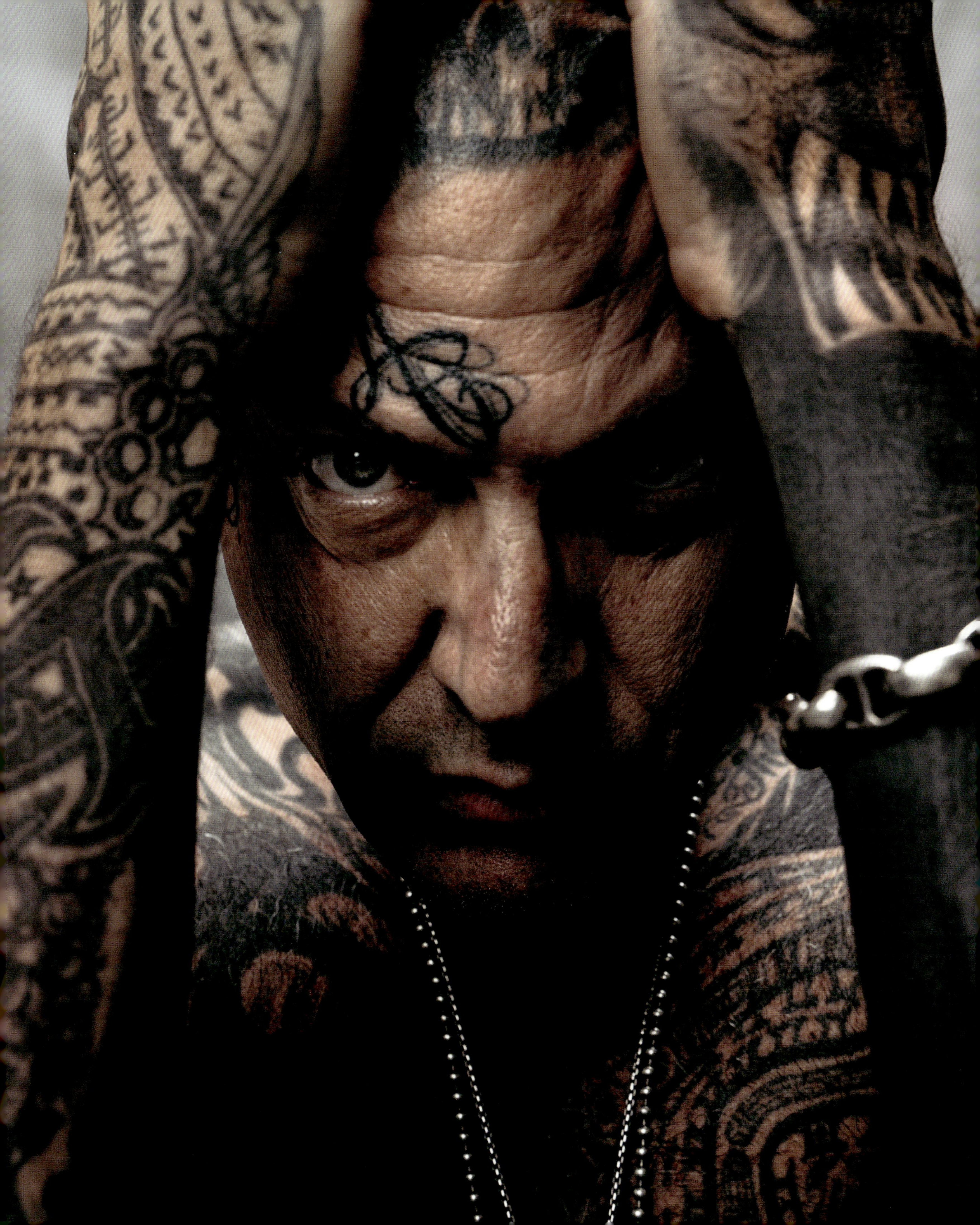

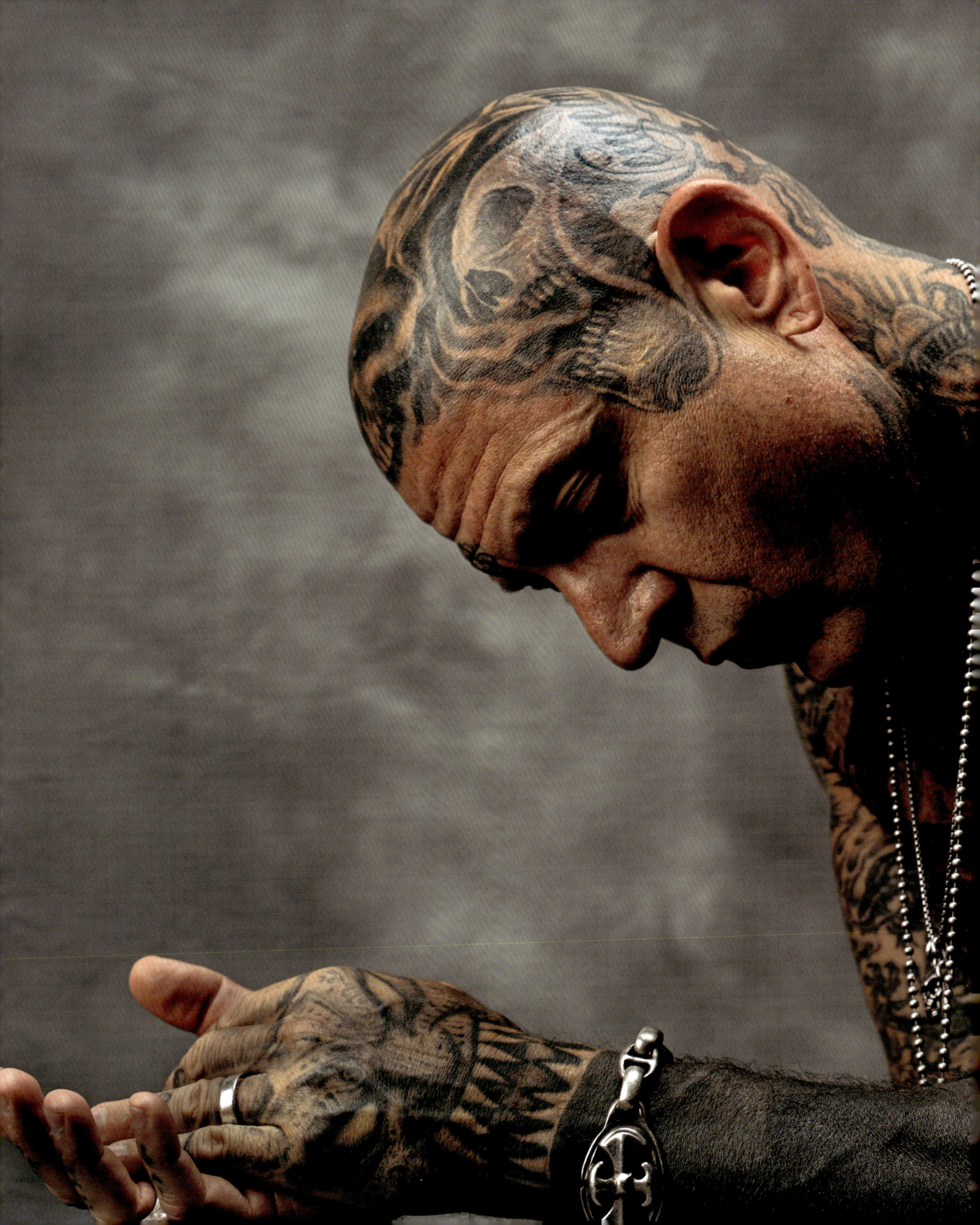

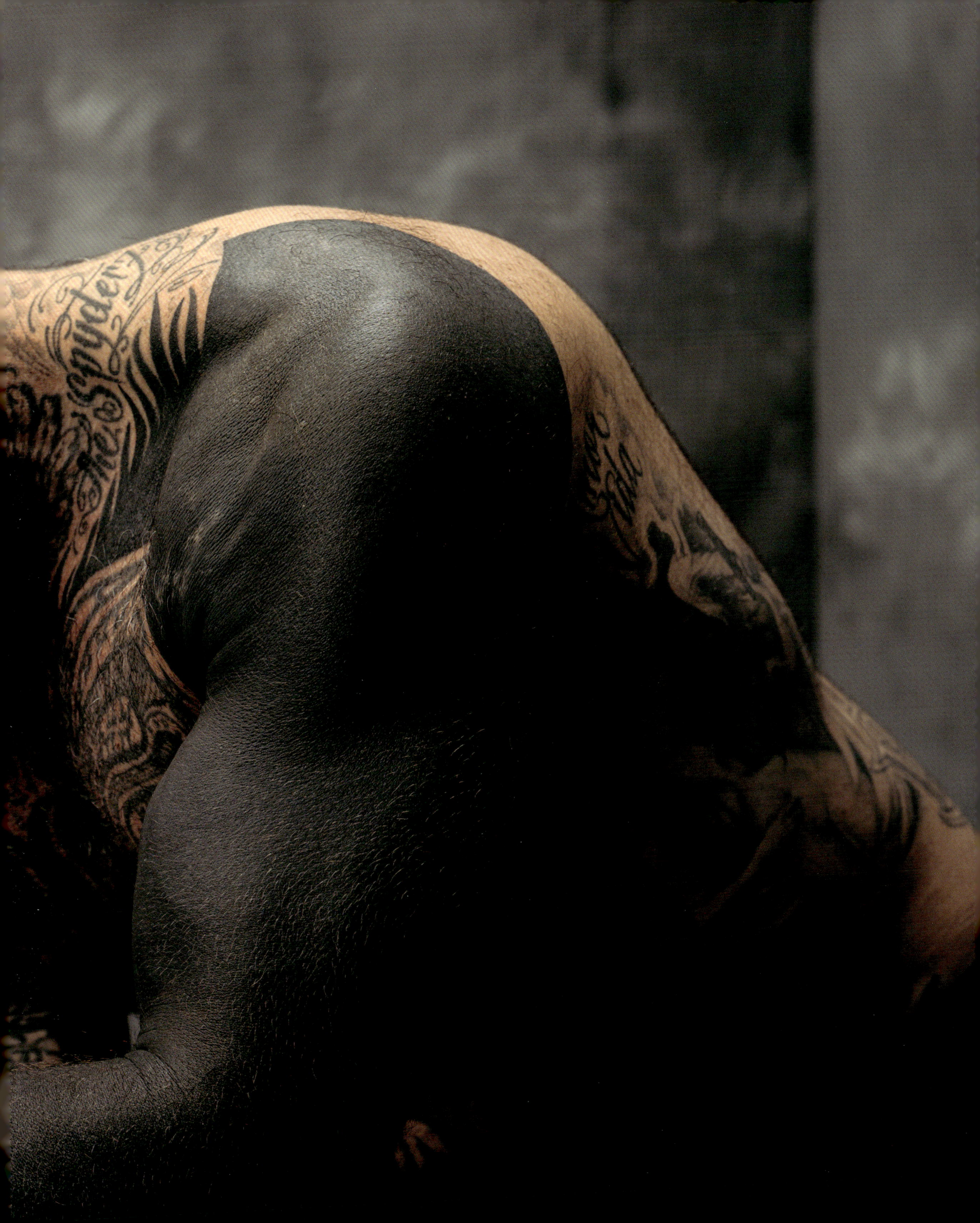

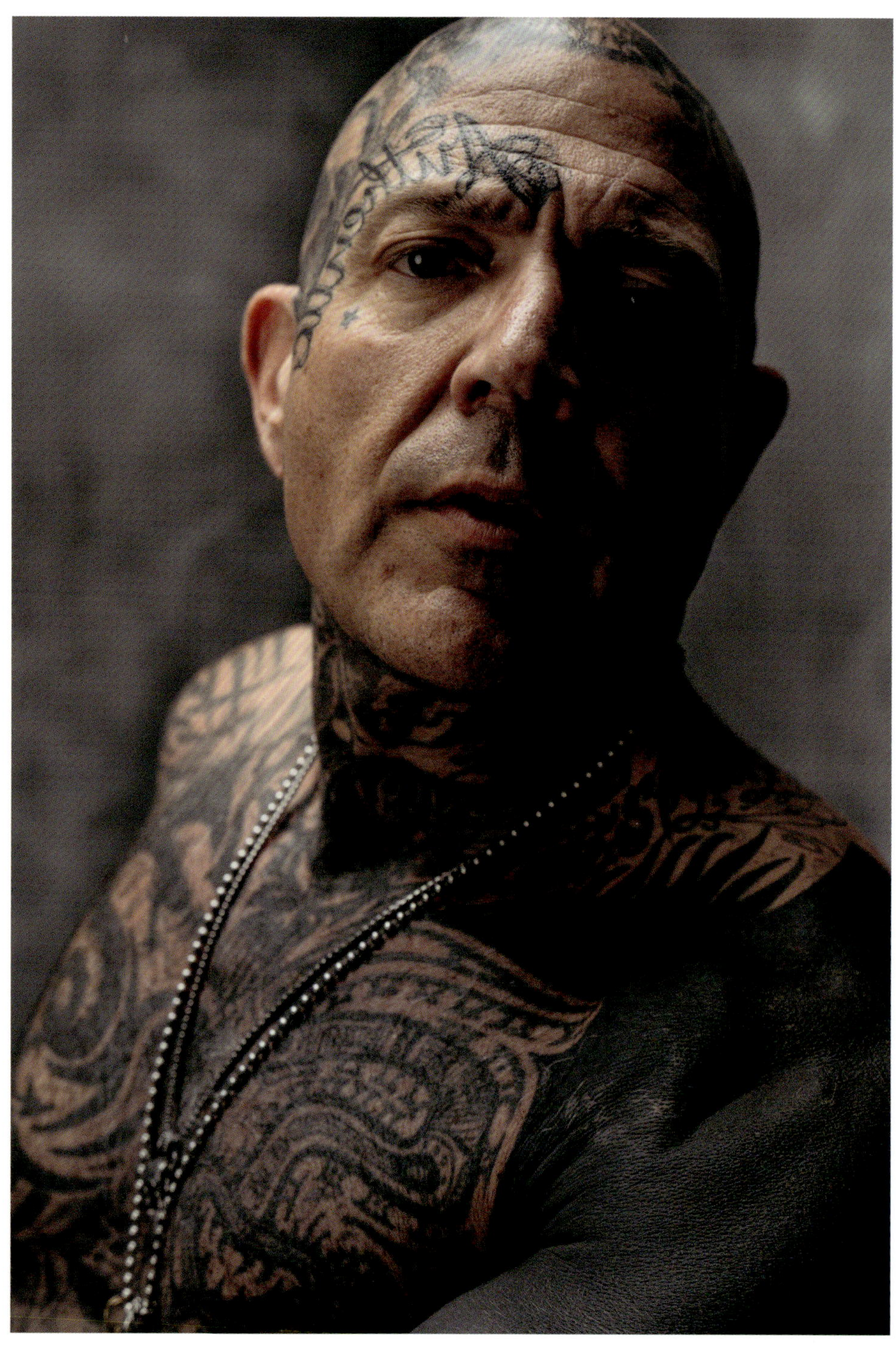

Fernie Andrade tattooed the portrait of Seinfeld's wife with angel wings that reads "Mi Amor, Mi Vida."

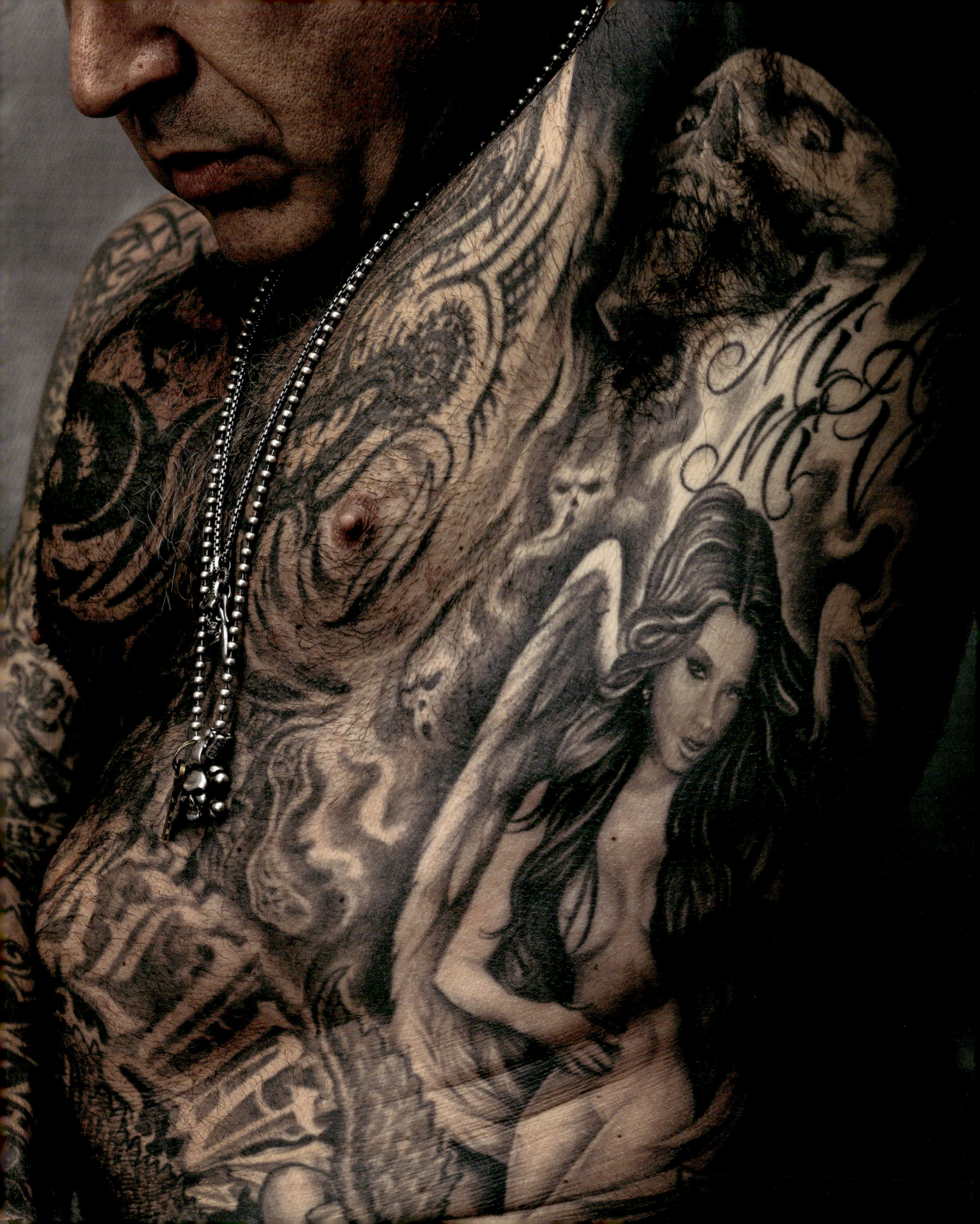

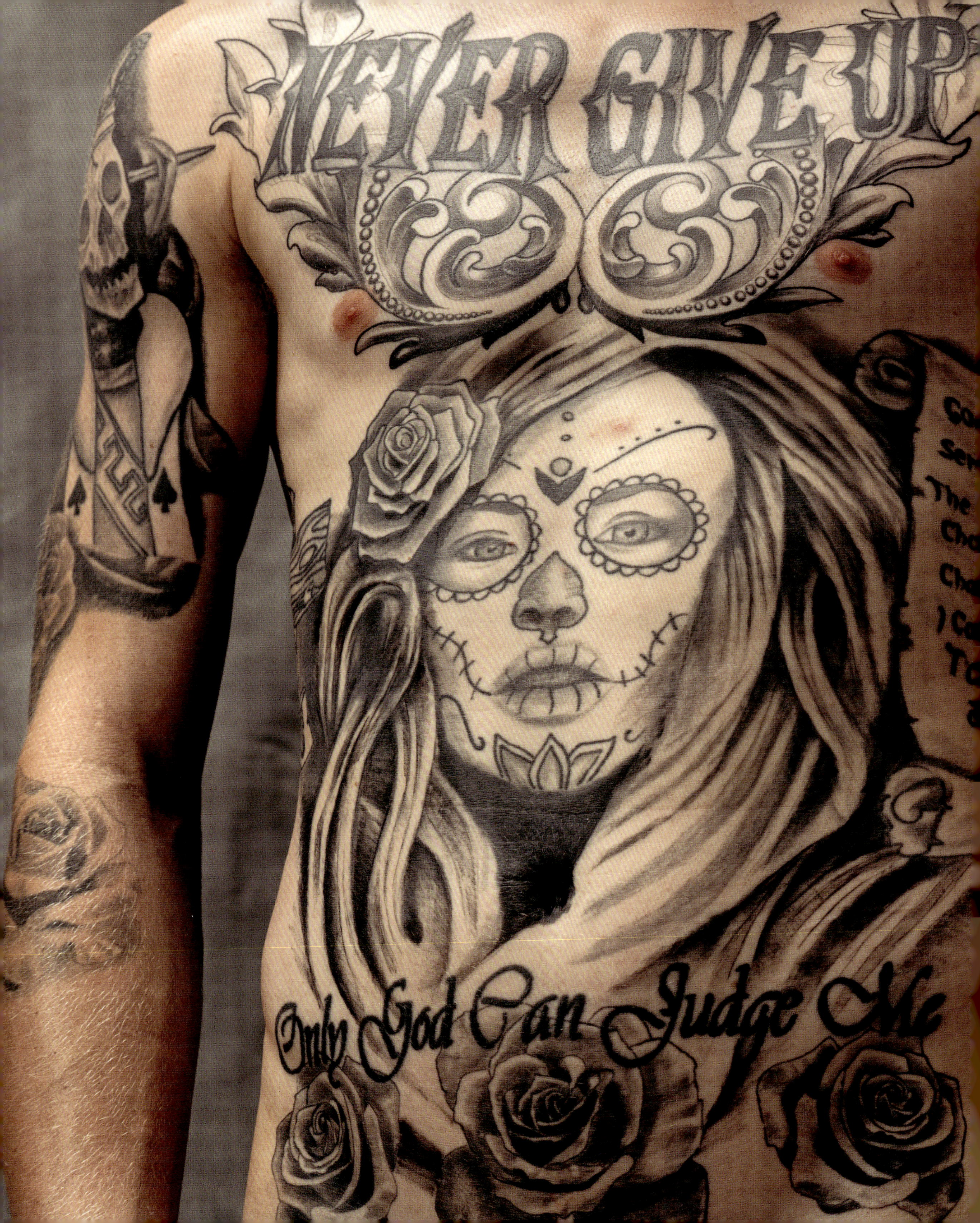
NEVER GIVE UP
Only God Can Judge Me

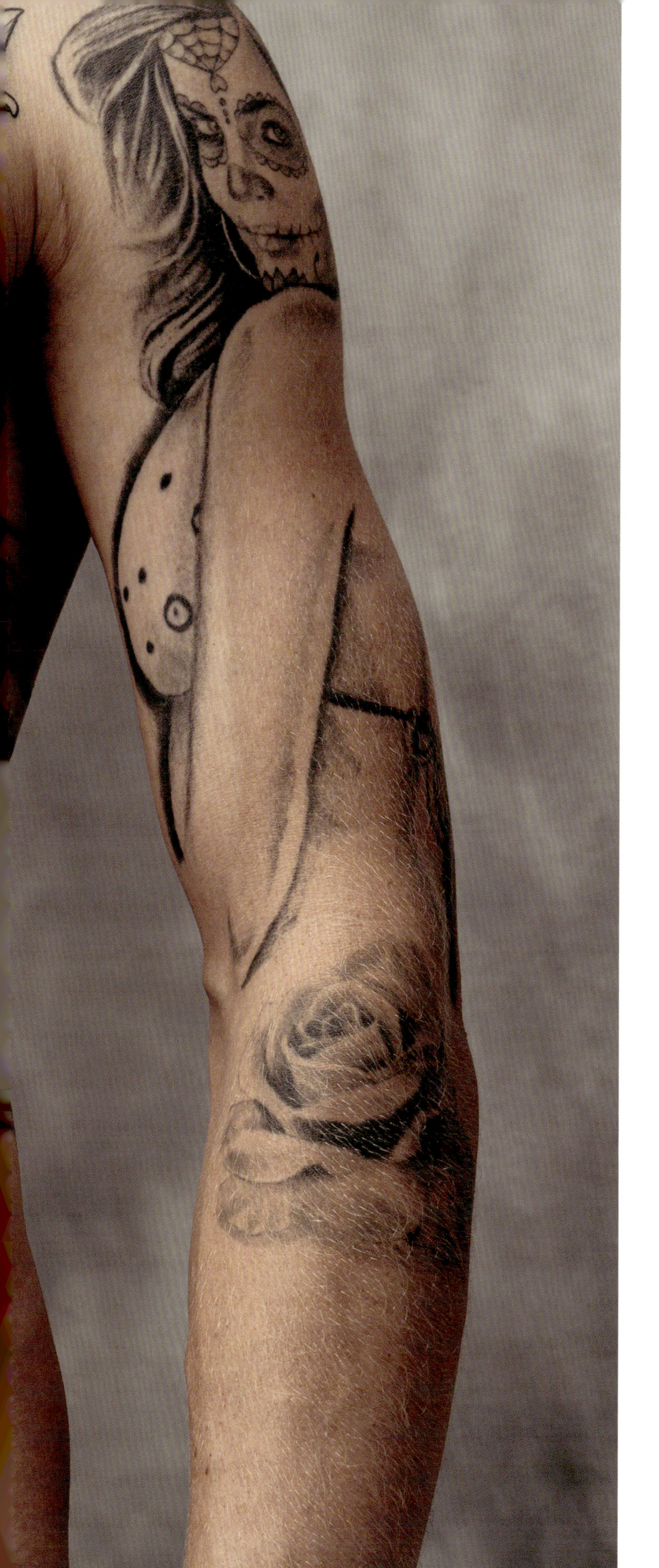

Pages 60–61: Artist Greg Skibo illustrated Devon Colegate's first tattoo, as well as his second piece, on his chest.

Opposite: After a motocross accident, Colegate had to quit riding, but with the help of artist John Eckles, getting tattooed has brought Colegate happiness and stress relief.

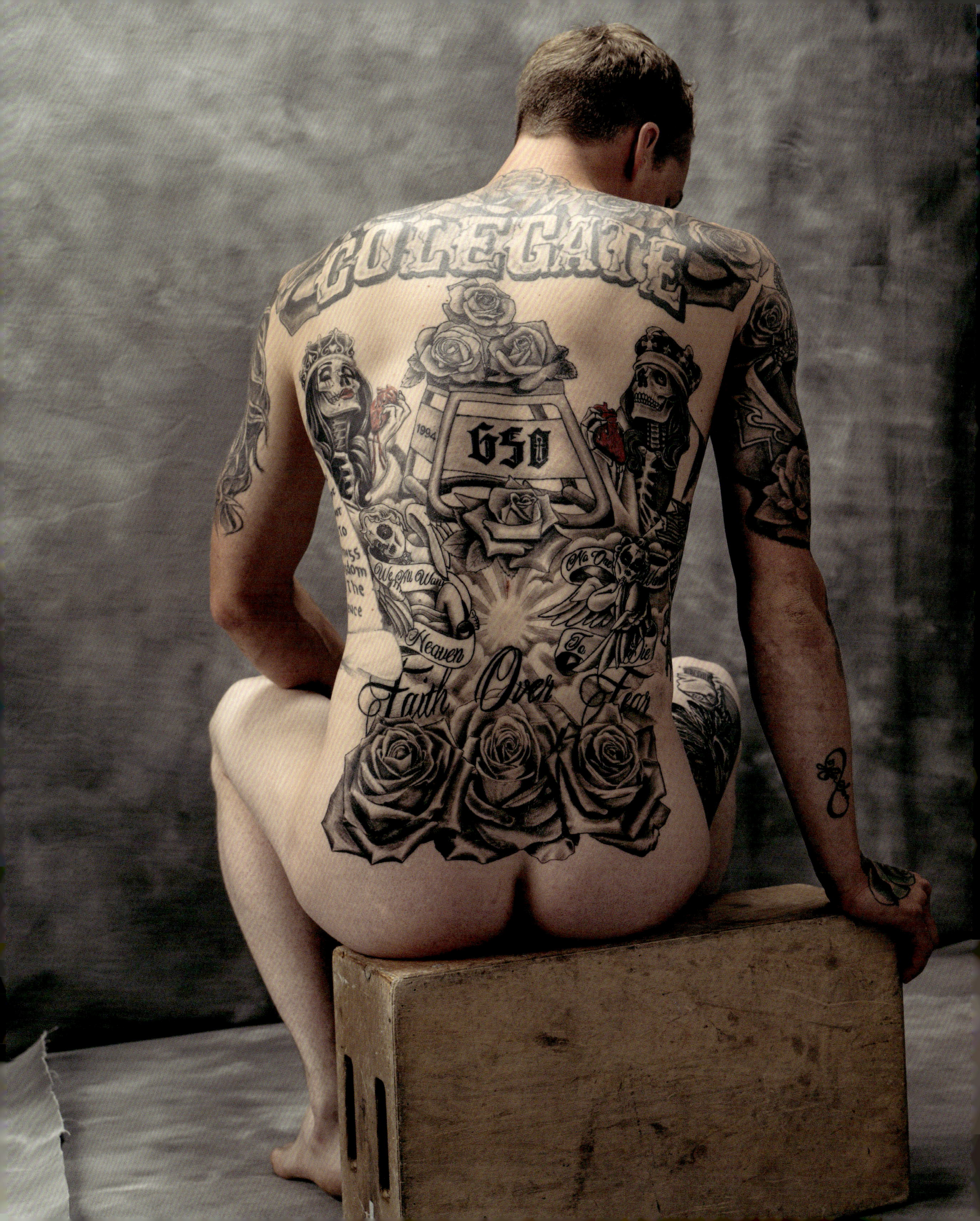
COLEGATE
1994
650
Heaven
Faith Over Fear

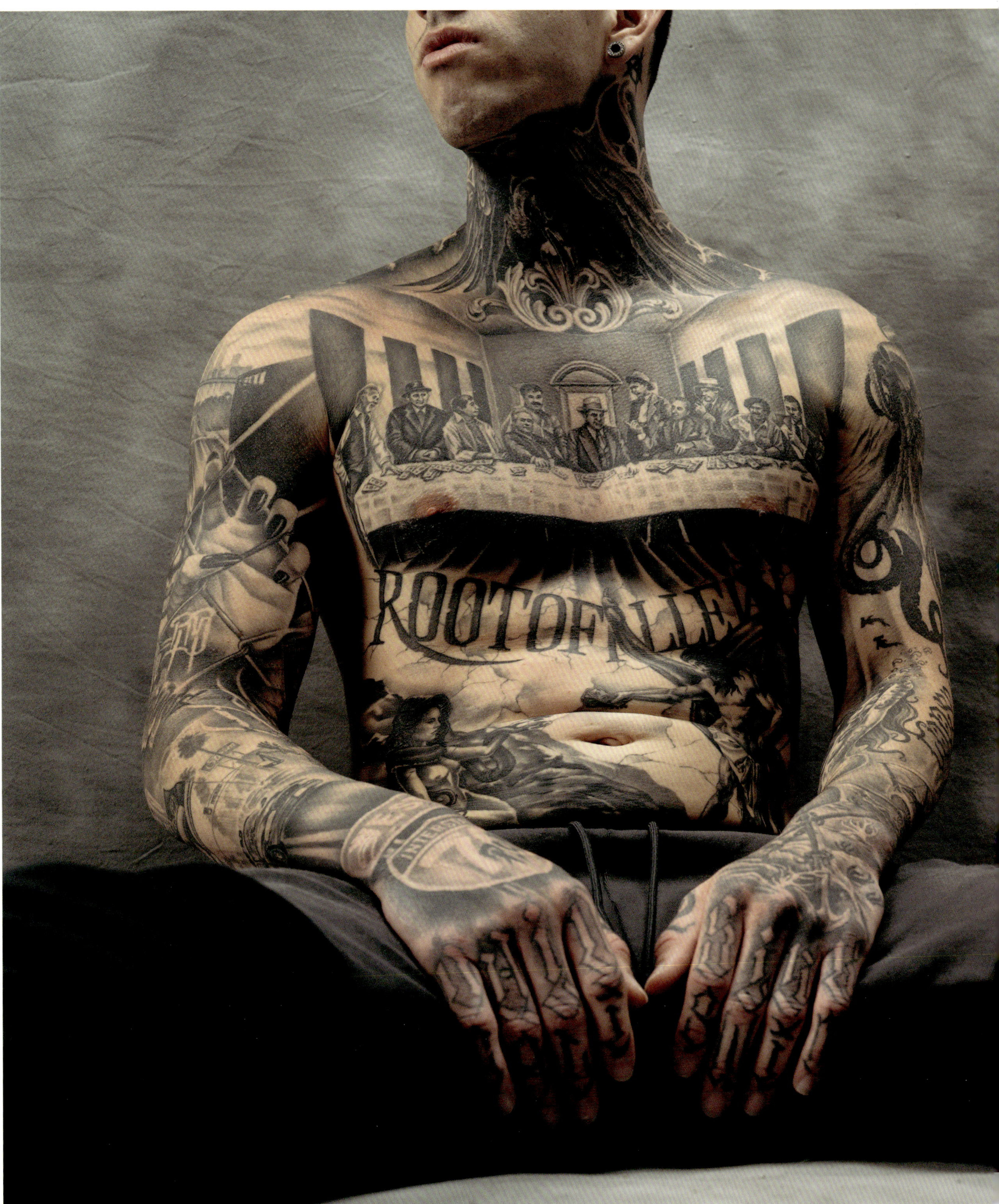

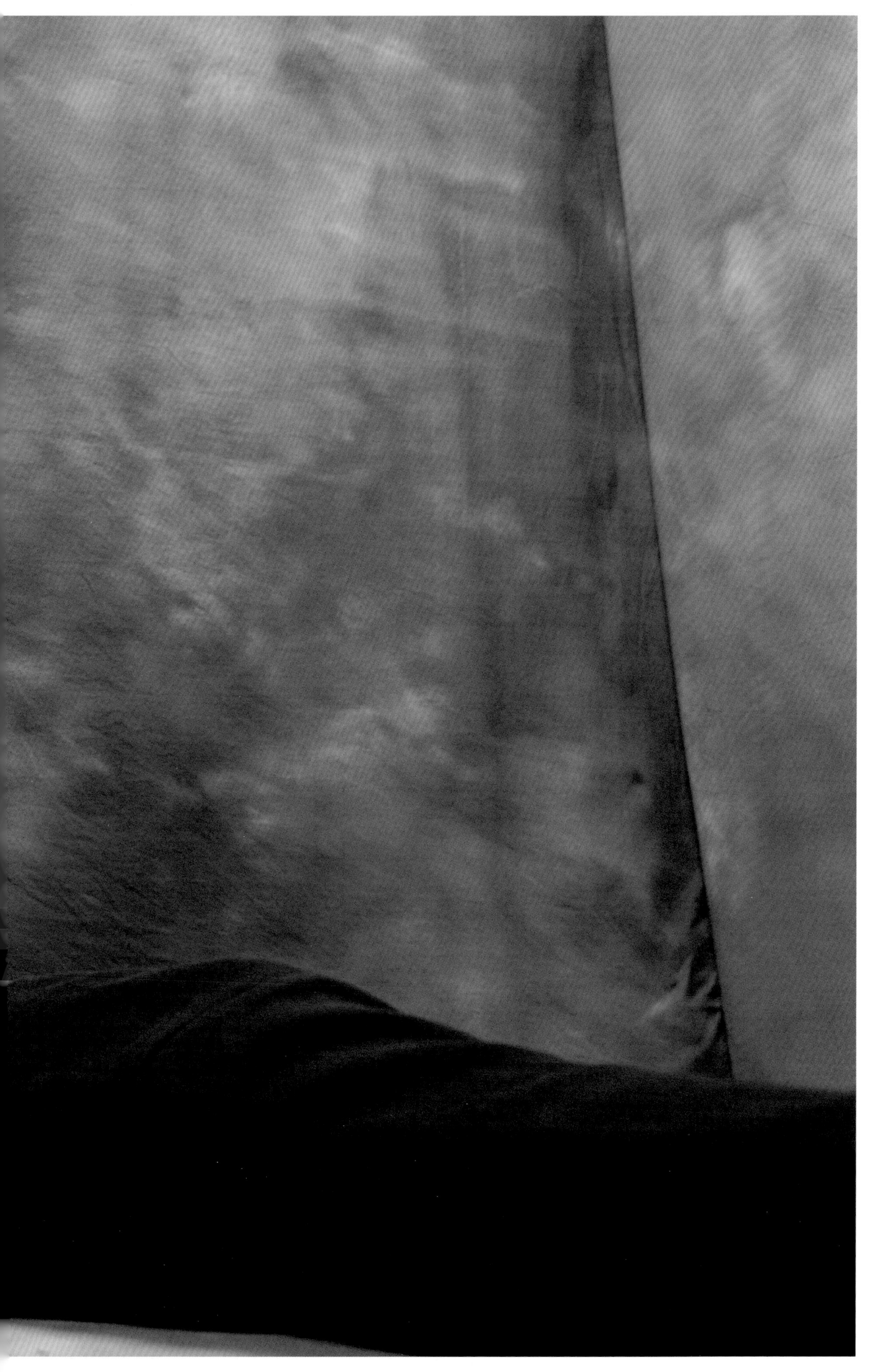

Pages 64–65: Artist Angel Rose's take on the Last Supper on collector Brady Storm, nicknamed Bodysuitbrady, features America's infamous gangsters: (left to right) Big Meech, John Dillinger, Pablo Escobar, Machine Gun Kelly, Frank Costello, Clyde Barrow, Al Capone, El Chapo, John Gotti, Henry Hill, Carlo Gambino, and Vinny Ocean.

Opposite: DJ Sev-One's favorite tattoo of his collection was done by Jeff Saunders: of DJ Sev-One's father at nine years old, the same age Sev was when he passed away.

Pages 68–69: DJ Sev-One, whose own graffiti has kept him running from the police throughout his life, also wears work from Sasha Konkin, Big Toons, and Shane Bonham.

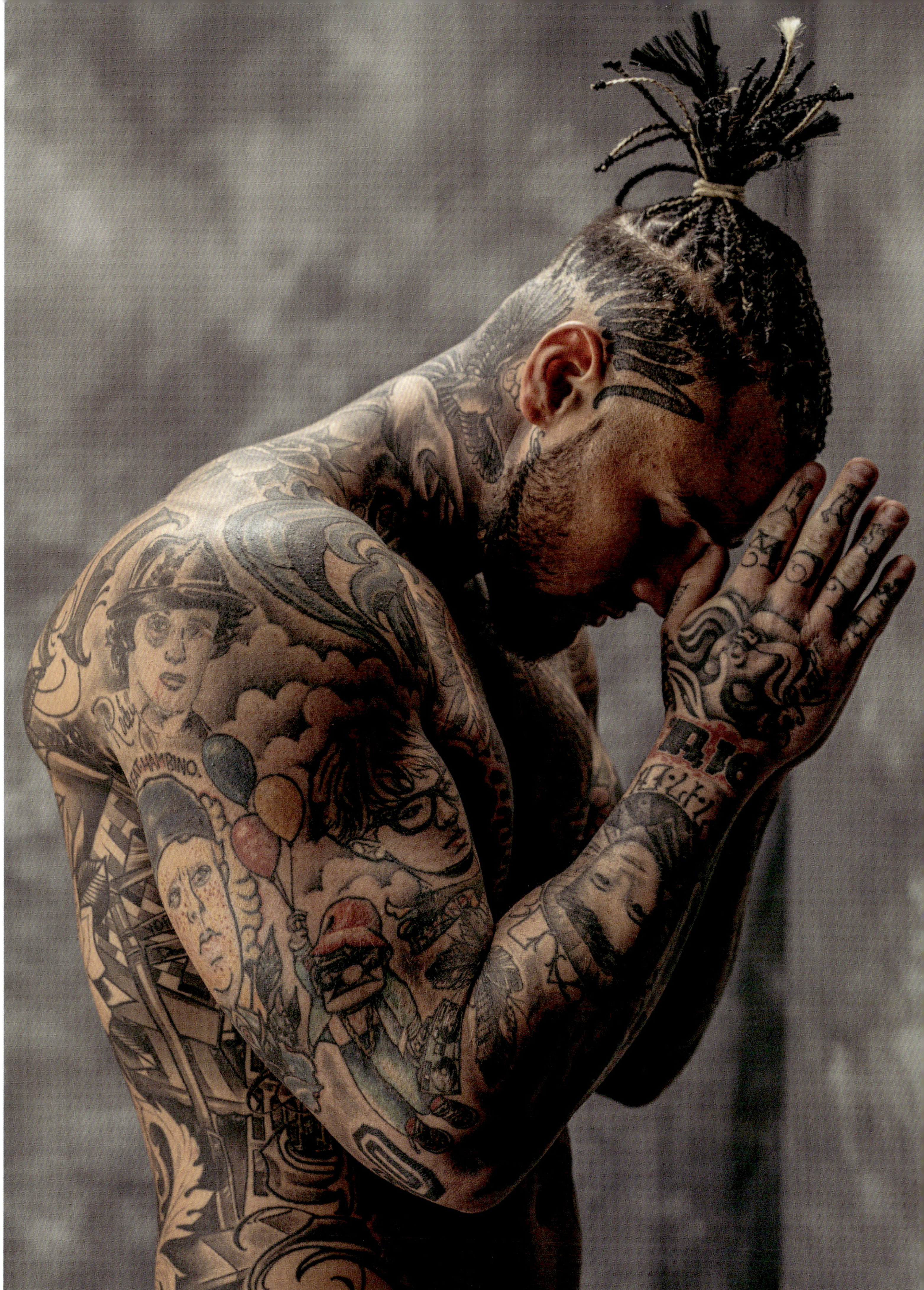

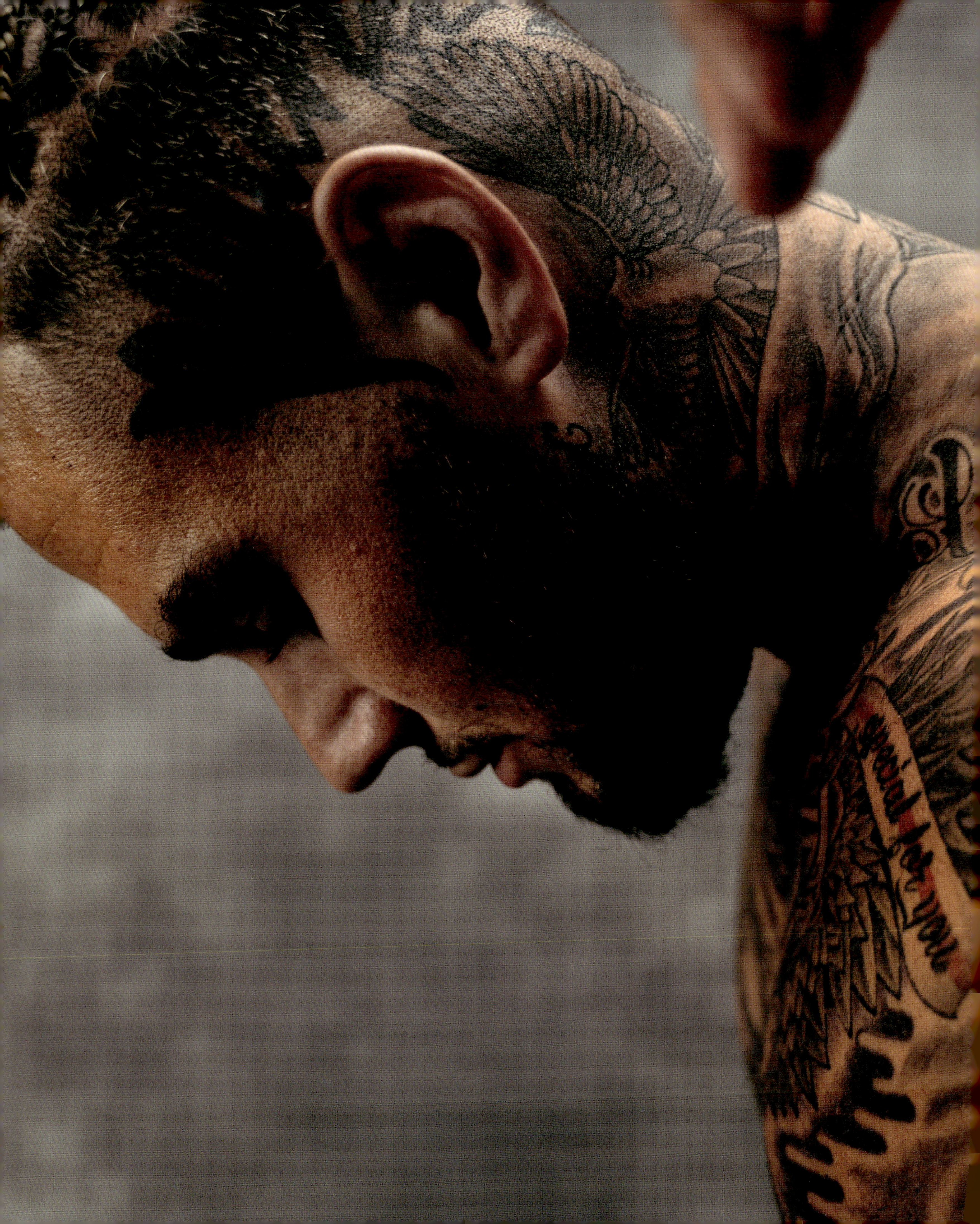

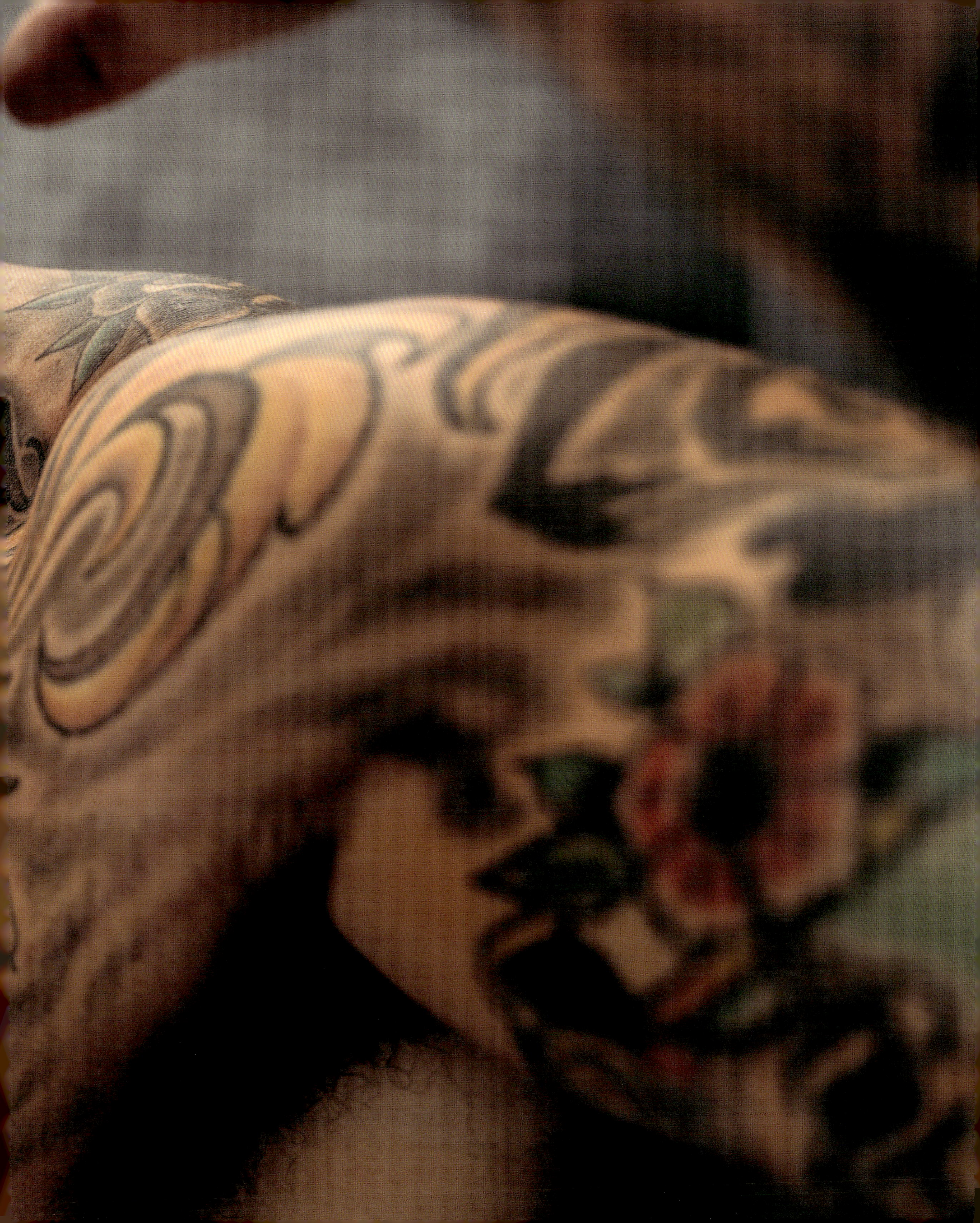

Joseph Cucurillo's Japanese-style bodysuit was tattooed by Bill Canales at Full Circle Tattoo in San Diego, California. Angel Mancini's collection includes work from Angel Reynosa, Joey Ortega, Jadd McElroy, Omar Sanchez, and Lara Scotton.

Pages 72–73: Mancini's first tattoo, of a martian lady on her arm, was illustrated by her go-to artist, Devx Ruiz. Cucurillo's bodysuit took about 265 hours to complete, done over the course of nineteen months, from February 2016 to August 2018.

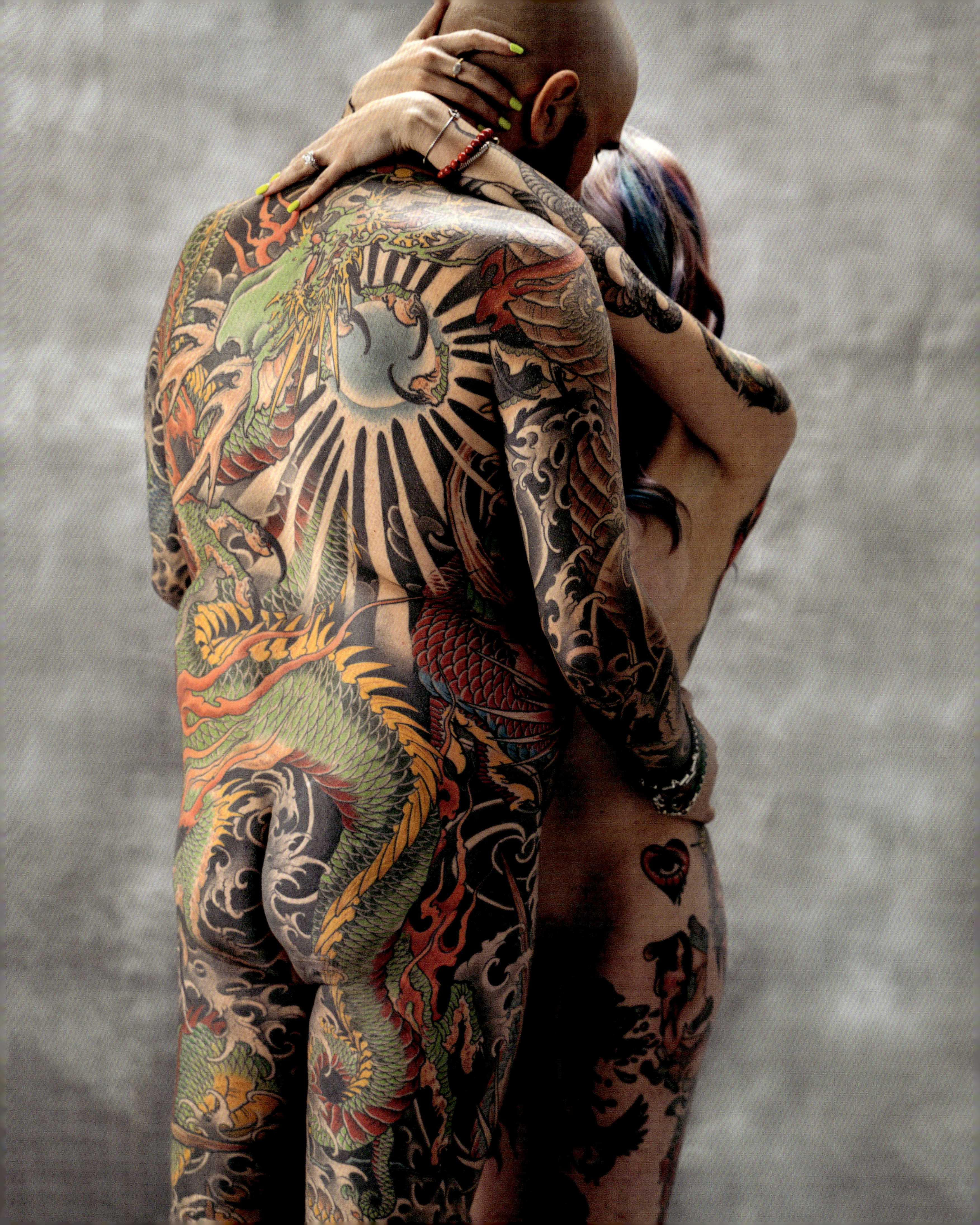

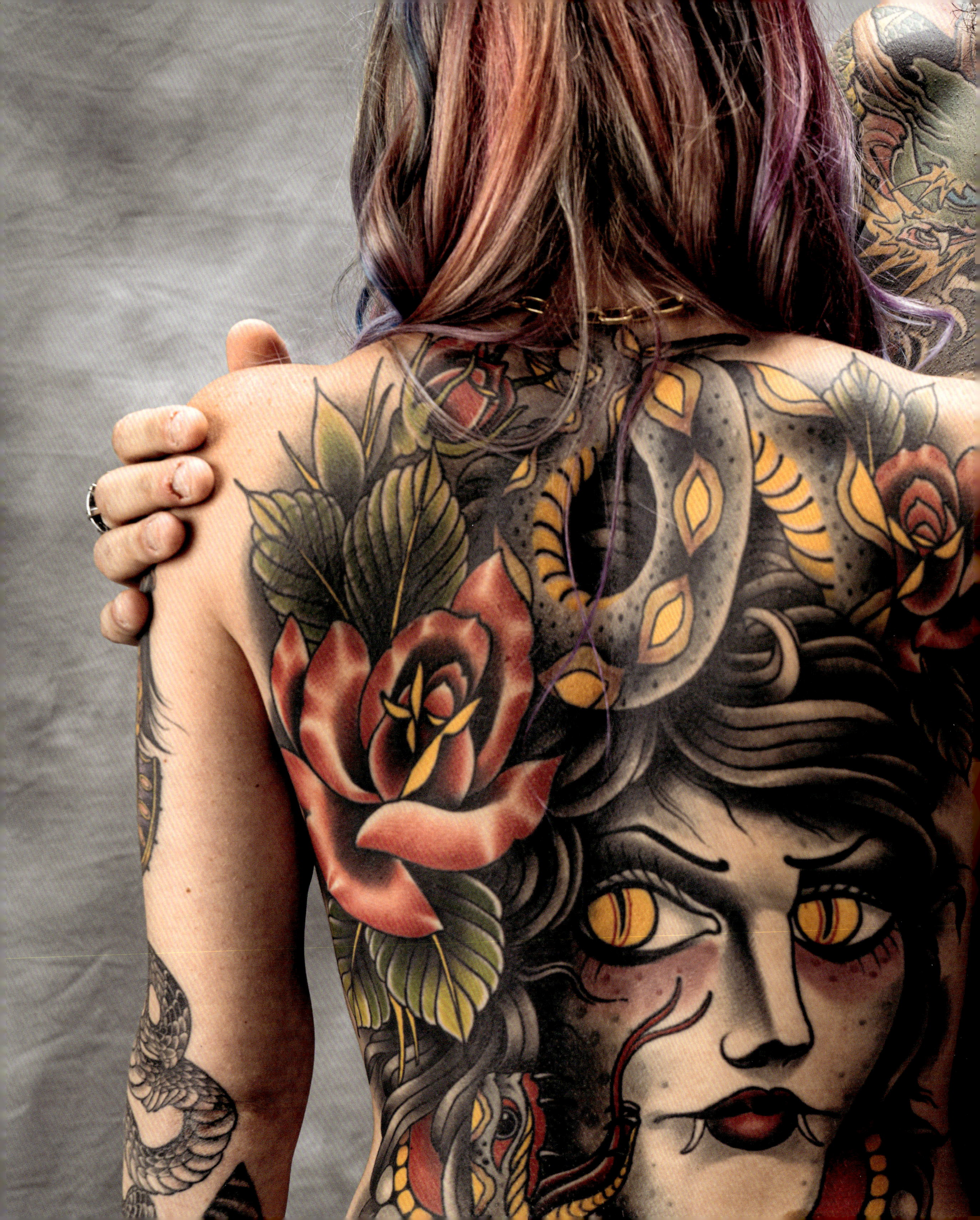

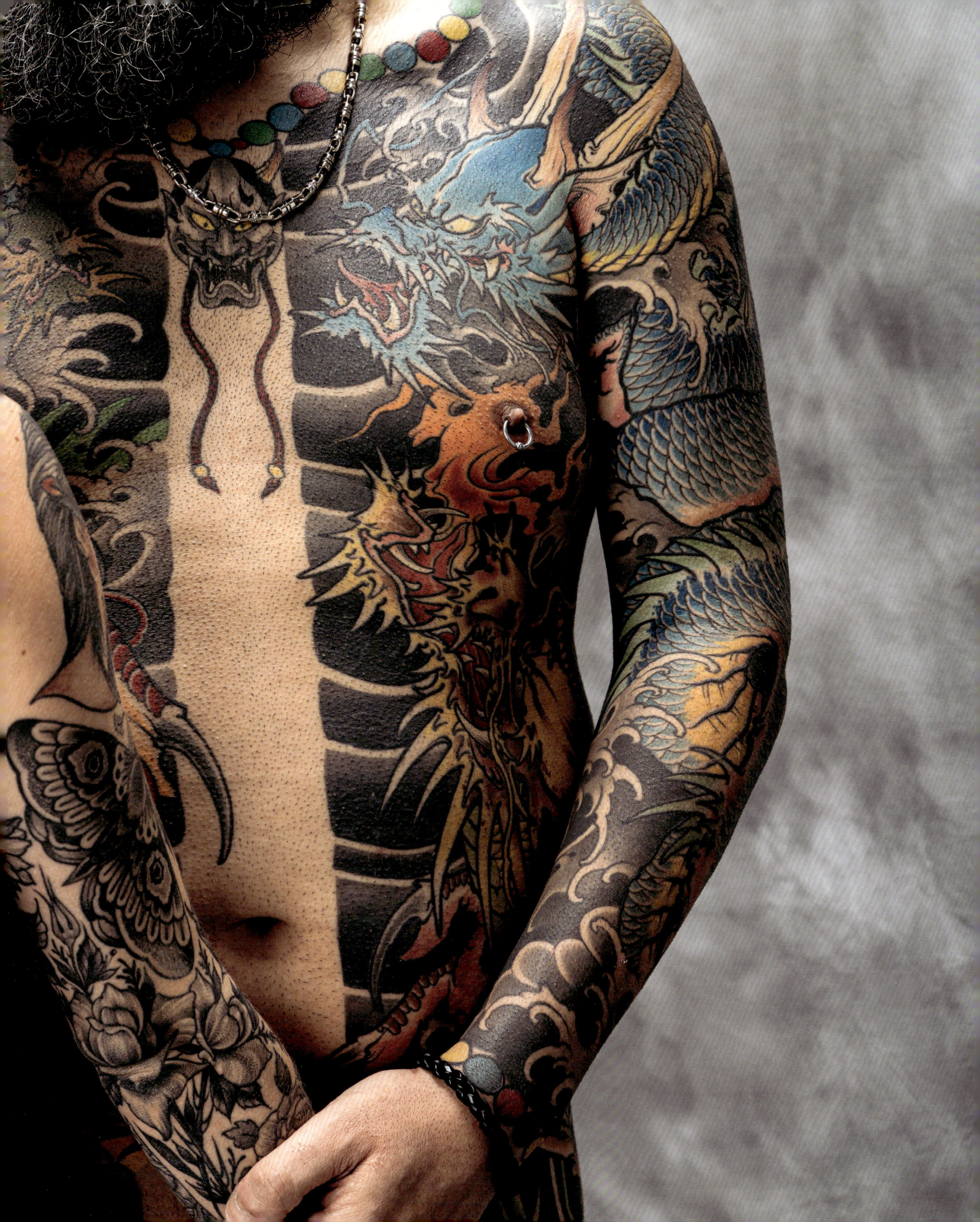

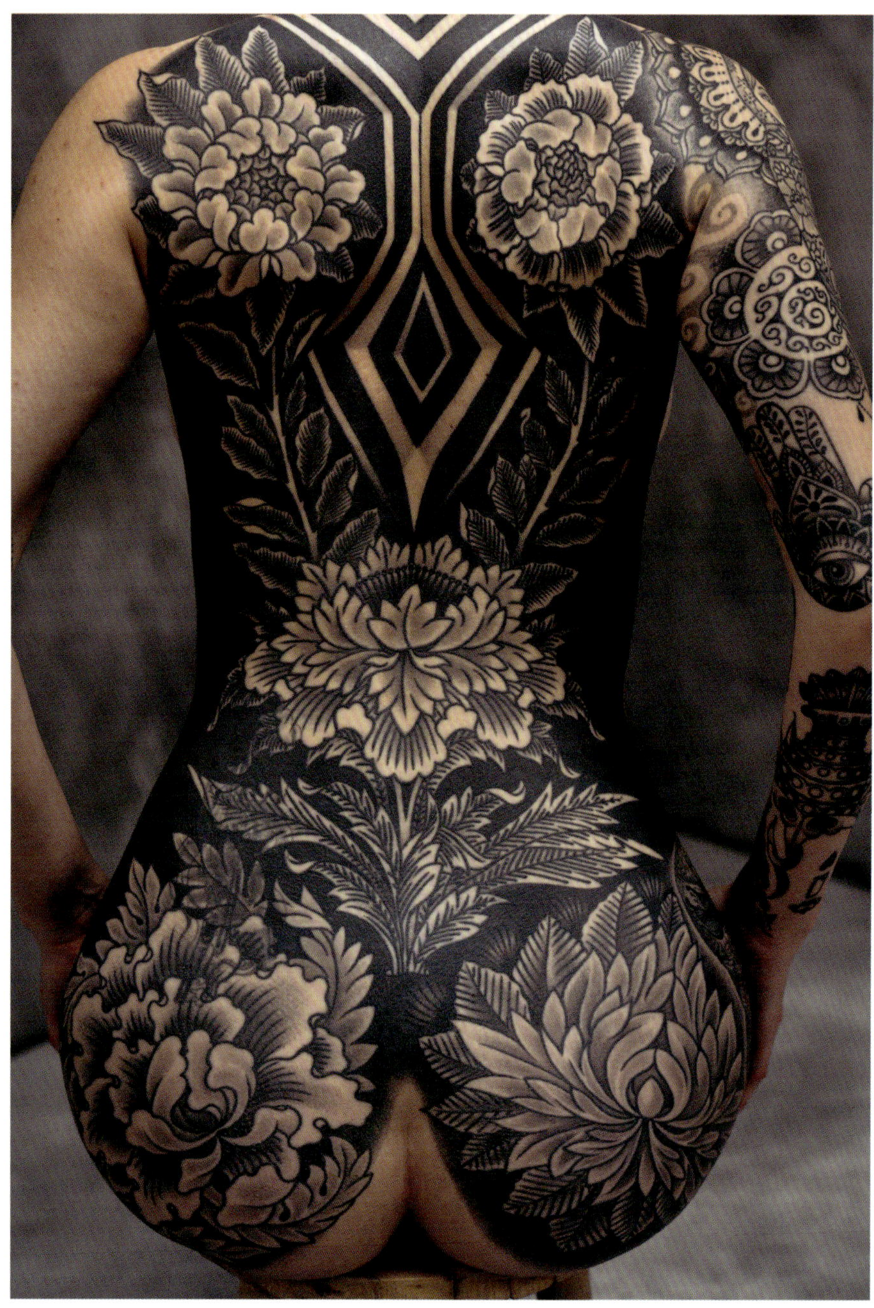

Octavia Plach is proud of her blackwork and patterned-tattoo collection by Hoode, Mony, Zakk Ross, Kyle Fitzpatrick, and Andrew Borisyuk. Her back and butt were done by Hoode, while her chest was done by Mony.

Pages 76–77: "There's an ecstasy to collecting different art pieces to cultivate one large canvas," shares Plach, who loves the blackwork-style look.

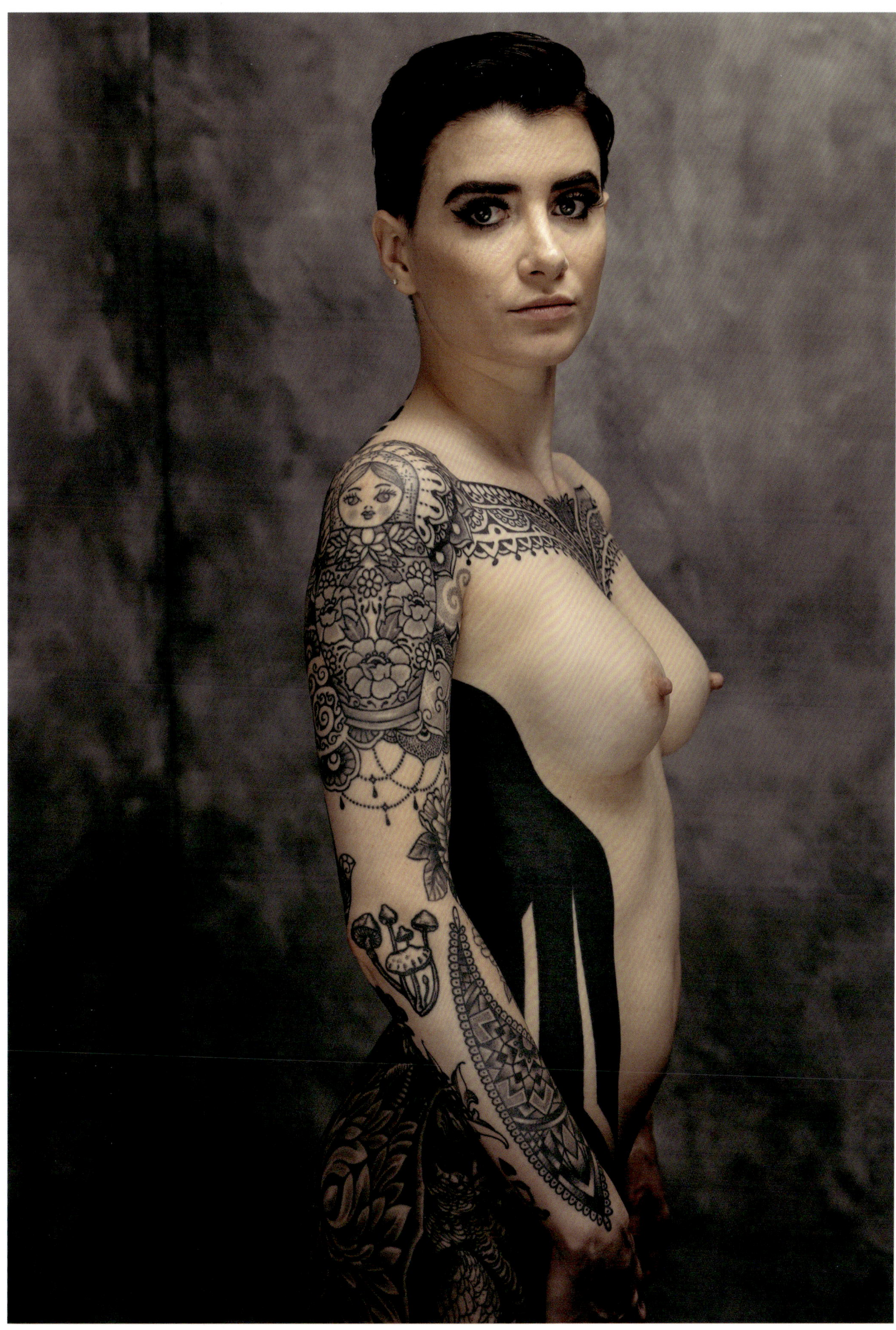

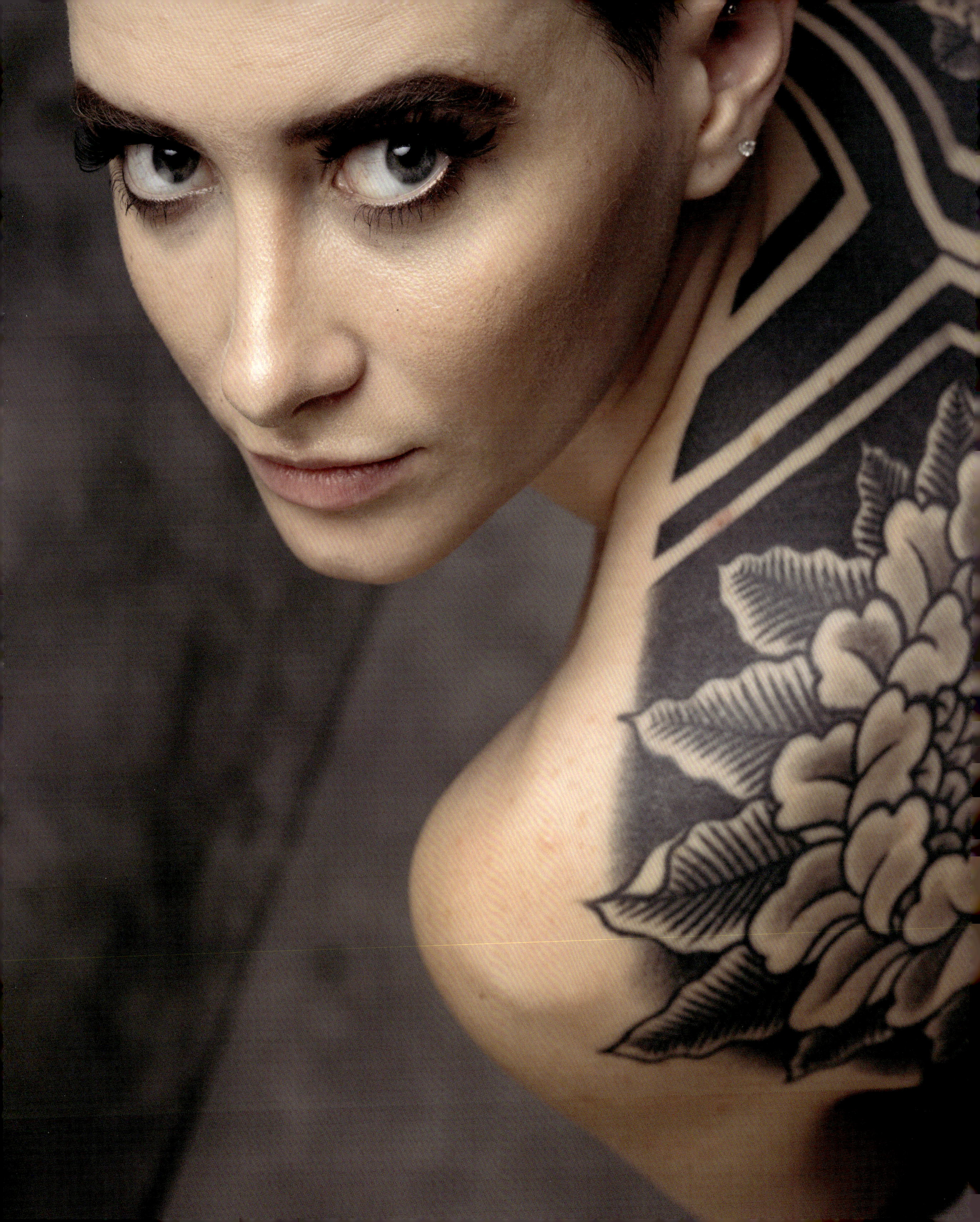

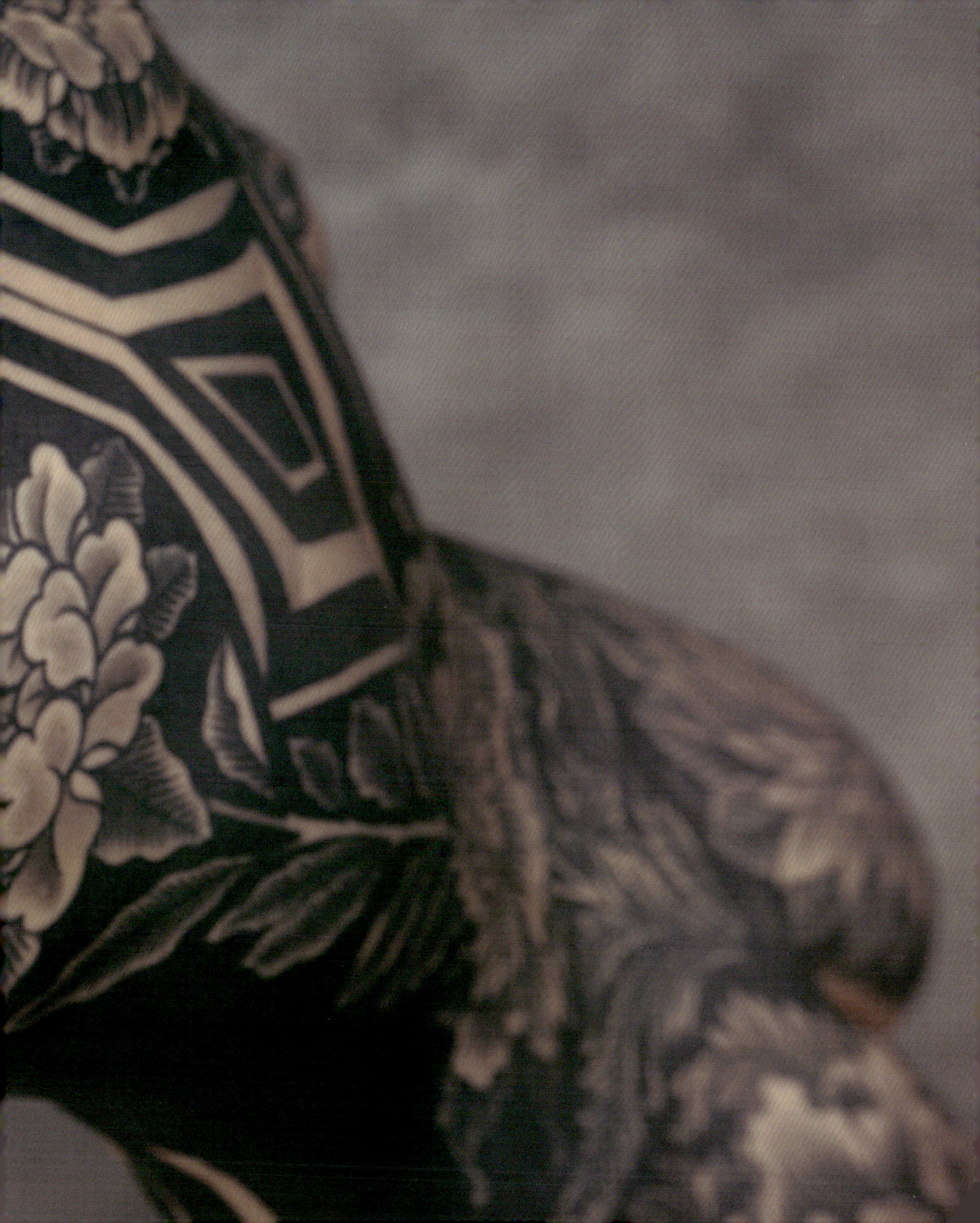

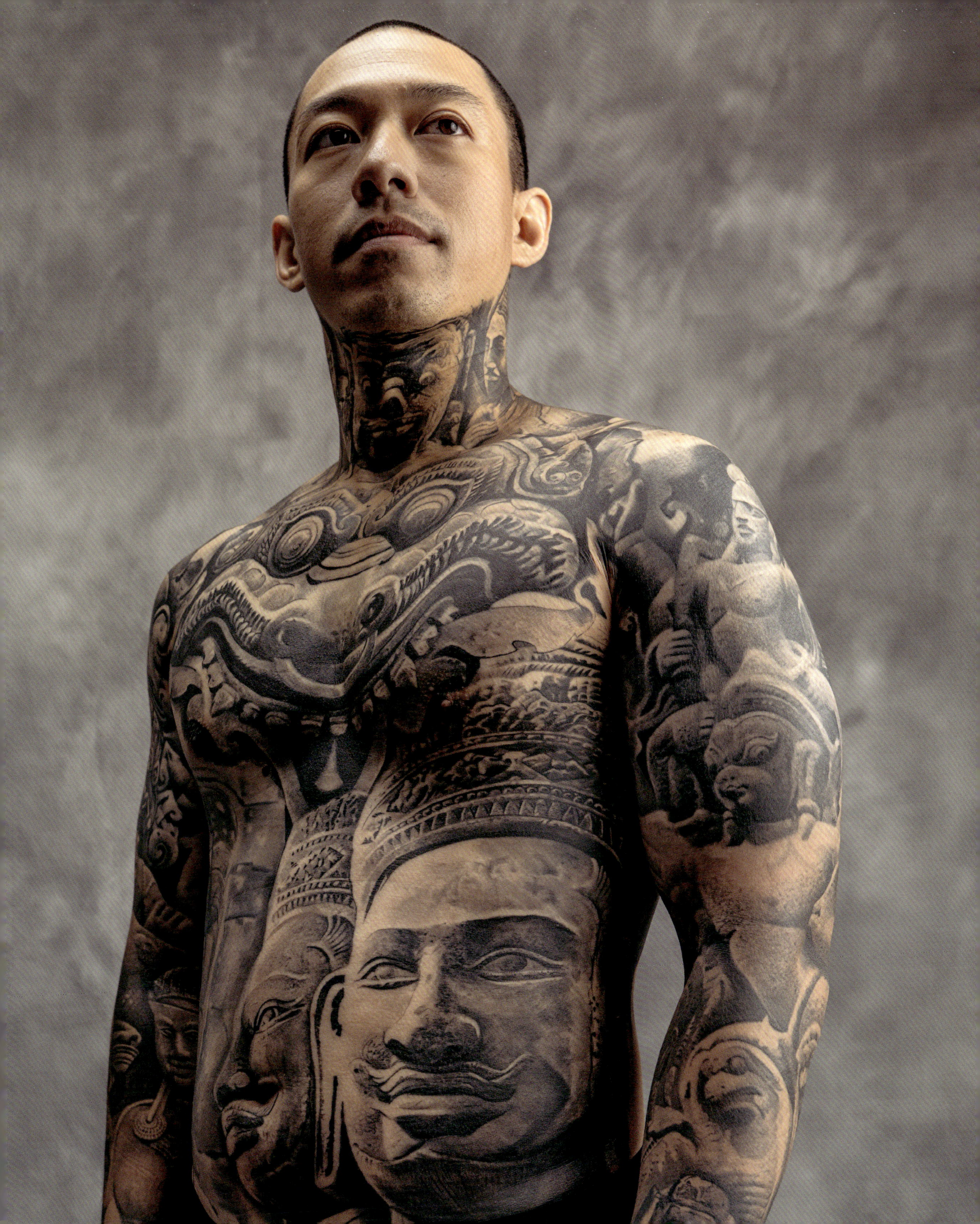

Pages 78–79: Tattoo collector and artist Andy Pho wears an Angkorian bodysuit, illustrated and tattooed by his brother and mentor, Robert Pho.

Opposite: "Being a tattoo collector is both powerful and vulnerable," says Quest G. His most meaningful tattoos include the names of his mom, his sisters, and all of his ex-girlfriends.

Page 82–83: Quest G wears work by artists Joshua Stallworth, Big Toons, Joseph Haefs, Joey Mullen, and Moriel "El Mori" Seror.

Pages 84–85: Billy Bartow, prison guard for the California Department of Corrections and Rehabilitation, wears knuckle tattoos by Layne Furniss, with his front primarily tattooed by Thomas Young.

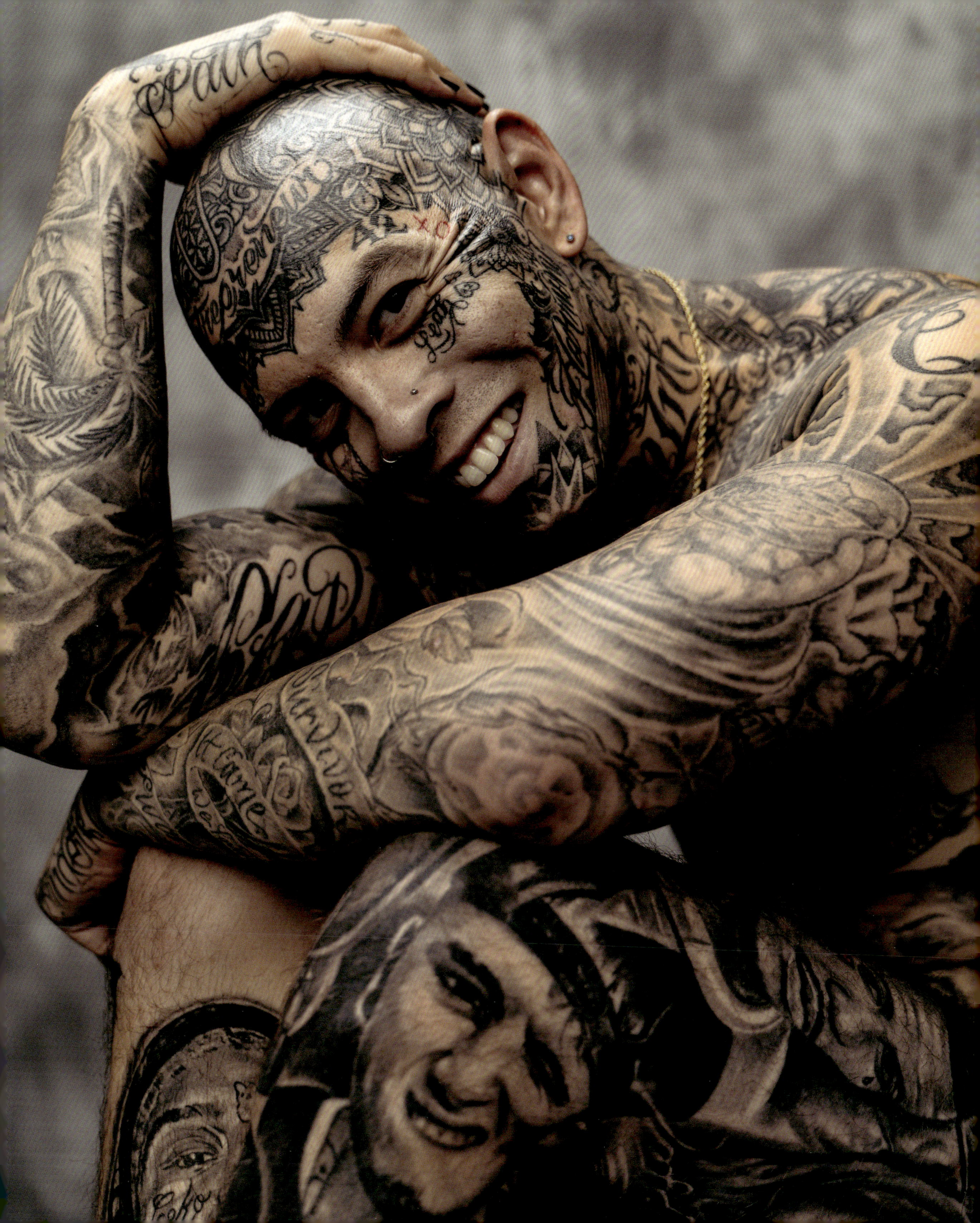
Path

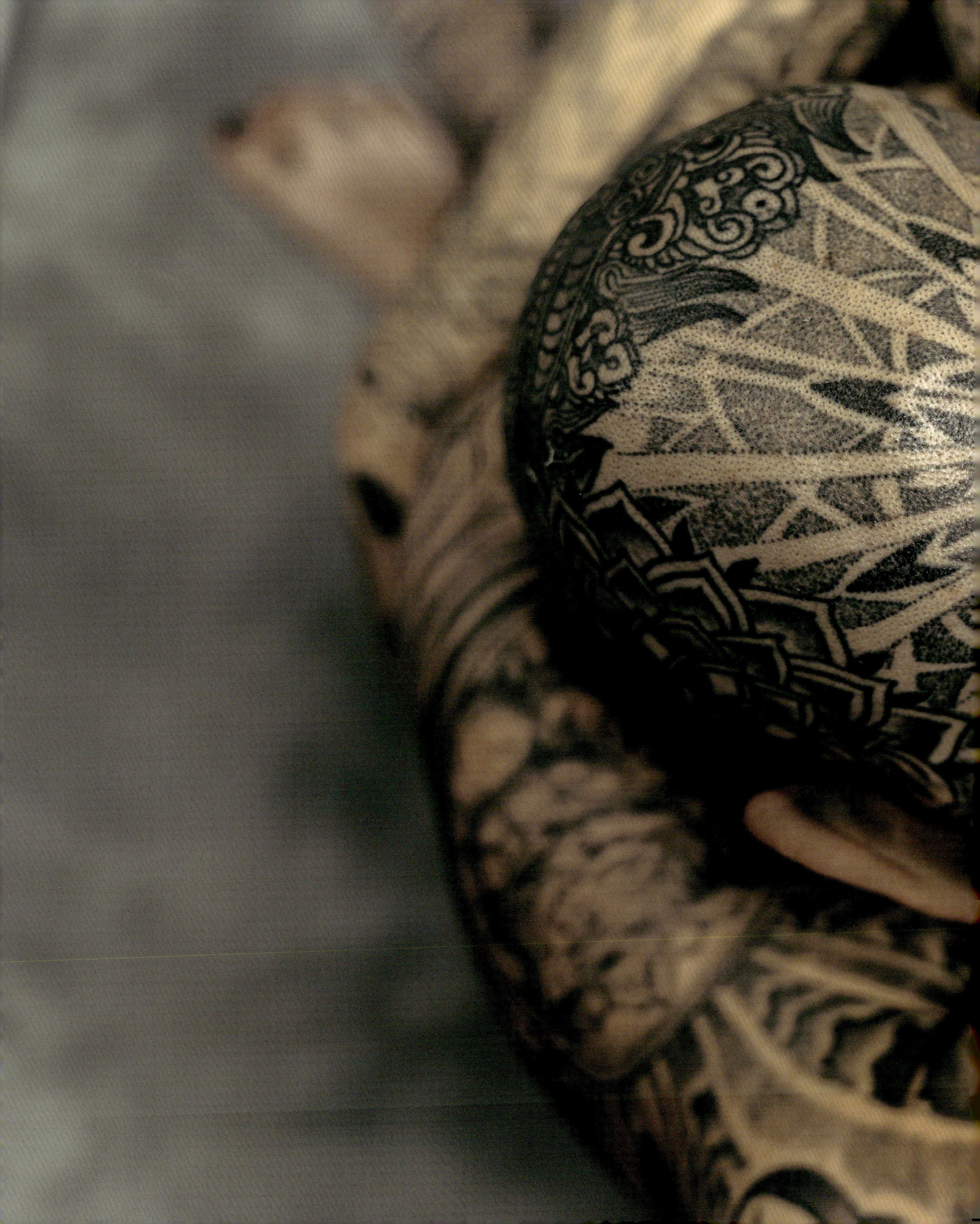

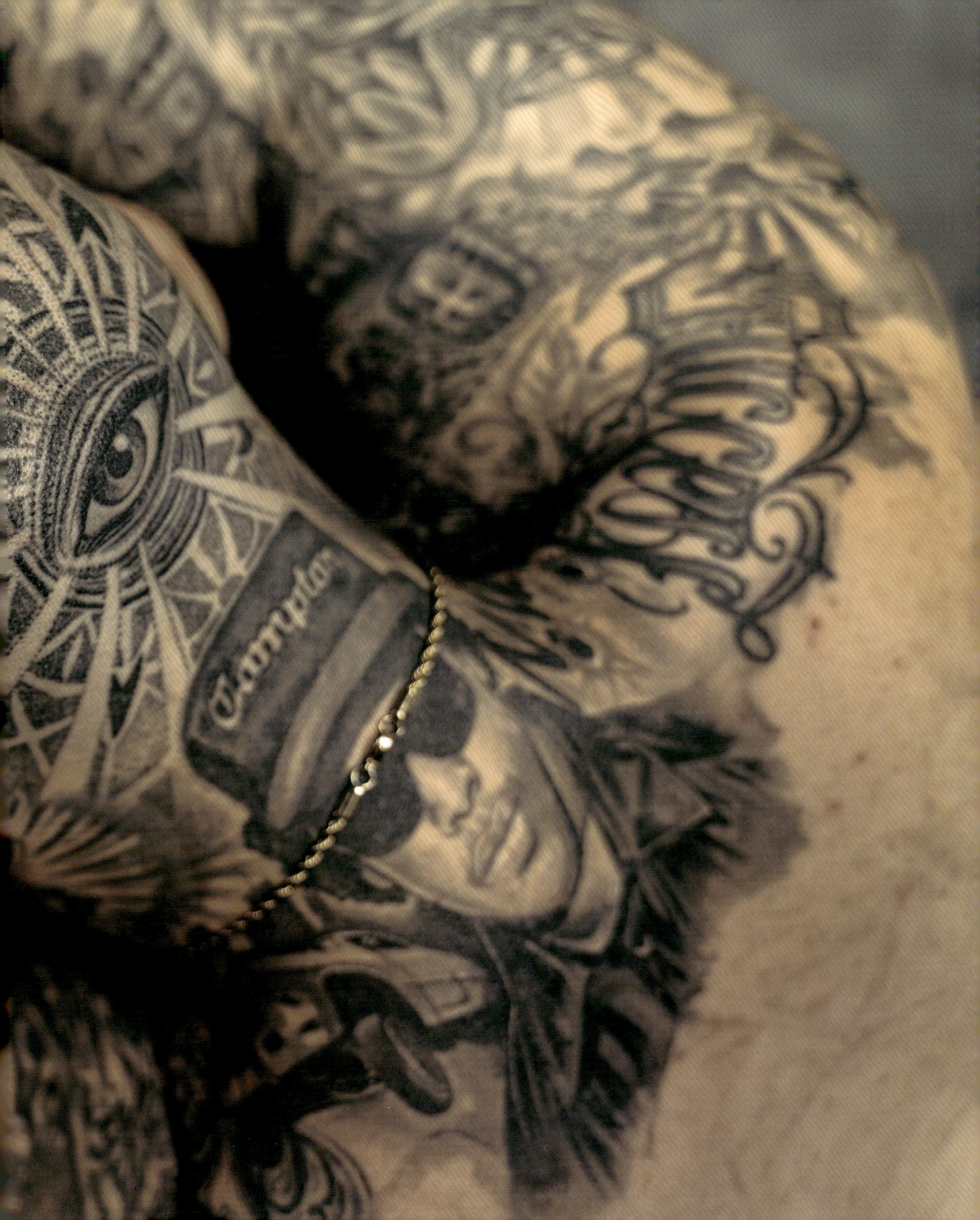

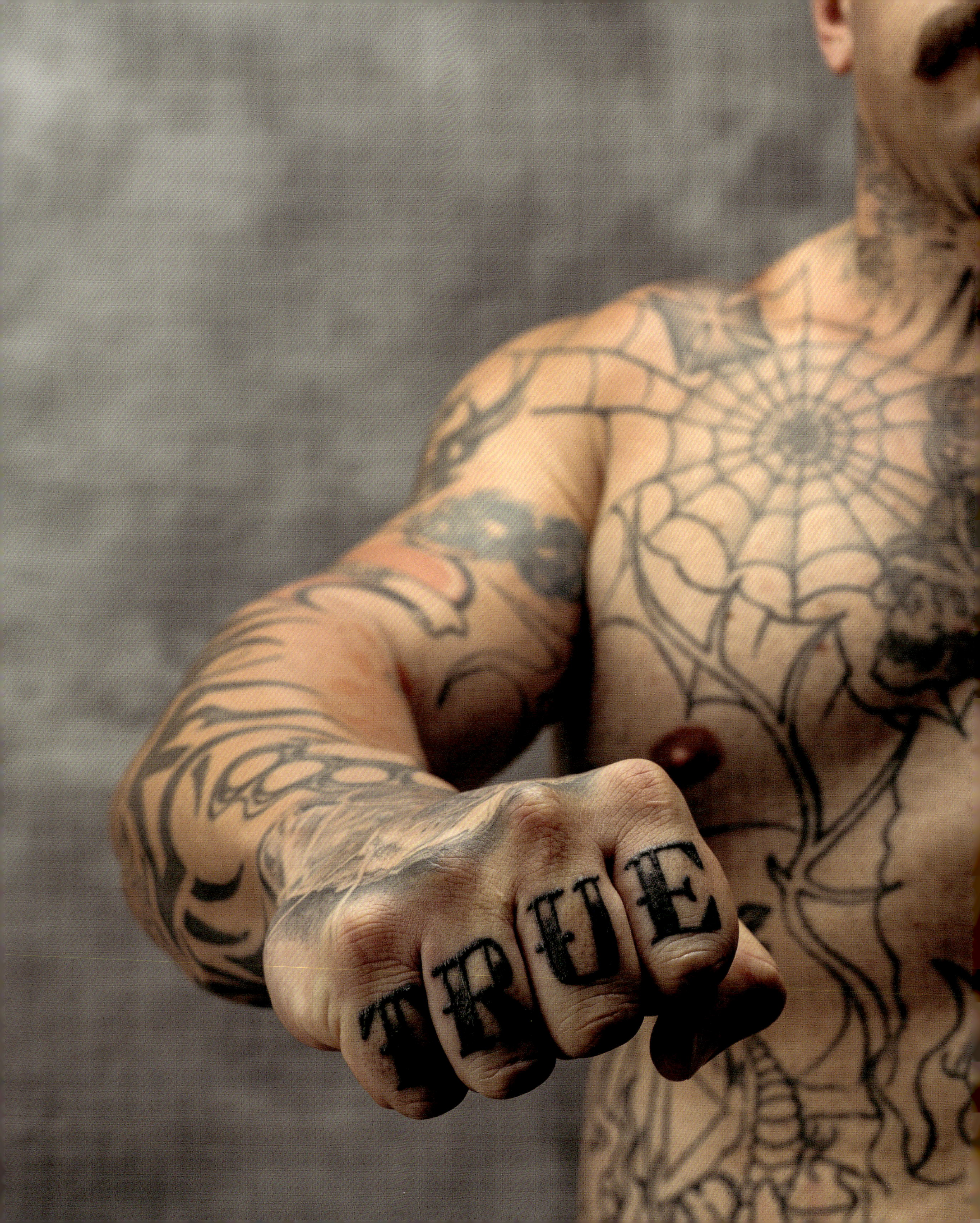
TRUE

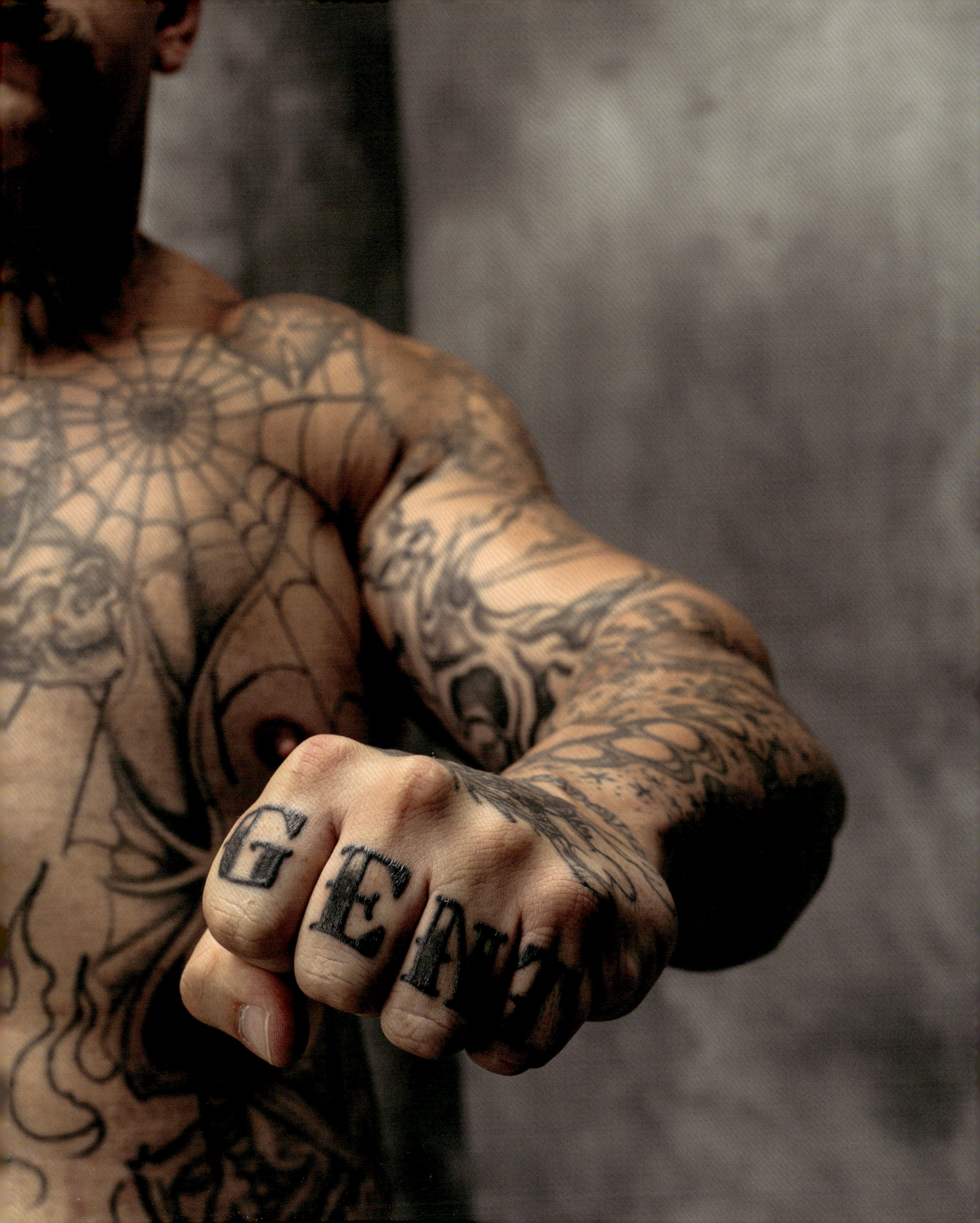

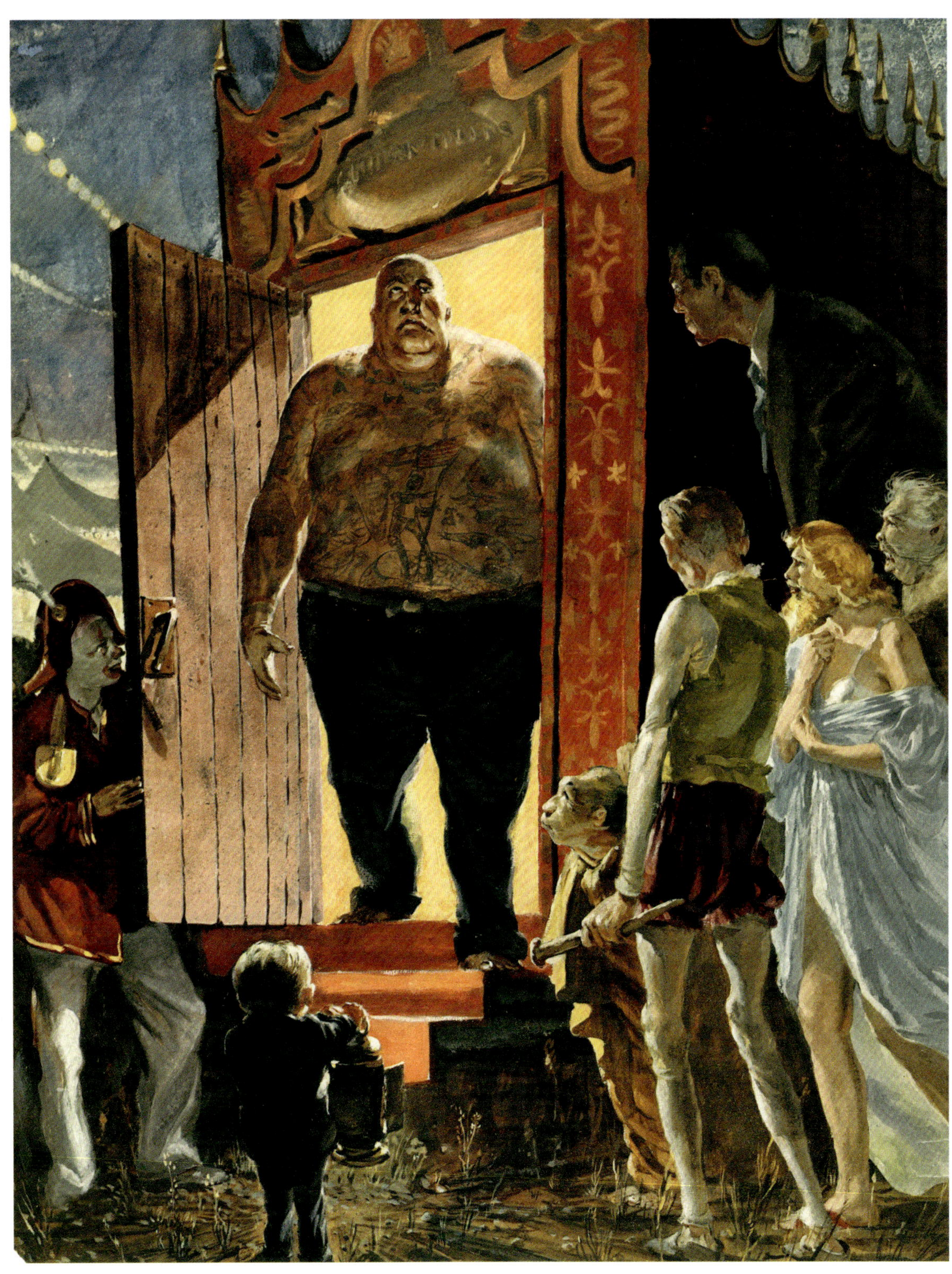

Stanley Meltzoff's illustration for *Esquire* magazine's publication of the short story "The Illustrated Man," July 1950.

RAY BRADBURY

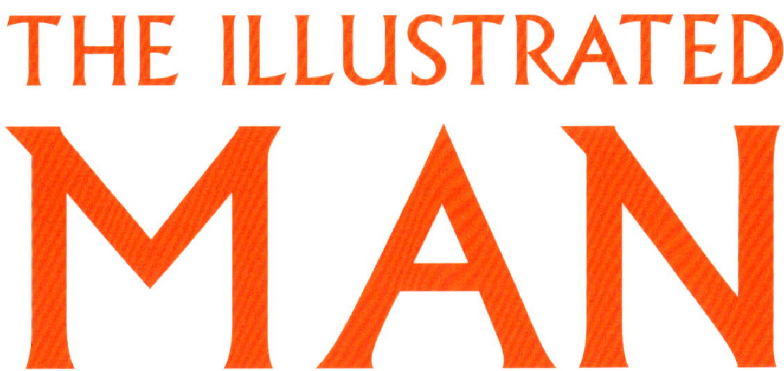

"Hey, the Illustrated Man!"

A calliope screamed, and Mr. William Philippus Phelps stood, arms folded, high on the summer-night platform, a crowd unto himself.

He was an entire civilization. In the Main Country, his chest, the Vasties lived – nipple-eyed dragons swirling over his flesh-pot, his almost feminine breasts. His navel was the mouth of a slit-eyed monster – an obscene, in-sucked mouth, toothless as a witch. And there were secret caves where the Darklings, eyes jealously ablaze, peered out through rank creeper and hanging vine.

Mr. William Philippus Phelps leered down from his freak platform with a thousand peacock eyes. Across the sawdust meadow he saw his wife, Lisabeth, far away, ripping tickets in half, staring at the silver belt buckles of passing men.

Mr. William Philippus Phelps' hands were tattooed roses. At the sight of his wife's interest, the roses shriveled, as with the passing of sunlight.

A year before, when he had led Lisabeth to the marriage bureau to watch her work her name in ink, slowly, on the form, his skin had been pure and white and clean. He glanced down at himself in sudden horror. Now he was like a great painted canvas, shaken in the night wind! How had it happened? Where had it all begun?

It had started with the arguments, and then the flesh, and then the pictures. They had fought deep into the summer nights, she like a brass trumpet forever blaring at him. And he had gone out to eat five thousand steaming hot dogs, ten million hamburgers, and a forest of green onions, and to drink vast red seas of orange juice. Peppermint candy formed his brontosaur bones, the hamburgers shaped his balloon flesh, and strawberry pop pumped in and out of his heart valves sickeningly, until he weighed three hundred pounds.

"William Philippus Phelps," Lisabeth said to him in the eleventh month of their marriage, "you're dumb and fat."

That was the day the carnival boss handed him the blue envelope.

"Sorry, Phelps. You're no good to me with all that gut on you."

"Wasn't I always your best tent man, boss?"

"Once. Not anymore. Now you sit, you don't get the work out."

"Let me be your fat man."

"I got a fat man. Dime a dozen." The boss eyed him up and down. "Tell you what, though. We ain't had a Tattooed Man since Gallery Smith died last year..."

That had been a month ago. Four short weeks. From someone, he had learned of a tattoo artist far out in the rolling Wisconsin country, an old woman, they said, who knew her trade. If he took the dirt road and turned right at the river and then turned left...

He had walked across a yellow meadow, which was crisp from the sun. Red flowers blew and bent in the wind as he walked, and he came to the old shack, which looked as if it had stood in a million rains.

Inside the door was a silent, bare room, and in the center of the bare room sat an ancient woman.

Her eyes were stitched with red resin-thread. Her nose was sealed with black wax-twine. Her ears were sewn, too, as if a darning-needle dragonfly had stitched all her senses shut. She sat, not moving, in the vacant room. Dust lay in a yellow flour all about, unfoot-printed in many weeks; if she had moved it would have shown, but she had not moved. Her hands touched each other like thin, rusted instruments. Her feet were naked and obscene as rain rubbers, and near them sat vials of tattoo milk — red, lightning-blue, brown, cat-yellow. She was a thing sewn tight into whispers and silence.

Only her mouth moved, unsewn. "Come in. Sit down. I'm lonely here." He did not obey.

"You came for the pictures," she said in a high voice. "I have a picture to show you first."

She tapped a blind finger to her thrust-out palm. "See!" she cried. It was a tattoo-portrait of William Philippus Phelps.

"Me!" he said.

Her cry stopped him at the door. "Don't run."

He held to the edges of the door, his back to her. "That's me, that's me on your hand!"

"It's been there fifty years." She stroked it like a cat, over and over.

He turned. "It's an *old* tattoo." He drew slowly nearer. He edged forward and bent to blink at it. He put out a trembling finger to brush the picture. "Old. That's impossible! You don't know *me*. I don't know you. Your eyes, all sewed shut."

"I've been waiting for you," she said. "And many people." She displayed her arms and legs, like the spindles of an antique chair. "I have pictures on me of people who have already come here to see me. And there are other pictures of other people who are coming to see me in the next one hundred years. And you, you have come."

"How do you know it's me? You can't see!"

"You *feel* like the lions, the elephants, and the tigers to me. Unbutton your shirt. You need me. Don't be afraid. My needles are as clean as a doctor's fingers. When I'm finished with illustrating you, I'll wait for someone else to walk along out here and find me. And someday, a hundred summers from now, perhaps, I'll just go lie down in the forest under some white mushrooms, and in the spring you won't find anything but a small blue cornflower..."

He began to unbutton his sleeves.

"I know the Deep Past and the Clear Present and the even Deeper Future," she whispered, eyes knotted into blindness, face lifted to this unseen man. "It is on my flesh. I will paint it on yours, too. You will be the only *real* Illustrated Man in the universe. I'll give you special pictures you will never forget. Pictures of the Future on your skin."

She pricked him with a needle.

He ran back to the carnival that night in a drunken terror and elation. Oh, how quickly the old dust-witch had stitched him with color and design. At the end of a long afternoon of being bitten by a silver snake, his body was alive with portraiture. He looked as if he had dropped and been crushed between the steel rollers of a print press, and come out like an incredible rotogravure. He was clothed in a garment of trolls and scarlet dinosaurs.

"Look!" he cried to Lisabeth. She glanced up from her cosmetics table as he tore his shirt away. He stood in the naked bulb-light of their car-trailer, expanding his impossible chest. Here, the Tremblies, half-maiden, half-goat, leaping when his biceps flexed. Here, the Country of Lost Souls, his chins. In so many accordion pleats of fat, numerous small scorpions, beetles, and mice were crushed, held, hid, darting into view, vanishing, as he raised or lowered his chins.

"My God," said Lisabeth. "My husband's a freak."

She ran from the trailer and he was left alone to pose before the mirror. Why had he done it? To have a job, yes, but, most of all, to cover the fat that had larded itself impossibly over his bones. To hide the fat under a layer of color and fantasy, to hide it from his wife, but most of all from himself.

He thought of the old woman's last words. She had needled him two *special* tattoos, one on his chest, another for his back, which she would not let him see. She covered each with cloth and adhesive.

"You are not to look at these two," she had said.

"Why?"

"Later, you may look. The Future is in these pictures. You can't look now or it may spoil them. They are not quite finished. I put ink on your flesh, and the sweat of you forms the rest of the picture, the Future—your sweat and your thought." Her empty mouth grinned. "Next Saturday night, you may advertise! The Big Unveiling! Come see the Illustrated Man unveil his picture! You can make money in that way. You can charge admission to the Unveiling, like to an art gallery. Tell them you have a picture that even *you* never have seen, that *nobody* has seen yet. The most unusual picture ever painted. Almost alive. And it tells the Future. Roll the drums and blow the trumpets. And you can stand there and unveil at the Big Unveiling."

"That's a good idea," he said.

"But only unveil the picture on your chest," she said. "That is first. You must save the picture on your back, under the adhesive, for the following week. Understand?"

"How much do I owe you?"

"Nothing," she said. "If you walk with these pictures on you, I will be repaid with my own satisfaction. I will sit here for the next two weeks and think how clever my pictures are, for I make them fit each man himself and what is inside him. Now, walk out of this house and never come back. Good-bye."

"Hey! The big unveiling!"

The red signs blew in the night wind: NO ORDINARY TATTOOED MAN! THIS ONE IS "ILLUSTRATED!" GREATER THAN MICHELANGELO! TONIGHT! ADMISSION 10 CENTS!

Now the hour had come. Saturday night, the crowd stirring their animal feet in the hot sawdust.

"In one minute—" the carny boss pointed his cardboard megaphone—"in the tent immediately to my rear, we will unveil the Mysterious Portrait upon the Illustrated Man's chest! Next Saturday night, the same hour, same location, we'll unveil the Picture upon the Illustrated Man's *back*! Bring your friends!"

There was a stuttering roll of drums. Mr. William Philippus Phelps jumped back and vanished; the crowd poured into the tent, and, once inside, found him re-established upon another platform, the band brassing out a jig-time melody.

He looked for his wife and saw her, lost in the crowd, like a stranger, come to watch a freakish thing, a look of contemptuous curiosity upon her face. For, after all, he was her husband, this was a thing she didn't know about him herself. It gave him a feeling of great height and warmness and light to find himself the center of the jangling universe, the carnival world, for one night. Even the other freaks—the Skeleton, the Seal Boy, the Yoga, the Magician, and the Balloon—were scattered through the crowd.

"Ladies and gentlemen, the great moment!"

A trumpet flourish, a hum of drumsticks on tight cowhide.

Mr. William Philippus Phelps let his cape fall. Dinosaurs, trolls, and half-woman-half-snakes withered on his skin in the stark light.

Ah, murmured the crowd, for surely there had never been a tattooed man like this! The beast eyes seemed to take red fire and blue fire, blinking and twisting. The roses on his fingers seemed to expel a sweet pink bouquet.

The Tyrannosaurus rex reared up along his leg, and the sound of the brass trumpet in the boat in the hot tent heavens was a prehistoric cry from the red monster throat. Mr. William Philippus Phelps was a museum jolted to life. Fish swam in seas of electric-blue ink. Fountains sparkled under yellow suns. Ancient buildings stood in meadows of harvest wheat. Rockets burned across spaces of muscle and flesh. The slightest inhalation of his breath threatened to make chaos of the entire printed universe. He seemed afire, the creatures flinching from the flame, drawing back from the great heat of his pride, as he expanded under the audience's rapt contemplation.

The carny boss laid his fingers to the adhesive. The audience rushed forward, silent in the oven vastness of the night tent.

"You ain't seen nothing yet!" cried the carny boss.

The adhesive ripped free.

There was an instant in which nothing happened. An instant in which the Illustrated Man thought that the Unveiling was a terrible and irrevocable failure.

But then the audience gave a low moan.

The carny boss drew back, his eyes fixed.

Far out at the edge of the crowd, a woman, after a moment, began to cry, began to sob, and did not stop.

Slowly, the Illustrated Man looked down at his naked chest and stomach.

The thing that he saw made the roses on his hands discolor and die. All of his creatures seemed to wither, turn inward, shrivel with the arctic coldness that pumped from his heart outward to freeze and destroy them. He stood trembling. His hand floated up to touch that incredible picture, which lived, moved and shivered with life. It was like gazing into a small room, seeing a thing of someone else's life so intimate, so impossible that one could not believe and one could not long stand to watch without turning away.

It was a picture of his wife, Lisabeth, and himself.

And he was killing her.

Before the eyes of a thousand people in a dark tent in the center of a black-forested Wisconsin land, he was killing his wife.

His great flowered hands were upon her throat, and her face was turning dark and he killed her and he killed her and did not ever in the next minute stop killing her. It was real. While the crowd watched, she died, and he turned very sick. He was about to fall straight down into the crowd. The tent whirled like a monster bat wing, flapping grotesquely. The last thing he heard was a woman, sobbing, far out on the shore of the silent crowd.

And the crying woman was Lisabeth, his wife.

In the night, his bed was moist with perspiration. The carnival sounds had melted away, and his wife, in her own bed, was quiet now, too. He fumbled with his chest. The adhesive was smooth. They had made him put it back.

He had fainted. When he revived, the carny boss had yelled at him, "Why didn't you say what the picture was like?"

"I didn't know, I didn't," said the Illustrated Man.

"Good God!" said the boss. "Scare hell outa everyone. Scared hell outa Lizzie, scared hell outa me. Christ, where'd you *get* that damn tattoo?" He shuddered. "Apologize to Lizzie, now."

His wife stood over him.

"I'm sorry, Lisabeth," he said, weakly, his eyes closed. "I didn't know."

"You did it on purpose," she said. "To scare me."

"I'm sorry."

"Either it goes or I go," she said.

"Lisabeth."

"You heard me. That picture comes off or I quit this show."

"Yeah, Phil," said the boss. "That's how it is."

"Did you lose money? Did the crowd demand refunds?"

"It ain't the money, Phil. For that matter, once the word got around, hundreds of people wanted in. But I'm runnin' a clean show. That tattoo comes off! Was this your idea of a practical joke, Phil?"

He turned in the warm bed. No, not a joke. Not a joke at all. He had been as terrified as anyone. Not a joke. That little old dust-witch, what had she *done* to him and how had she done it? Had she put the picture there? No; she had said that the picture was unfinished, and that he himself, with his thoughts and perspiration, would finish it. Well, he had done the job all right.

But what, if anything, was the significance? He didn't want to kill anyone. He didn't want to kill Lisabeth. Why should such a silly picture burn here on his flesh in the dark?

He crawled his fingers softly, cautiously down to touch the quivering place where the hidden portrait lay. He pressed tight, and the temperature of that spot was enormous.

He could almost feel that little evil picture killing and killing and killing all through the night.

I don't wish to kill her, he thought, insistently, looking over at her bed.

And then, five minutes later, he whispered aloud: "Or *do* I?"

"What?" she cried, awake.

"Nothing," he said, after a pause, "Go to sleep."

The man bent forward, a buzzing instrument in his hand. "This cost five bucks an inch. Costs more to peel tattoos off than put 'em on. Okay, jerk the adhesive."

The Illustrated Man obeyed.

The skin man sat back. "Christ! No wonder you want that off! That's ghastly. *I* don't even want to look at it." He flicked his machine. "Ready? This won't hurt."

The carny boss stood in the tent flap, watching. After five minutes, the skin man changed the instrument head, cursing. Ten minutes later he scraped his chair back and scratched his head. Half an hour passed and he got up, told Mr. William Philippus Phelps to dress, and packed his kit.

"Wait a minute," said the carny boss. "You ain't done the job."

"And I ain't going to," said the skin man.

"I am paying good money. What's wrong?"

"Nothing except that damn picture just won't come off. Damn thing must go right down to the bone."

"You're crazy."

"Mister, I'm in business thirty years and never seen a tattoo like this. An inch deep, if it's anything."

"But I have to get it off!" cried the Illustrated Man.

The skin man shook his head. "Only one way to get rid of that."

"How?"

"Take a knife and cut off your chest. You won't live long, but the picture'll be gone."

"Come back here!"

But the skin man walked away.

They could hear the big Sunday-night crowd, waiting.

"That's a big crowd," said the Illustrated Man.

"But they ain't going to see what they came to see," said the carny boss.

"You ain't going out there, except with the adhesive. Hold still now, I'm curious about this *other* picture, on your back. We might be able to give 'em an unveiling on this one instead."

"She said it wouldn't be ready for a week or so. The old woman said it would take time to set, make a pattern."

There was a soft ripping as the carny boss pulled aside a flap of white tape on the Illustrated Man's spine.

"What do you see?" gasped Mr. Phelps, bent over.

The carny boss replaced the tape. "Buster, as a Tattooed Man, you're a washout, ain't you? Why'd you let that old dame fix you up this way?"

"I didn't know who she was."

"She sure cheated you on this one. No design to it. Nothing. No picture at all."

"It'll come clear. You wait and see."

The boss laughed. "Okay. Come on. We'll show the crowd part of you, anyway."

They walked out into an explosion of brassy music.

He stood monstrous in the middle of the night, putting out his hands like a blind man to balance himself in a world now tilted, now rushing, now threatening to spin him over and down into the mirror before which he raised his hands. Upon the flat, dimly lighted tabletop were peroxide, acids, silver razors, and squares of sandpaper. He took each of them in turn. He soaked the vicious tattoo upon his chest, he scraped at it. He worked steadily for an hour.

He was aware, suddenly, that someone stood in the trailer door behind him. It was three in the morning. There was a faint odor of beer. She had come home from town. He heard her slow breathing. He did not turn. "Lisabeth?" he said.

"You'd better get rid of it," she said, watching his hand move the sandpaper. She stepped into the trailer.

"I didn't want the picture this way," he said.

"You did," she said. "You planned it."

"I didn't."

"I know you," she said. "Oh, I know you hate me. Well, that's nothing. I hate you. I've hated you a long time now. Good God, when you started putting on the fat, you think anyone could love you then? I could teach you some things about hate. Why don't you ask me?"

"Leave me alone," he said.

"In front of that crowd, making a spectacle out of me!"

"I didn't know what was under the tape."

She walked around the table, hands fitted to her hips talking to the beds, the walls, the table, talking it all out of her. And he thought: *Or did I know? Who made this picture, me or the witch? Who formed it? How? Do I really want her dead? No! And yet . . .* He watched his wife draw nearer, nearer, he saw the ropy strings of her throat vibrate to her shouting. This and this and *this* was wrong with him! That and that and *that* was unspeakable about him! He was a liar, a schemer, a fat, lazy, ugly man, a child. Did he think he could compete with the carny boss or the tent peggers? Did he think he was sylphine and graceful, did he think he was a framed El Greco? DaVinci, huh! Michelangelo, my eye! She brayed. She showed her teeth. "Well, you can't scare me into staying with someone I don't want touching me with their slobby paws!" she finished, triumphantly.

"Lisabeth," he said.

"Don't Lisabeth me!" she shrieked. "I know your plan. You had that picture put on to scare me. You thought I wouldn't *dare* leave you. Well!"

"Next Saturday night, the Second Unveiling," he said. "You'll be proud of me."

"Proud! You're silly and pitiful. God, you're like a whale. You ever see a beached whale? I saw one when I was a kid. There it was, and they came and shot it. Some lifeguards shot it. Jesus, a whale!"

"Lisabeth."

"I'm leaving, that's all, and getting a divorce."

"Don't."

"And I'm marrying a man, not a fat woman — that's what you are, so much fat on you there ain't no sex!"

"You can't leave me," he said.

"Just watch!"

"I love you," he said.

"Oh," she said. "Go look at your pictures."

He reached out.

"Keep your hands off," she said.

"Lisabeth."

"Don't come near. You turn my stomach."

"Lisabeth."

All the eyes of his body seemed to fire, all the snakes to move, all the monsters to seethe, all the mouths to widen and rage. He moved toward her — not like a man, but a crowd. He felt the great blooded reservoir of orangeade pump through him now, the sluice of cola and rich lemon pop pulse in sickening sweet anger through his wrists, his legs, his heart. All of it, the oceans of mustard and relish and all the million drinks he had drowned himself in in the last year were aboil; his face was the color of a steamed beef. And the pink roses of his hands became those hungry, carnivorous flowers kept long years in tepid jungle and now let free to find their way on the night air before him.

He gathered her to him, like a great beast gathering in a struggling animal. It was a frantic gesture of love, quickening and demanding, which, as she struggled, hardened to another thing. She beat and clawed at the picture on his chest.

"You've got to love me, Lisabeth."

"Let go!" she screamed. She beat at the picture that burned under her fists. She slashed at it with her fingernails.

"Oh, Lisabeth," he said, his hands moving up her arms.

"I'll scream," she said, seeing his eyes.

"Lisabeth." The hands moved up to her shoulders, to her neck. "Don't go away."

"Help!" she screamed. The blood ran from the picture on his chest.

He put his fingers about her neck and squeezed.

She was a calliope cut in mid-shriek.

Outside, the grass rustled. There was the sound of running feet.

Mr. William Philippus Phelps opened the trailer door and stepped out.

They were waiting for him. Skeleton, Midget, Balloon, Yoga, Electra, Popeye, Seal Boy. The freaks, waiting in the middle of the night, in the dry grass.

He walked toward them. He moved with a feeling that he must get away; these people would understand nothing, they were not thinking people. And because he did not flee, because he only walked, balanced, stunned, between the tents, slowly, the freaks moved to let him pass. They watched him, because their watching guaranteed that he would not escape. He walked out across the black meadow, moths fluttering in his face. He walked steadily as long as he was visible, not knowing where he was going. They watched him go, and then they turned. All of them shuffled to the silent car-trailer together and pushed the door slowly wide....

The Illustrated Man walked steadily in the dry meadows beyond the town.

“He went that way!” a faint voice cried. Flashlights bobbled over the hills. There were dim shapes, running.

Mr. William Philippus Phelps waved to them. He was tired. He wanted only to be found now. He was tired of running away. He waved again.

“There he is!” The flashlights changed direction. “Come on! We’ll get the bastard!”

When it was time, the Illustrated Man ran again. He was careful to run slowly. He deliberately fell down twice. Looking back, he saw the tent stakes they held in their hands.

He ran toward a far crossroads lantern, where all the summer night seemed to gather: merry-go-rounds of fireflies whirling, crickets moving their song toward that light, everything rushing, as if by some midnight attraction, toward that one high-hung lantern—the Illustrated Man first, the others close at his heels.

As he reached the lights and passed a few yards under and beyond it, he did not need to look back. On the road ahead, in silhouette, he saw the upraised tent stakes sweep violently up, up, and then *down*!

A minute passed.

In the country ravines, the crickets sang. The freaks stood over the sprawled Illustrated Man, holding their tent stakes loosely.

Finally they rolled him over on his stomach. Blood ran from his mouth.

They ripped the adhesive from his back. They stared down for a long moment at the freshly revealed picture. Someone whispered. Someone else swore, softly. The Thin Man pushed back and walked away and was sick. Another and another of the freaks stared, their mouths trembling, and moved away, leaving the Illustrated Man on the deserted road, the blood running from his mouth.

In the dim light, the unveiled Illustration was easily seen.

It showed a crowd of freaks bending over a dying fat man on a dark and lonely road, looking at a tattoo on his back which illustrated a crowd of freaks bending over a dying fat man on a…

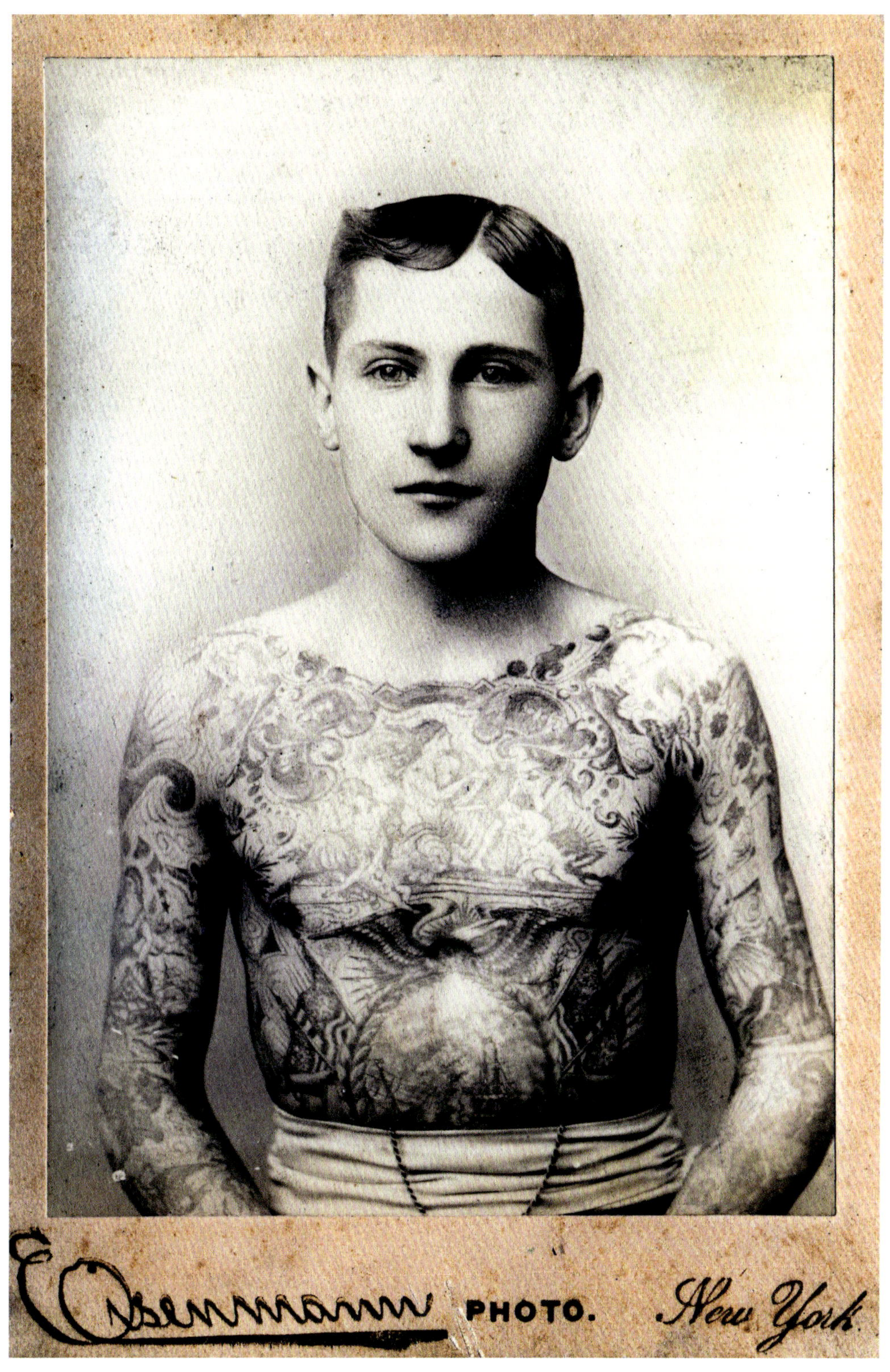

A sideshow boy performer photographed by Charles Eisenmann, ca. 1885.

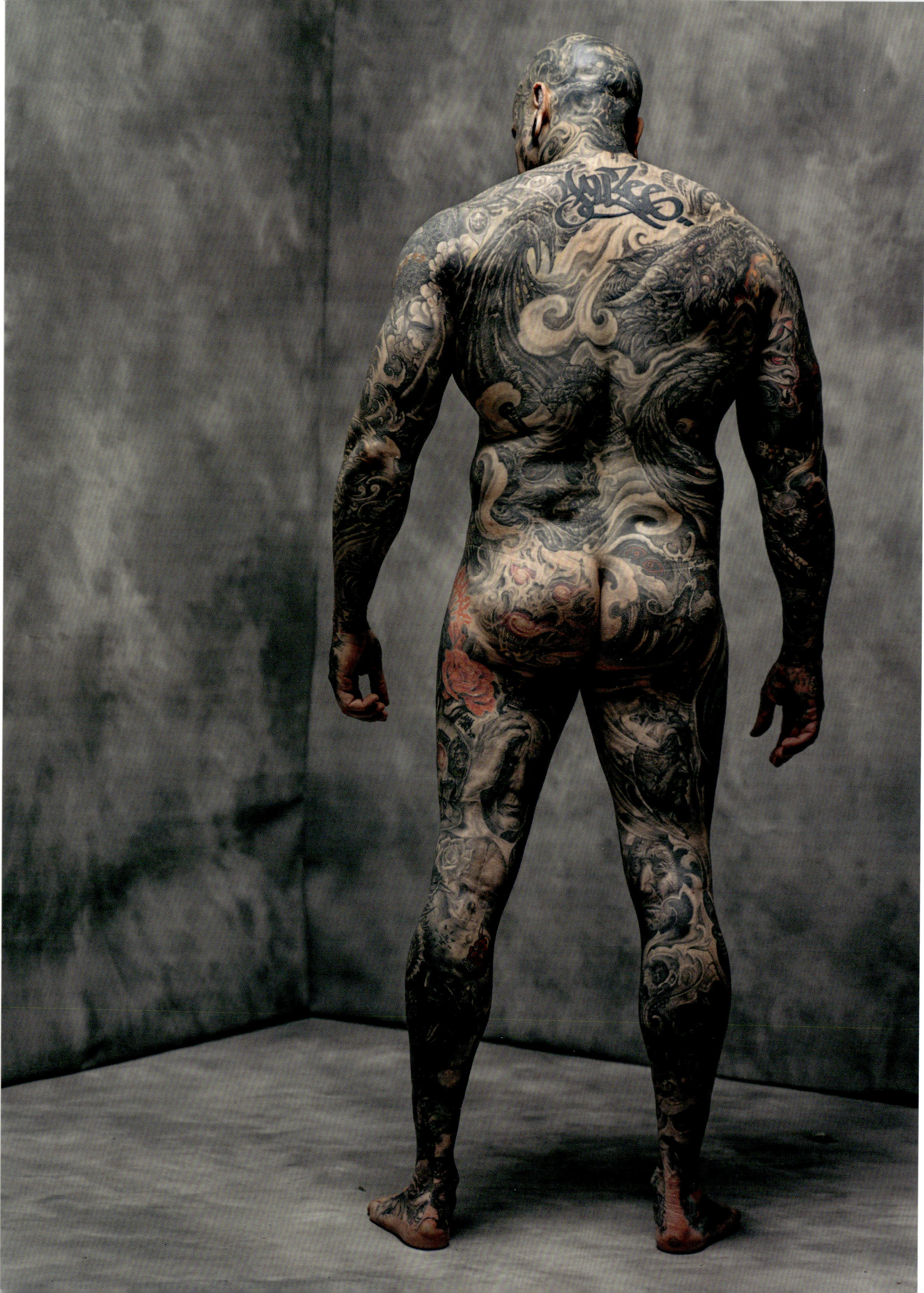

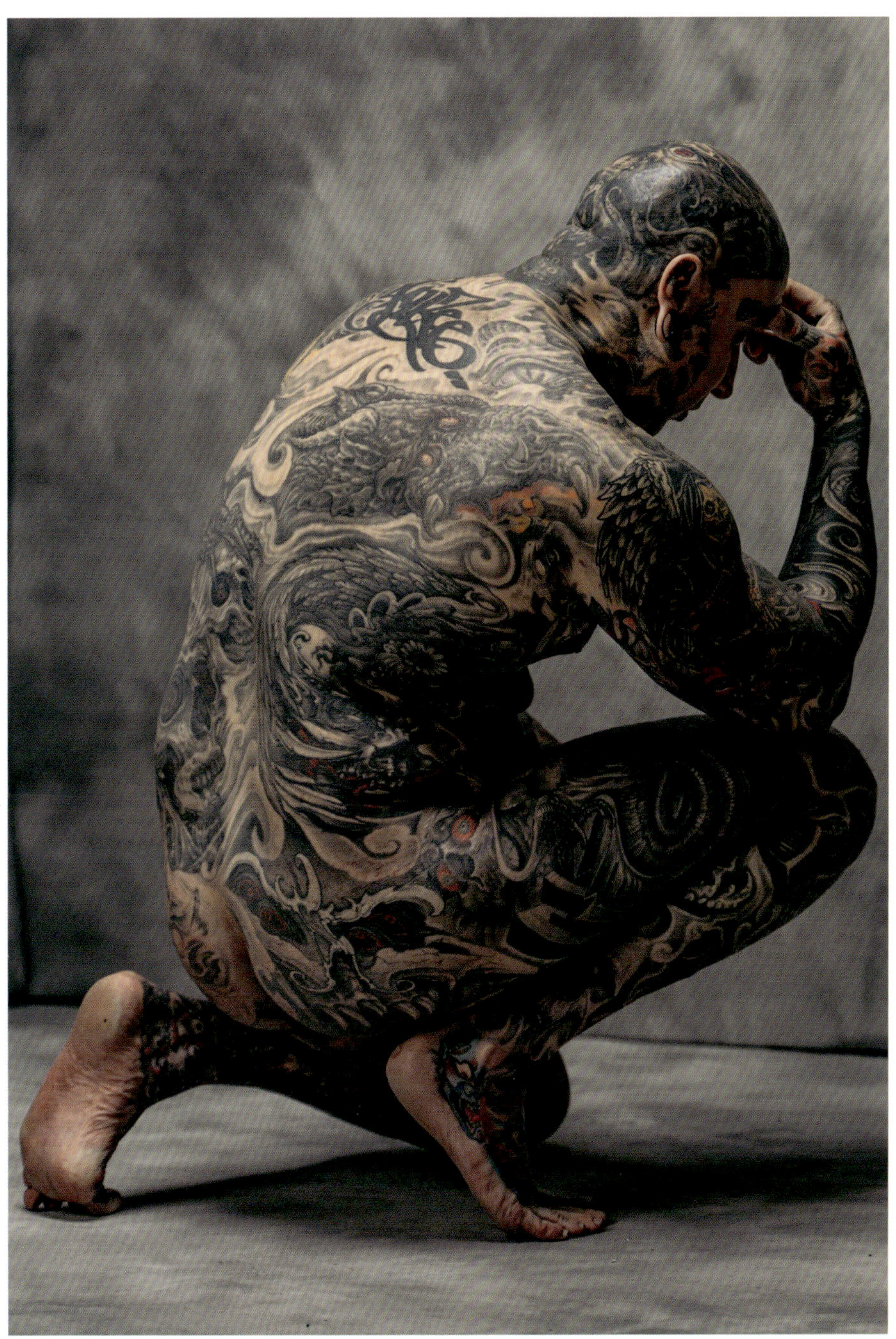

His eponymous back tag is by Juan R. López. Yallzee also wears work by Robert Hernandez, Stefano Alcantara, Myke Chambers, and Axel López.

Pages 106–107: "I love all my tattoo work, from the biggest ones to the smallest," says Yallzee, whose most painful tattoos were his eyelids and head. "It's my journey."

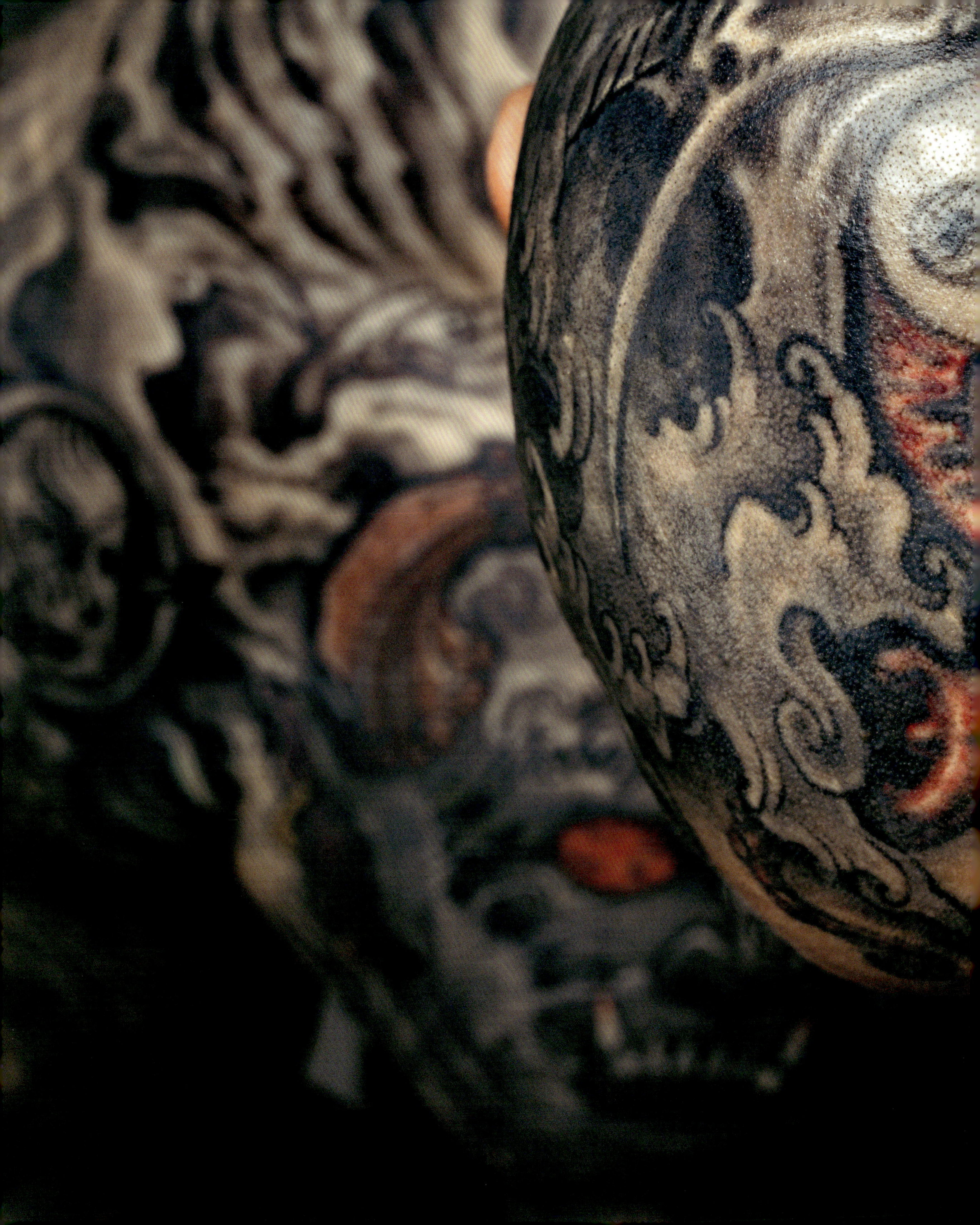

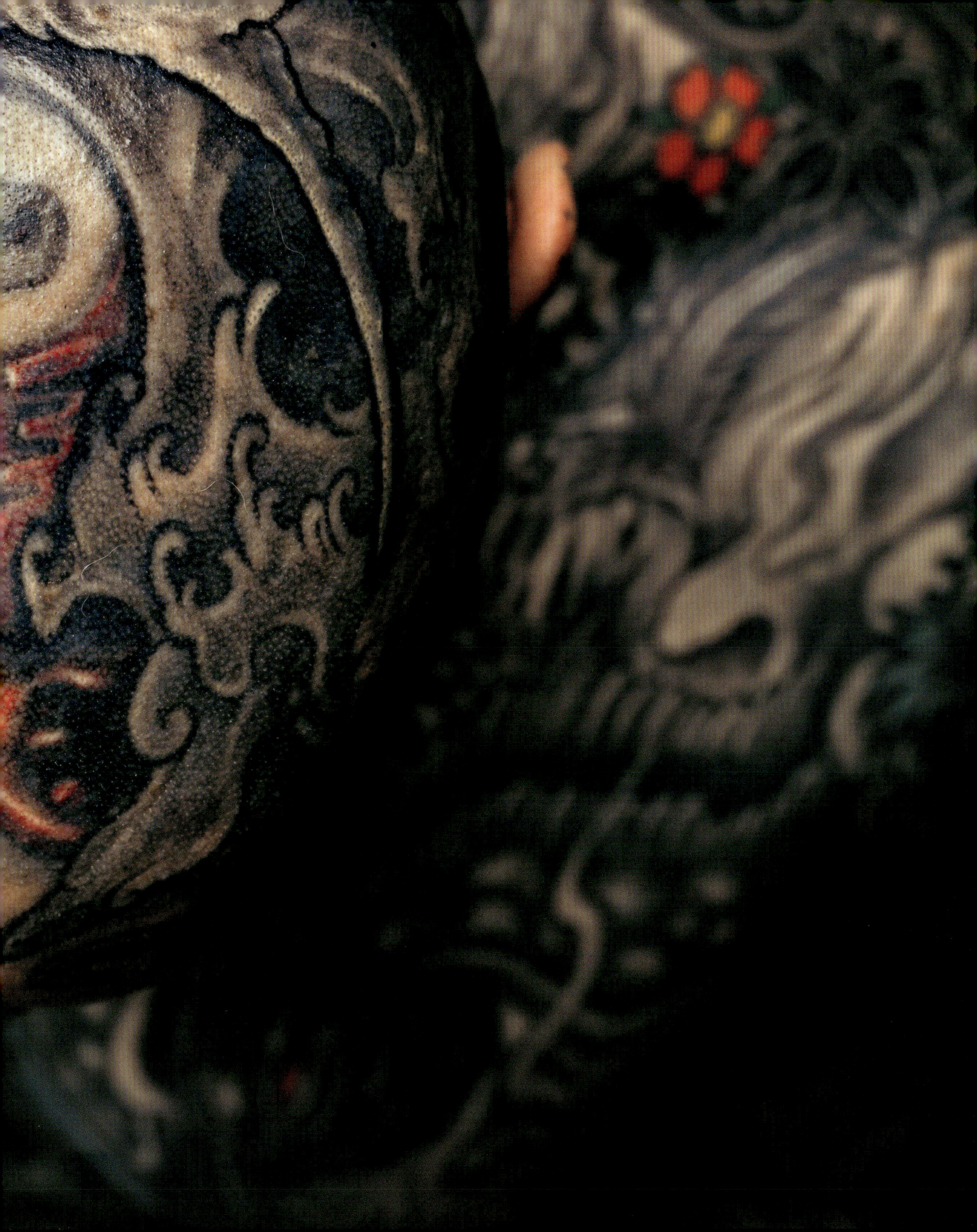

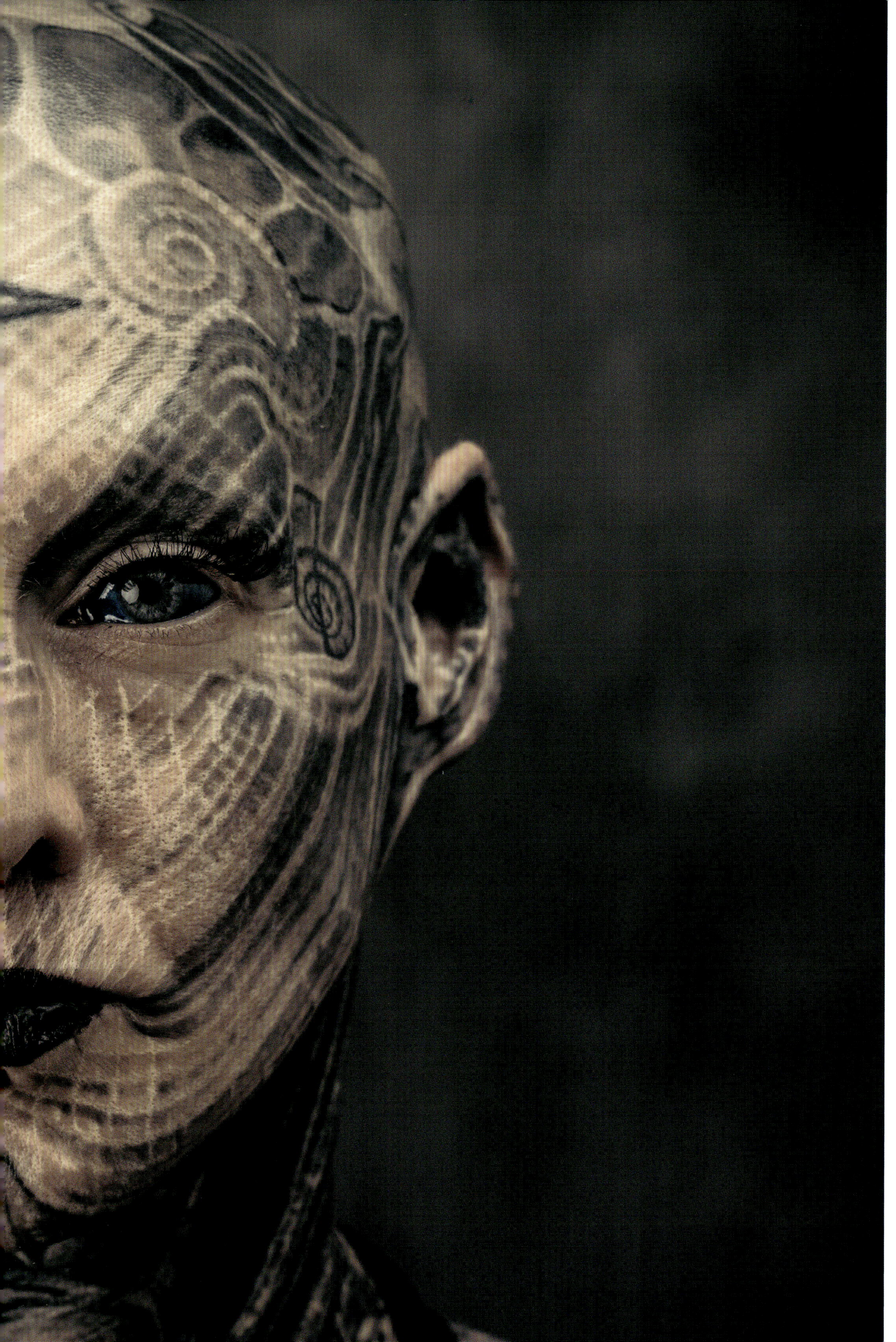

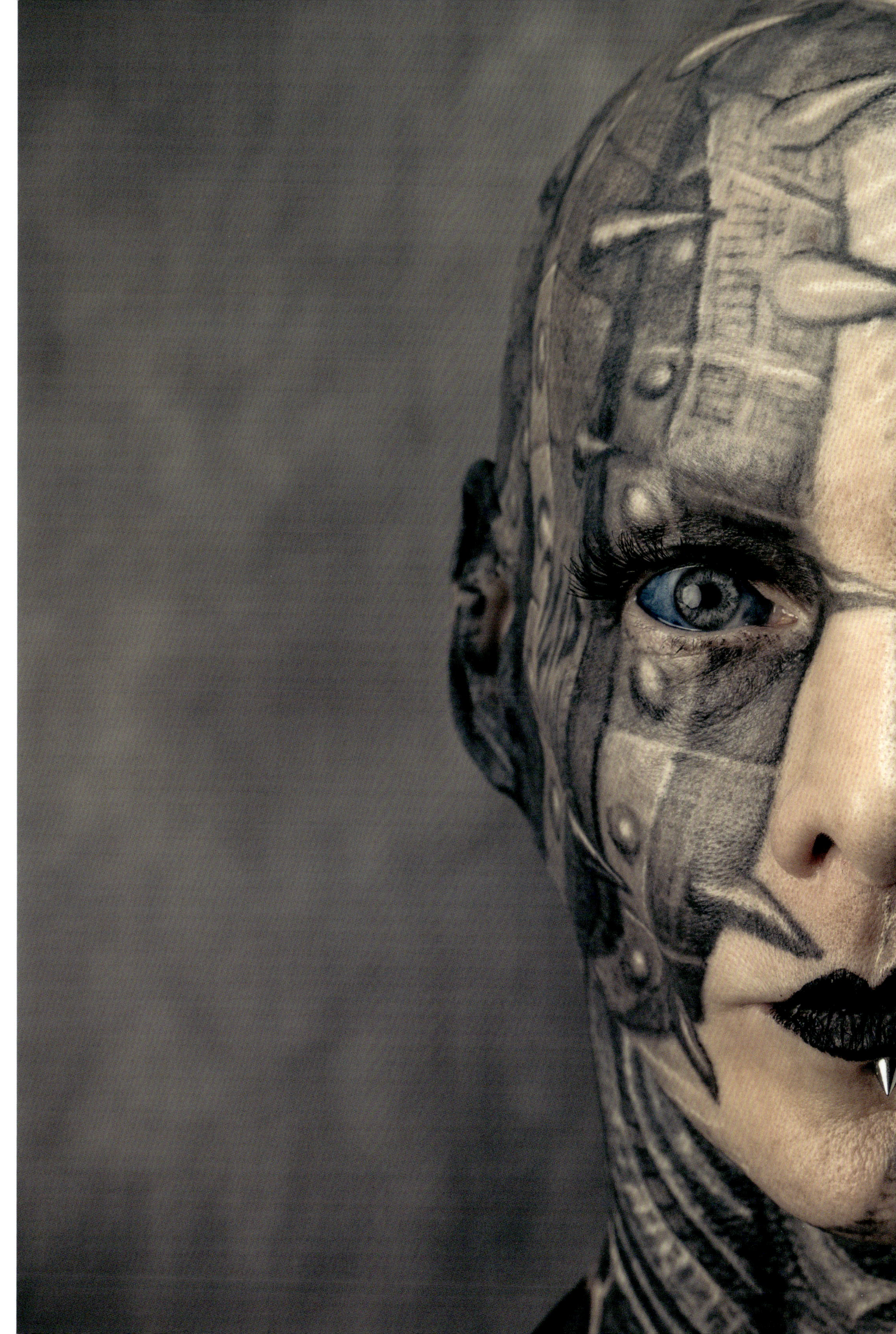

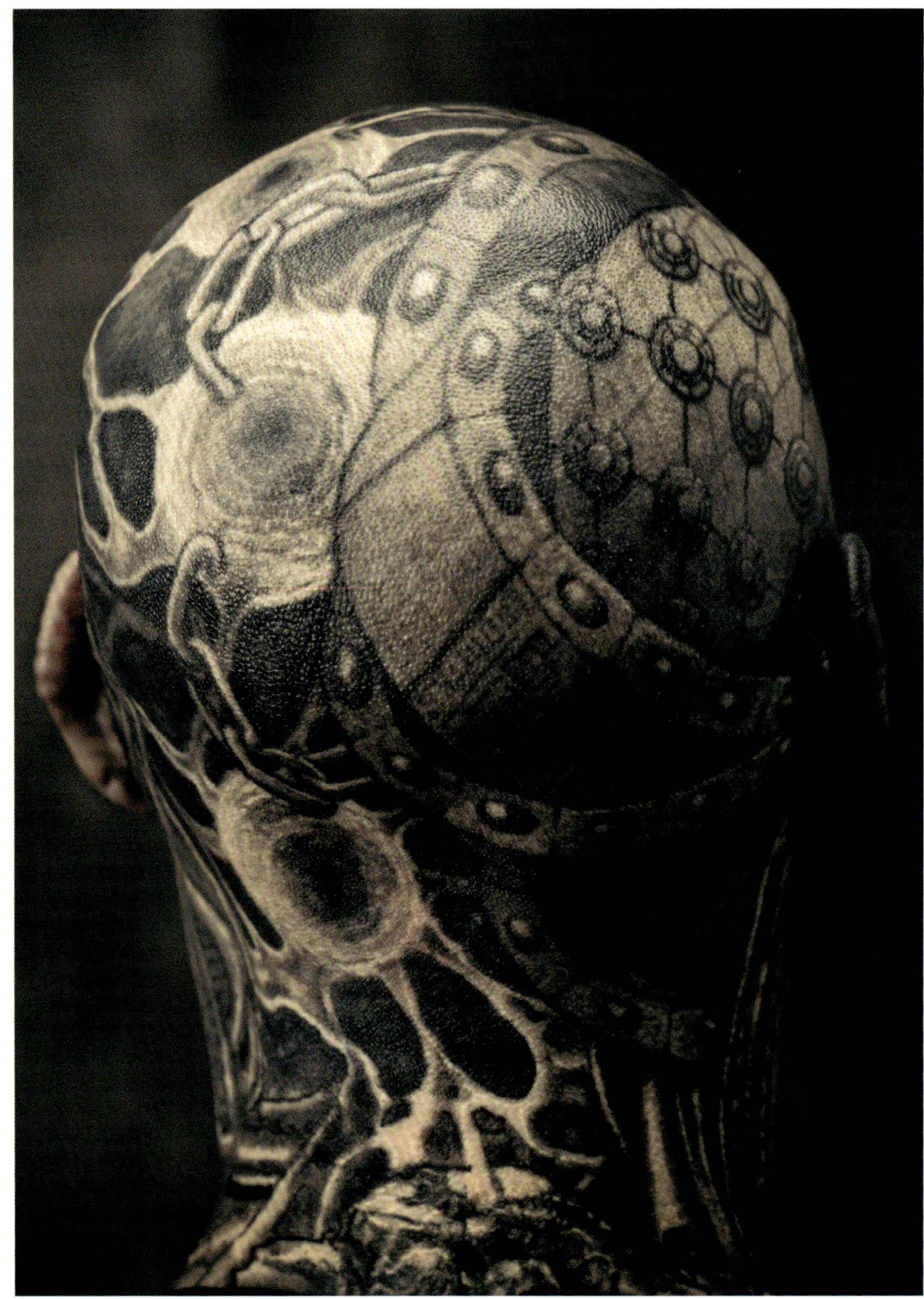

Pages 108–109: Kris Kai dedicated her head and face to Paul Booth's illustrations because of his incredible portfolio, as well as their shared love of banjos. With sclera tattoos by Luna Cobra, Kai believes her tattoos give her superhuman strength.

Above and opposite: Kai does not identify as a tattoo addict and says she can stop at any time. She believes the more ink a person has, the more intelligent they become.

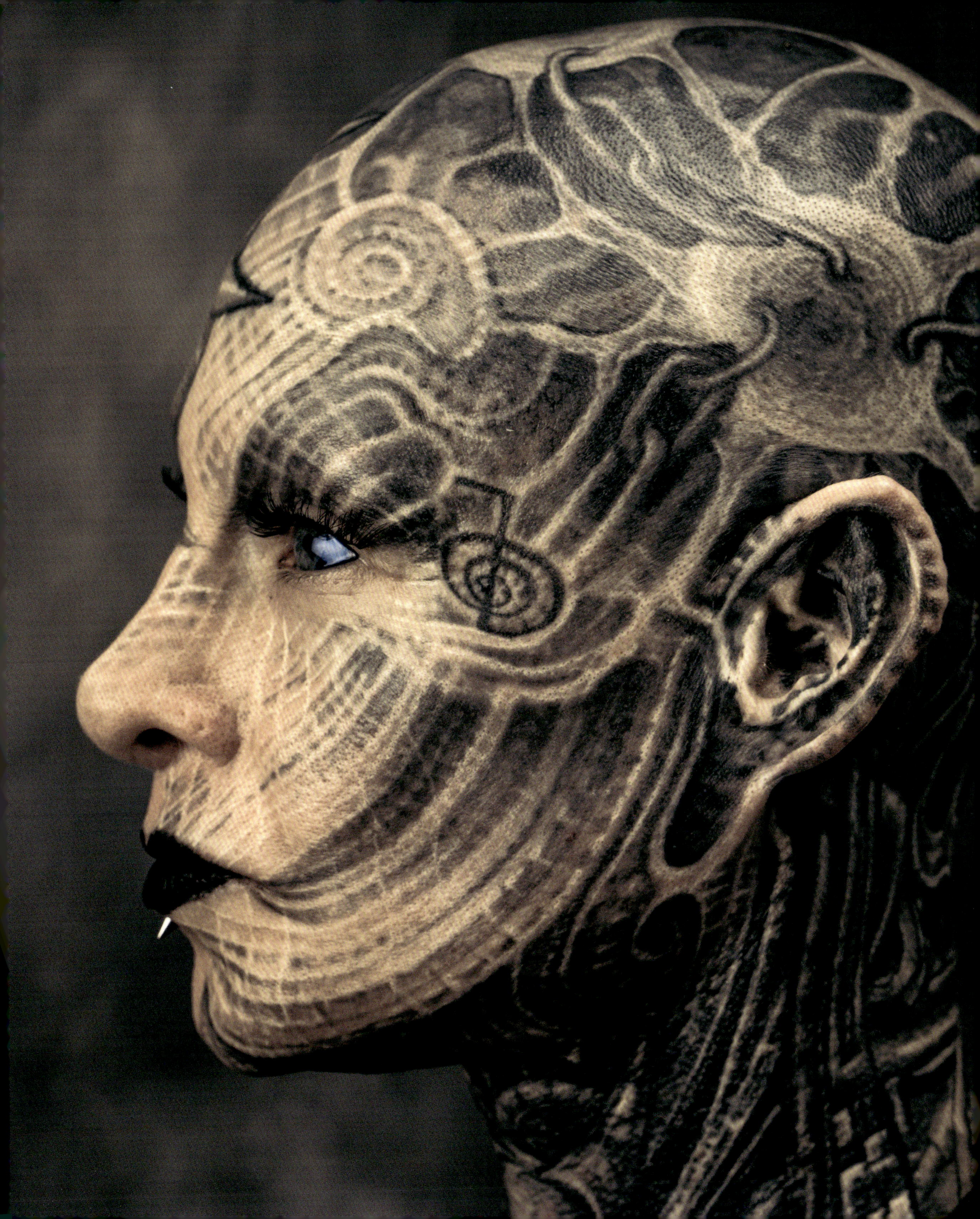

Representing the story of Kinnara, Brandon Lee's full cover-up backpiece, illustrated and tattooed by DJ Tambe, is inspired by Wat Rong Khun, the White Temple, in Thailand.

Pages 114–115: Lee also collects illustrations from Nikko Hurtado, Kip Delaney, Jamie Schene, and Mike Giant, who did his tree tattoo. Leanne Osborn's backpiece (right), done by DJ Tambe in roughly thirty hours, is of the Buddha statue in the Todaiji Temple in Nara, Japan, where her grandmother is from.

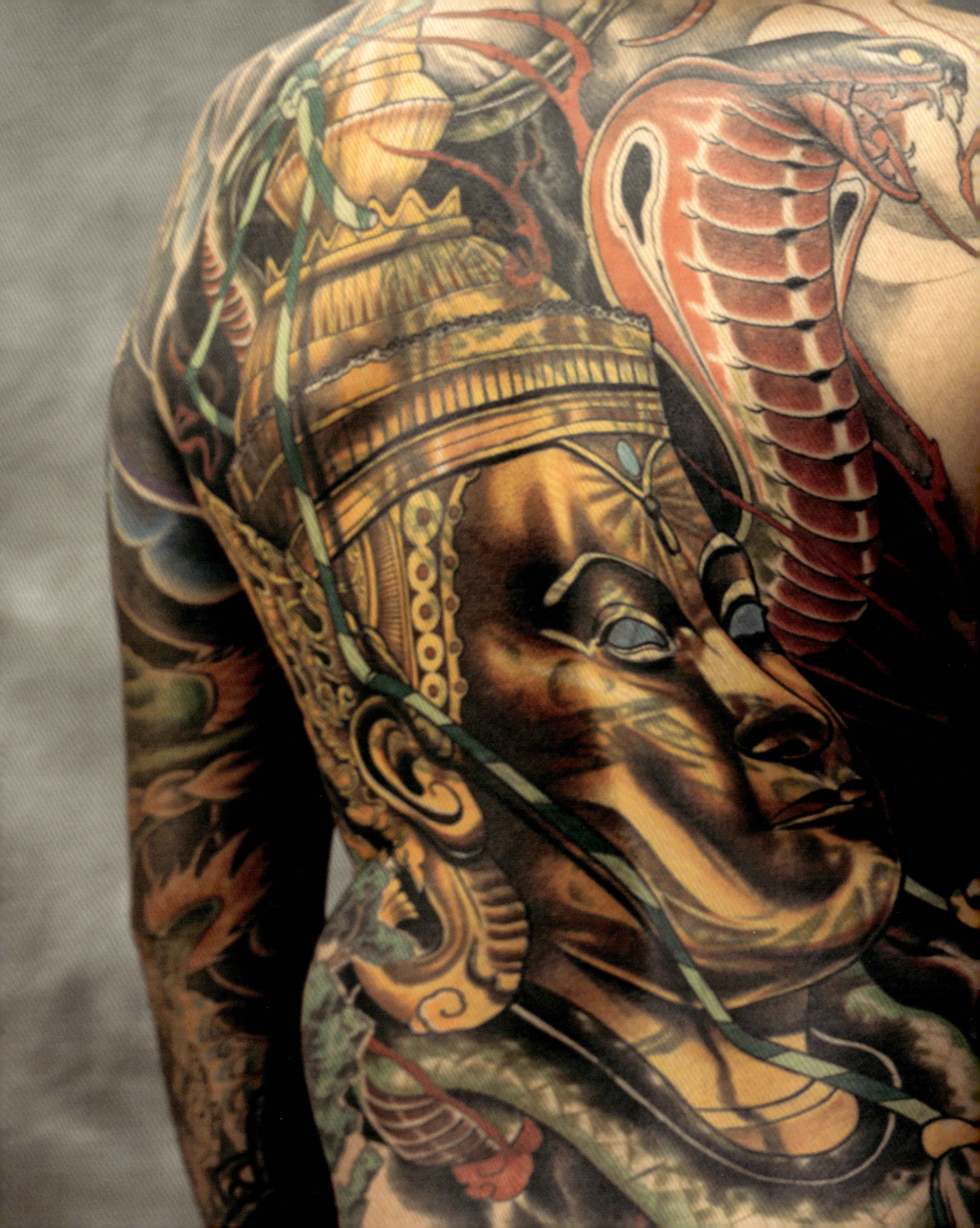

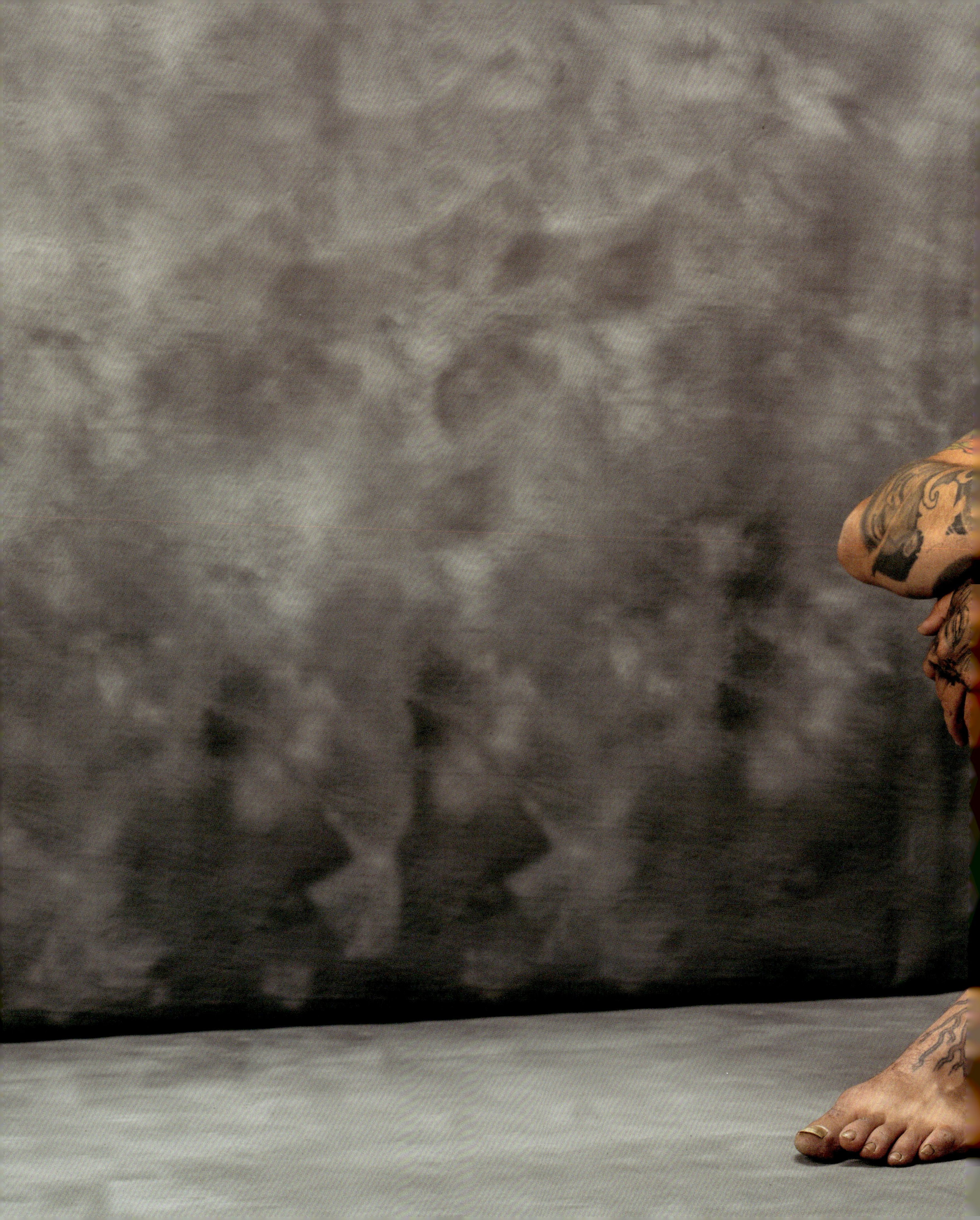

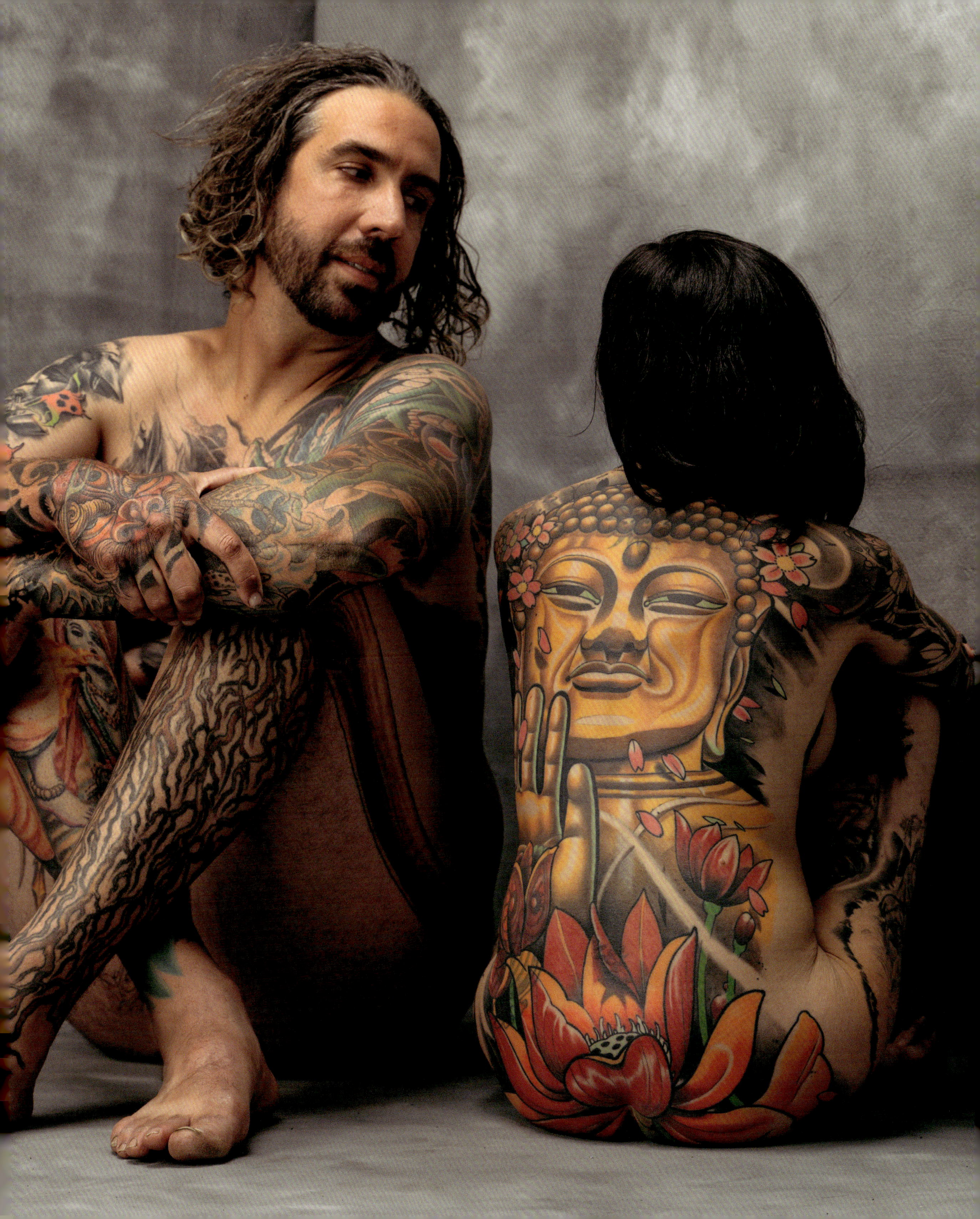

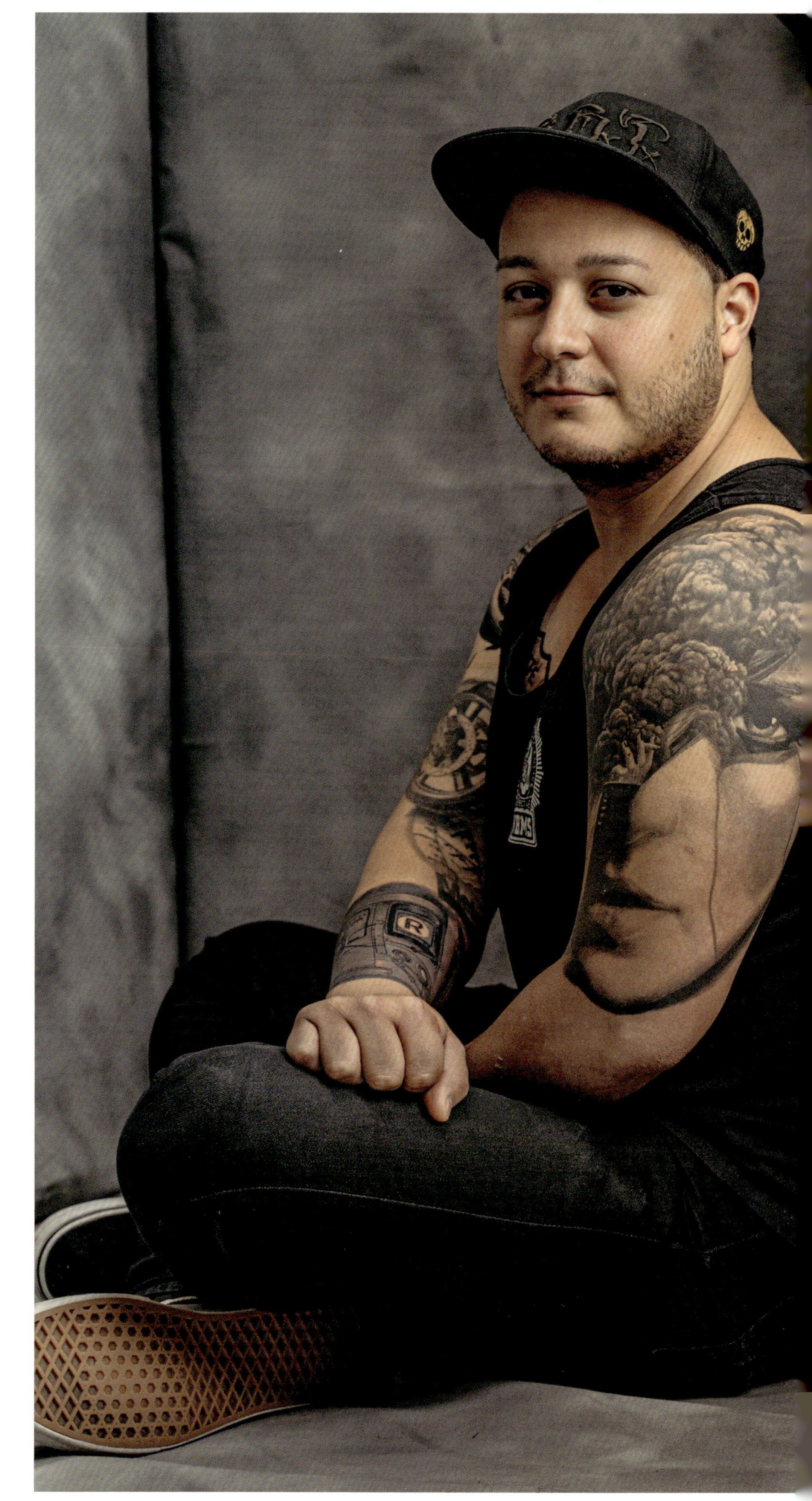

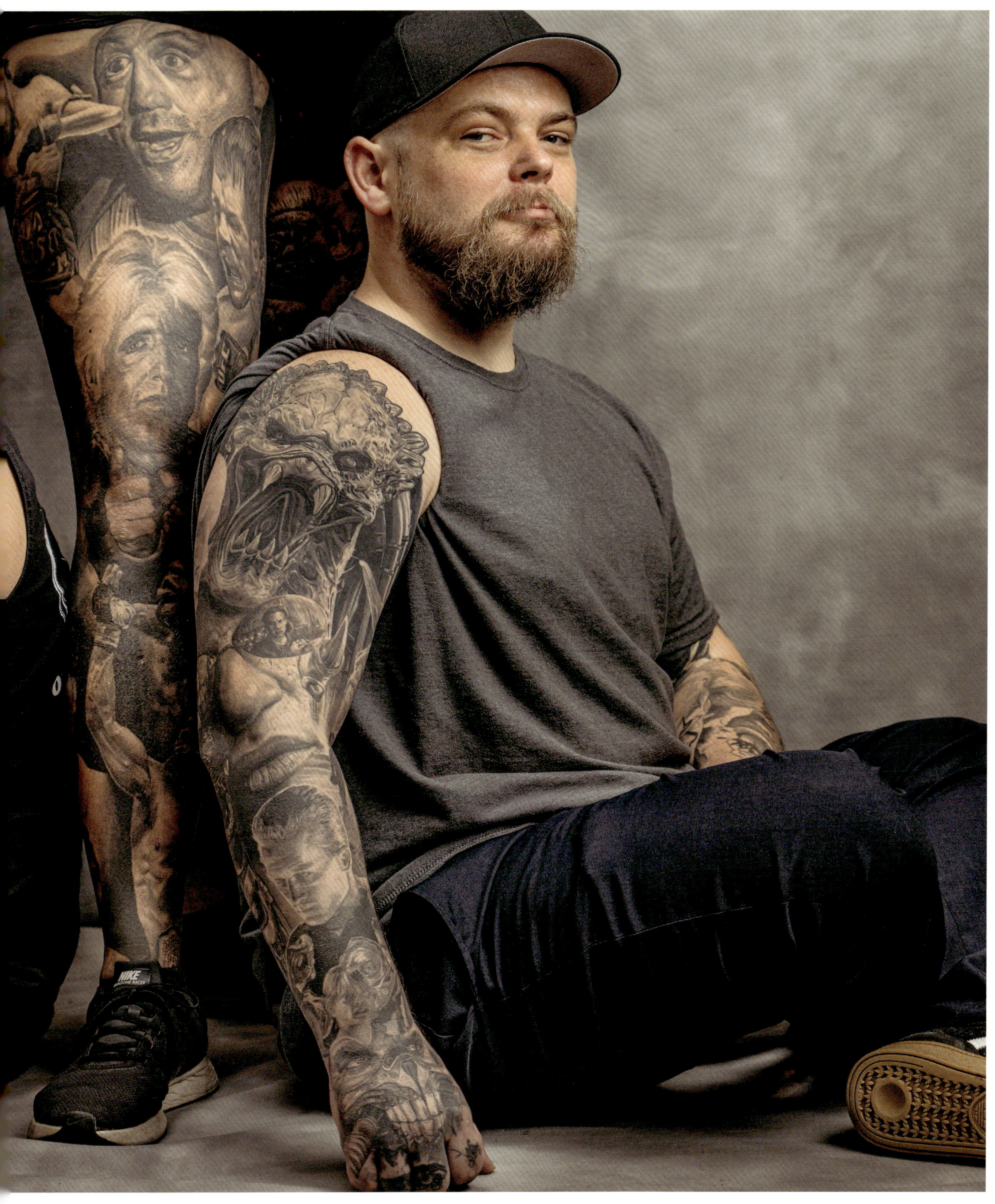
NIKE

Pages 116–117: Benny Lopez, Patrick C. Tran, and Jake Ingersoll (left to right) all feature work by Andy Pho. Pho illustrated Lopez's left arm, which depicts a fusion of seductive women at different points in their lives, and completed Tran's leg sleeve and Ingersoll's right arm.

Opposite: Tattoo artist and collector Ryan Ashley Malarkey inked her own illustrations on the front of her legs, while Tyler Pawelzik did her stomach and face tattoos.

Pages 120–121: Bob Lewis illustrated Malarkey's chest, throat, and left armpit, which features a bat, with Ethan Morgan designing the rams on her upper left arm. Her legs are marked with the works of Jacob Sheffield, TeeJ Poole, Marc Roy, and Ron Russo.

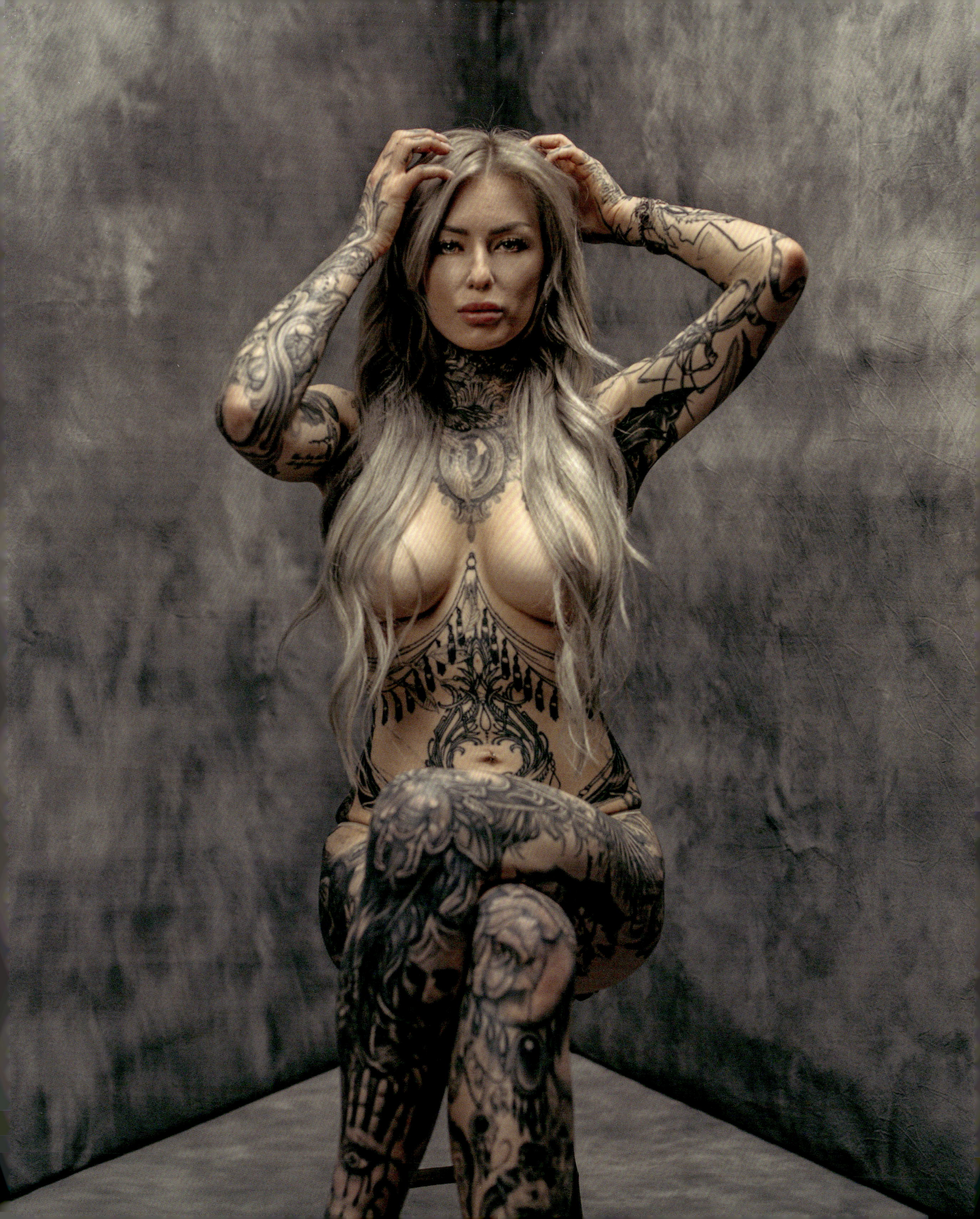

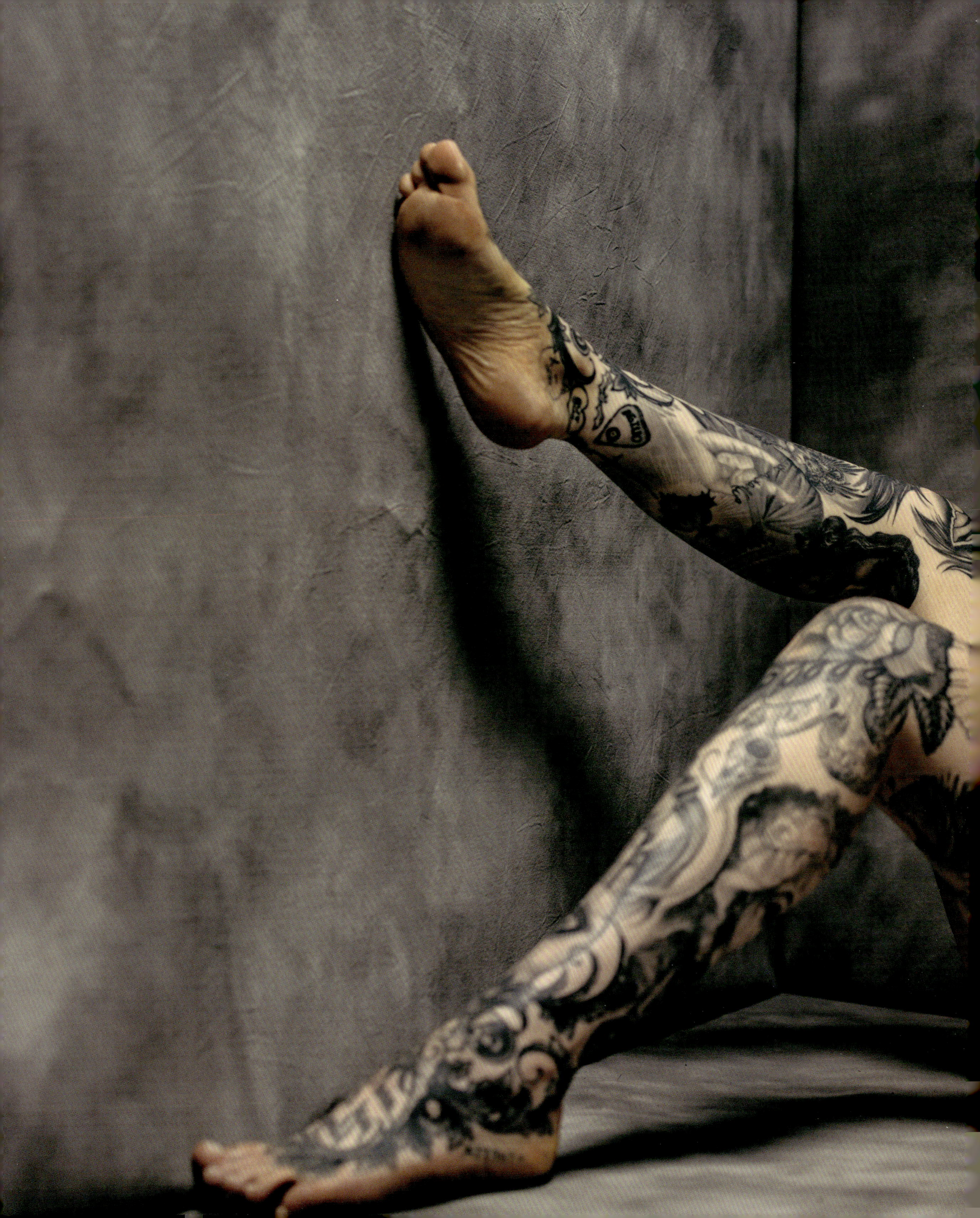

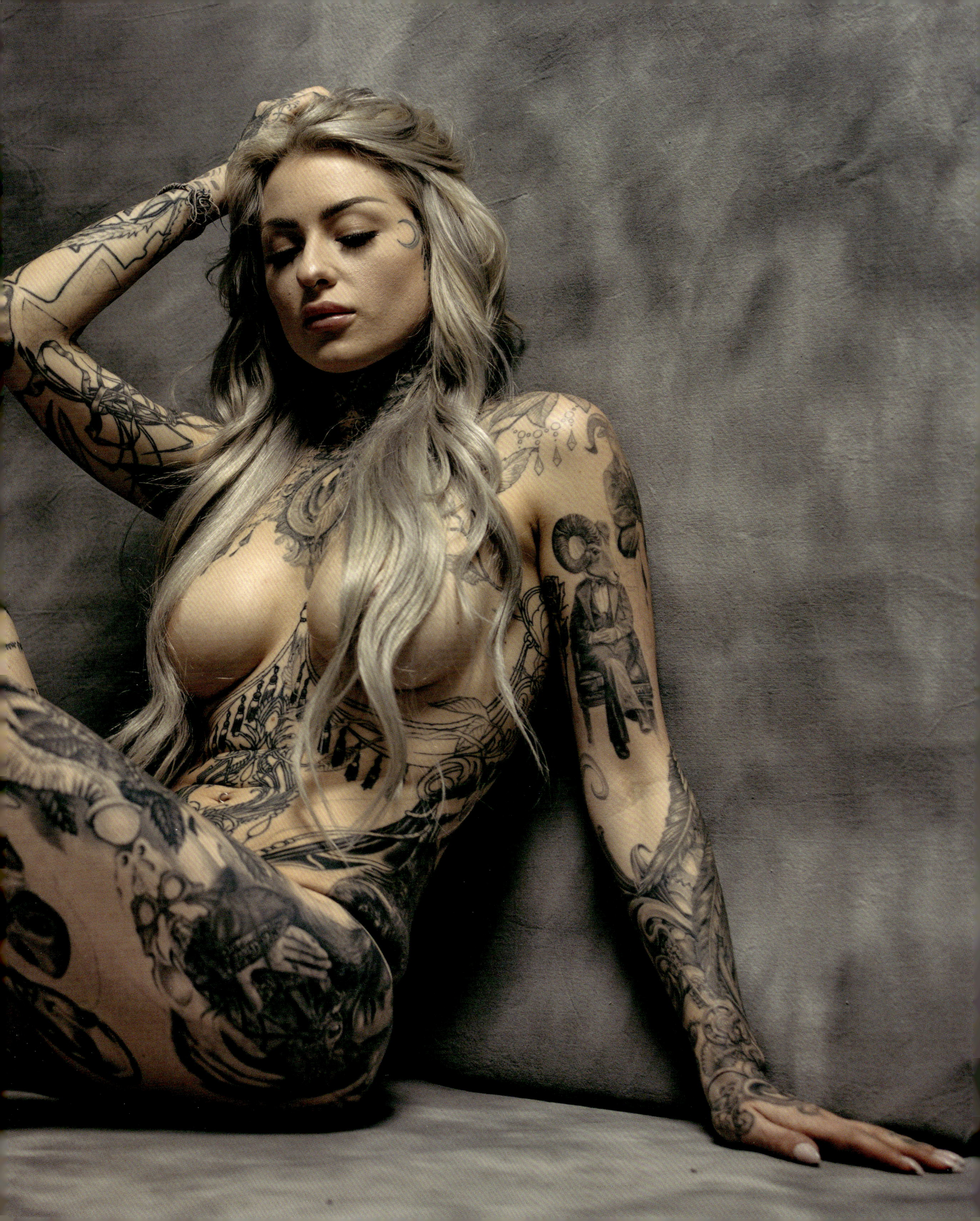

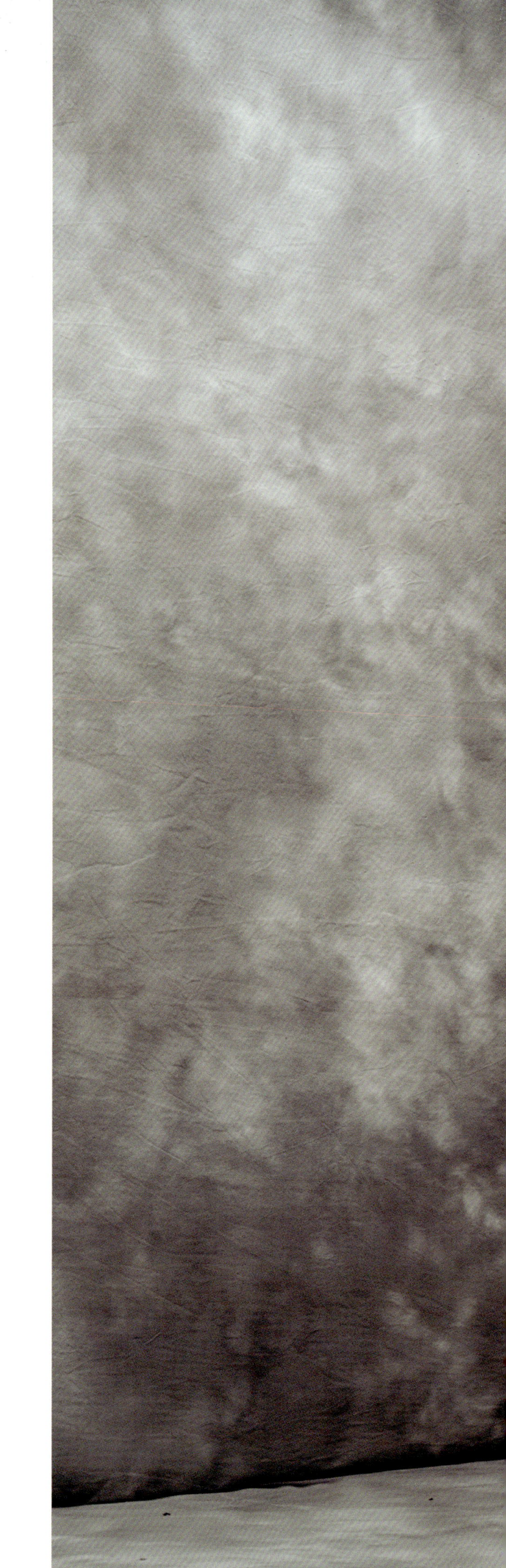

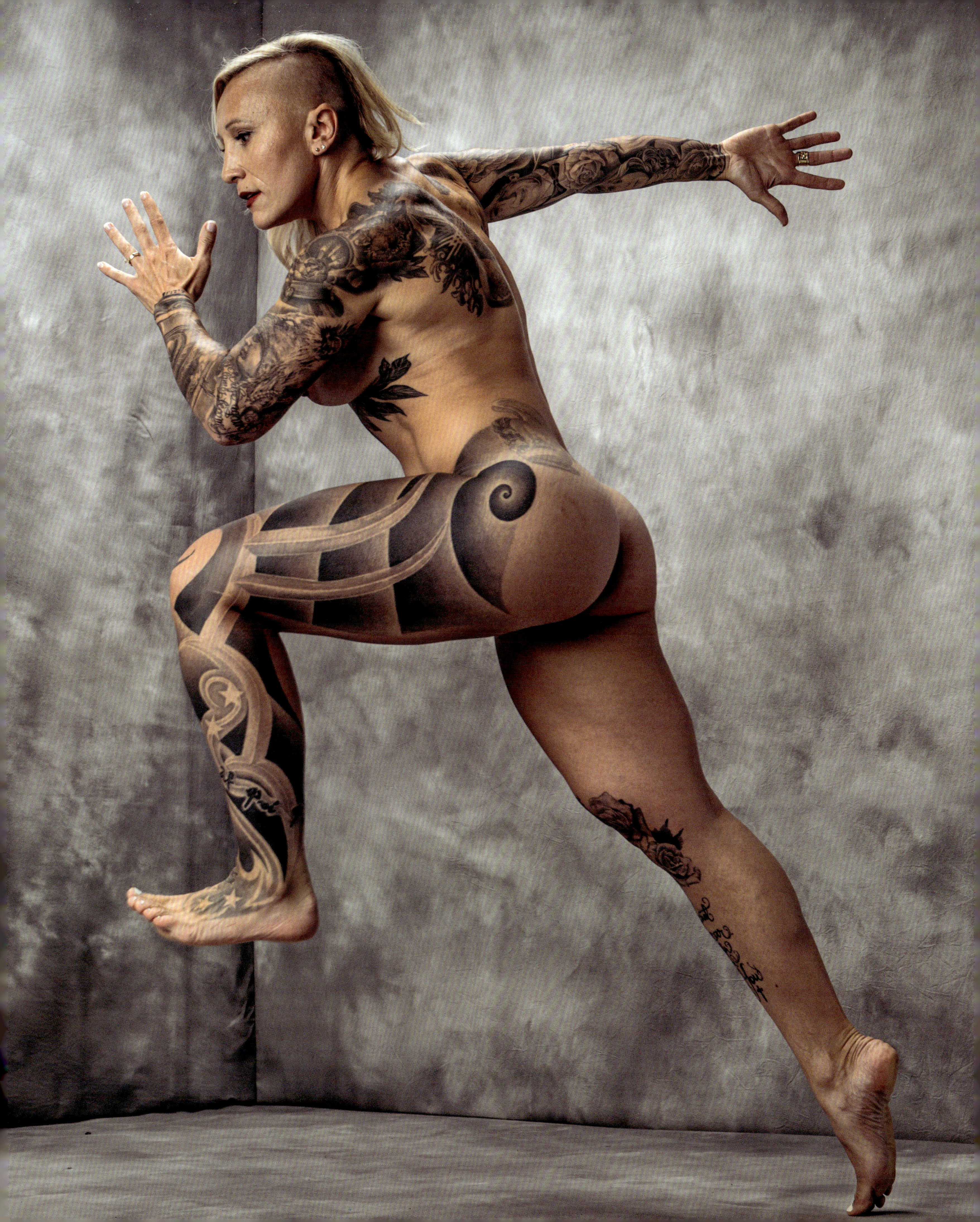

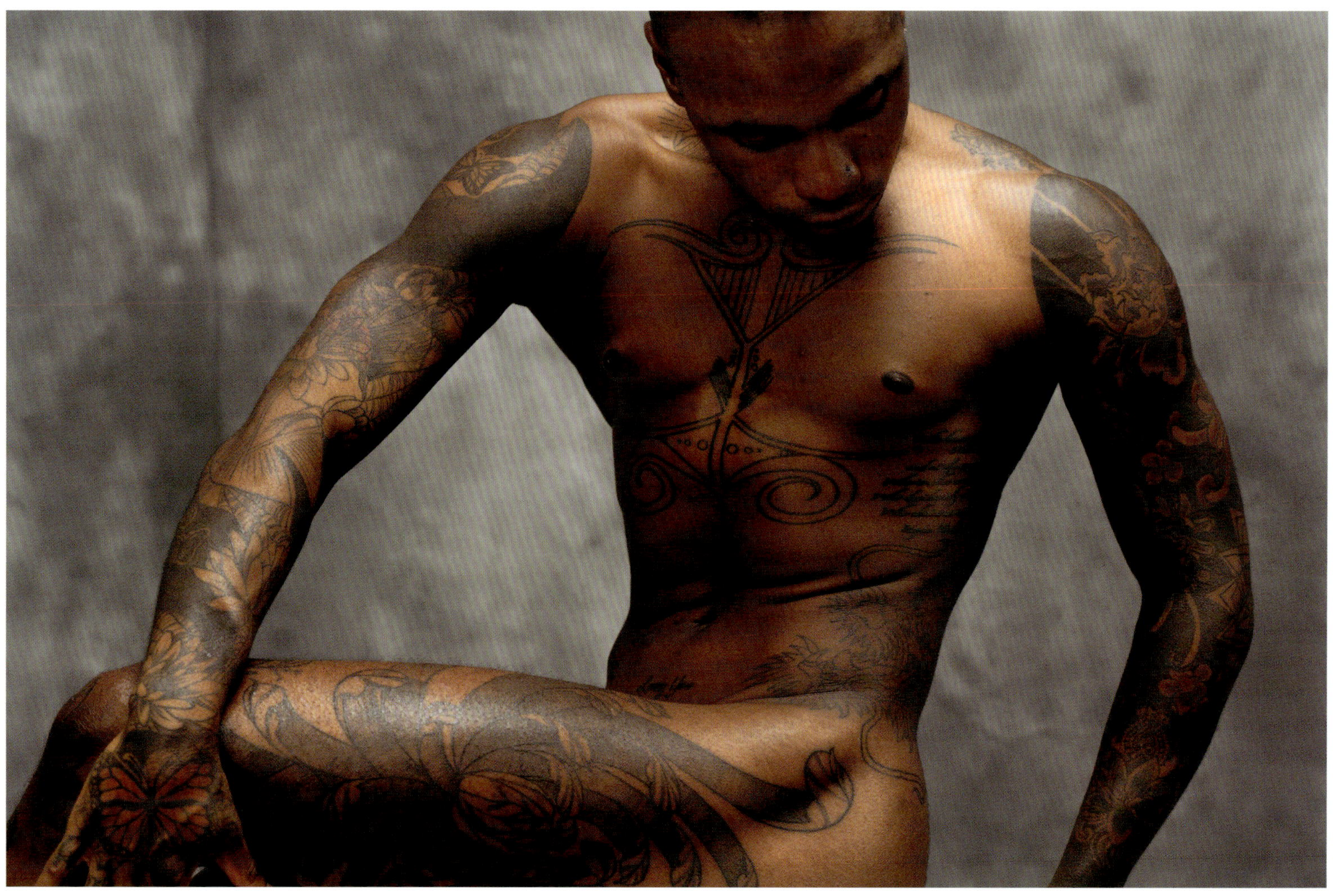

Pages 122–123: Olympic bobsled athlete Kaillie Humphries has work by Donavan Moore on her left leg, Jun Cha on her right arm (representing family), and Niki Norberg on her left sleeve. The right sleeve started as a representation of herself and ended with a memorial piece for her late uncle and grandfather, who passed suddenly.

Above and opposite: Sahir Watson's Japanese-inspired collection, tattooed by Jessa Bigelow, includes his head, neck, arm and leg sleeves, right hand, and fingers. Stephanie Tamez and his main artist, Bigelow, whom he says he shares a sibling-like bond with, tattooed his left hand.

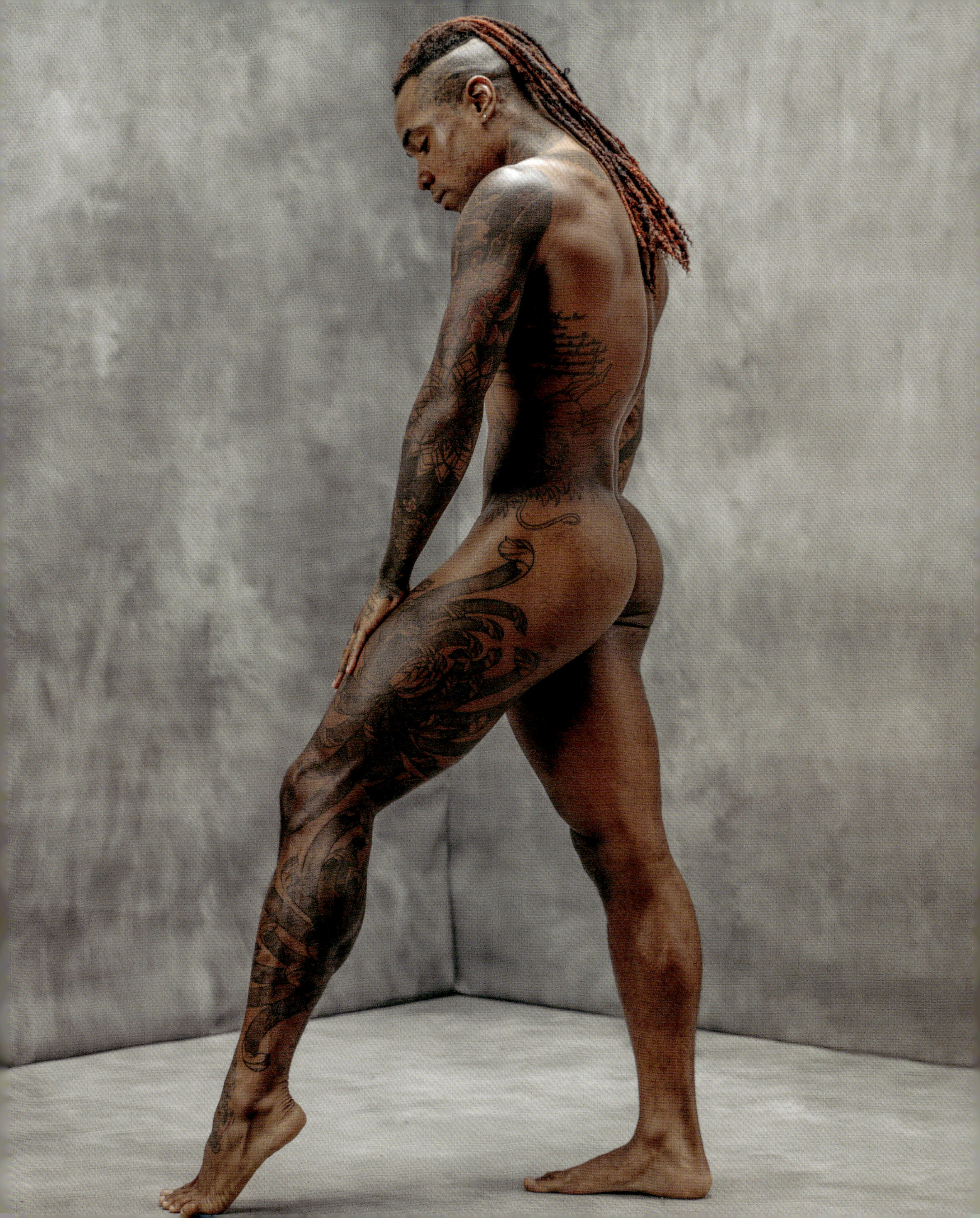

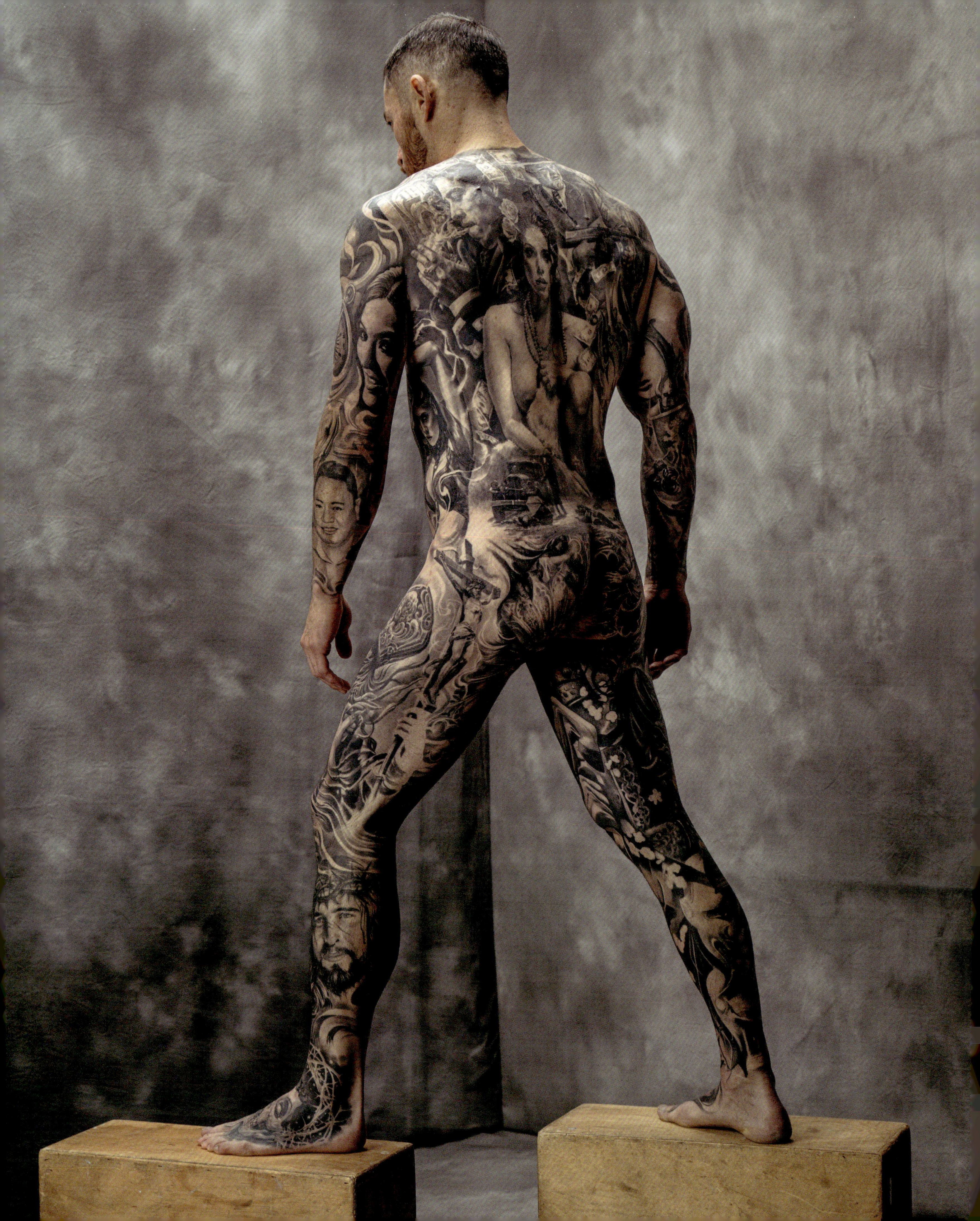

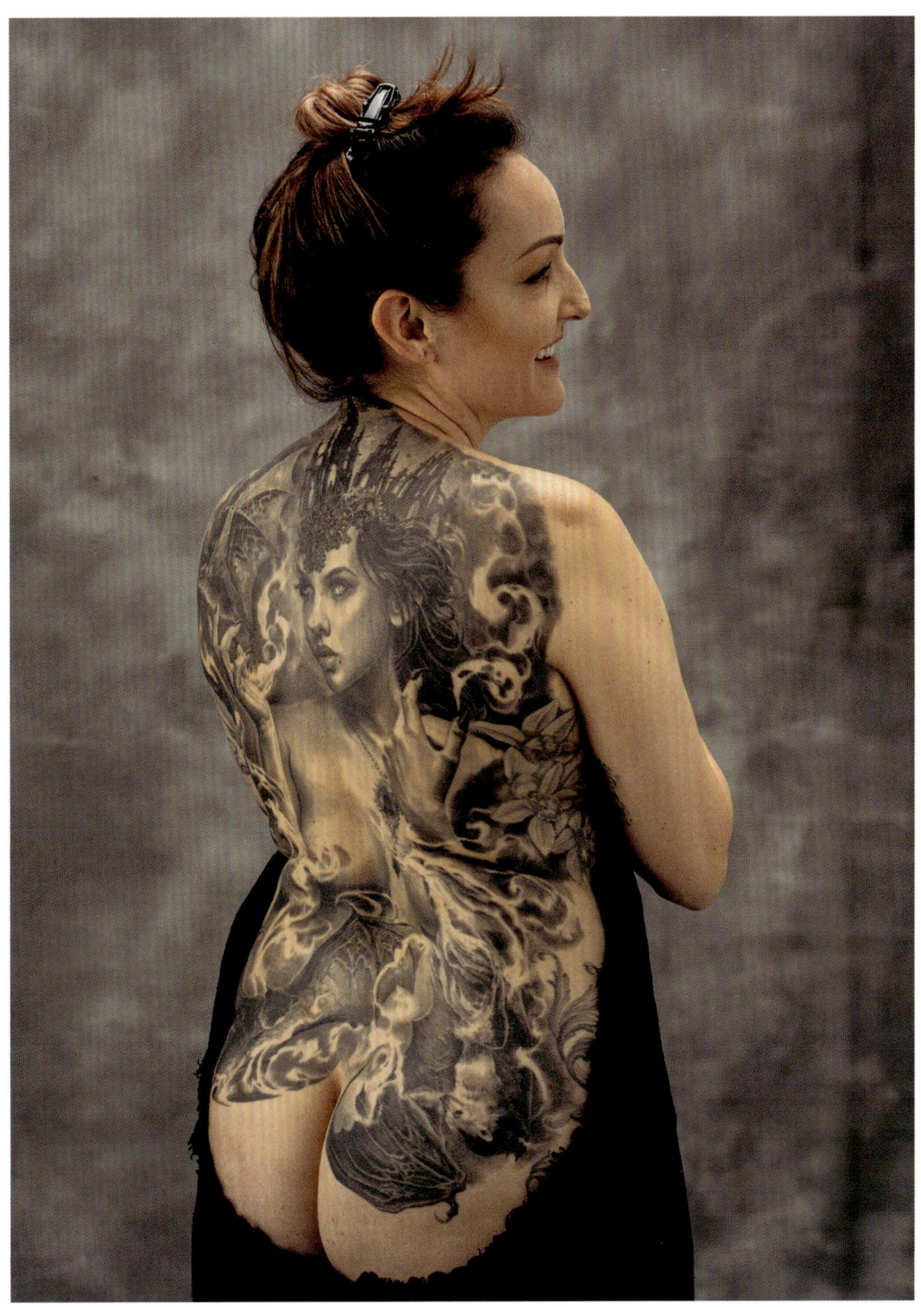

Opposite: Patrick Eidson wears a mobster-themed backpiece tattooed by Carlos Torres. His leg sleeves feature different inspirations: The right, by Robert Pho, shows Japanese influences; the left, by Ivano Natale, is religious in nature.

Above: Before managing Carlos Torres' studio, The Raven and The Wolves, Juliette Peat was a social worker. Her backpiece, by Torres, was completed with free rein.

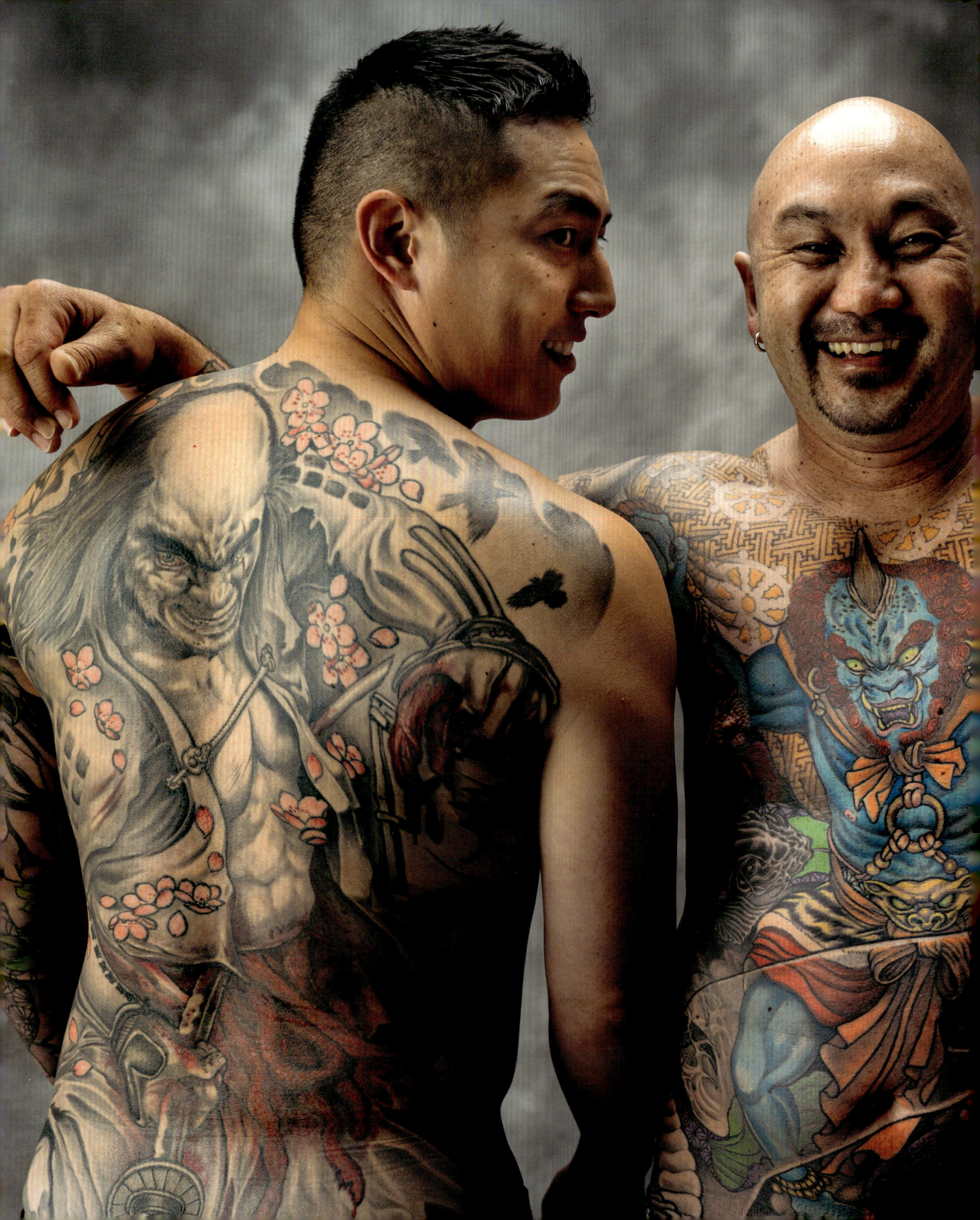

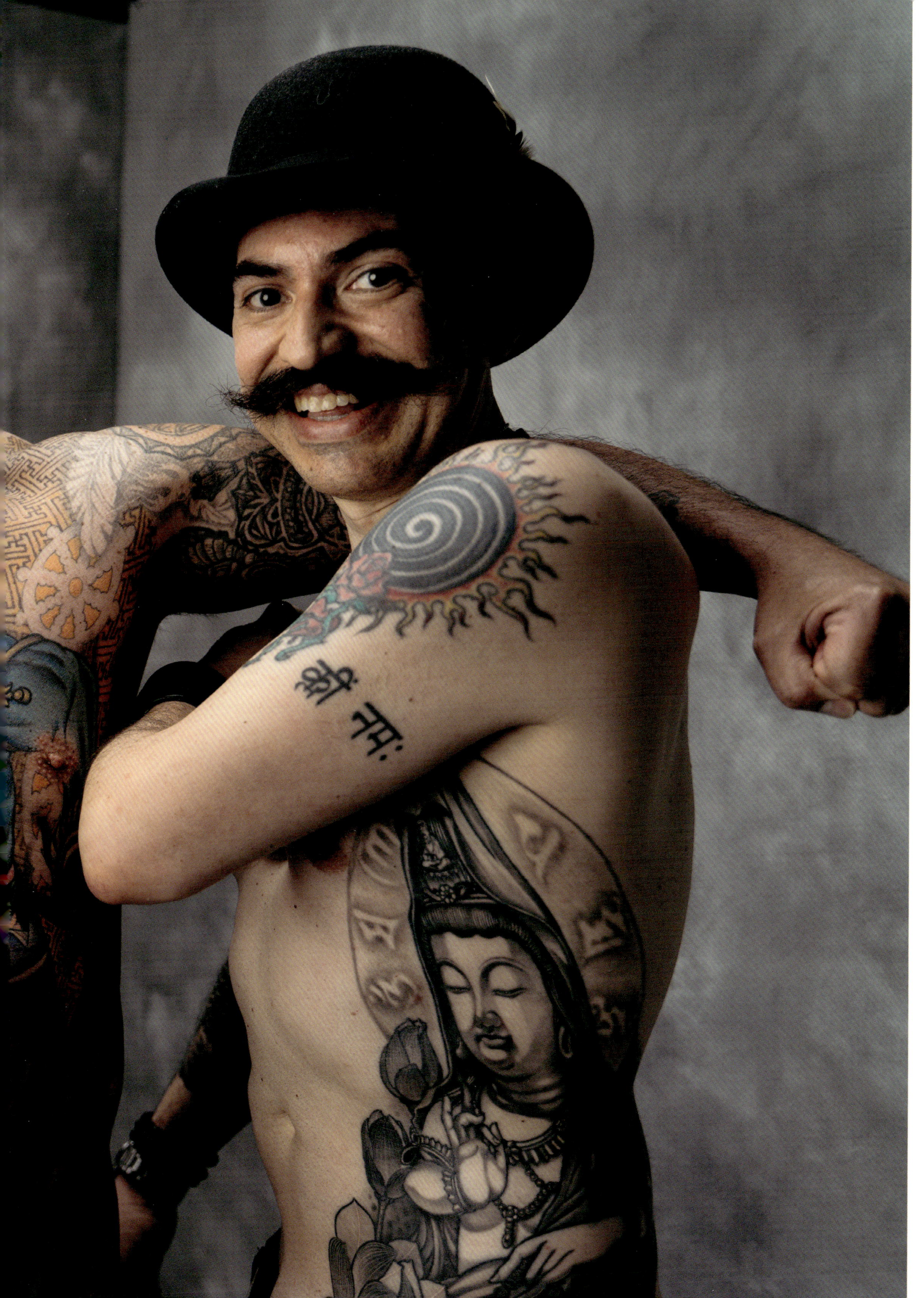
क्लीं नमः

Pages 128–129: The bodysuits of Clinton Ino (left) and Sheldon Hayashi (middle) were illustrated by Jess Yen, who also tattooed the Chinese goddess Guanyin on the rib cage of Tim Barreto (right). Barreto says it magnified his healing abilities as a chiropractor, because he can feel Yen's energy through the ink.

Opposite: Born and raised in Taiwan, Jonson wears a bodysuit by Jess Yen of mythical Taiwanese creatures that represent his family.

Pages 132–133: David and Cassandra Mendoza have primarily been tattooed by Carlos Torres. Her backpiece depicts the ancient story of Lilith, who represents feminine equality versus inferiority.

Pages 134–135: Beau Butcher (left) and Brent Frodge (right) have been collecting TeeJ Poole's illustrations since they discovered the artist's work. Frodge's entire bodysuit has taken Poole over eight years to complete.

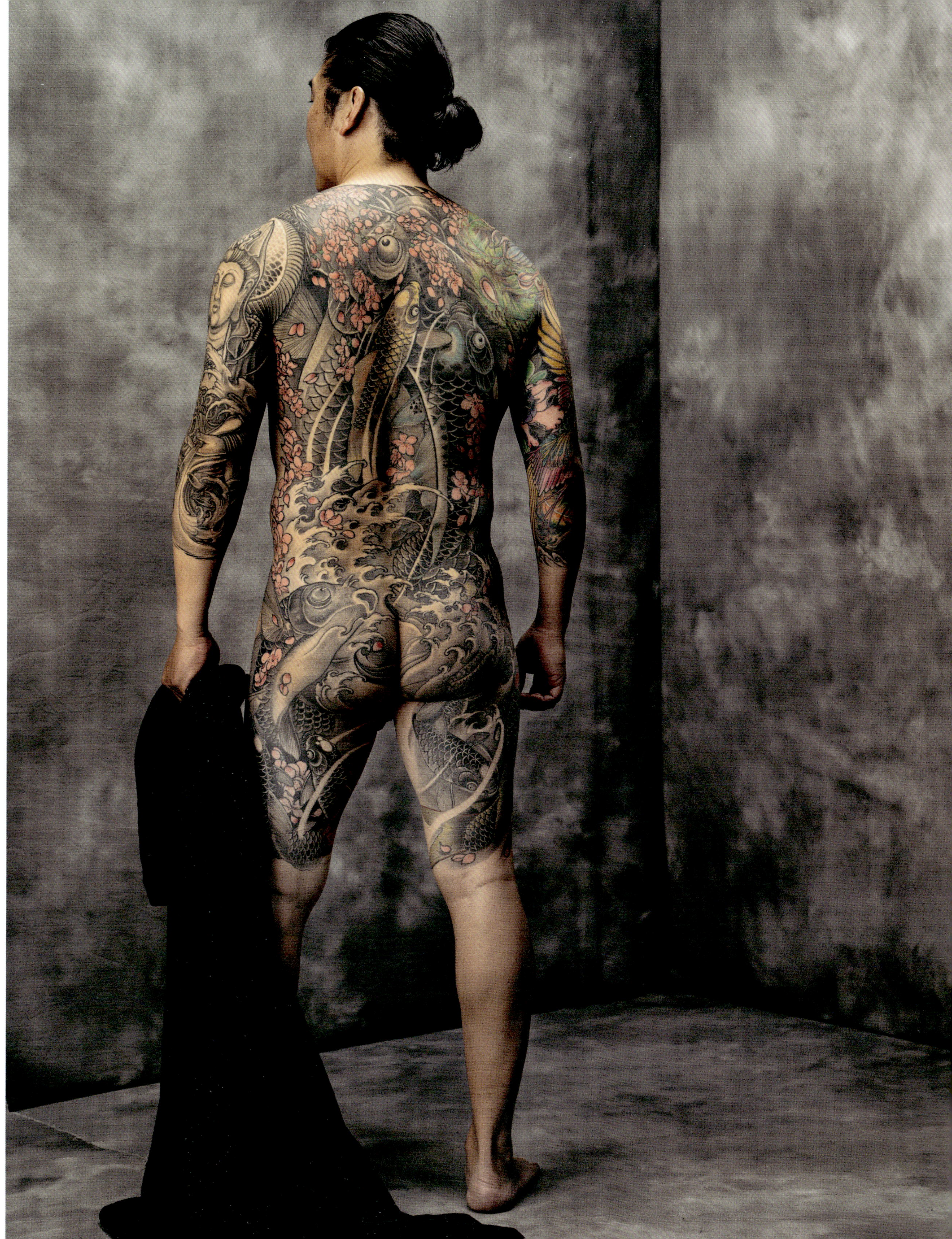

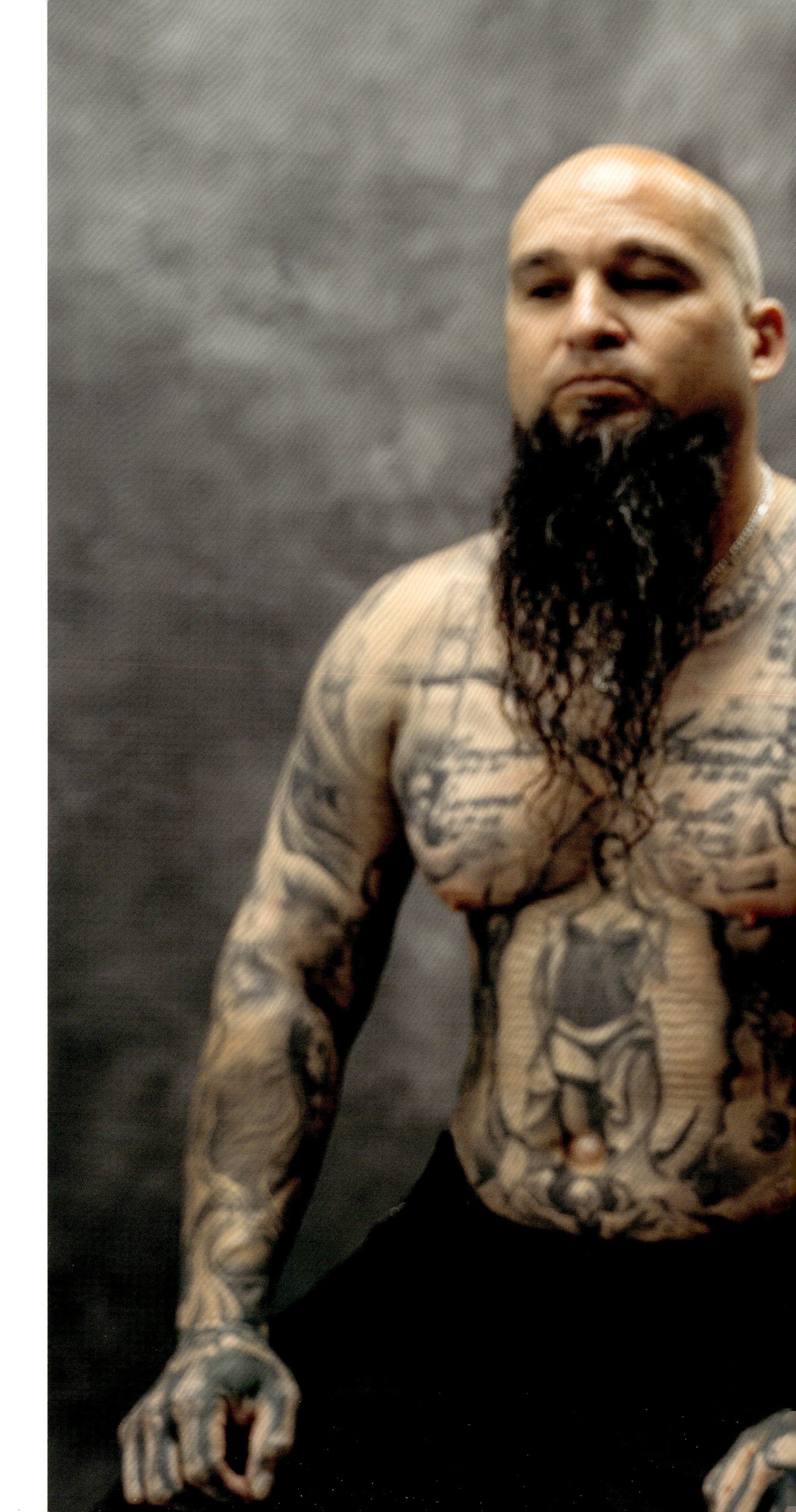

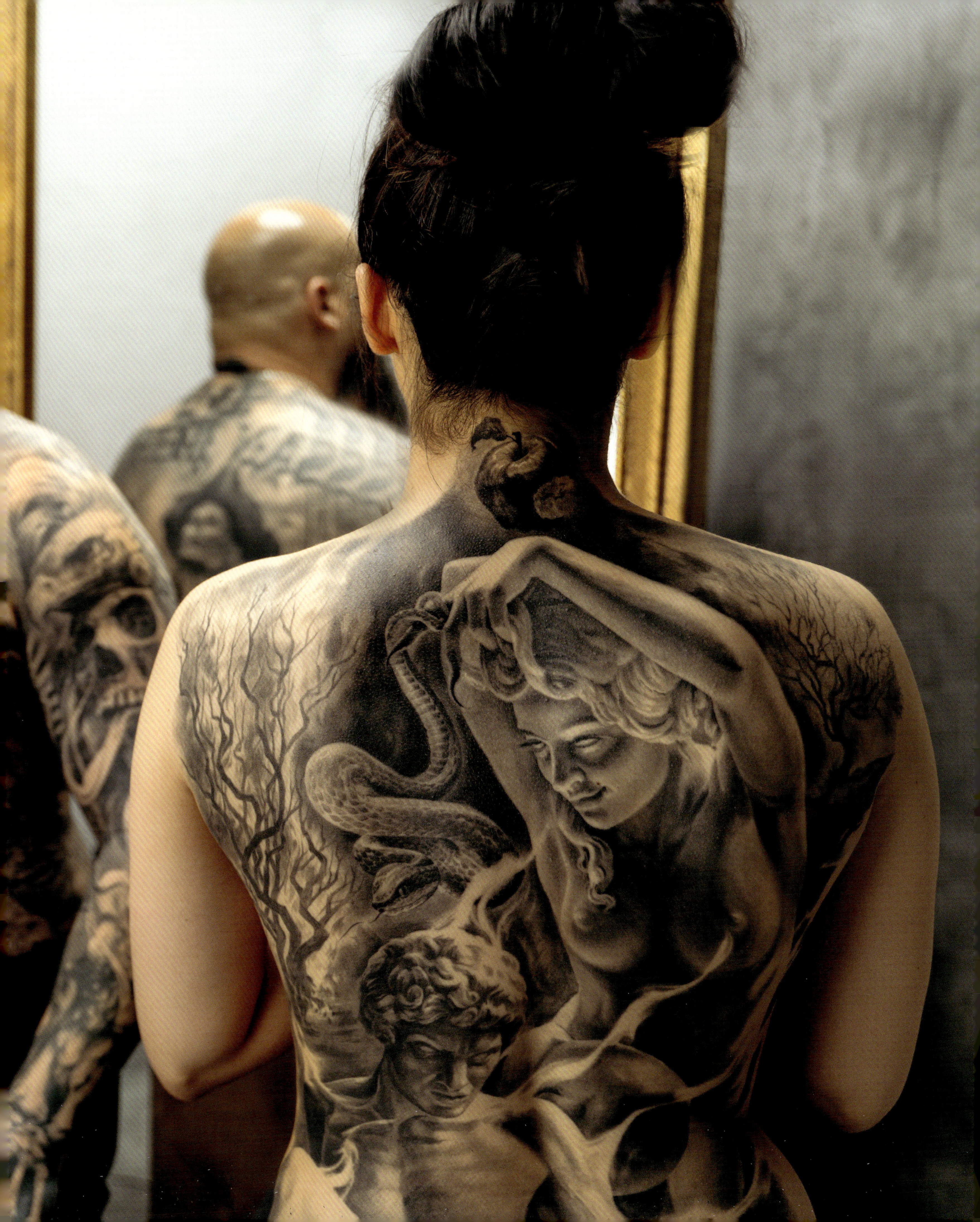

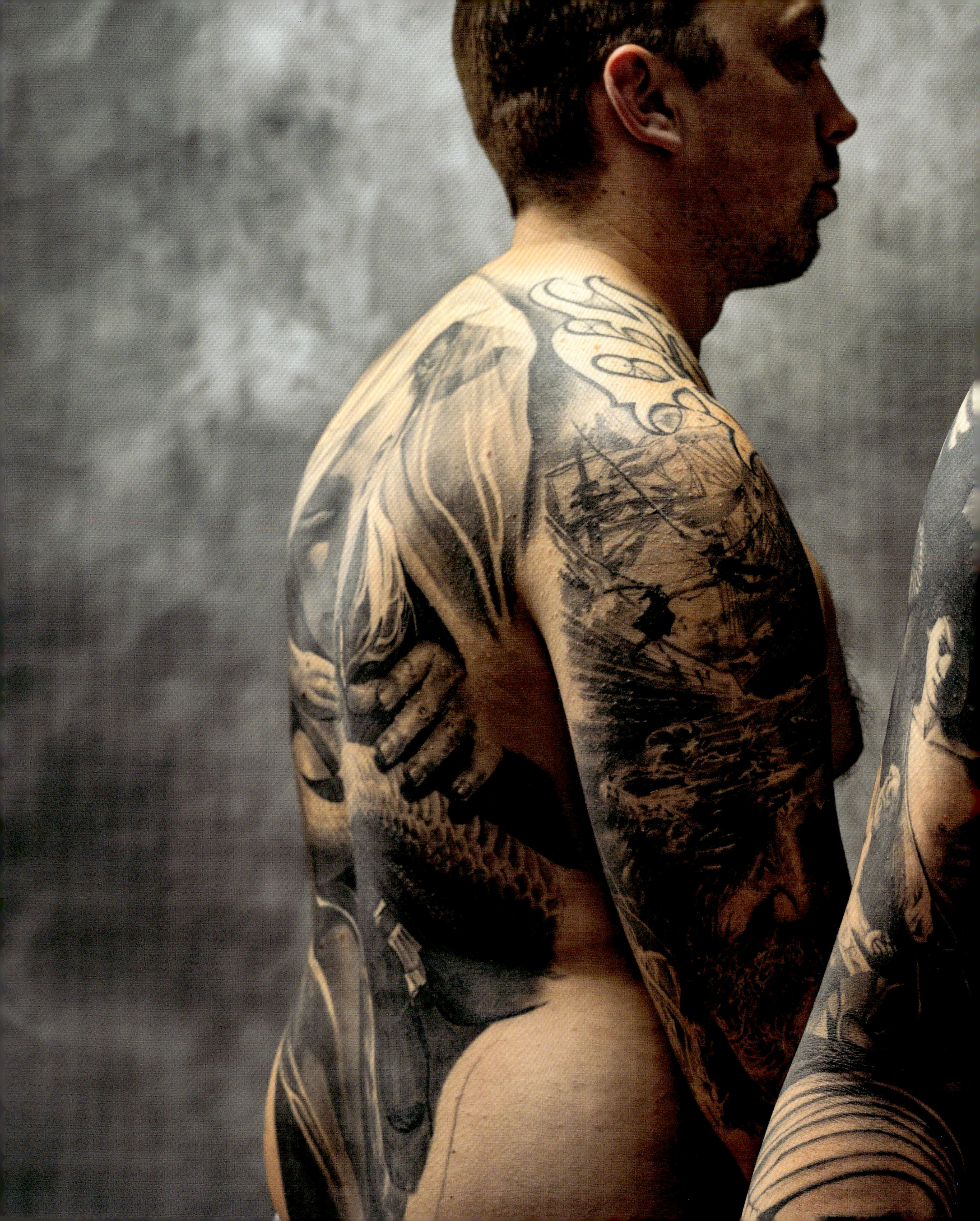

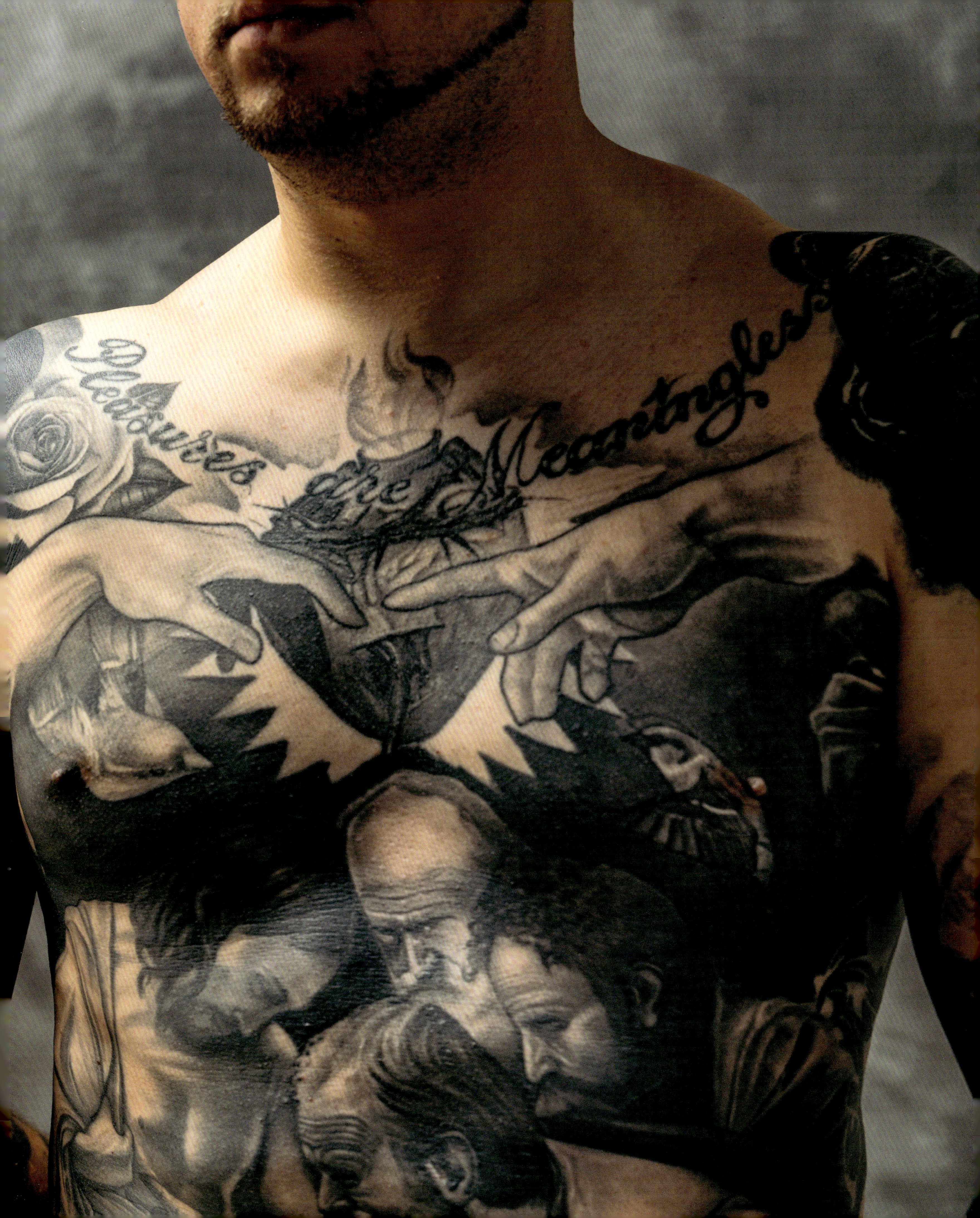

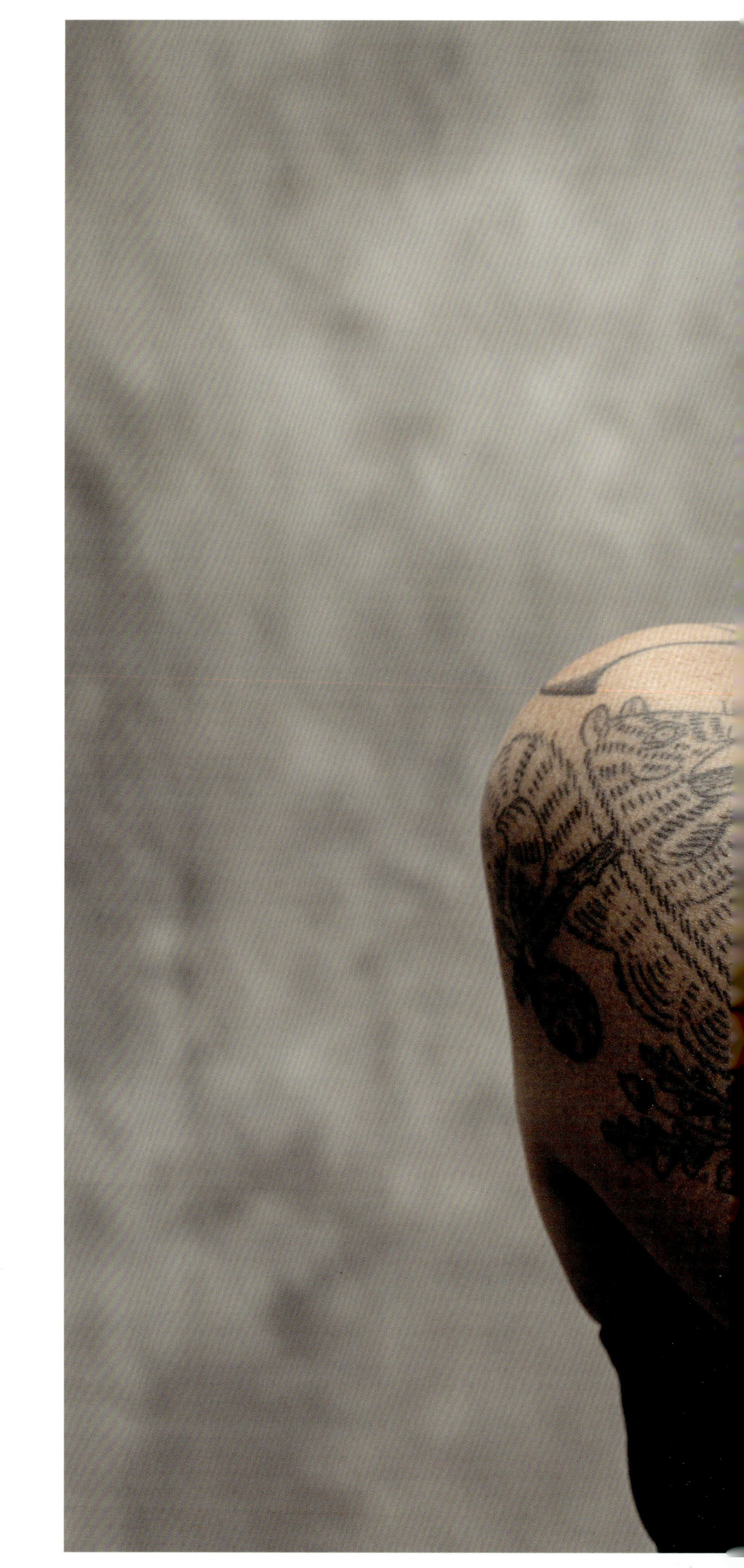

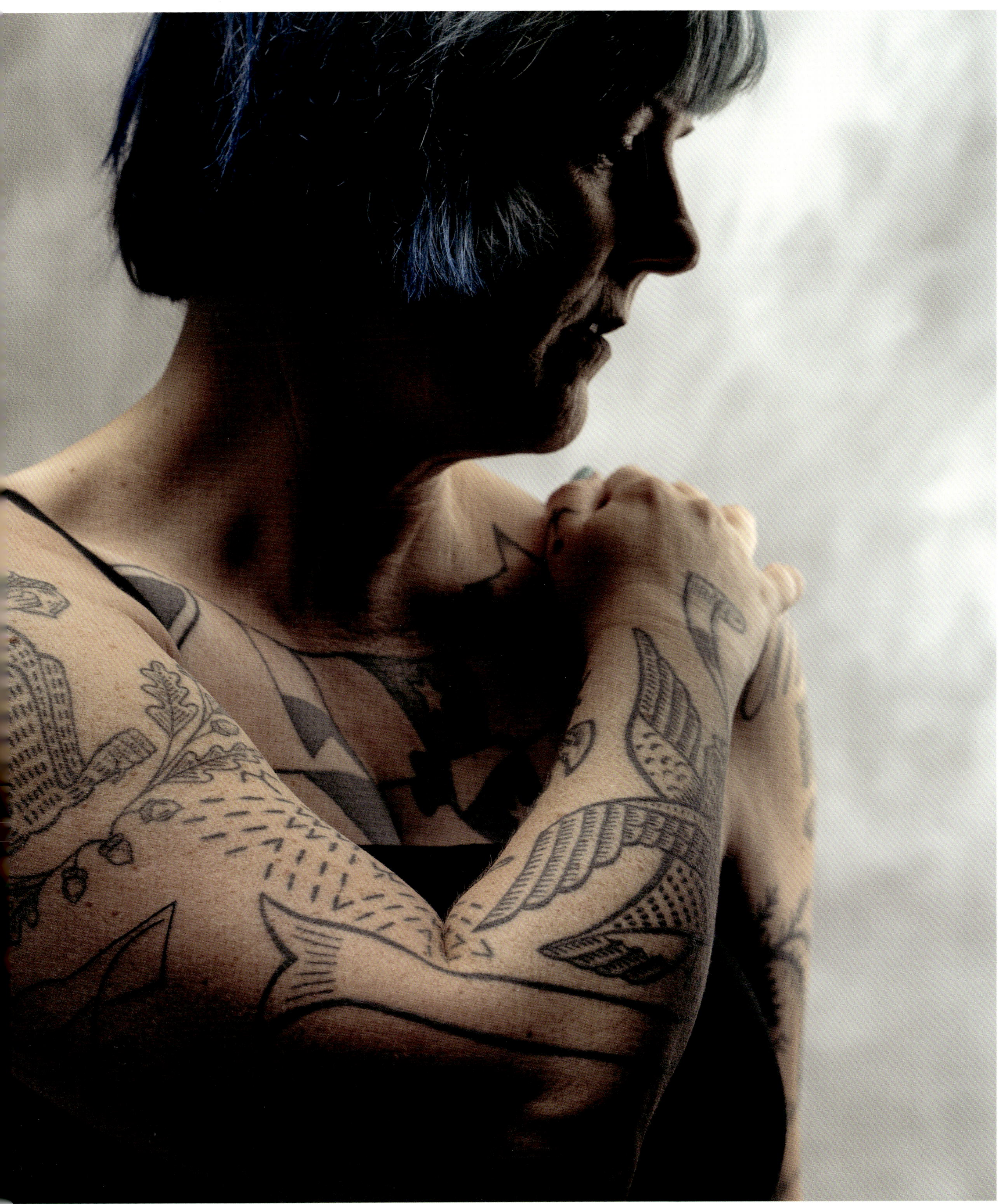

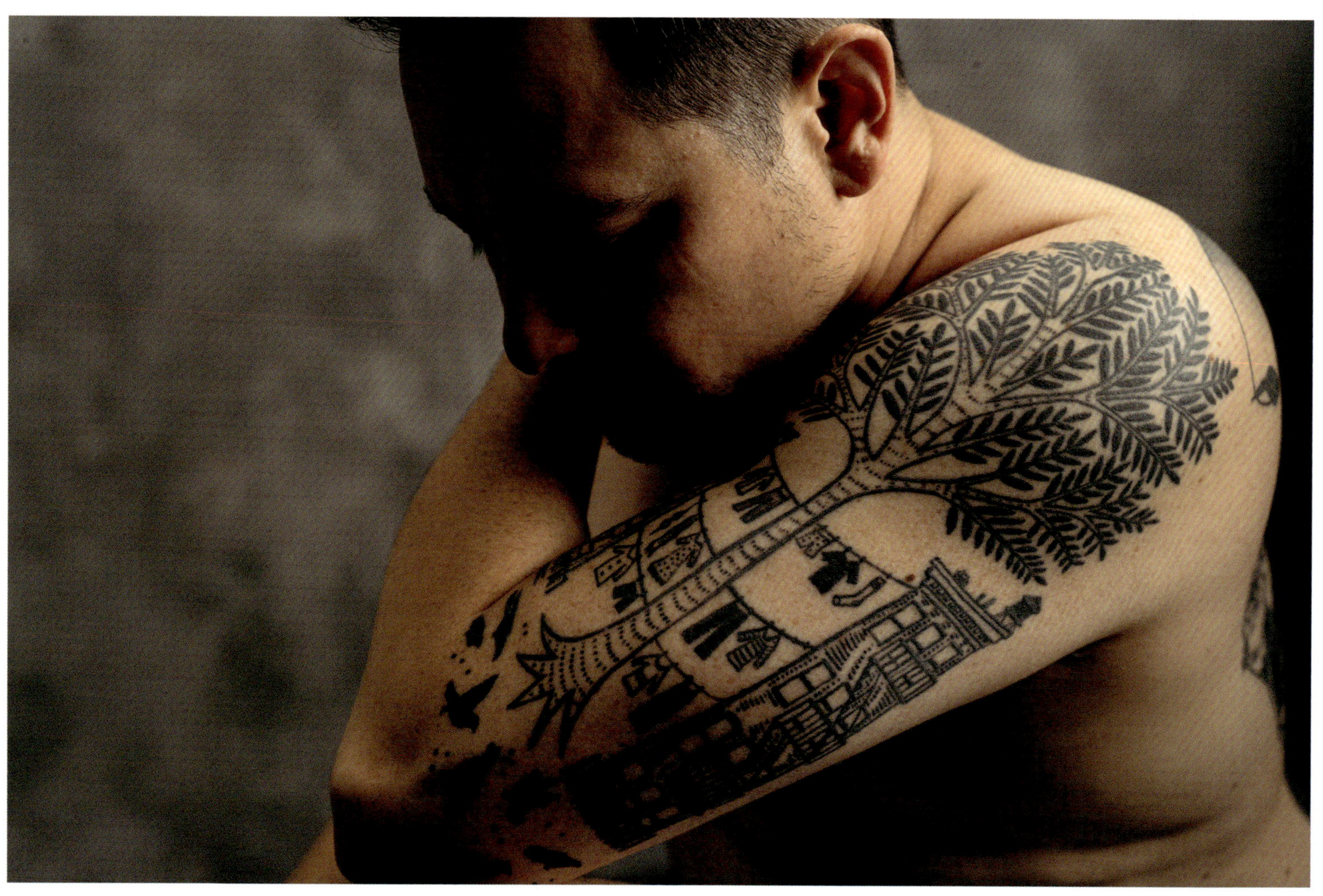

Pages 136–137: Predominantly illustrated by Duke Riley, Kitty Joe Sainte-Marie wears black linework, florals, and birds.

Above: Riley illustrated the ailanthus tree growing between two tenement buildings on Jae Mosc.
It stands as a symbol of perseverance and finding beauty in unexpected places.

Opposite: Stephanie H. Shih's body is almost exclusively a canvas for Riley.
Her backpiece of a pheasant, wolf, and bear trap represents a fable about fortitude and survival.

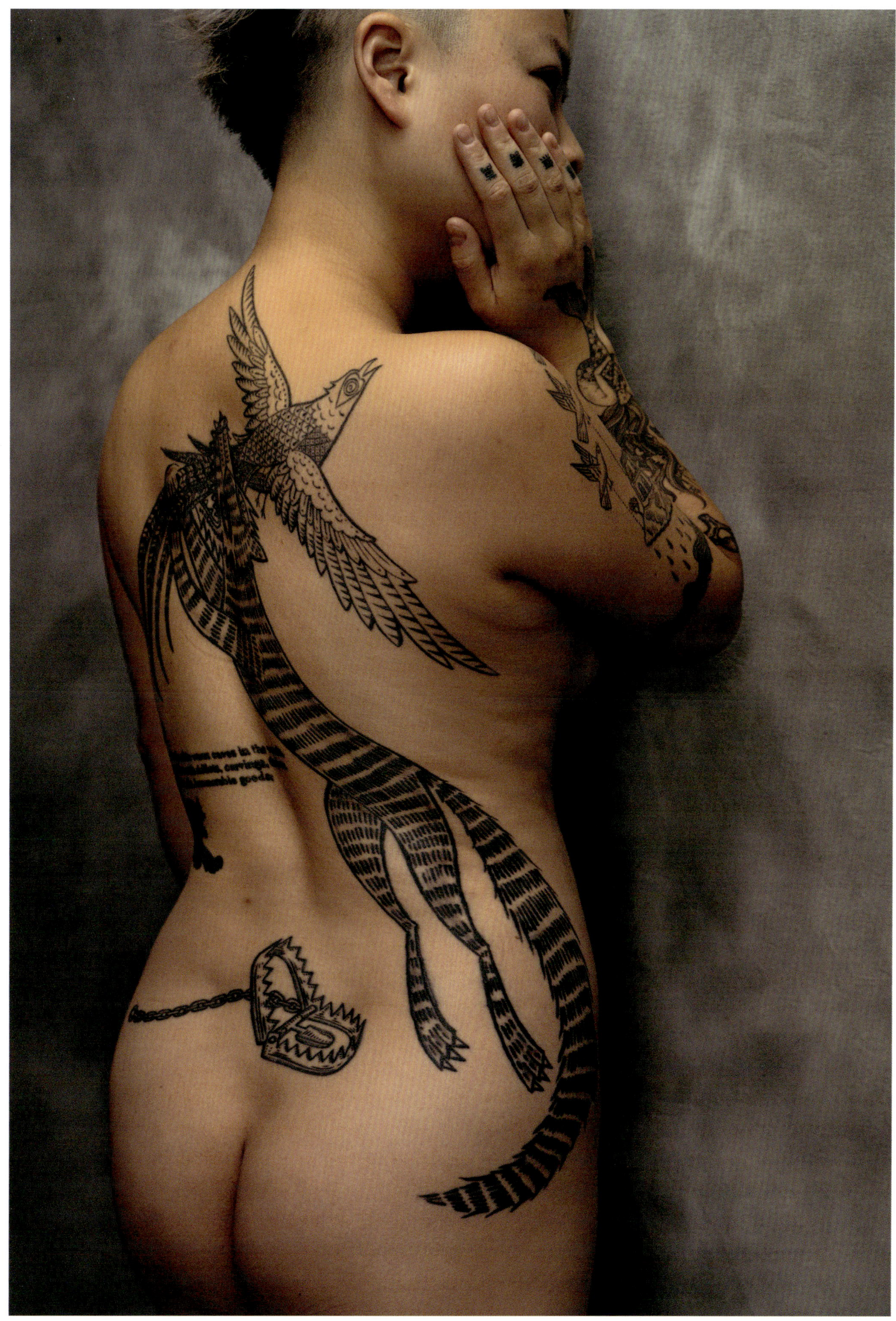

While Jim Miner is Cigno's main artist, she also wears work from Giuseppe Strambini, Christopher Vaughn Gay, Ryan Wiebusch, and Yorick Fauquant.

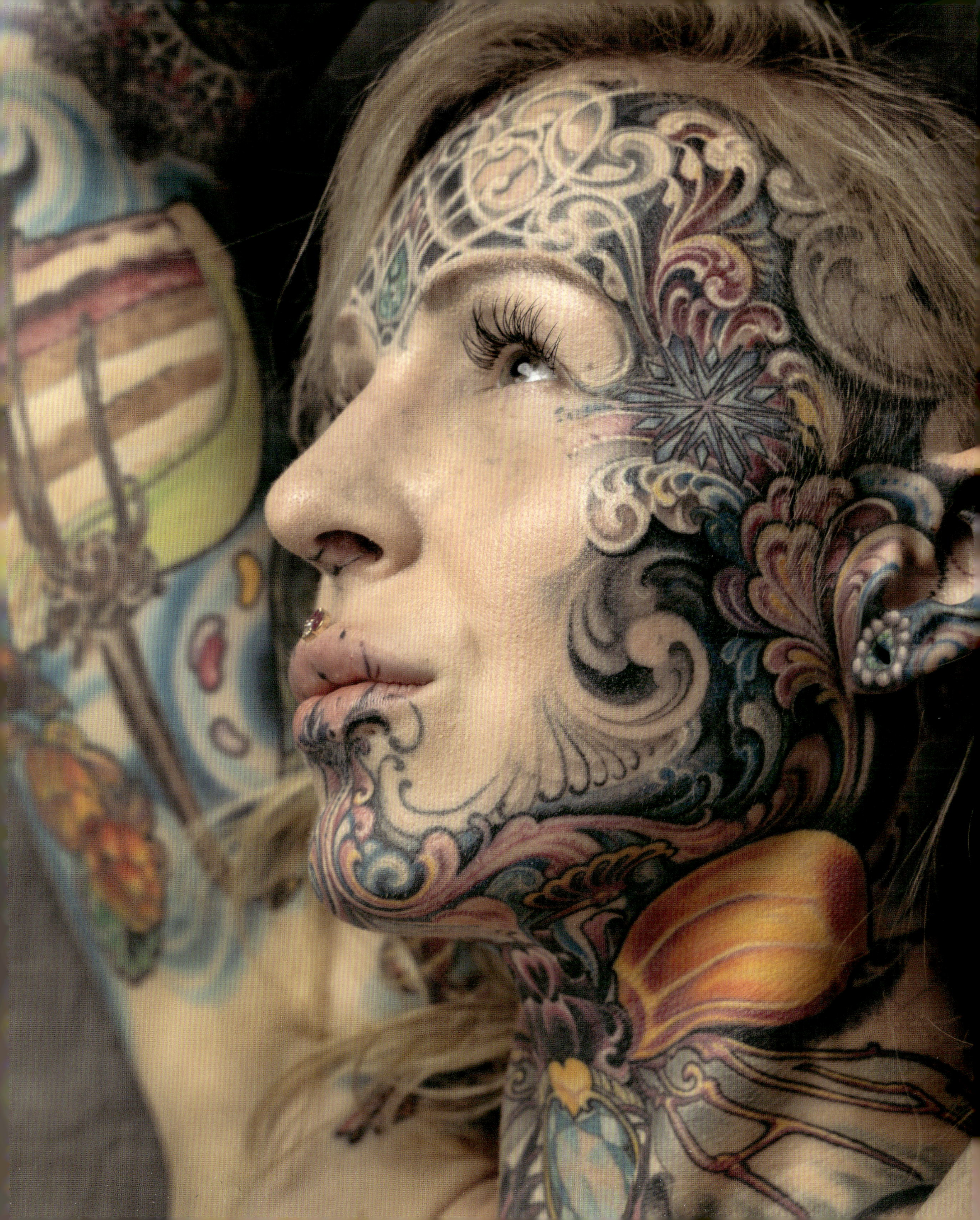

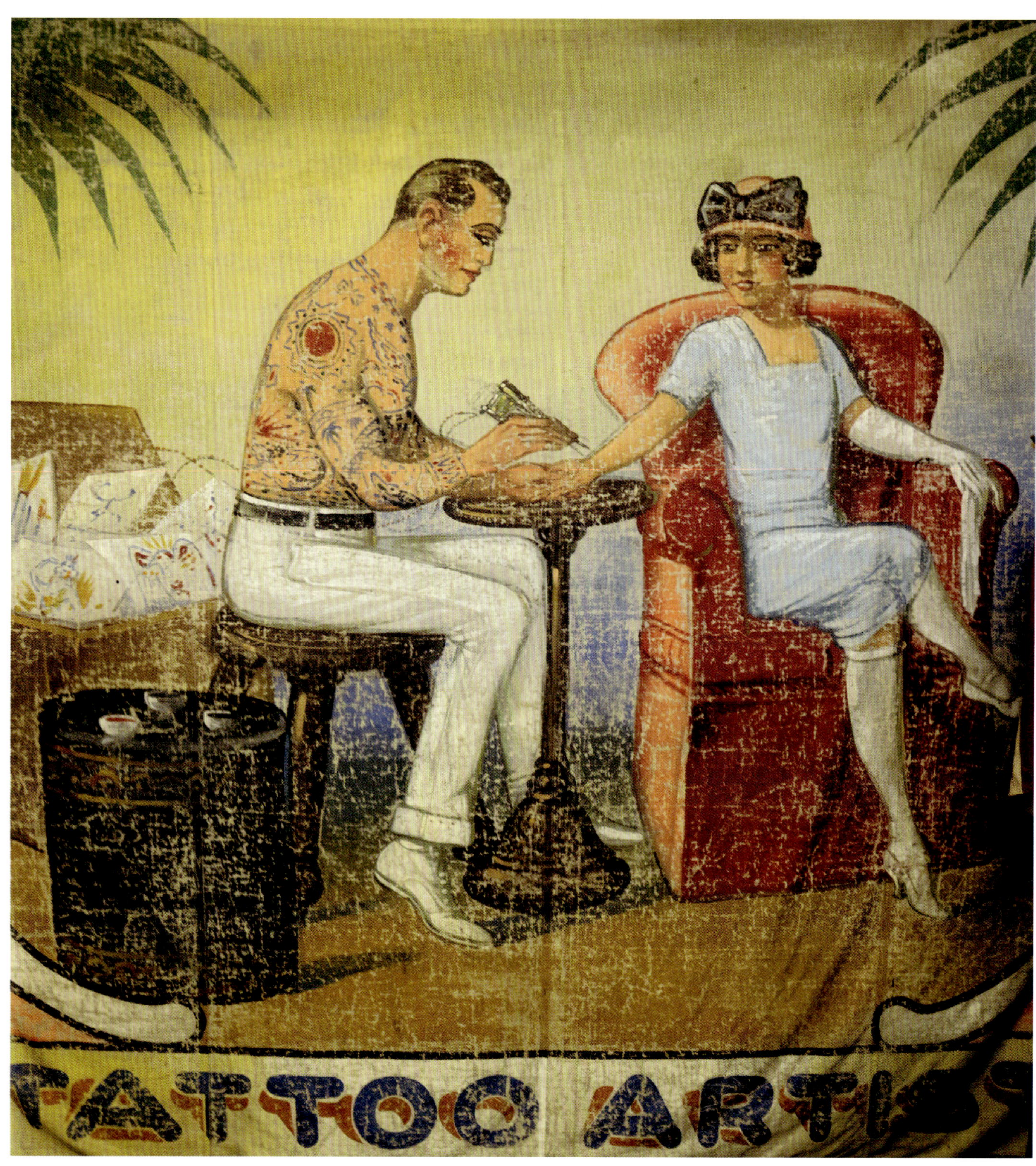

Sideshow banner, 1925, Chicago's Driver Brothers company.

RAY BRADBURY

THE ILLUSTRATED WOMAN

When a new patient wanders into the office and stretches out to stutter forth a compendious ticker-tape of free-association, it is up to the psychiatrist immediately beyond, behind, and above to decide at just which points of the anatomy the client is in touch with the couch.

In other words, where does the patient make contact with reality?

Some people seem to float half an inch above any surface whatsoever. They have not seen earth in so long they have become somewhat airsick.

Still others so firmly weight themselves down, clutch, thrust, heave their bodies toward reality that long after they are gone you find their tiger shapes and claw marks in the upholstery.

In the case of Emma Fleet, Dr. William C. George was a long time deciding which was furniture and which was woman and where what touched which.

For, to begin with, Emma Fleet resembled a couch.

"Mrs. Emma Fleet, doctor," announced his receptionist.

Dr. William C. George gasped.

And it was a traumatic experience, seeing this woman shunt herself through the door without benefit of railroad switchman or the ground crews who rush about under Macy's Easter balloons, heaving on lines, guiding the massive images to some eternal hangar off beyond.

In came Emma Fleet, as quick as her name, the floor shifting like a huge scale under her weight.

Dr. George must have gasped again, guessing her at four hundred on the hoof, for Emma Fleet smiled as if reading his mind.

"Four hundred two and one-half pounds, to be exact," she said.

He found himself staring at his furniture.

"Oh, it'll hold all right," said Mrs. Fleet intuitively.

She sat down.

The couch yelped like a cur.

Dr. George cleared his throat. "Before you make yourself comfortable," he said, "I feel I should say immediately and honestly that we in the psychiatric field have had little success in inhibiting appetites. The whole problem of weight and food has so far eluded our ability for coping. A strange admission, perhaps, but unless we put our frailties forth, we might be in danger of fooling ourselves and thus taking money under false pretenses. So, if you are here seeking help for your figure, I must list myself among the nonplussed."

"Thank you for your honesty, doctor," said Emma Fleet. "However, I don't wish to lose. I'd prefer your helping me *gain* another one hundred or two hundred pounds."

"Oh, no!" Dr. George exclaimed.

"Oh, yes. But my heart will not allow what my deep dear soul would most gladly endure. My physical heart might fail at what my loving heart and mind would ask of it."

She sighed. The couch sighed.

"Let me brief you. I'm married to Willy Fleet. We work for the Dillbeck-Horsemann Traveling Shows. I'm known as Lady Bountiful. And, Willy…?"

She swooned up out of the couch and glided or rather escorted her shadow across the floor. She opened the door.

Beyond, in the waiting room, a cane in one hand, a straw hat in the other, seated rigidly, staring at the wall, was a tiny man with tiny feet and tiny hands and tiny bright blue eyes in a tiny head. He was, at the most, one would guess, three feet high, and probably weighed sixty pounds in the rain. But there was a proud, gloomy, almost violent look of genius blazing in that small but craggy face.

"That's Willy Fleet," said Emma lovingly, and shut the door.

The couch, sat on, cried again.

Emma beamed at the psychiatrist, who was still staring, in shock, at the door.

"No children, of course," he heard himself say.

"No children." Her smile lingered. "But that's not my problem, either. Willy, in a way, is my child. And I, in a way, besides being his wife, am his mother. It all has to do with size, I imagine, and we're happy with the way we've balanced things off."

"Well, if your problem isn't children, or your size or his, or controlling weight, then what...?"

Emma Fleet laughed lightly, tolerantly. It was a nice laugh, like a girl's somehow caught in that great body and throat.

"Patience, doctor. Mustn't we go back down the road to where Willy and I first met?"

The doctor shrugged, laughed quietly himself, and relaxed, nodding. "You must."

"During high school," said Emma Fleet, "I weighed one-eighty and tipped the scales at two-fifty when I was twenty-one. Needless to say, I went on few summer excursions. Most of the time I was left in dry dock. I had many girlfriends, however, who liked to be seen with me. They weighed one-fifty, most of them, and I made them feel svelte. But...that's a long time ago. I don't worry over it any more. Willy changed all that."

"Willy sounds like a remarkable man," Dr. George found himself saying, against all the rules.

"Oh he is, he is! He—*smoulders*—with ability, with talent as yet undiscovered, untapped!" she said, quickening warmly. "God bless him, he leaped into my life like summer lightning! Eight years ago I went with my girlfriends to the visiting Labor Day carnival. By the end of the evening, the girls had all been seized away from me, by the running boys who, rushing by, grabbed and took them off into the night. There I was alone with three Kewpie dolls, a fake alligator handbag, and nothing to do but make the GUESS OUR WEIGHT man nervous by looking at him every time I went by and pretending like at any moment I might pay my money and dare him to guess.

"But, the GUESS OUR WEIGHT man wasn't nervous! After I had passed three times I saw him staring at me. With awe, yes, with admiration! And who was this GUESS OUR WEIGHT man? Willy Fleet, of course. The fourth time I passed he called to me and said I could get a prize free if only I'd let him guess my weight. He was all feverish and excited. He danced around. I'd never been made over so much in my life. I blushed. I felt good. So I sat in the scales chair. I heard the pointer whizz up around and I heard Willy whistle with honest delight.

"'Two hundred and eighty-nine pounds!' he cried. 'Oh boy, oh boy, you're lovely!'

"'I'm *what*?' I said.

"'You're the loveliest woman in the whole world,' said Willy, looking me right in the eye.

"I blushed again. I laughed. We both laughed. Then I must have cried, for the next thing, sitting there, I felt him touch my elbow with concern. He was gazing into my face, faintly alarmed.

"'I haven't said the wrong thing—?' he asked.

"'No,' I sobbed and then grew quiet. 'The right thing, only the right thing. It's the first time anyone ever—'

"'What?' he said.

"'Ever put up with my fat,' I said.

"'You're not fat,' he said. 'You're large, you're big, you're wonderful. Michelangelo would have loved you. Titian would have loved you. Da Vinci would have loved you. They knew what they were doing in those days. Size. Size is everything. I should know. Look at me. I traveled with Singer's Midgets for six seasons, known as Jack Thimble. And Oh my God, dear lady, you're right out of the most glorious part of the Renaissance. Bernini, who built those colonnades around the front of Saint Peter's and inside at the altar, would have lost his everlasting soul just to know someone like you...'

"'Don't!' I cried. 'I wasn't meant to feel this happy. It'll hurt so much when you stop.'

"'I won't stop, then,' he said. 'Miss...?'

"'Emma Gertz.'

"'Emma,' he said, 'are you married?'

"'Are you kidding?' I said.

"'Emma, do you like to travel?'

"'I've never traveled.'

"'Emma,' he said, 'this old carnival's going to be in your town one more week. Come down every night, every day, why not? Talk to me, know me. At the end of the week, who can tell, maybe you'll travel with me.'

"'What are you suggesting?' I said, not really angry or irritated or anything but fascinated and intrigued that anyone would offer anything to Moby Dick's daughter.

"'I mean marriage!' Willy Fleet looked at me, breathing hard, and I had the feeling that he was dressed in a mountaineer's rig, alpine hat, climbing boots, spikes, and a rope slung over his baby shoulder. And if I should ask him, 'Why are you saying this?' he might well answer, 'Because you're *there*.'

"But I didn't ask, so he didn't answer. We stood there in the night, at the center of the carnival, until at last I started off down the midway, swaying. 'I'm drunk!' I cried. 'Oh, so very drunk, and I've had nothing to drink.'

"'Now that I've found you,' called Willy Fleet after me, 'you'll never escape me, remember!'

"Stunned and reeling, blinded by this large man's words sung out in his soprano voice, I somehow blundered from the carnival grounds and trekked home.

"The next week, we were married."

Emma Fleet paused and looked at her hands.

"Would it bother you if I told you about the honeymoon?" she asked shyly.

"No," said the doctor, then lowered his voice, for he was responding all too quickly to the details. "Please *do* go on."

"The honeymoon." Emma sounded her *vox humana*. The response from all the chambers of her body vibrated the couch, the room, the doctor, the dear bones within the doctor.

"The honeymoon...was not usual."

The doctor's eyebrows lifted the faintest touch. He looked from the woman to the door beyond which, in miniature, sat the image of Edward Hillary, he of Everest.

"You have never seen such a rush as Willy spirited me off to his home, a lovely doll-house, really, with one large normal-sized room that was to be mine, or, rather, ours. There, very politely, always the kind, the thoughtful, the quiet gentleman, he asked for my blouse, which I gave him, my skirt, which I gave him. Right down the list, I handed him the garments that he named, until at last... Can one blush from head to foot? One can. One did. I stood like a veritable hearth-fire stoked by a blush of all-encompassing and ever-moving color that surged and resurged up and down my body in tints of pink and rose and then pink again.

"'My God!' cried Willy, 'you're the loveliest grand camellia that ever did unfurl!' Whereupon new tides of blush moved in hidden avalanches within, showing only to color the tent of my body, the outermost and, to Willy anyway, most precious skin.

"What did Willy do then? Guess."

"I daren't," said the doctor, flustered himself.

"He walked around and around me."

"*Circled* you?"

"Around and around, like a sculptor gazing at a huge block of snow-white granite. He said so himself. Granite or marble from which he might shape images of beauty as yet unguessed. Around and around he walked, sighing and shaking his head happily at his fortune, his little hands clasped, his little eyes bright. Where to begin, he seemed to be thinking, where, where to begin!?

"He spoke at last. 'Emma,' he asked, 'why, why do you think I've worked for years as the GUESS OUR WEIGHT man at the carnival? Why? Because I have been searching my lifetime through for such as you. Night after night, summer after summer, I've watched those scales jump and twitter! And now at last I've the means, the way, the wall, the canvas, whereby to express my genius!'

"He stopped walking and looked at me, his eyes brimming over.

"'Emma,' he said softly, 'may I have permission to do anything absolutely whatsoever at all with you?'

"'Oh, Willy, Willy,' I cried. 'Anything!'"

Emma Fleet paused.

The doctor found himself out at the edge of his chair. "Yes, yes. And then?"

"And then," said Emma Fleet, "he brought out all his boxes and bottles of inks and stencils and his bright silver tattoo needles."

"Tattoo needles?"

The doctor fell back in his chair.

"He…tattooed you?"

"He tattooed me."

"He was a tattoo artist?"

"He was, he is, an artist. It only happens that the form his art takes happens to be the tattoo."

"And you," said the doctor, slowly, "were the canvas for which he had been searching much of his adult life?"

"I was the canvas for which he had searched *all* of his life."

She let it sink, and it *did* sink, and keep on sinking, into the doctor. Then when she saw it had struck bottom and stirred up vast quantities of mud, she went serenely on.

"So our grand life began! I loved Willy and Willy loved me and we both loved this thing that was larger than ourselves that we were doing together. Nothing less than creating the greatest picture the world has ever seen. 'Nothing less than perfection!' cried Willy. 'Nothing less than perfection!' cried myself in response.

"Oh, it was a happy time. Ten thousand cozy busy hours we spent together. You can't imagine how proud it made me to be the vast shore along which the genius of Willy Fleet ebbed and flowed in a tide of colors.

"One year alone we spent on my right arm and my left, half a year on my right leg, eight months on my left, in preparation for the grand explosion of bright detail which erupted out along my collarbone and shoulderblades, which fountained upward from my hips to meet in a glorious July celebration of pinwheels, Titian nudes, Giorgione landscapes, and El Greco cross-indexes of lightning on my facade, prickling with vast electric fires up and down my spine.

"Dear me, there never has been, there never will be, a love like ours again, a love where two people so sincerely dedicated themselves to one task, of giving beauty to the world in equal portions. We flew to each other day after day, and if I ate more, grew larger, with the years, Willy approved, Willy applauded. Just that much more room, more space for his configurations to flower in. We could not bear to be apart, for we both felt, were certain, that once the Masterpiece was finished we could leave circus, carnival, or vaudeville forever. It was grandiose, yes, but we knew that once finished, I could be toured through the Art Institute in Chicago, the Kress Collection in Washington, the Tate Gallery in London, the Louvre, the Uffizi, the Vatican Museum! For the rest of our lives we would travel with the sun!

"So it went, year on year. We didn't need the world or the people of the world, we had each other. We worked at our ordinary jobs by day, and then till after midnight, there was Willy at my ankle, there was Willy at my elbow, there was Willy exploring up the incredible slope of my back toward the snowy-talcumed crest. Willy wouldn't let me see, most of the time. He didn't like me looking over his shoulder, he didn't like me looking over my shoulder, for that matter. Months passed before, curious beyond madness, I would be allowed to see his progress slow inch by inch as the brilliant inks inundated me and I drowned in the rainbow of his inspirations. Eight years, eight glorious wondrous years. And then at last, it was done, it was finished. And Willy threw himself down and slept for forty-eight hours straight. And I slept near him, the mammoth bedded with the black lamb. That was just four weeks ago. Four short weeks back, our happiness came to an end."

"Ah, yes," said the doctor. "You and your husband are suffering from the creative equivalent of the 'baby blues,' the depression a mother feels after her child is born. Your work is finished. A listless and somewhat sad period invariably follows. But, now, consider, you will reap the rewards of your long labor, surely? You *will* tour the world?"

"No," cried Emma Fleet, and a tear sprang to her eye. "At any moment, Willy will run off and never return. He has begun to wander about the city. Yesterday I caught him brushing off the carnival scales. Today I found him working, for the first time in eight years, back at his GUESS OUR WEIGHT booth!"

"Dear me," said the psychiatrist. "He's—?"

"Weighing new women, yes! Shopping for new canvas! He hasn't said, but I know, I know! This time he'll find a heavier woman yet, five hundred, six hundred pounds! I guessed this would happen, a month ago, when we finished the Masterpiece. So I ate still more, and stretched my skin still more, so that little places appeared here and there, little open patches that Willy had to repair, fill in with fresh detail. But now I'm done, exhausted, I've stuffed to distraction, the last fill-in work is done. There's not a millionth of an inch of space left between my ankles and my Adam's apple where we can squeeze in one last demon, dervish, or baroque angel. I am, to Willy, work over and done. Now he wants to move on. He will marry, I fear, four more times in his life, each time to a larger woman, a greater extension for a greater mural, and the grand finale of his talent. Then, too, in the last week, he has become critical."

"Of the Masterpiece with a capital M?" asked the doctor.

"Like all artists, he is a perfectionist. Now he finds little flaws, a face here done slightly in the wrong tint or texture, a hand there twisted slightly askew by my hurried diet to gain more weight and thus give him new space and renew his attentions. To him, above all, I was a beginning. Now he must move on from his apprenticeship to his true masterworks. Oh, doctor, I am about to be abandoned. Where is there for a woman who weighs four hundred pounds and is laved with illustrations? If he leaves, what shall I do, where go, who would want me now? Will I be lost again in the world as I was before my wild happiness?"

"A psychiatrist," said the psychiatrist, "is not supposed to give advice. But—"

"But, but, but?" she cried, eagerly.

"A psychiatrist is supposed to let the patient discover and cure himself. Yet, in this case—"

"This case, yes, go on!"

"It seems so simple. To keep your husband's love—"

"To keep his love, yes?"

The doctor smiled. "You must destroy the Masterpiece."

"What?"

"Erase it, get rid of it. Those tattoos *will* come off, won't they? I read somewhere once that—"

"Oh, doctor!" Emma Fleet leaped up. "That's *it*! It can be done! And best of all, Willy can do it! It will take three months alone to wash me clean, rid me of the very Masterpiece that irks him now. Then, virgin-white again, we can start another eight years, after that another eight and another. Oh, doctor, I know he'll do it! Perhaps he was only waiting for me to suggest—and I too stupid to guess! Oh, doctor, doctor!"

And she crushed him in her arms.

When the doctor broke happily free, she stood off, turning in a circle.

"How strange," she said. "In half an hour, you solve the next three thousand days and beyond, of my life. You're very wise. I'll pay you anything!"

"My usual modest fee is sufficient," said the doctor.

"I can hardly wait to tell Willy! But first," she said, "since you've been so wise, you deserve to see the Masterpiece before it is destroyed."

"That's hardly necessary, Mrs.—"

"You must discover for yourself the rare mind, eye, and artistic hand of Willy Fleet, before it is gone forever and we start anew!" she cried, unbuttoning her voluminous coat.

"It isn't really—"

"There!" she said, and flung her coat wide.

The doctor was somehow not surprised to see that she was stark naked beneath her coat.

He gasped. His eyes grew large. His mouth fell open. He sat down slowly, though in reality he somehow wished to stand, as he had in the fifth grade as a boy, during the salute to the flag, following which three dozen voices broke into an awed and tremulous song:

> *"Oh Beautiful for spacious skies,*
>
> *O'er amber waves of grain,*
>
> *For purple mountain majesties,*
>
> *Above the fruited plain..."*

But, still seated, overwhelmed, he gazed at the continental vastness of the woman.

Upon which nothing whatsoever was stitched, painted, water-colored or in any way tattooed.

Naked, unadorned, untouched, unlined, unillustrated.

He gasped again.

Now she had whipped her coat back about her with a winsome acrobat's smile, as if she had just performed a towering feat. Now she was sailing toward the door.

"Wait—" said the doctor.

But she was out the door, in the reception room, babbling, whispering, "Willy, Willy!" and bending to her husband, hissing in his tiny ear until *his* eyes flexed wide, and his firm and passionate mouth dropped open and he cried aloud and clapped his hands with elation.

"Doctor, doctor, thank you, thank you!"

He darted forward and seized the doctor's hand and shook it, hard. The doctor was surprised at the fire and rock hardness of that grip. It was the hand of a dedicated artist, as were the eyes burning up at him darkly from the wildly illuminated face.

"Everything's going to be fine!" cried Willy.

The doctor hesitated, glancing from Willy to the great shadowing balloon that tugged at him wanting to fly off away.

"We won't have to come back again, ever?"

Good Lord, the doctor thought, does *he* think that *he* has illustrated her from stem to stern, and does she humor him about it? Is *he* mad?

Or does *she* imagine that he has tattooed her from neck to toe-bone, and does he humor her? Is *she* mad?"

Or, most strange of all, do they *both* believe that he has swarmed, as across the Sistine Chapel ceiling, covering her with rare and significant beauties? Do they both believe, know, humor each other in their specially dimensioned world?

"Will we have to come back again?" asked Willy Fleet a second time.

"No." The doctor breathed a prayer. "I think not."

Why? Because by some idiot grace, he had done the right thing, hadn't he? By prescribing for an invisible cause he had made a full cure, yes? Regardless if she believed or he believed or both believed in the Masterpiece, by suggesting the pictures be erased, destroyed, the doctor had made her a clean, lovely, and inviting canvas again, if *she* needed to be. And if he, on the other hand, wished a new woman to scribble, scrawl, and pretend to tattoo on, well, that worked, too. For new and untouched she would be.

"Thank you, doctor, oh thank you, thank you!"

"Don't thank me," said the doctor. "I've done nothing." He almost said, it was all a fluke, a joke, a surprise! I fell downstairs and landed on my feet!

"Good-bye, good-bye!"

And the elevator slid down, the big woman and the little man sinking from sight into the now suddenly not-too-solid earth where the atoms opened to let them pass.

"Good-bye, thanks…thanks…"

Their voices faded, calling his name and praising his intellect long after they had passed the fourth floor.

The doctor looked around and moved unsteadily back into his office. He shut the door and leaned against it.

"Doctor," he murmured, "heal thyself."

He stepped forward. He did not feel real. He must lie down, if but for a moment.

Where?

On the couch, of course, on the couch.

Maud Wagner, ca. 1907, photo GraphialArtis / Getty Images

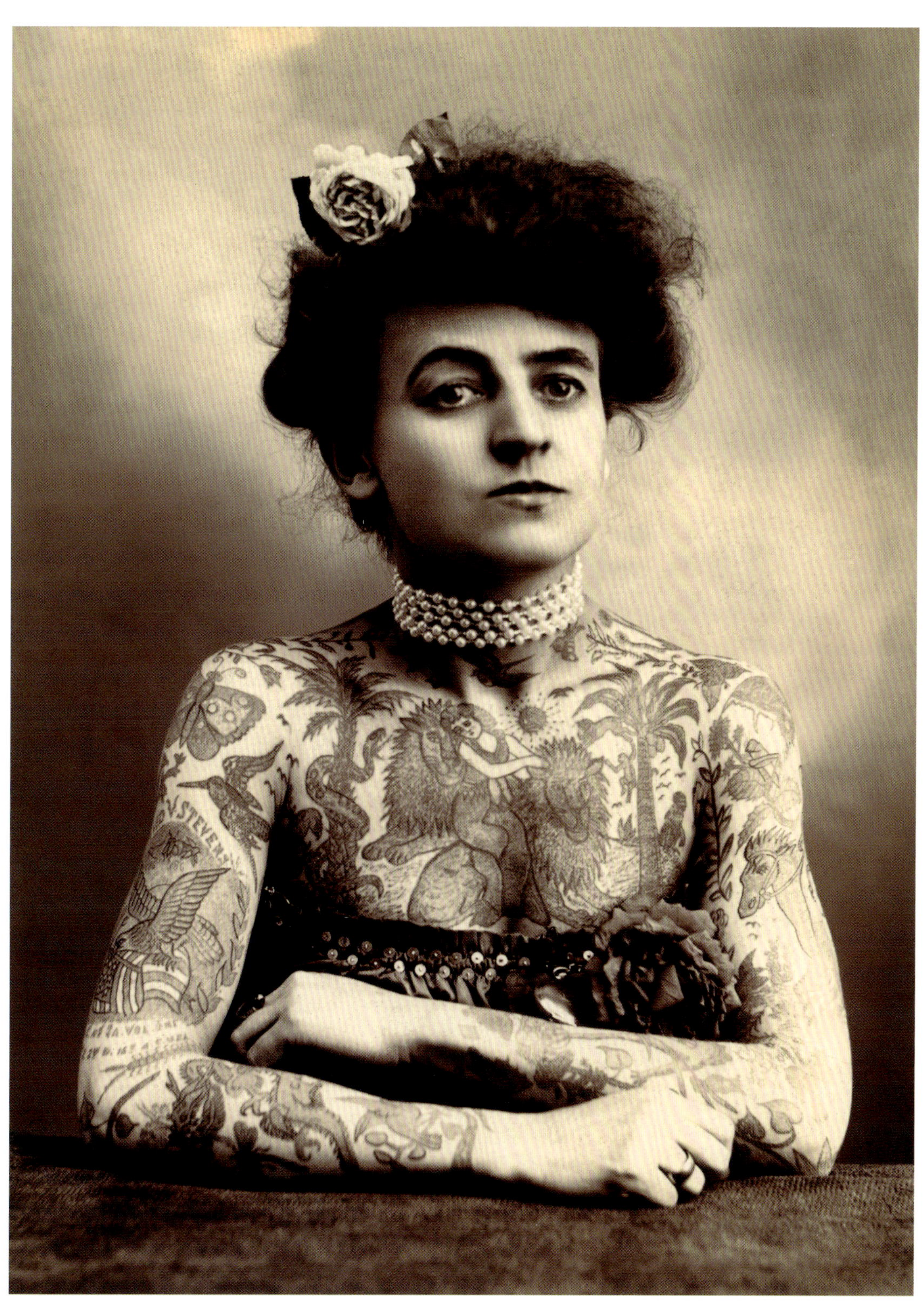

STEVENS

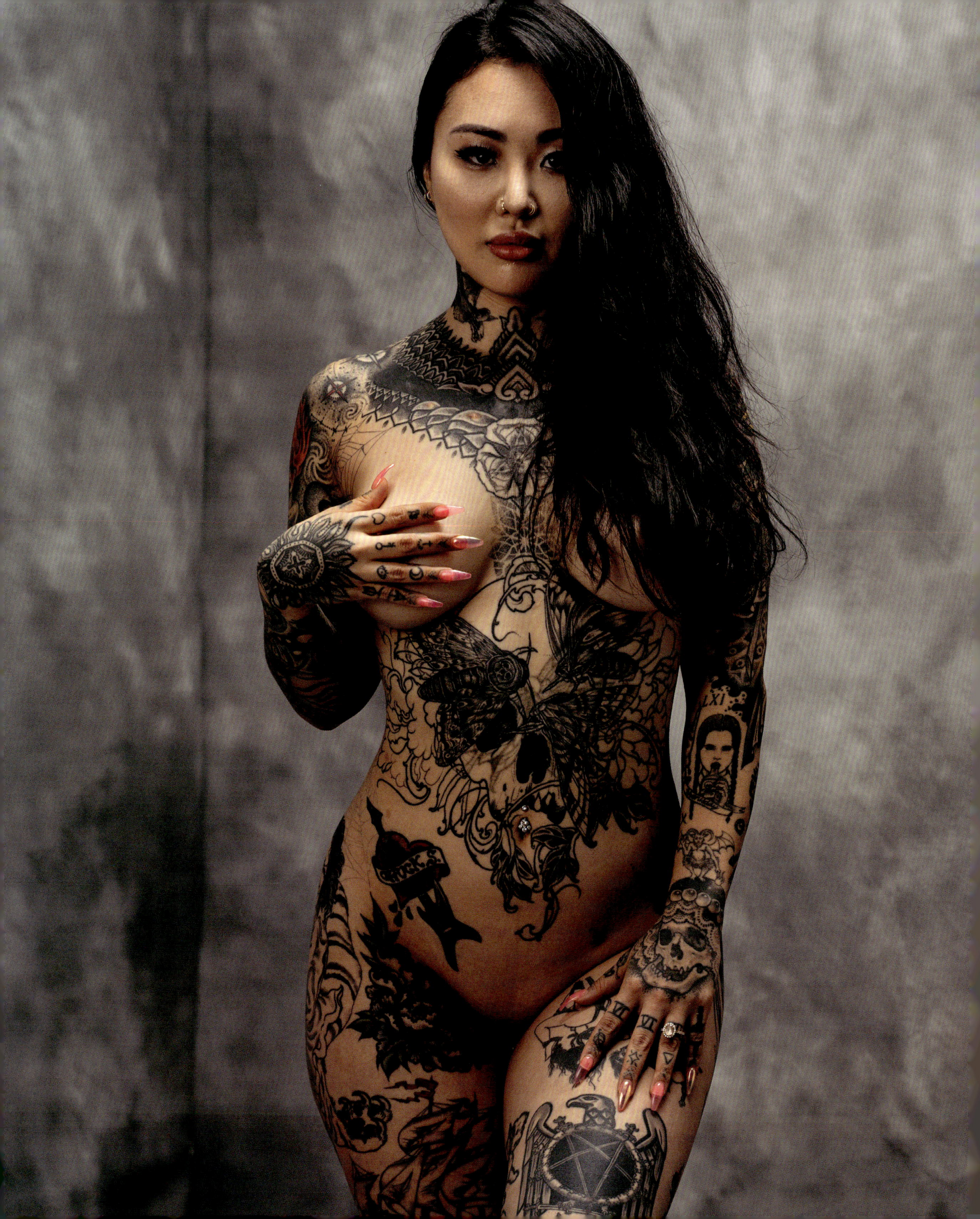

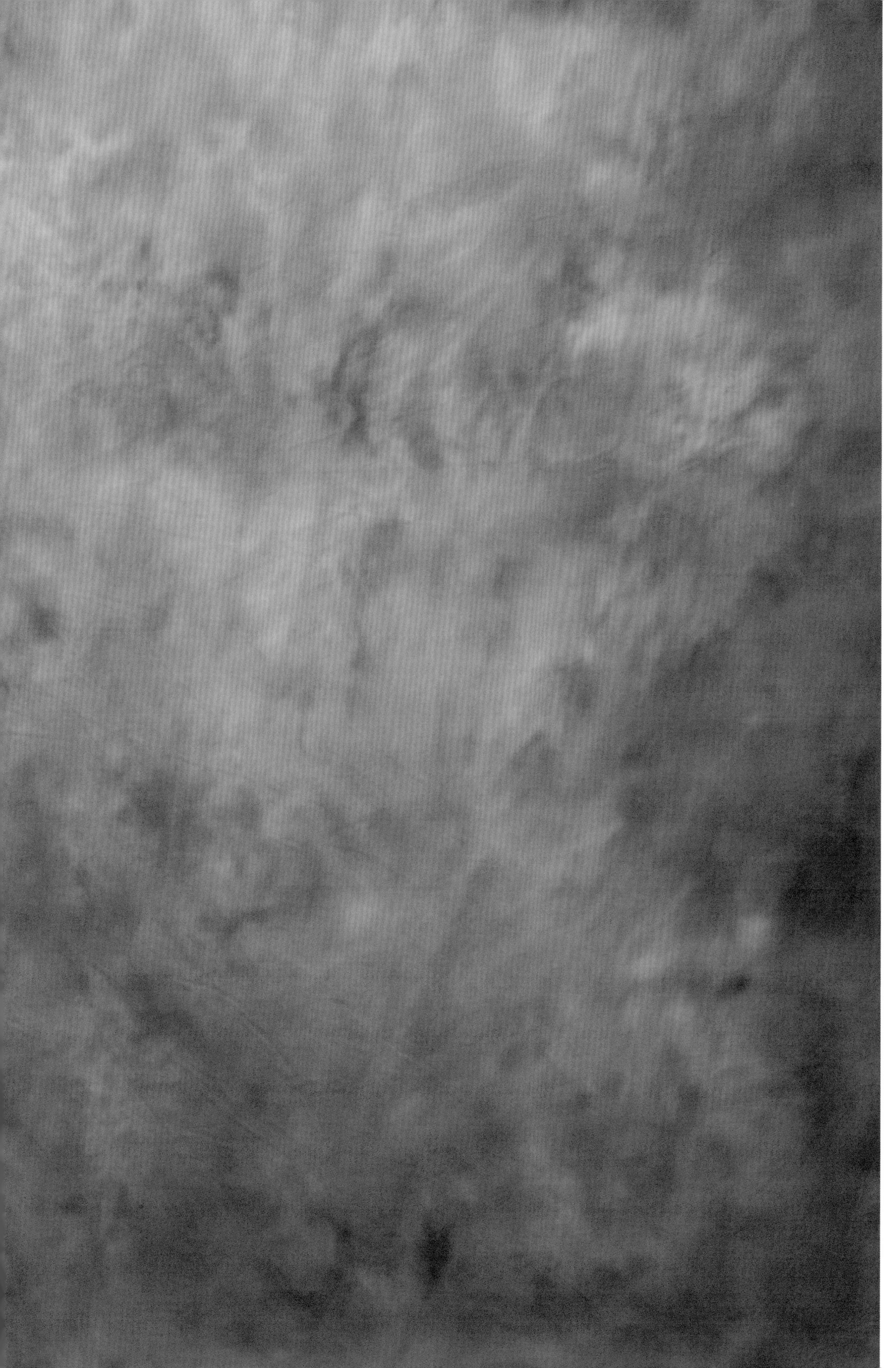

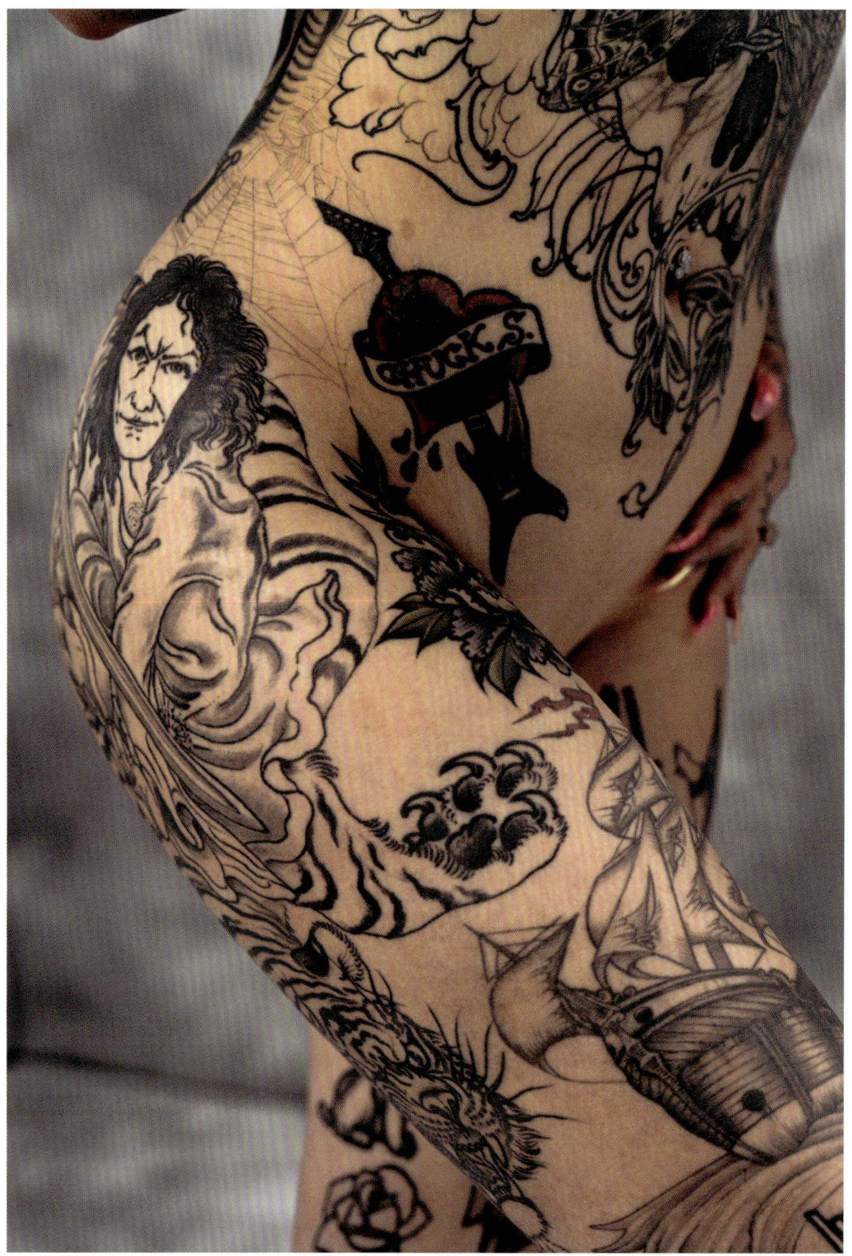

Pages 158–159: Alisha Gory's right sleeve, upper left arm, upper back, and the mandala tattoo on her right hand are by John Sultana. Her stomach cover-up, of a skull with moth, is by Camila Rocha, and her chest is by Peter Madsen, owner and tattoo artist of Meatshop Tattoo in Barcelona, Spain.

Above and opposite: Black Sabbath's Ronnie James Dio riding a tiger on Gory's hip was tattooed by Tim Lehi, while the Slayer piece and metal pickle were done by Jessica Veprovsky. Jon Mesa tattooed the octopus on Gory's leg, as well as the ram on her left hip.

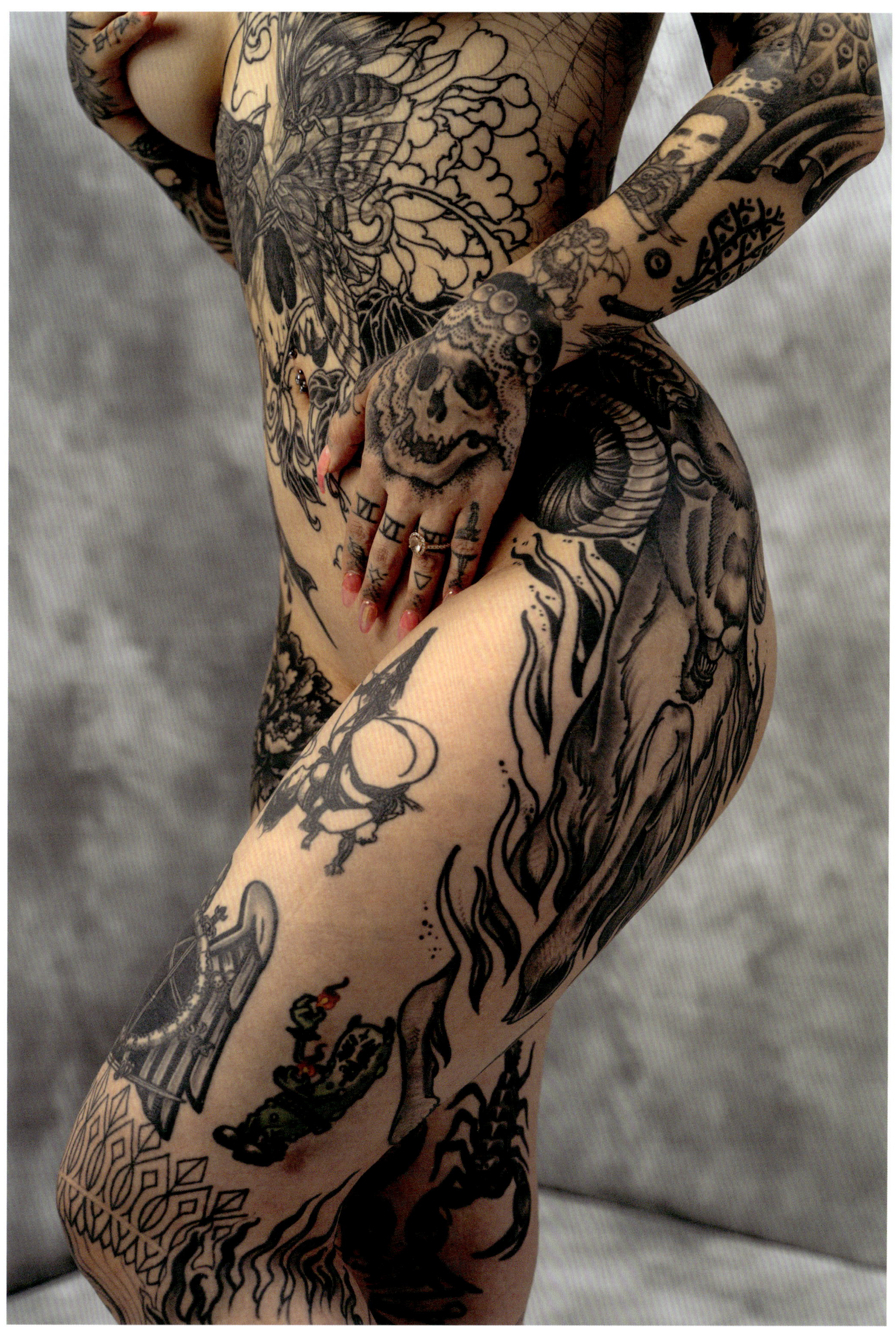

Anderson Luna illustrated and tattooed the gypsy on Gory's left leg, which represents her traveling lifestyle.

Pages 164–165: The feminine chest piece on tattoo collector and artist Jessa Bigelow, illustrated by David Osorio, represents her love for tattooing.

Pages 166–167: Osorio also tattooed her "horror" sleeve—featuring Nosferatu, Frankenstein, the Mummy, Dracula, Vampira, and Vincent Price—while she was studying under him.

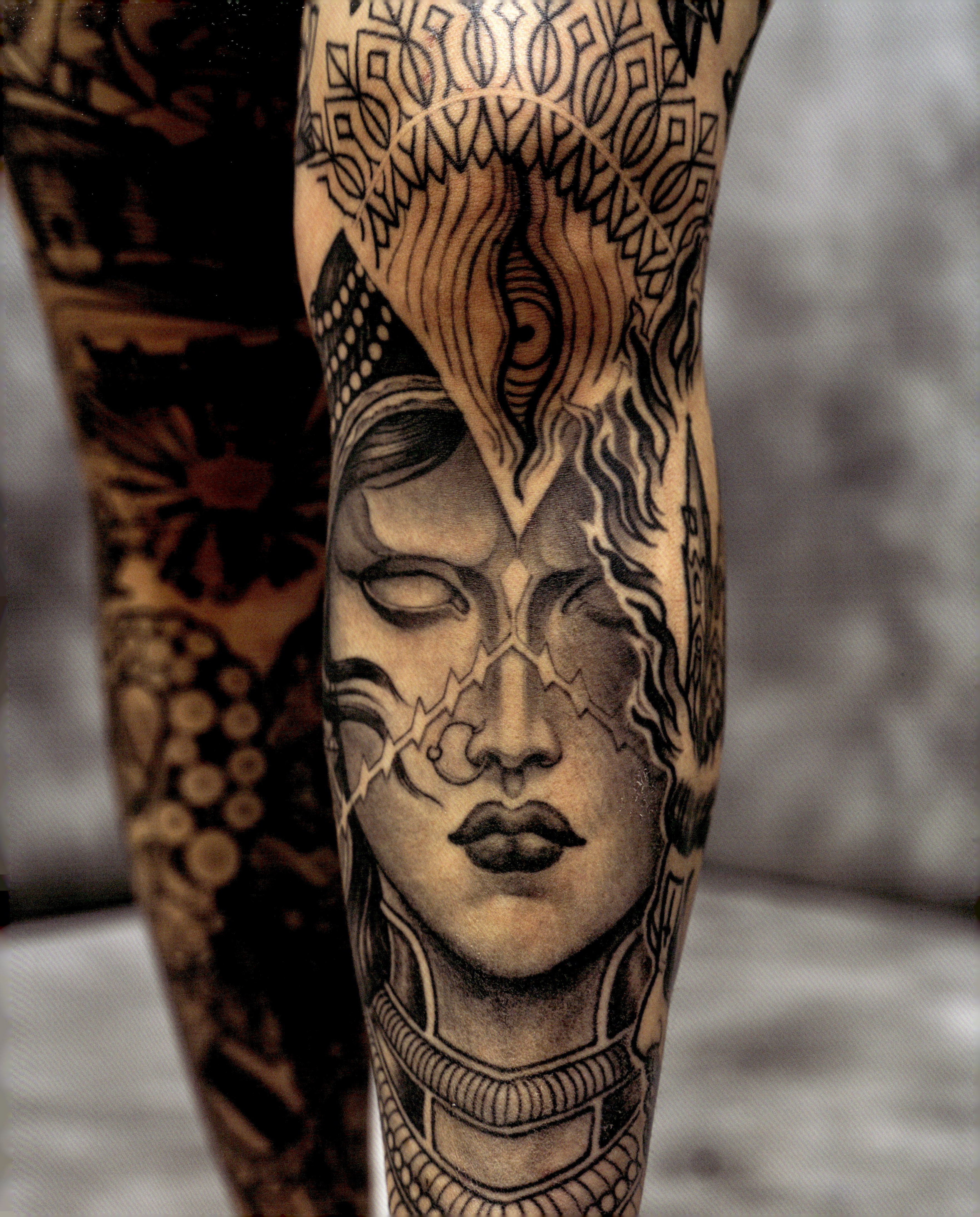

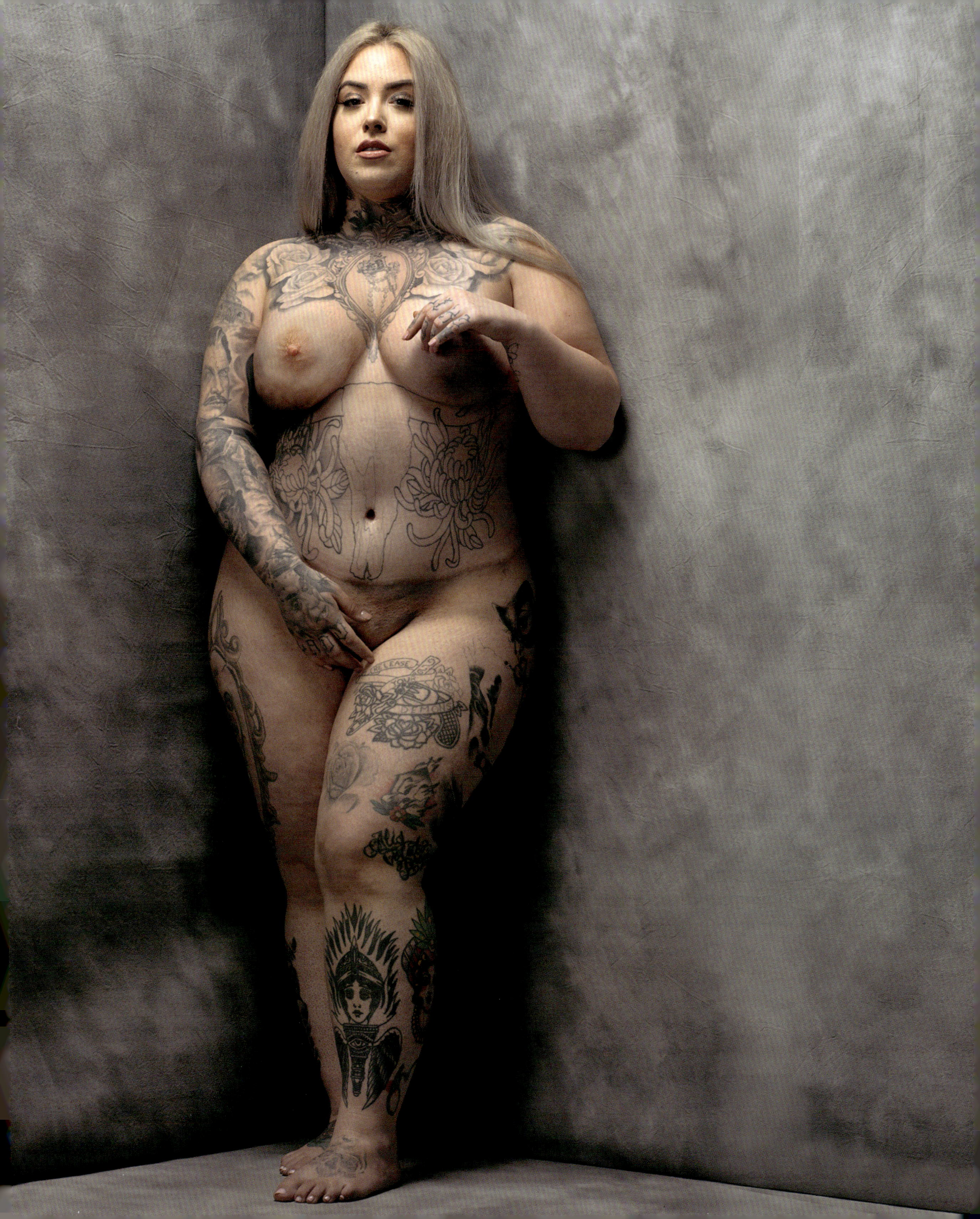

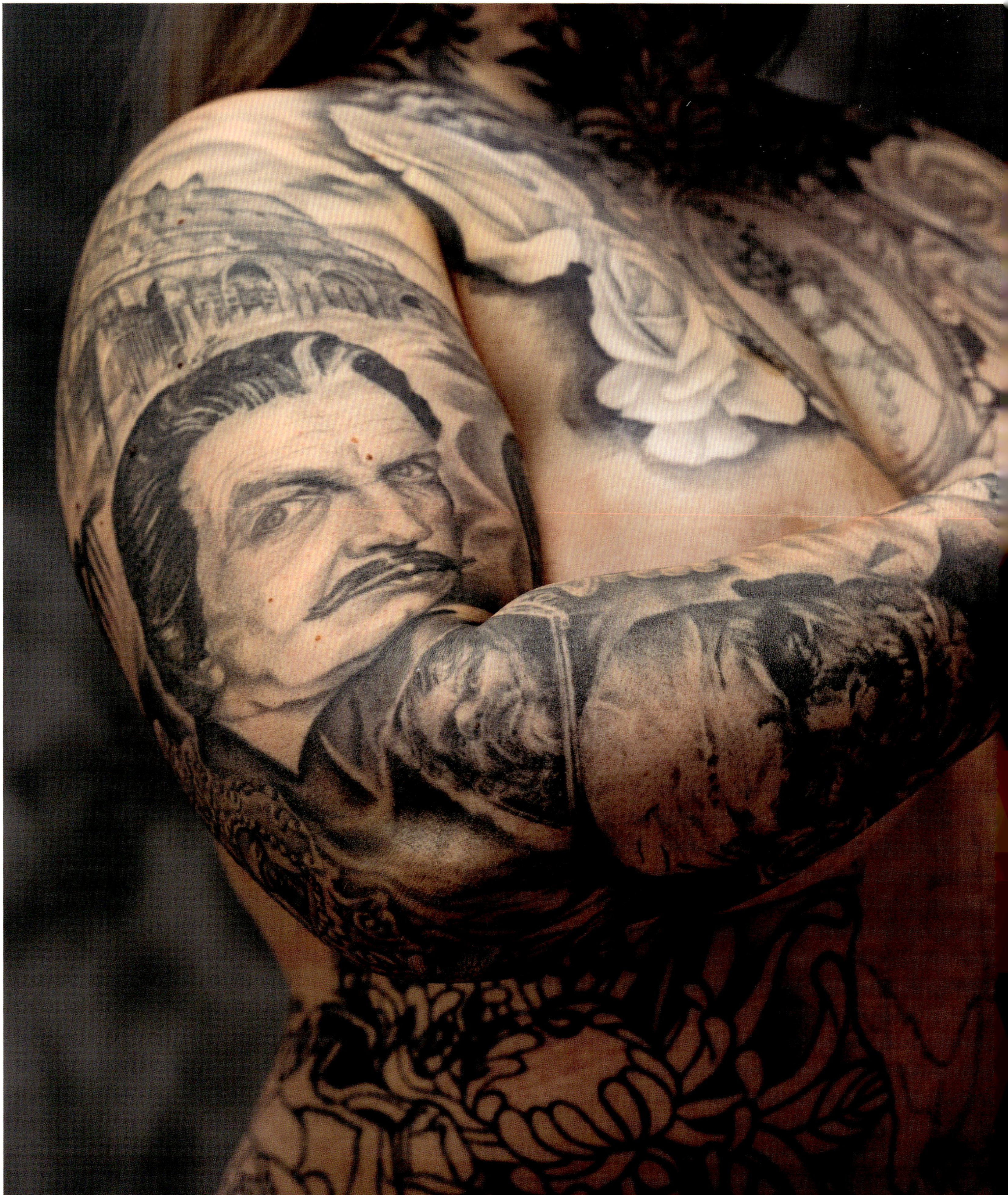

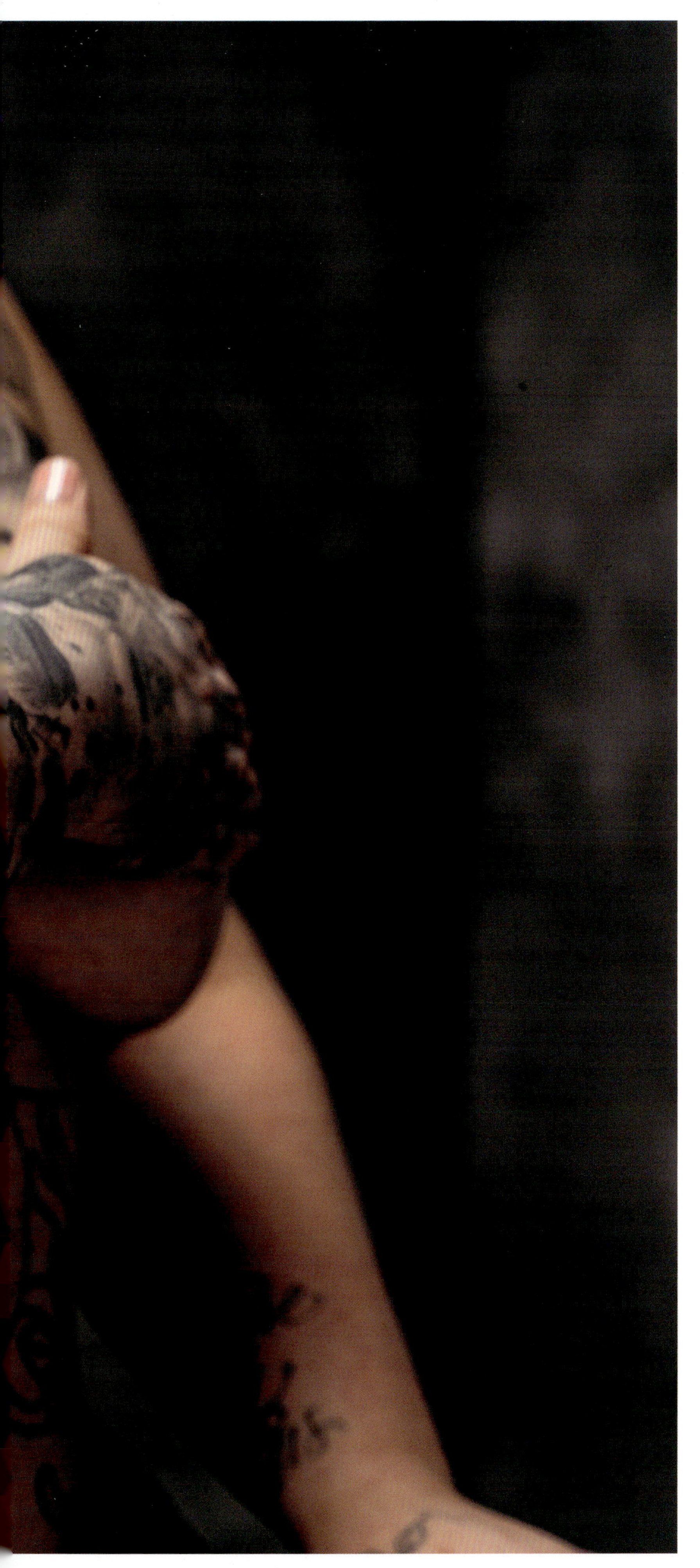

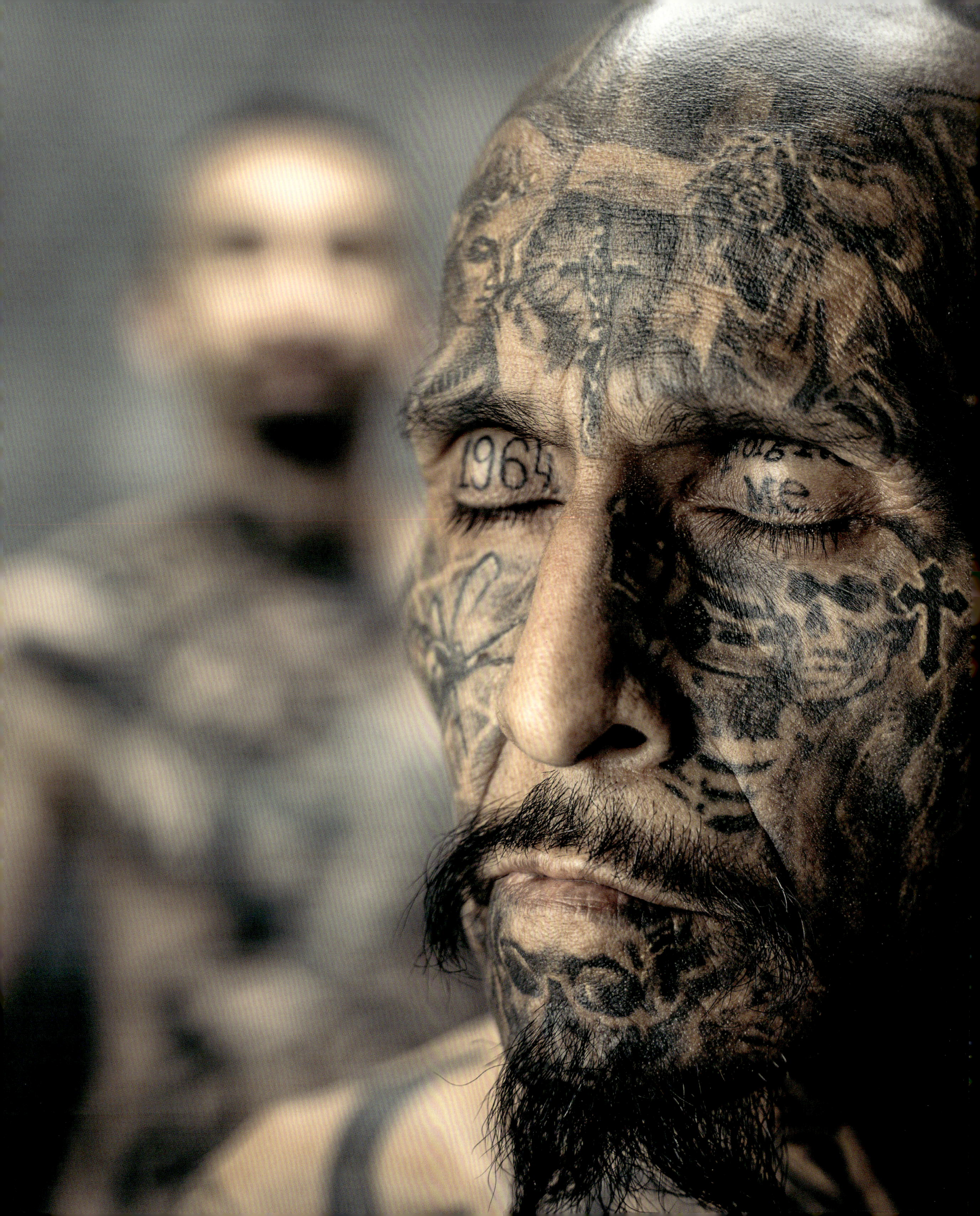
1964

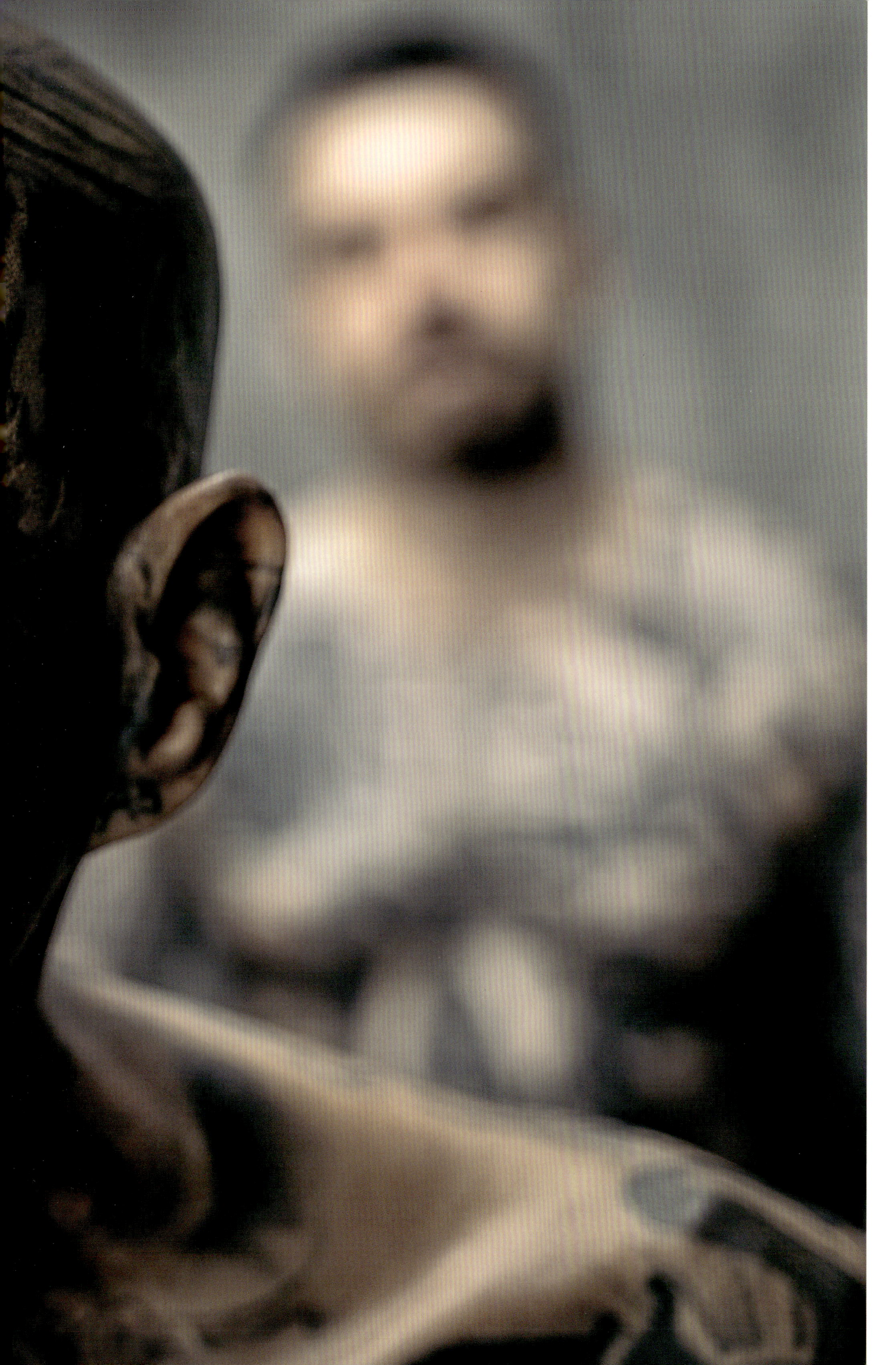

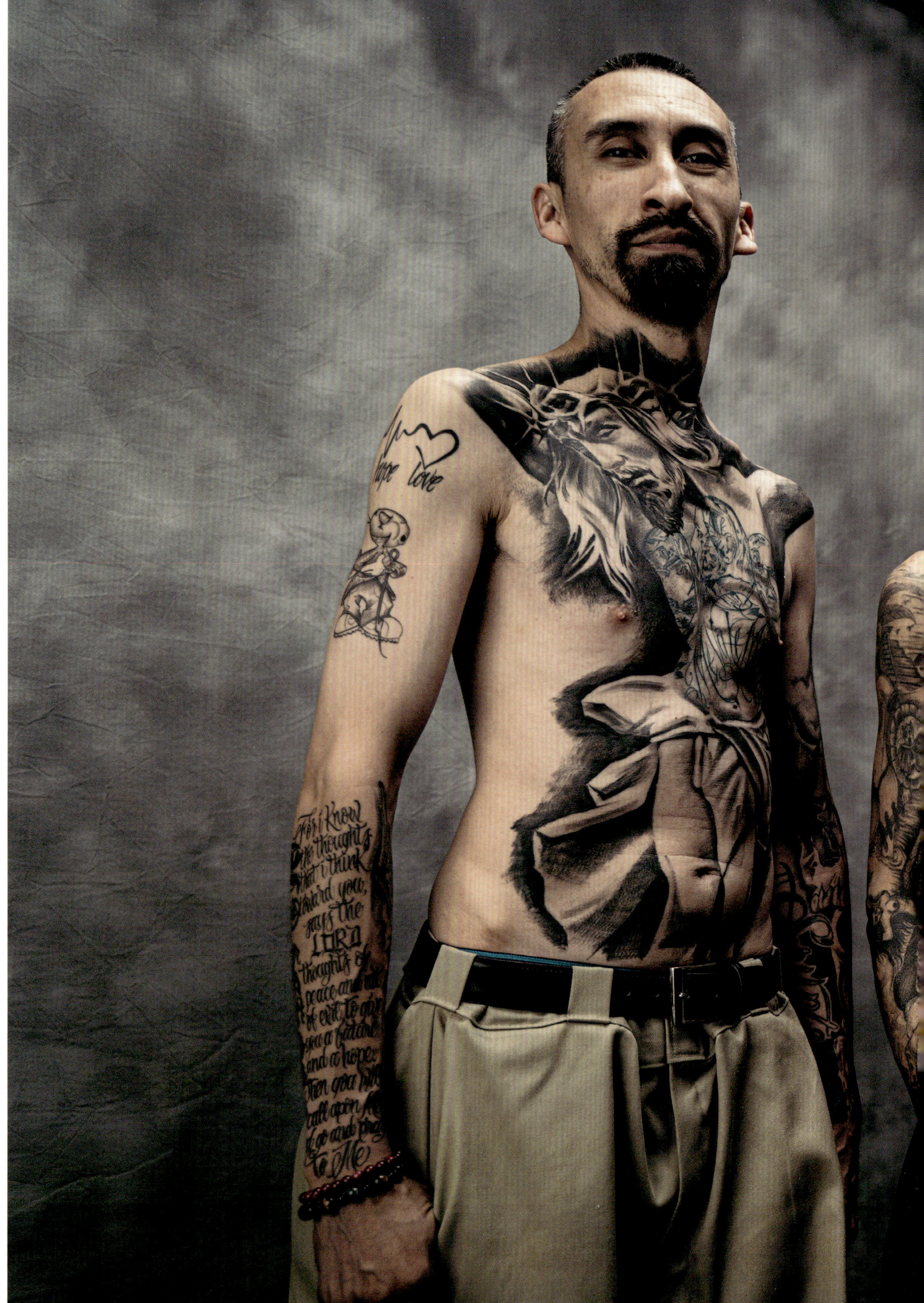
hope love
For I Know
the thoughts
that I think
toward you,
says the
LORD
and a hope.
To Me

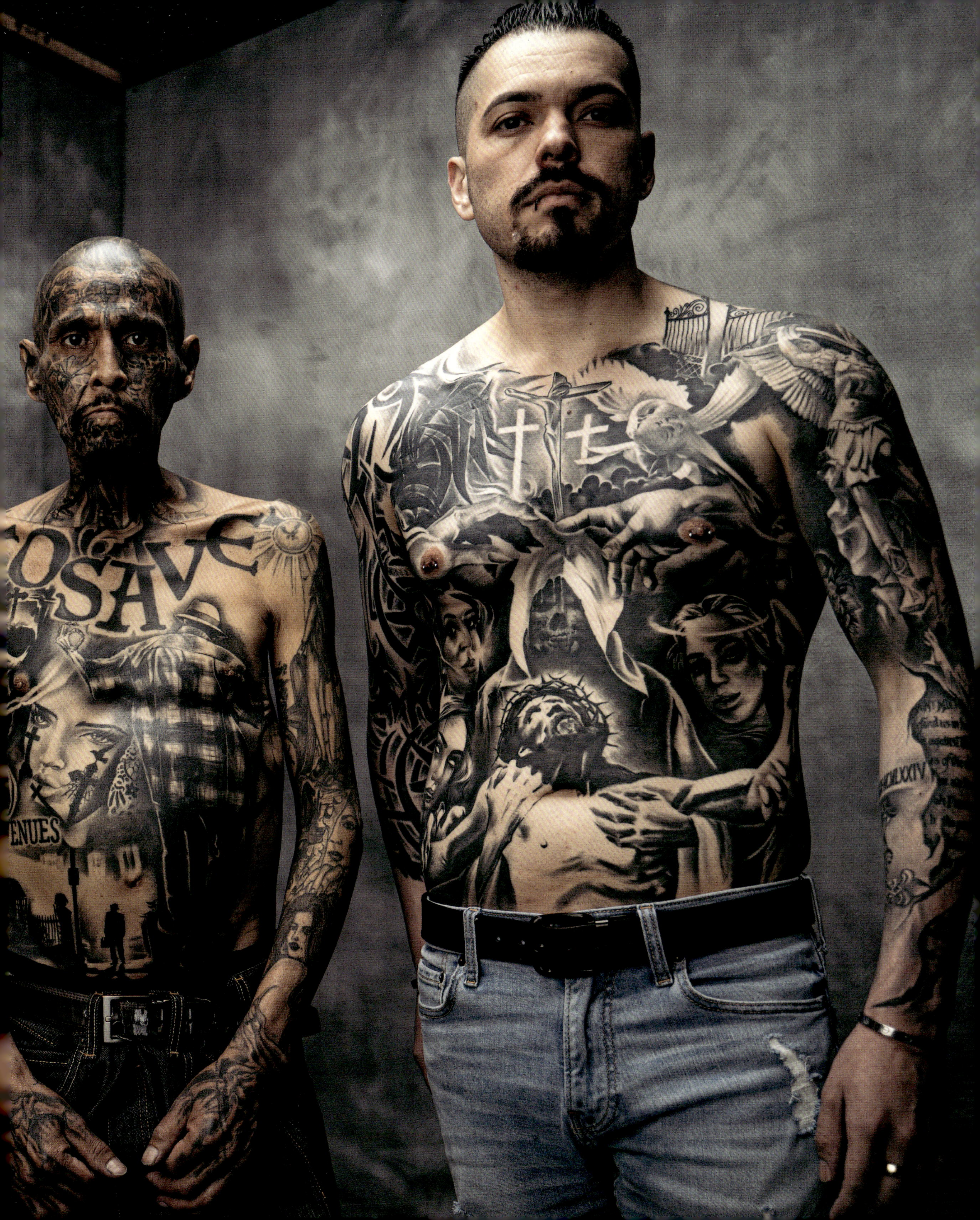
OSAVE
OSAV
ENUES

Pages 168–169: Predominantly inked by artists at Cryptic Tattoo, Rudy "Quiet" Berber's tattoos have given him peace and positivity. "In the name of Jesus Christ, Amen," he adds.

Page 170-171: Cryptic Tattoo's Carlos Macias did Anthony "Cricket" Dutcher's chest piece (left), most of Berber's body, and Frank Salazar's full body (right), with the exception of Salazar's tribal work on his right arm, which was done by Mando Garcia.

Opposite: Tattoo model and collector Yves Mathieu East has been tattooed by over 100 people, including Ja-Ryda, Mister Verona, and Grace Neutral.

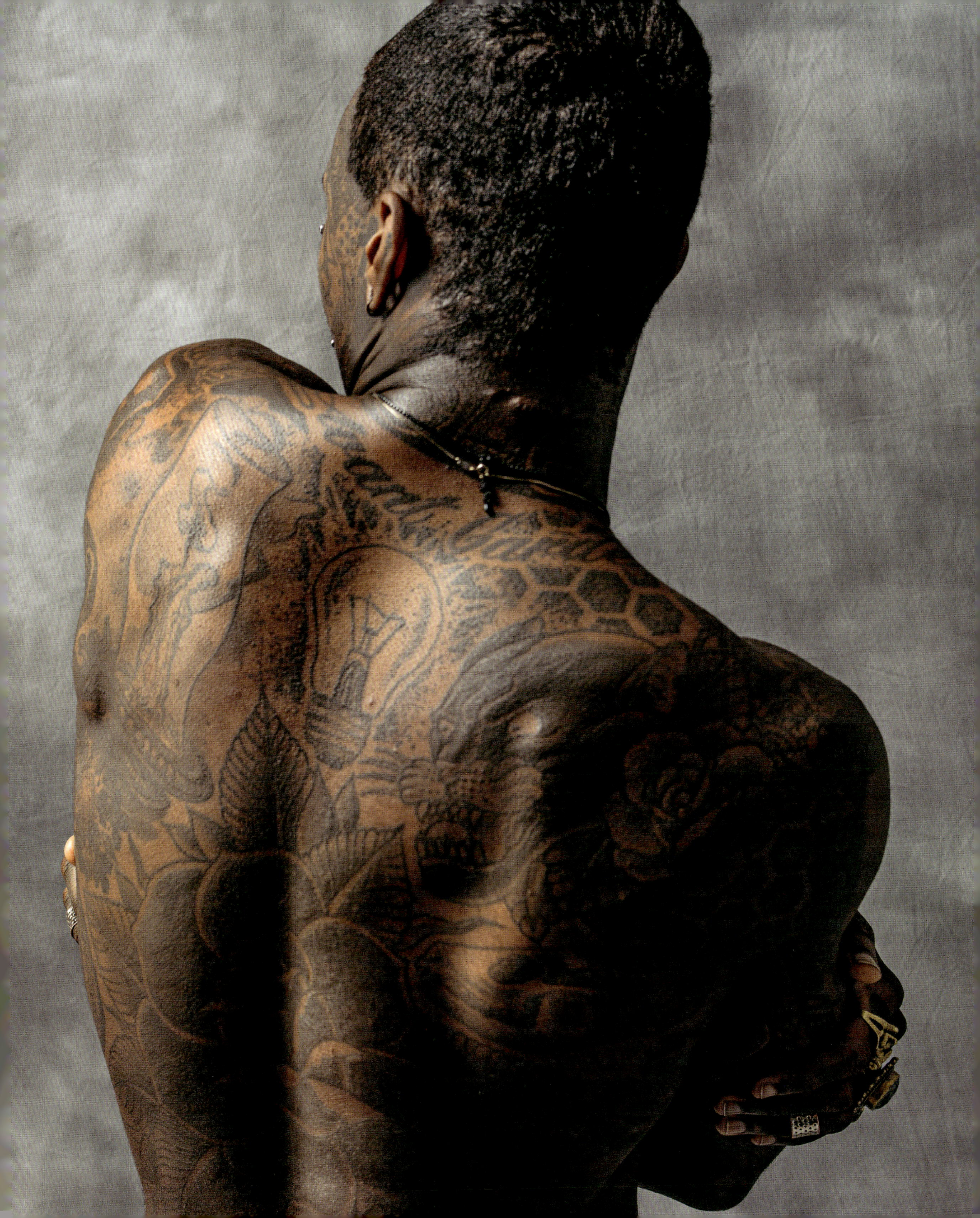

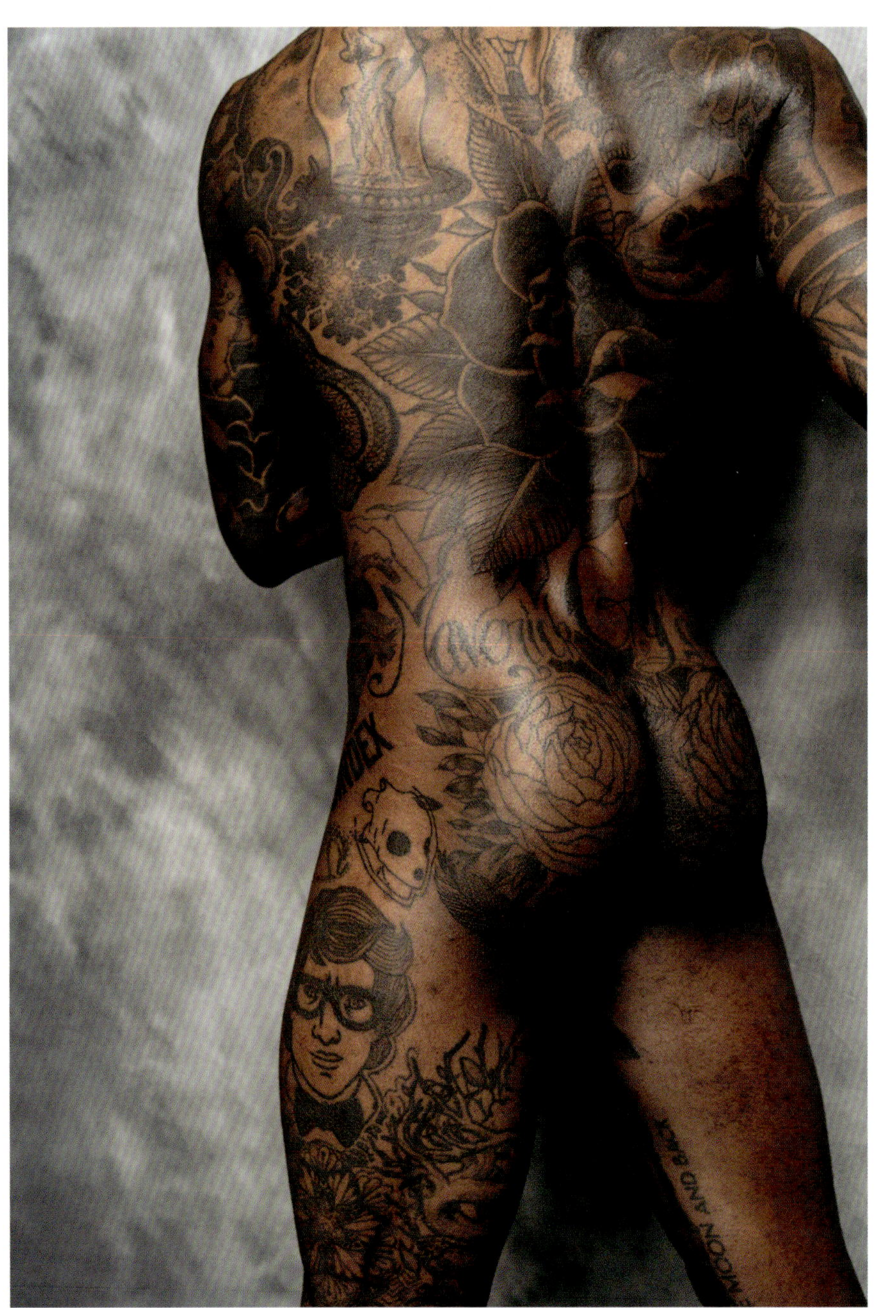

Above: East's traditional black rose tattoo on his back, by Marshall Rathburn, is a memorial piece, representing a year in his life when fourteen people close to him passed away.

Opposite: He finds the tattoo process therapeutic, describing his collection as "miscellaneous memories of morbid moments and also treasured times." His stomach was tattooed by Frankie Lambough, Cory Hand, Lady Mandala, and Dooz.

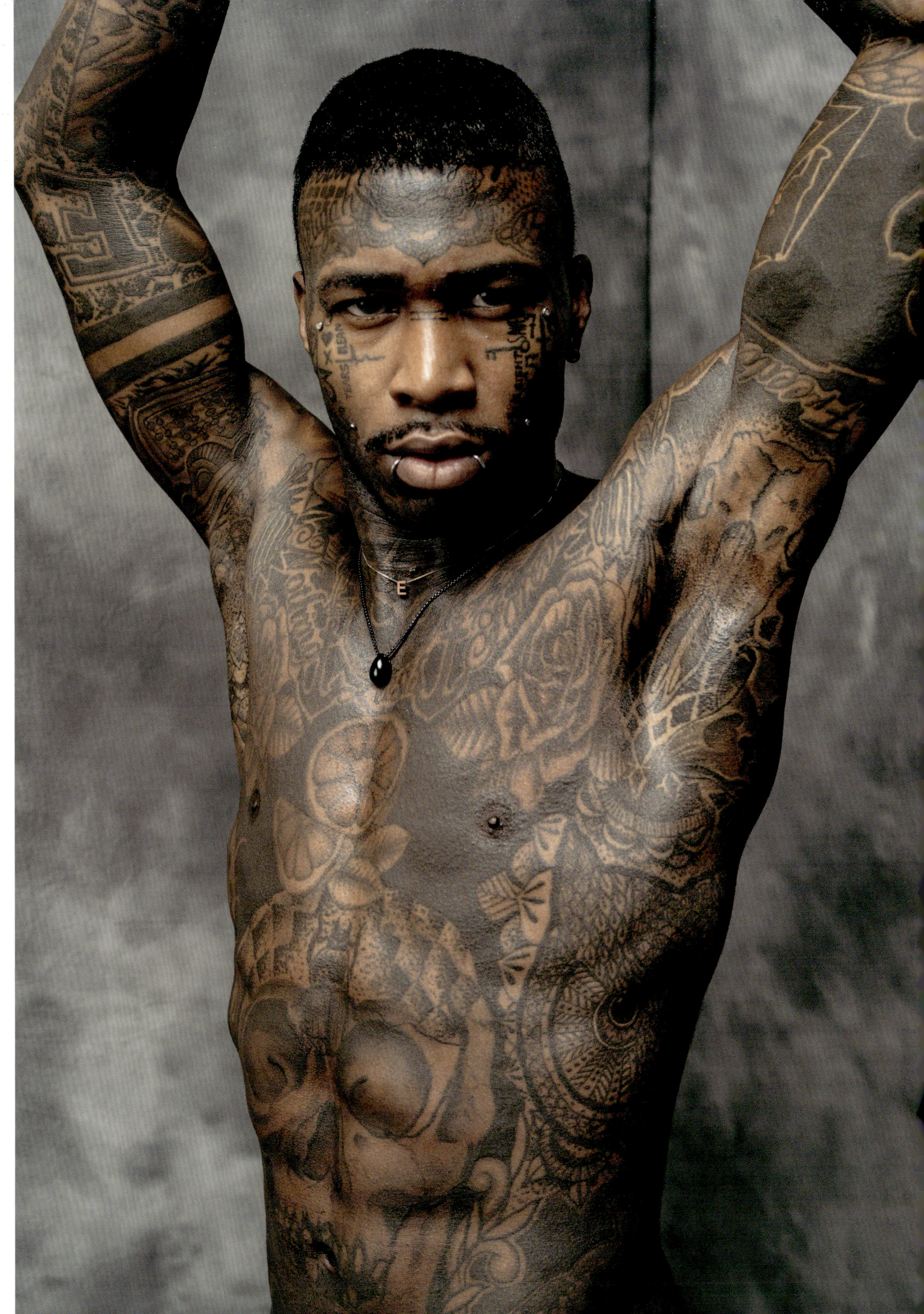

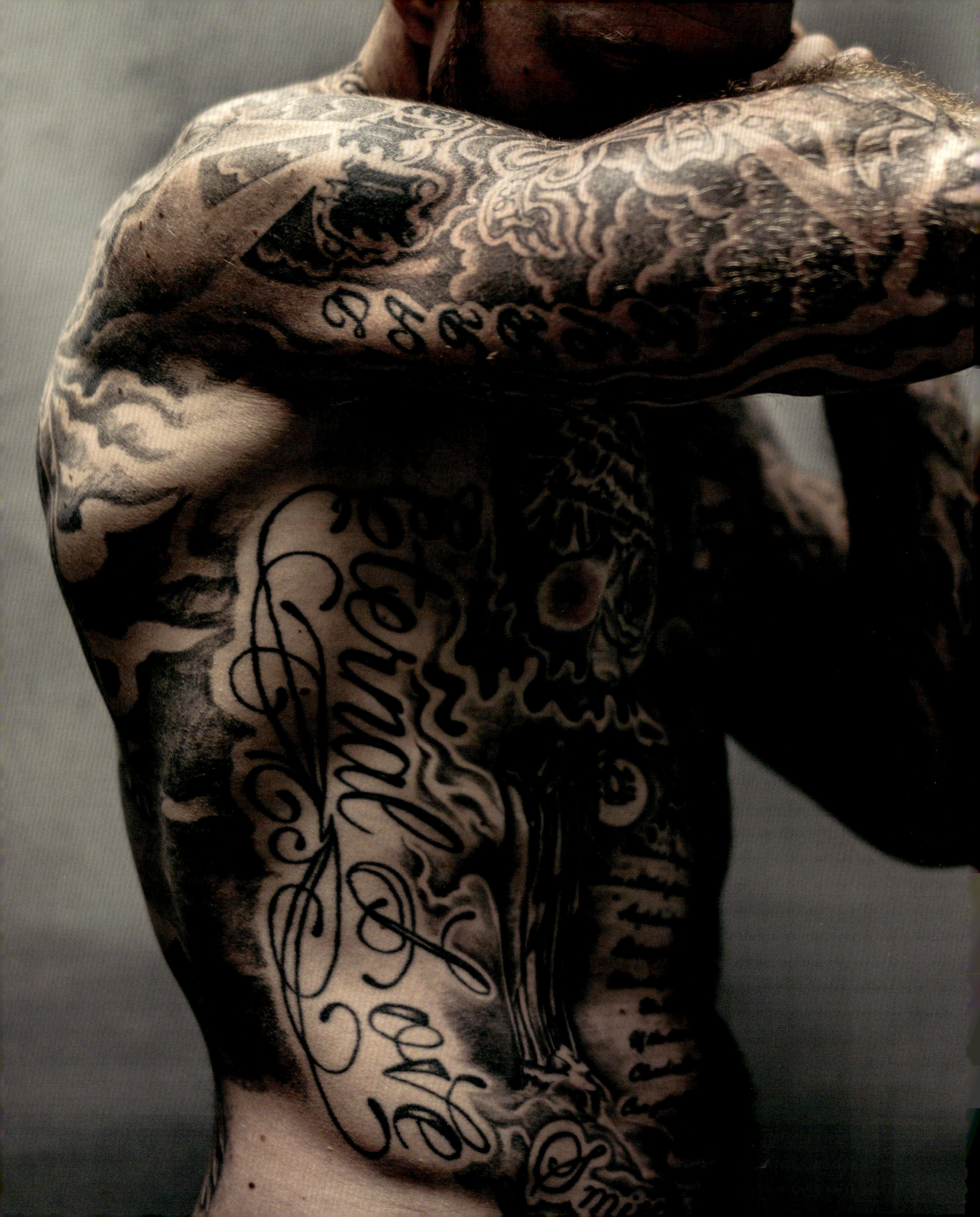
Eternal Love

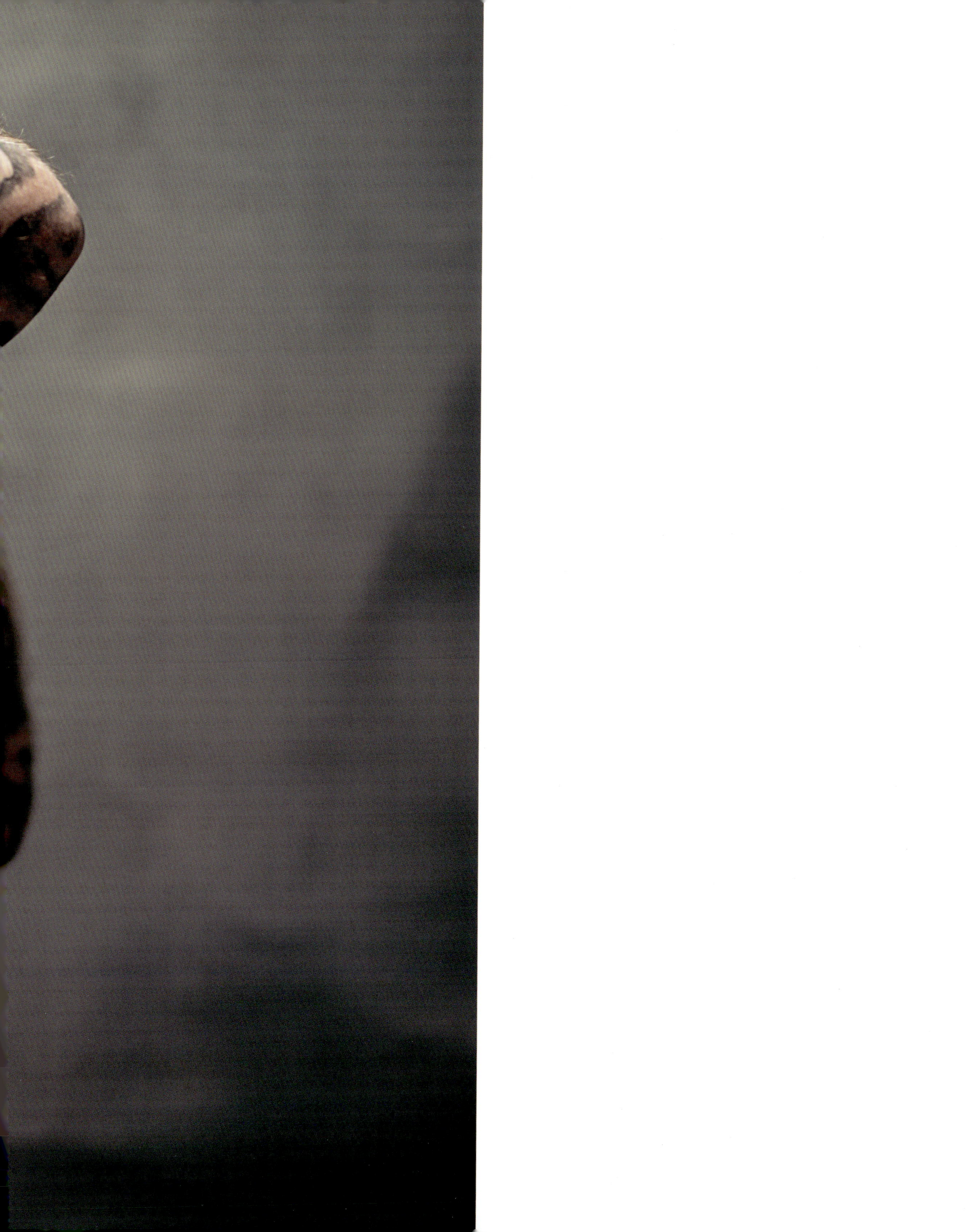

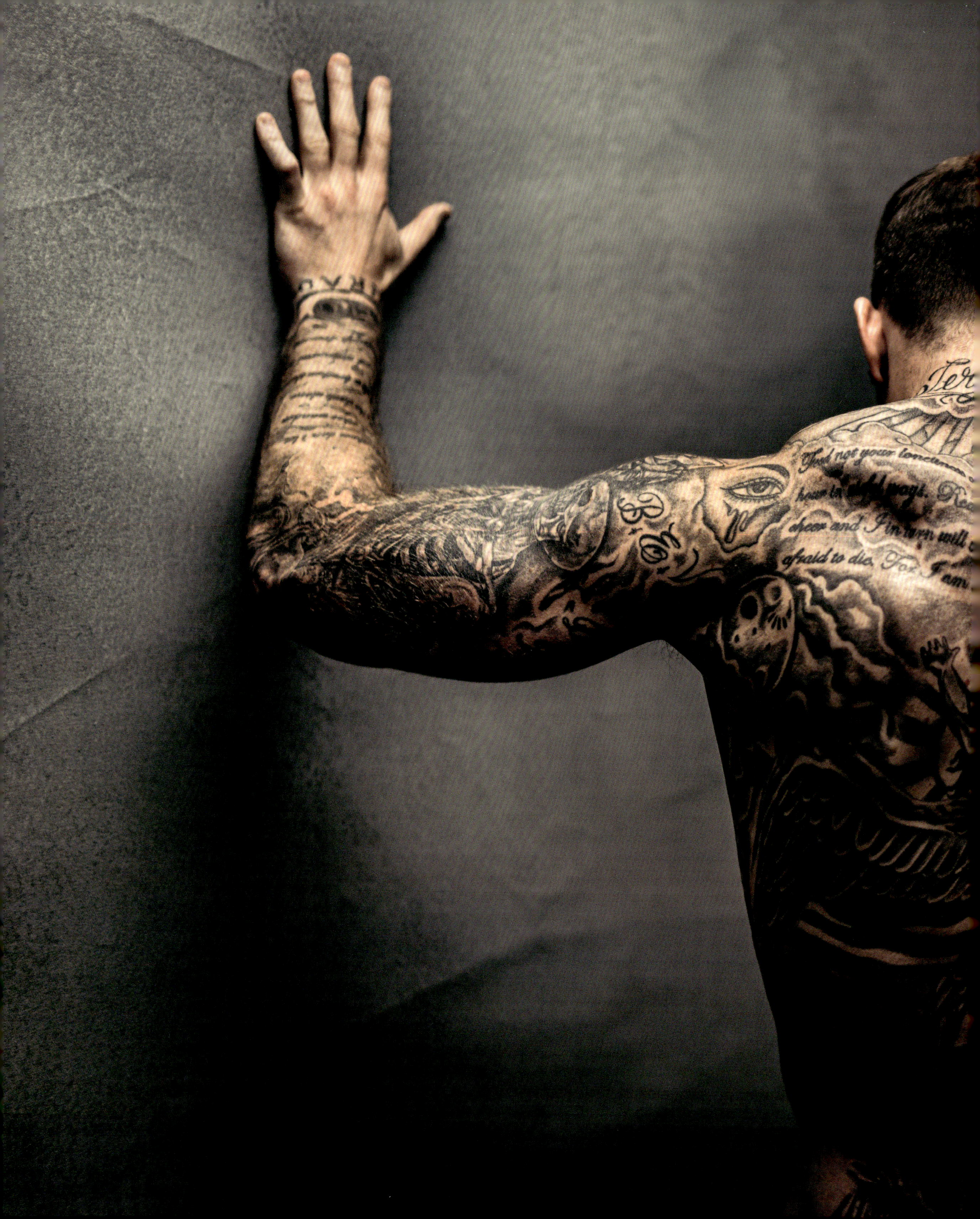

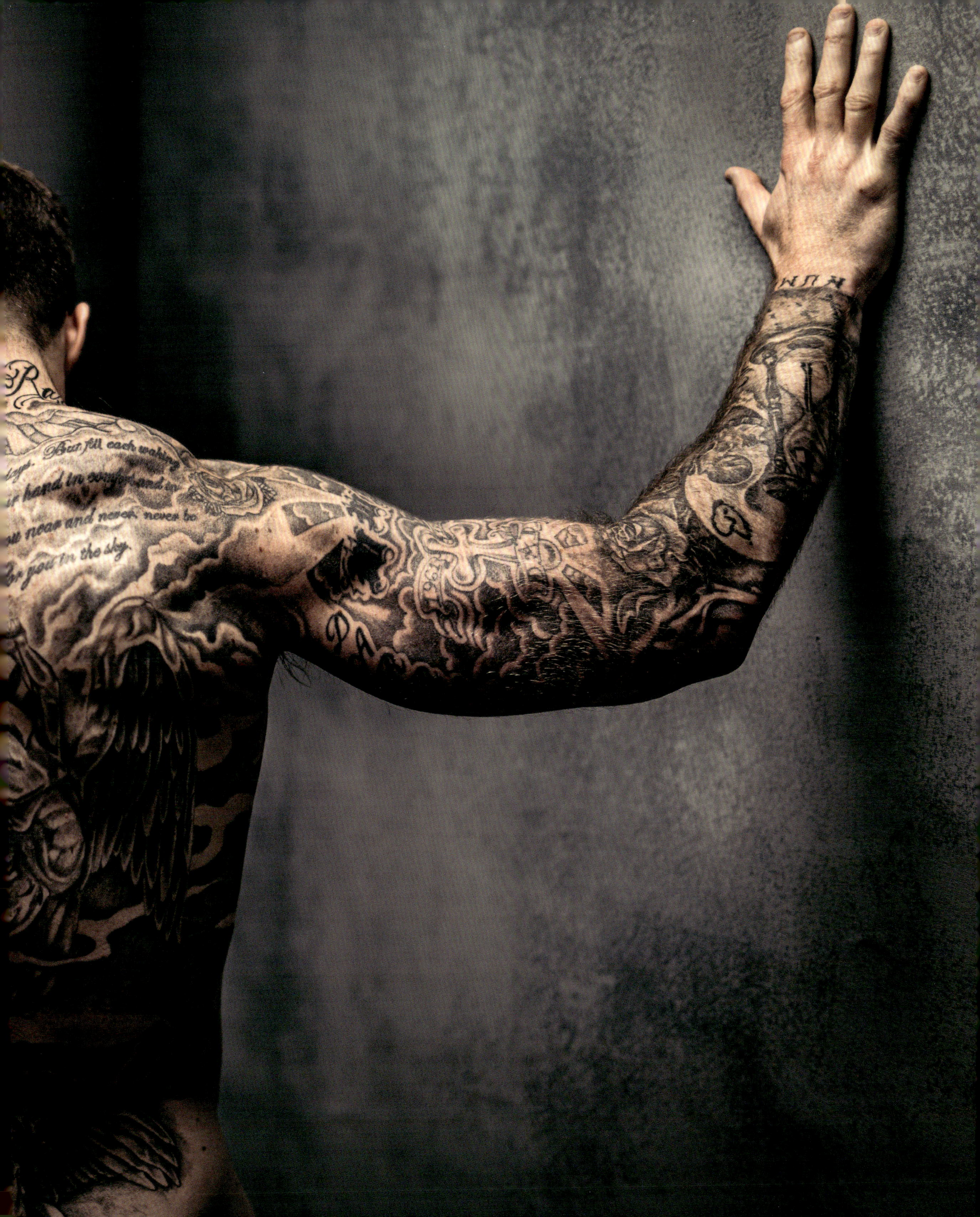
But fill each waking
near and never, never be
in the sky.

Pages 176–177: Predominantly illustrated by Alexis Miranda, artist Robert Kula started Jimmy Smith's tattoo story with a cross on his arm for his father who passed when Smith was twelve.

Pages 178–179: Smith's favorite tattoo, his Led Zeppelin angel backpiece, is also for his father, who named Smith after the band's guitarist, Jimmy Page.

Opposite: Becky Holt enjoys being a canvas for her main artist, TommiCrazy, who illustrated her from the waist down, for seven years. Her throat and chest piece were done by Raph Cemo.

Pages 182–183: Glenn Cuzen, Kingsley Hayward, and Martin Marshall tatooed her face, while her back was done by Dean Mclaughlin.

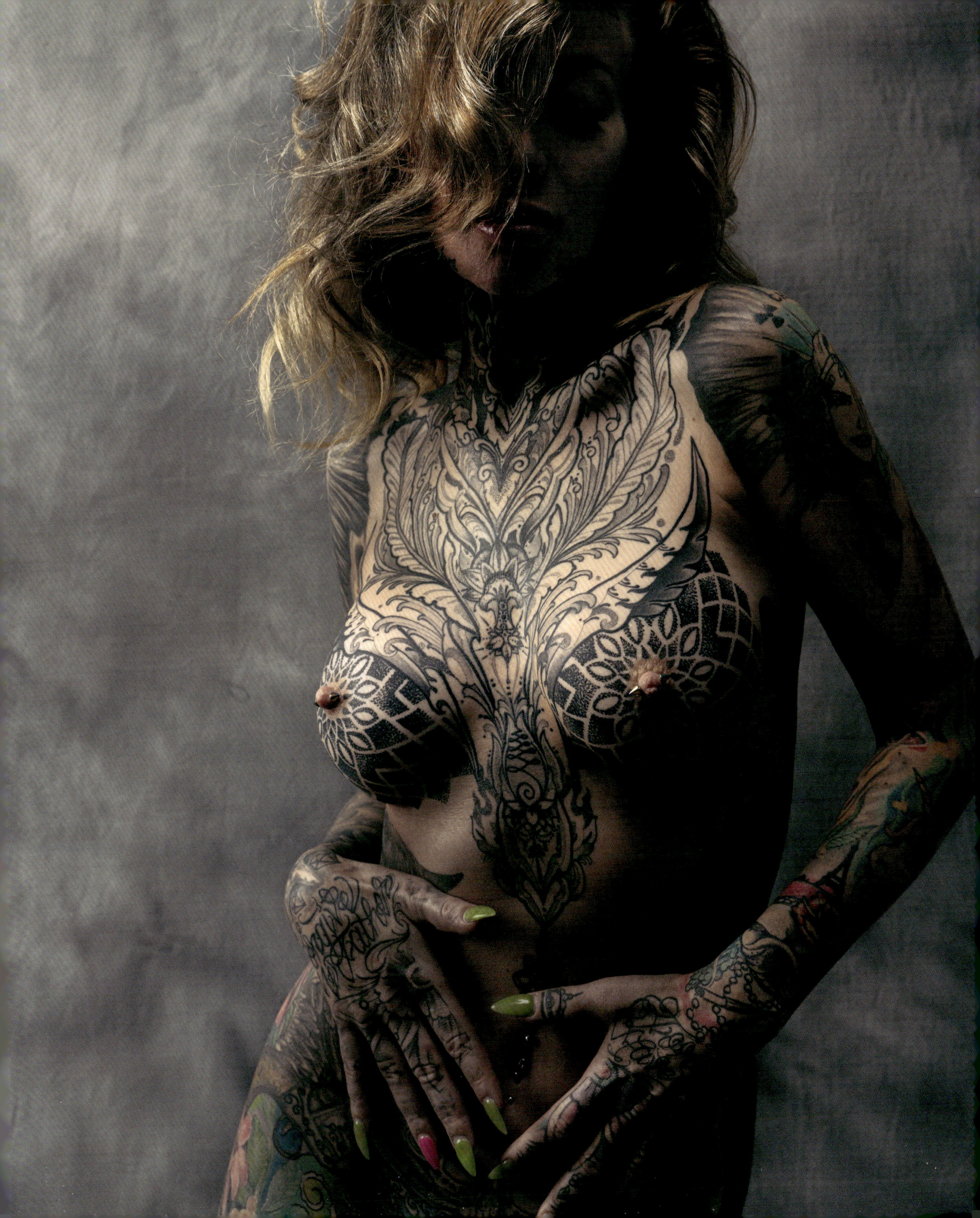

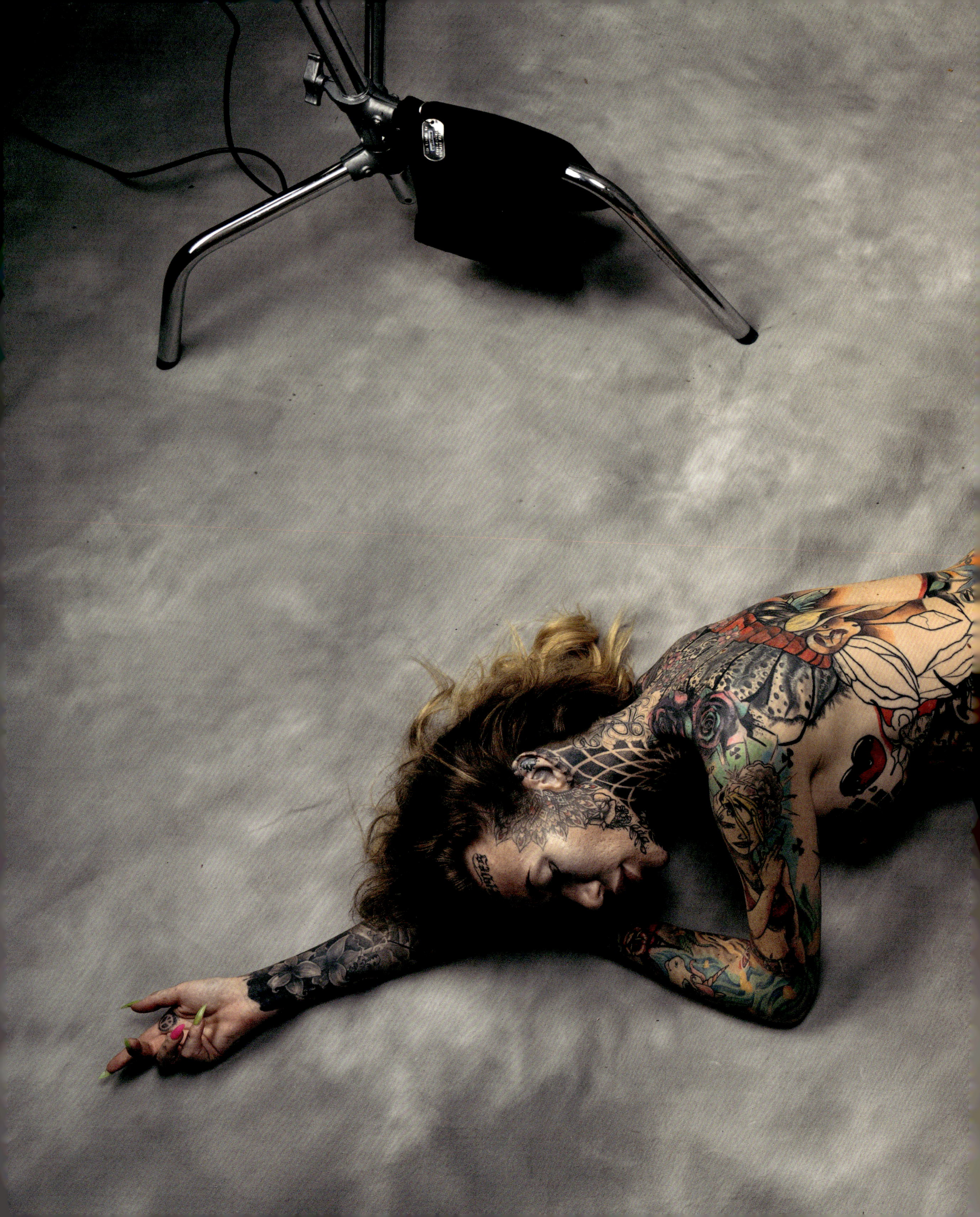

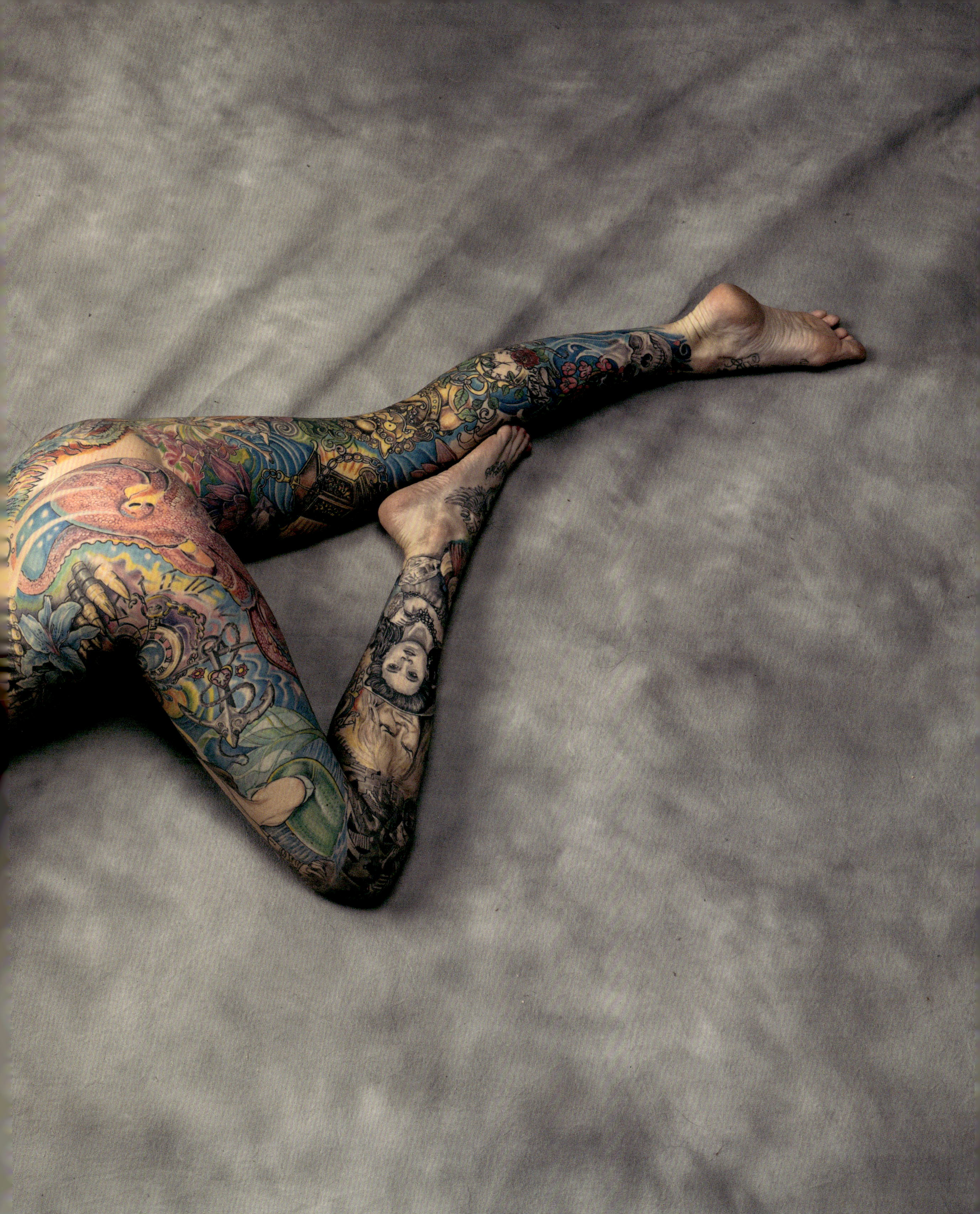

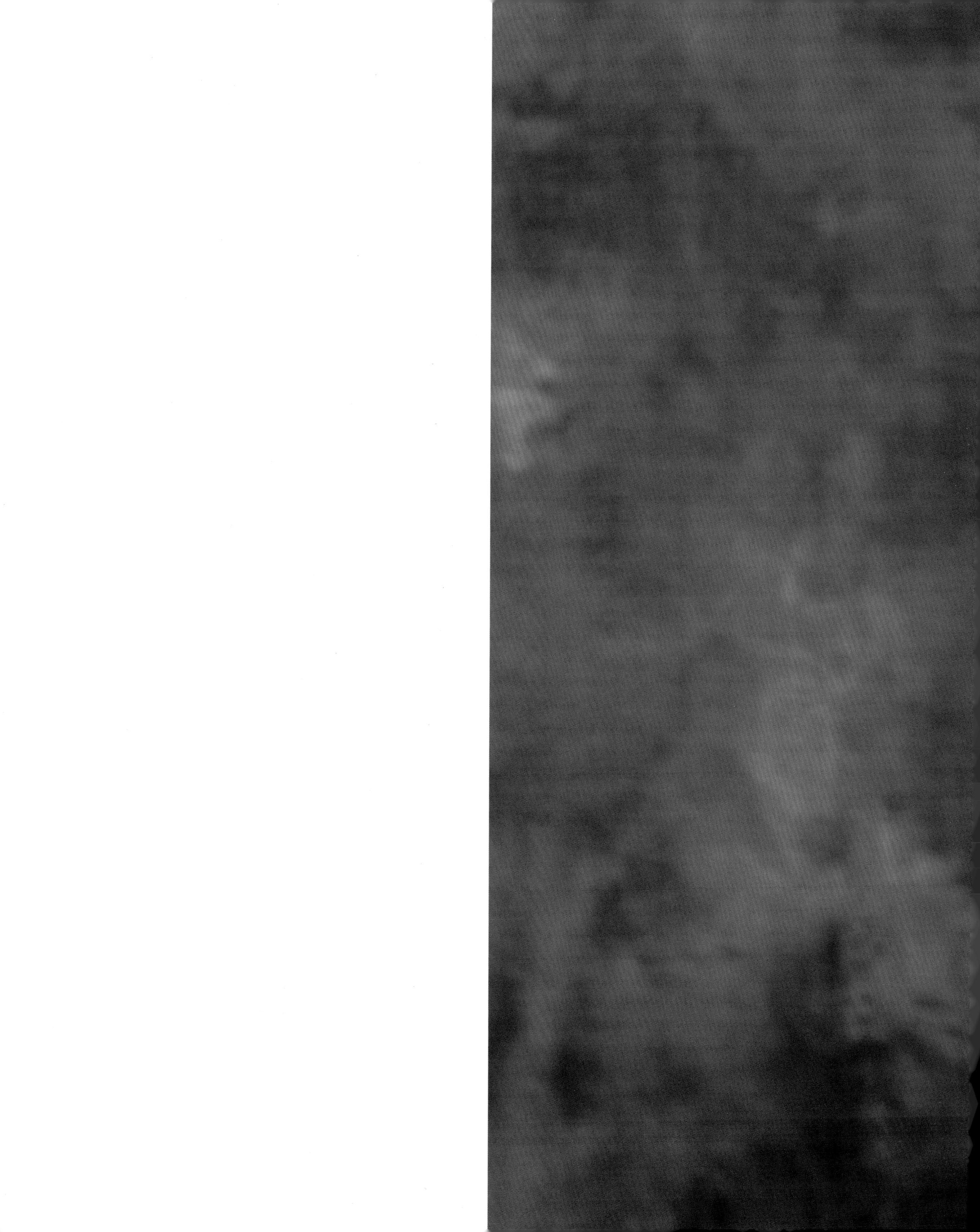

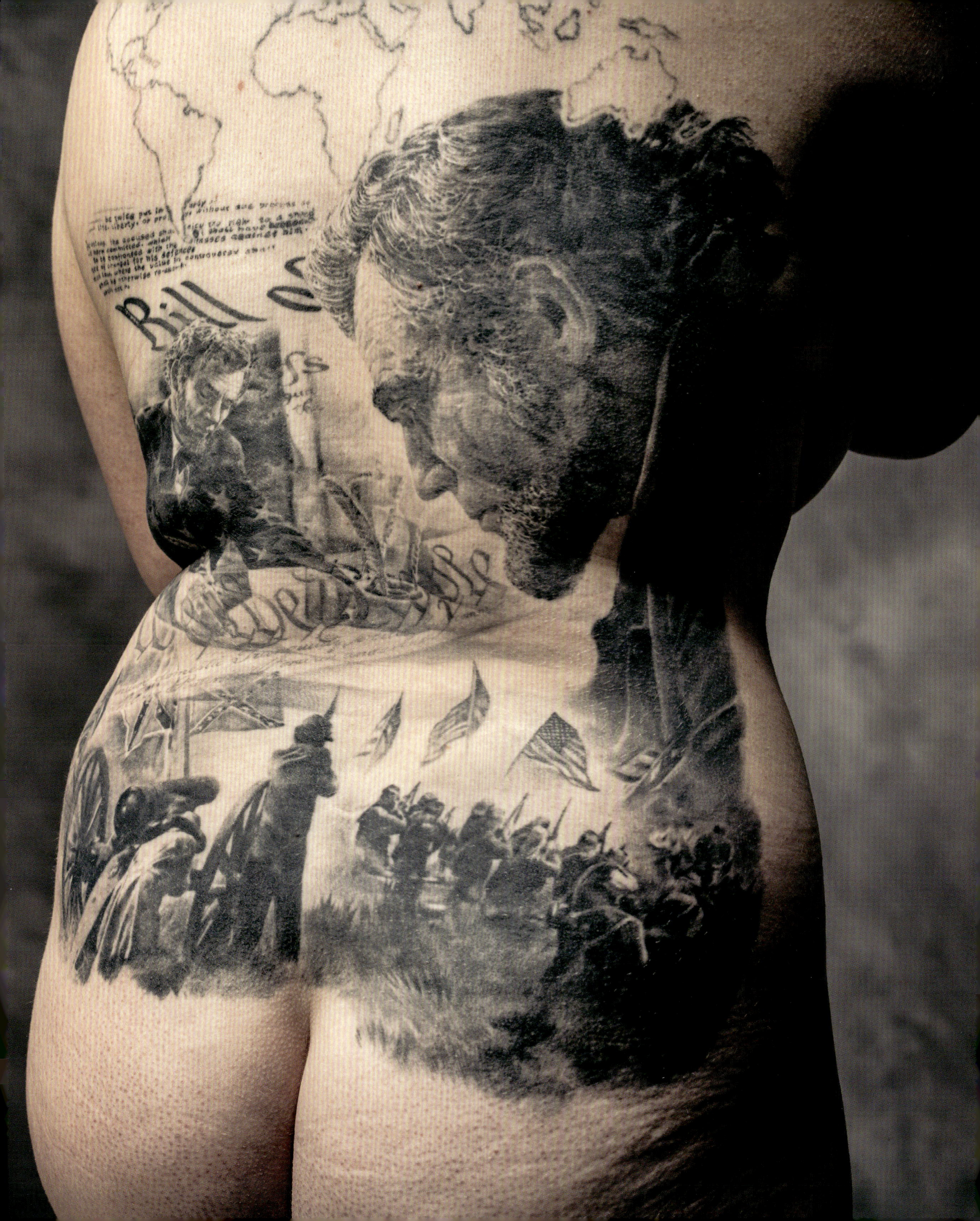
Bill

Pages 184–185: Julie Quinn graduated with a degree in American history, which inspired her backpiece that was illustrated and tattooed by Popo Zhang.

Opposite: Brooke Erickson's butterfly throat piece, tattooed by Jun Schilling, represents a loved one who passed away from cancer. She wanted something bold, beautiful, and painful to memorialize her with. Erickson's chest piece was tattooed by Ken Mattson.

Pages 188–189: Sabrina Sawyers started her tattoo journey at fifteen years old. Her chest and neck pieces were done by Jannik Perreault, and the tattooed lettering under her chin, by Homie Kwun.

Pages 190–191: Melissa Valiquette illustrated Sawyers' horror- and pinup-themed leg portraits, as well as her left arm, stomach, and ribs.

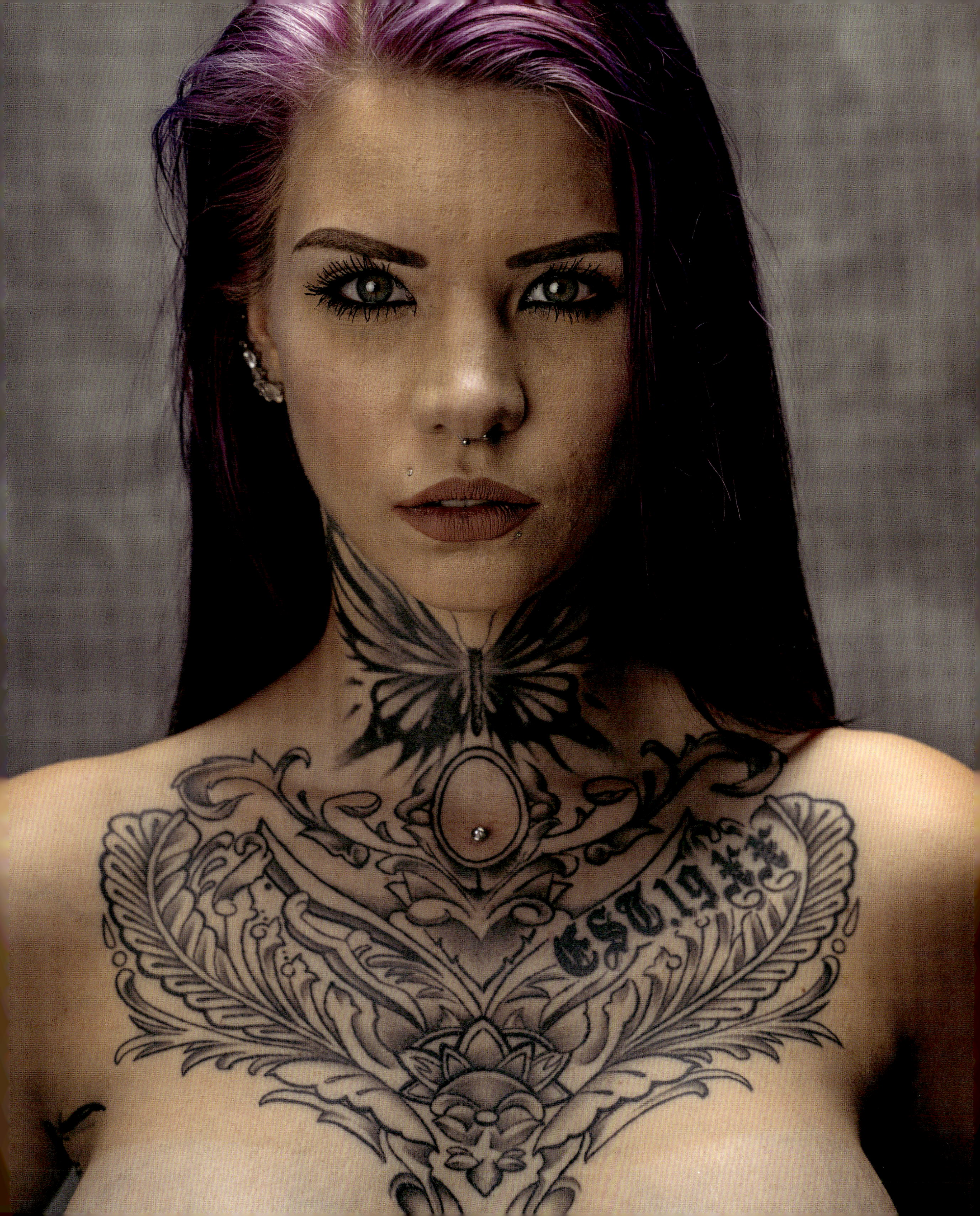

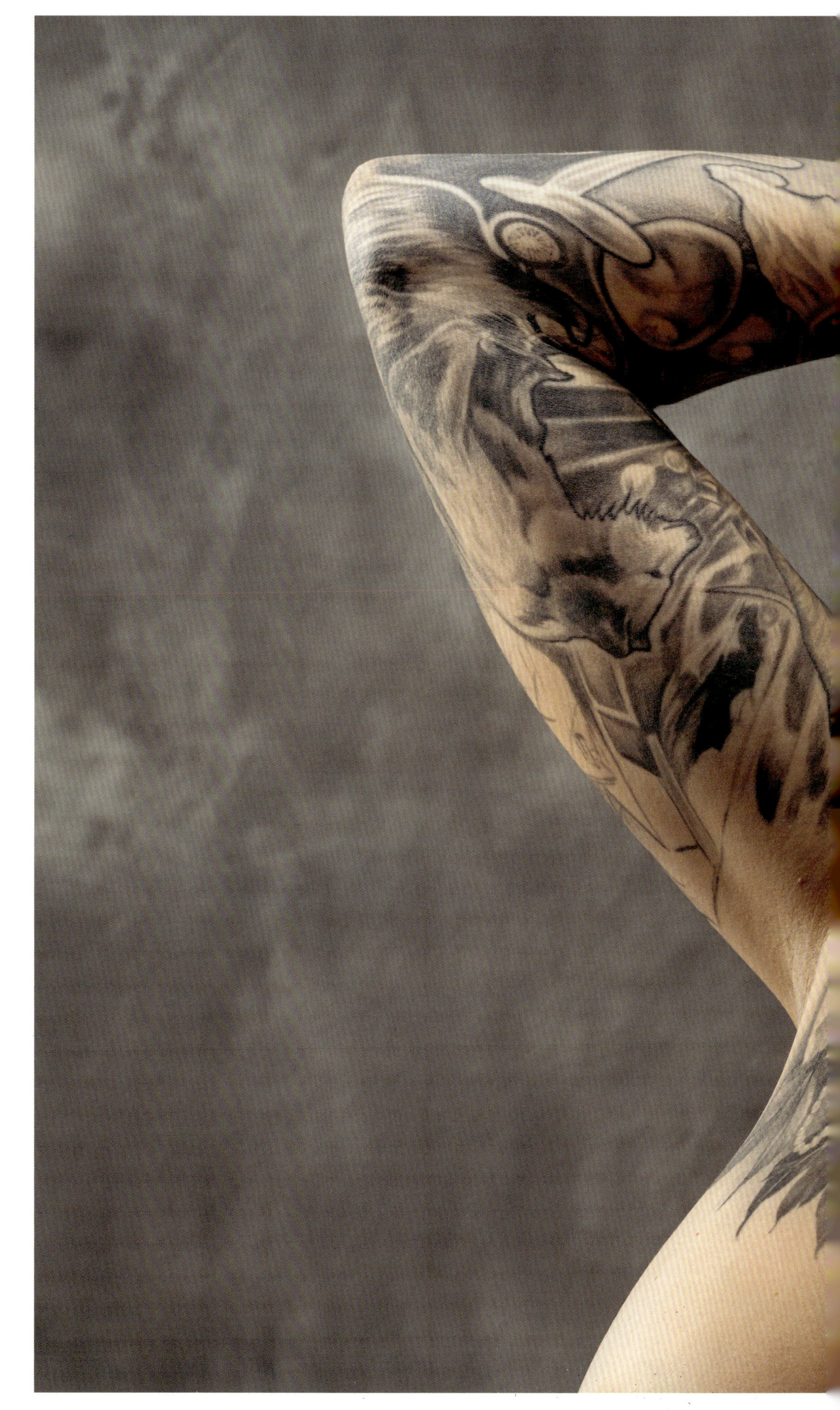

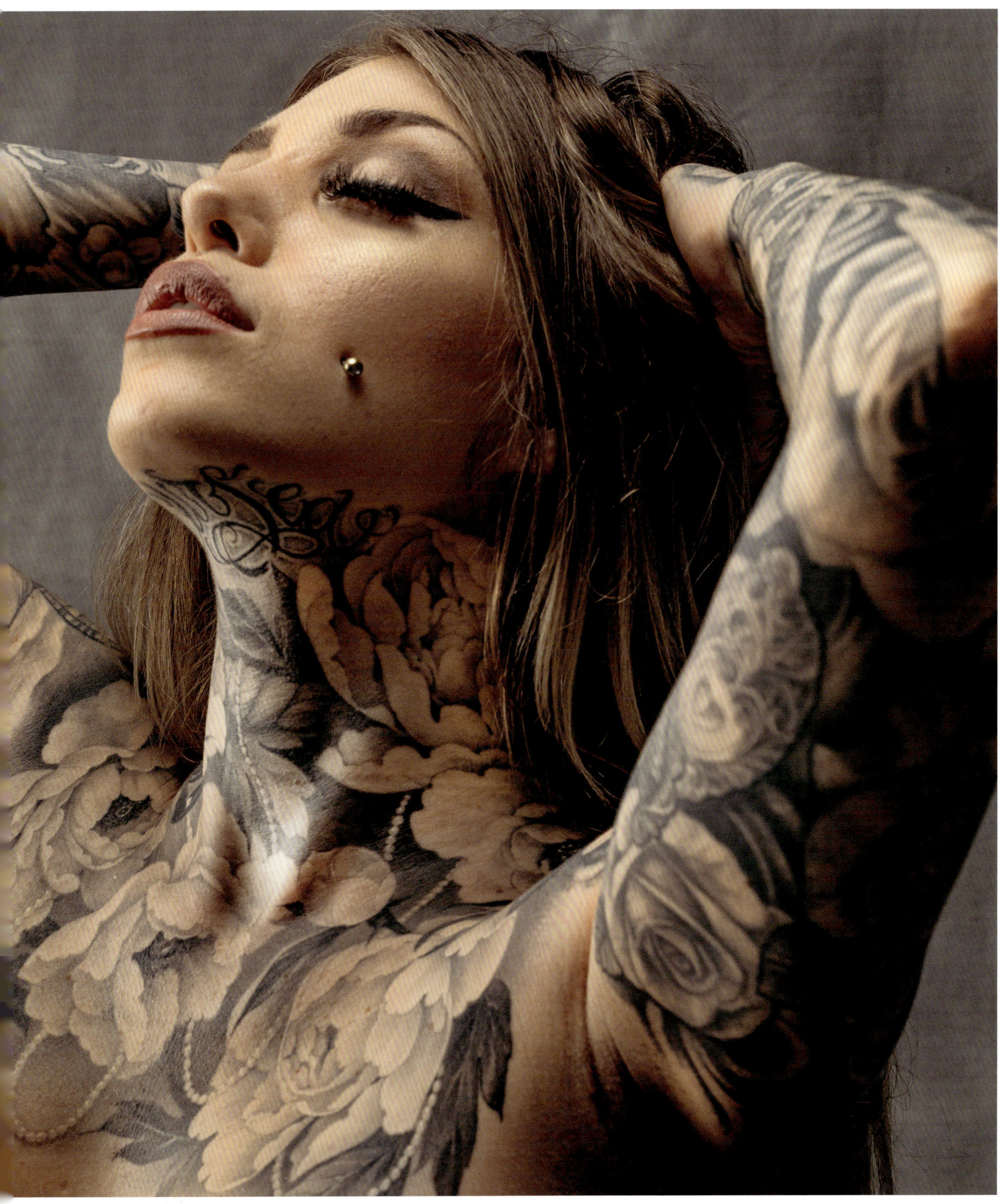

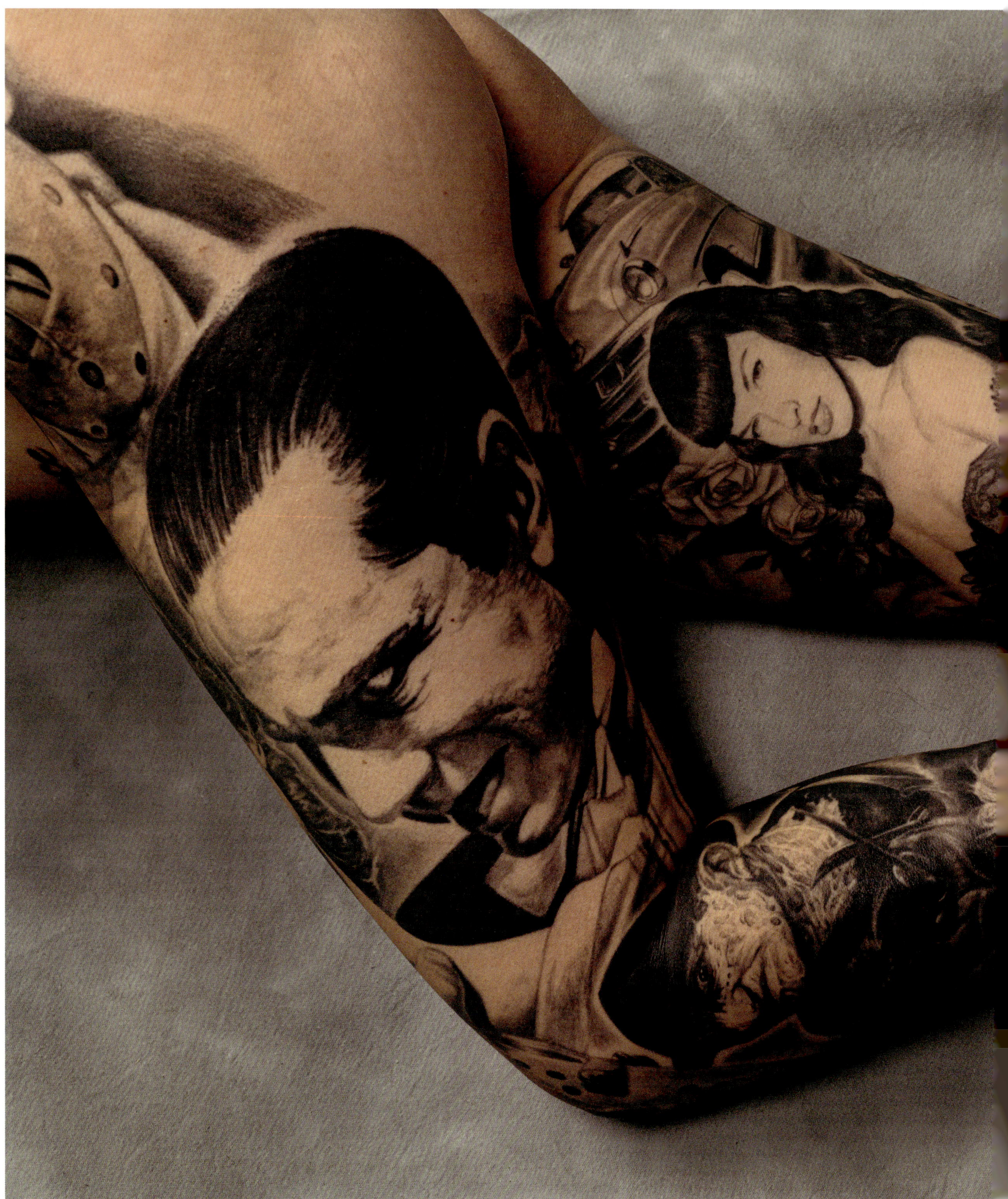

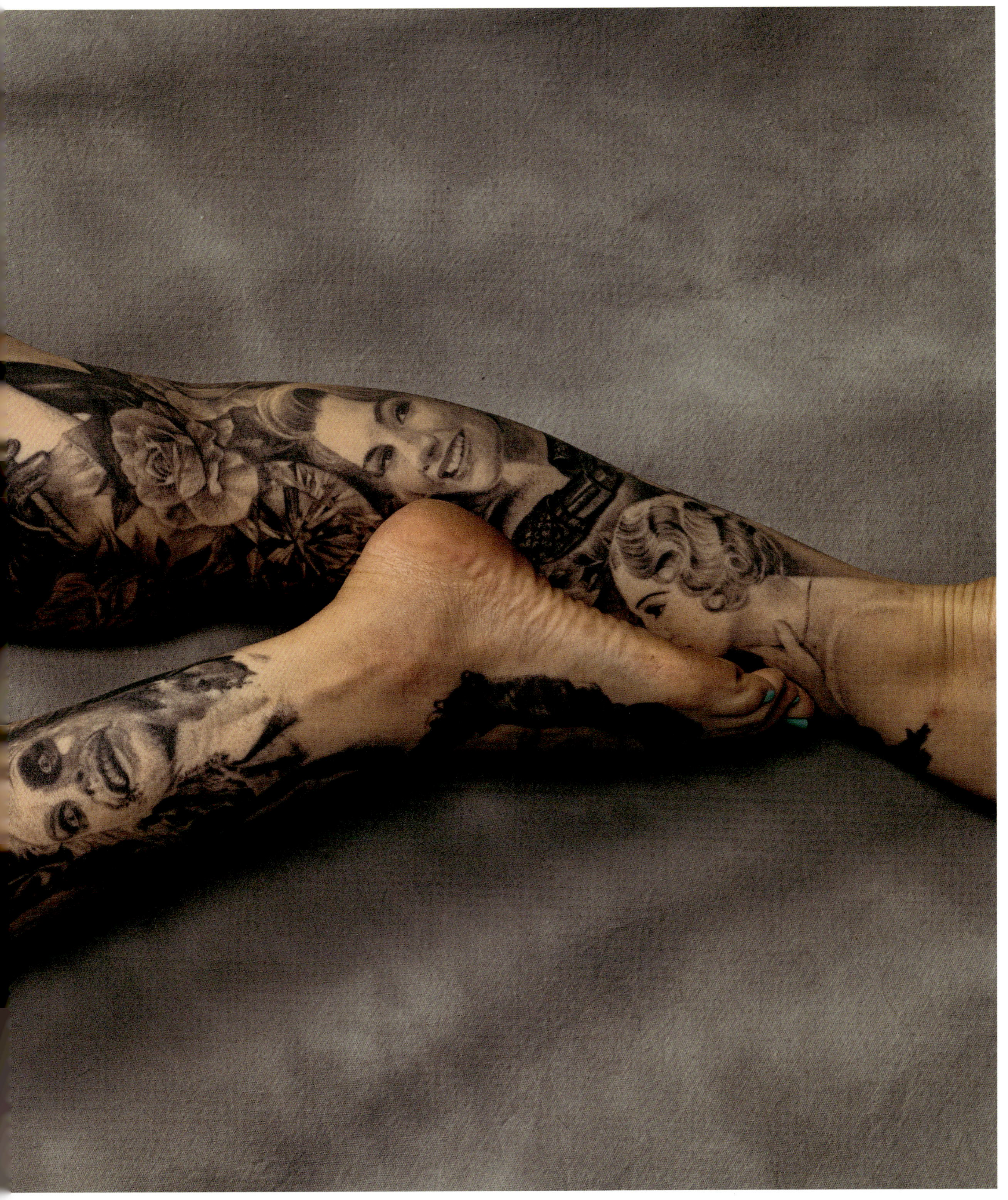

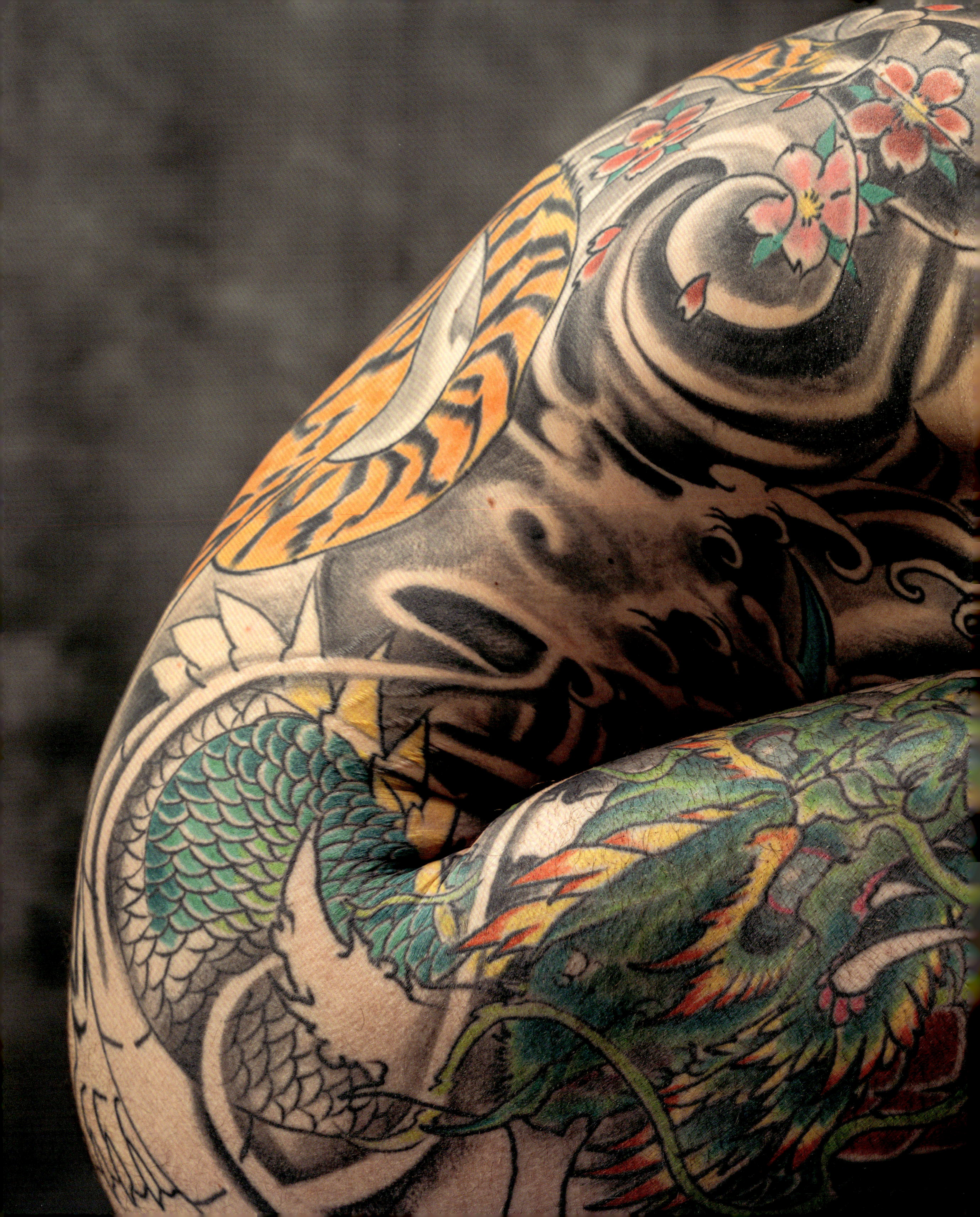

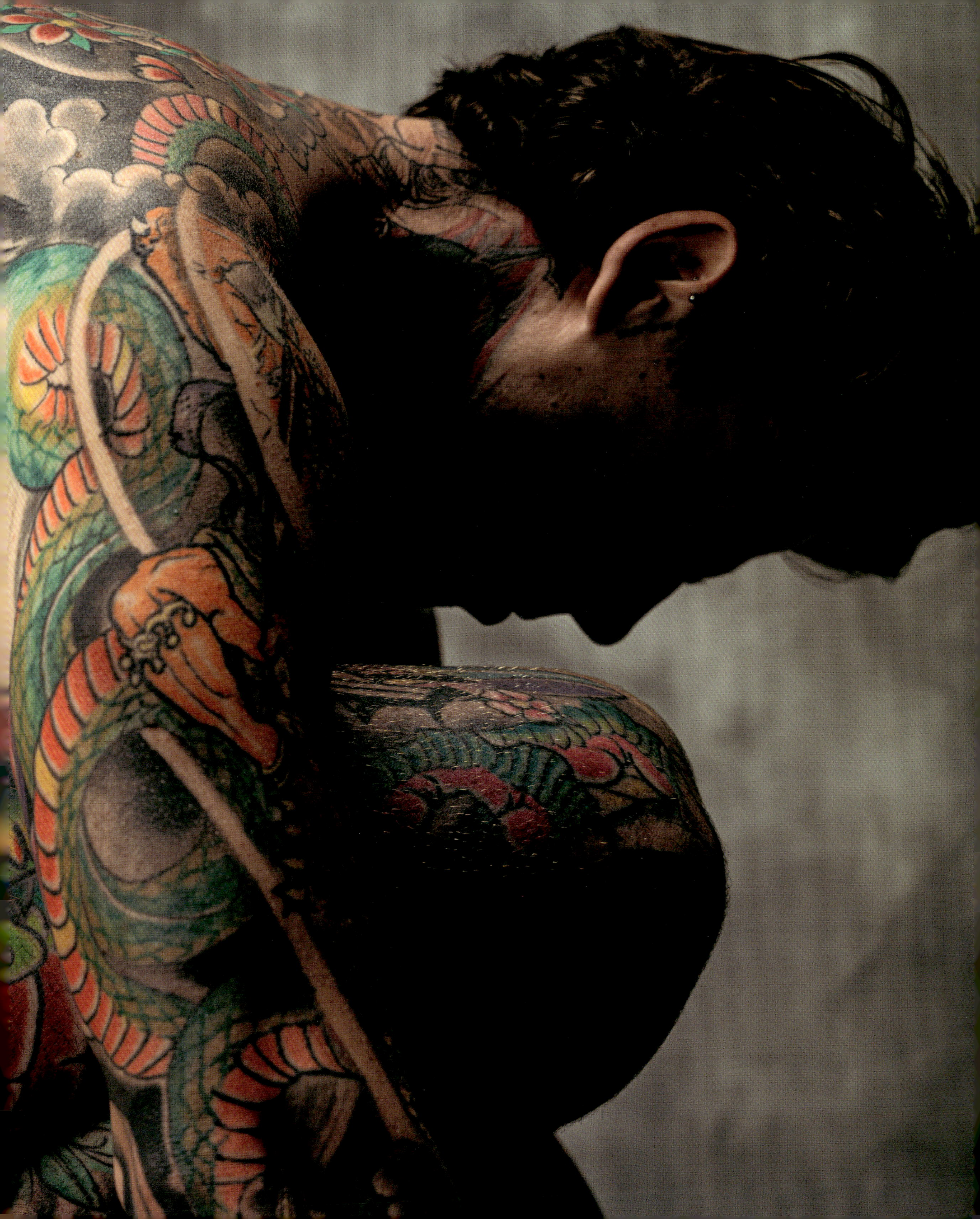

Pages 192–193: Sharky Edwards' tattoo collection was primarily illustrated by Nick White, while his neck, head, and leg work were done by Sasha Konkin. The quote under Edwards' chin, "Peace of Mind," was tattooed by Evan Weidner.

Opposite: Troy Denning collector Sven Pfeiffer wears a tiger to represent his father, which Pfeiffer had tattooed when his dad became terminally ill, and cherry blossoms for his mother.

Pages 196–197: Ludo Desvignes' backpiece, tattooed by Denning, depicts the Buddhist god Yamāntaka, Destroyer of Death, representing the collector's desire to channel his anger.

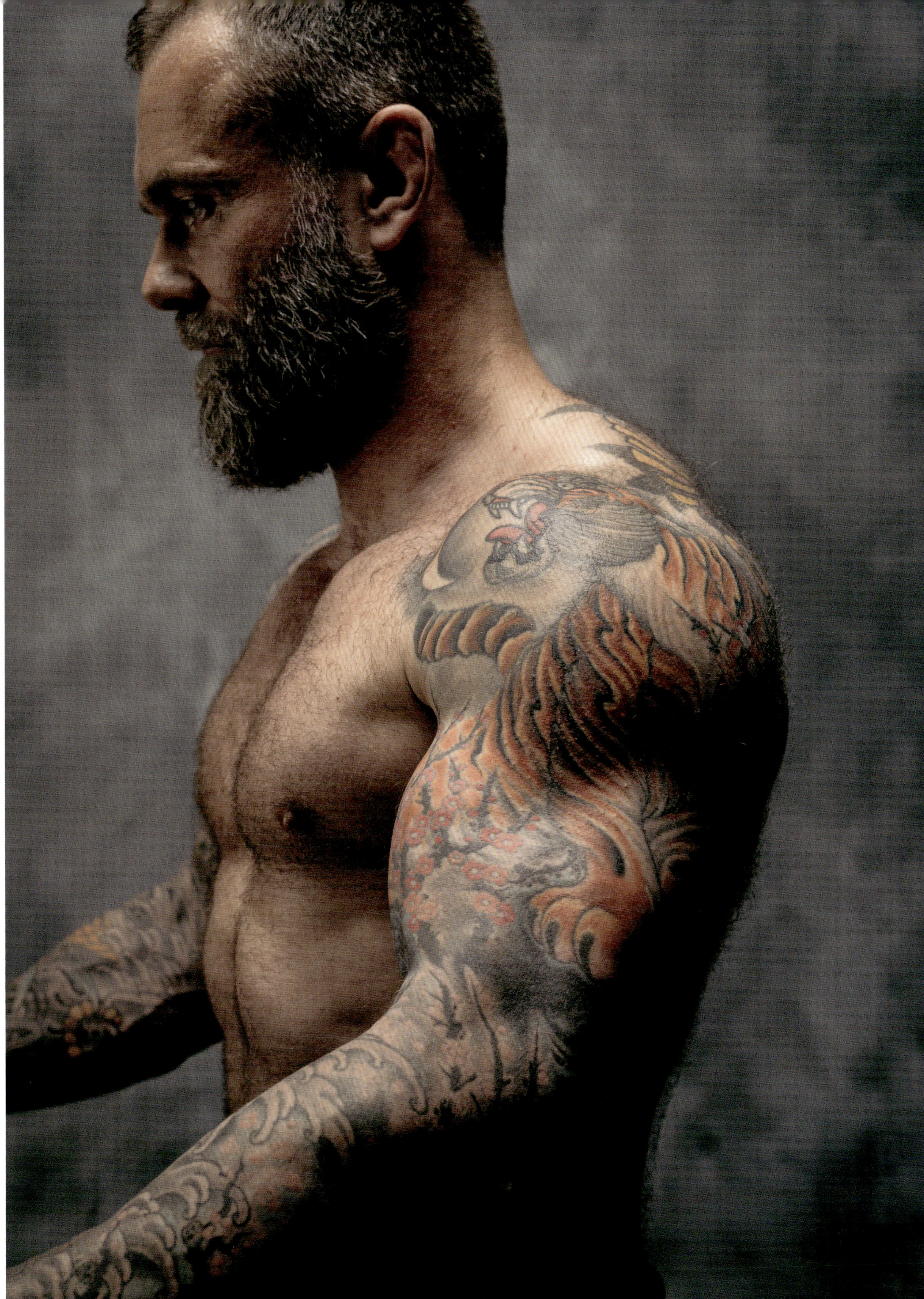

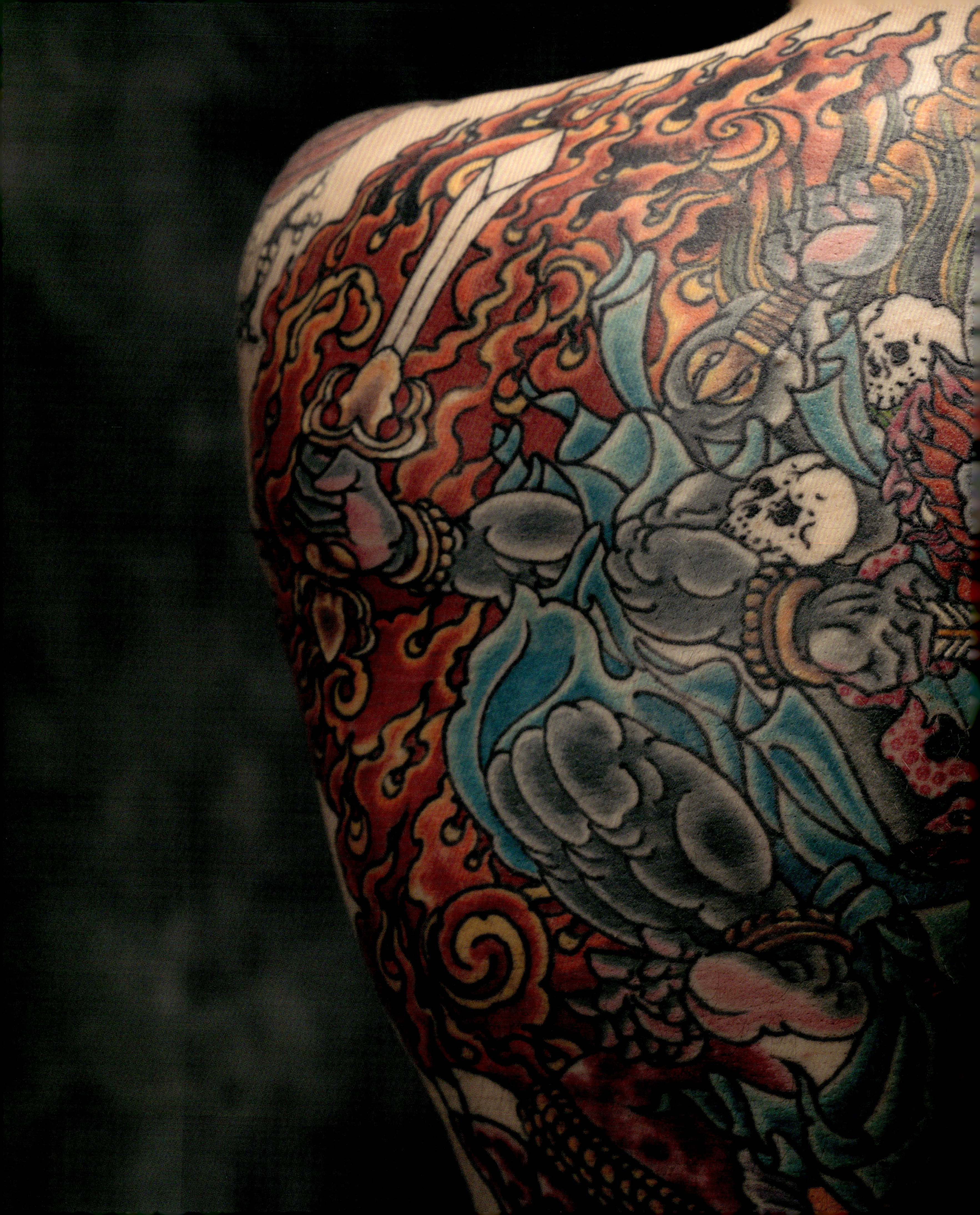

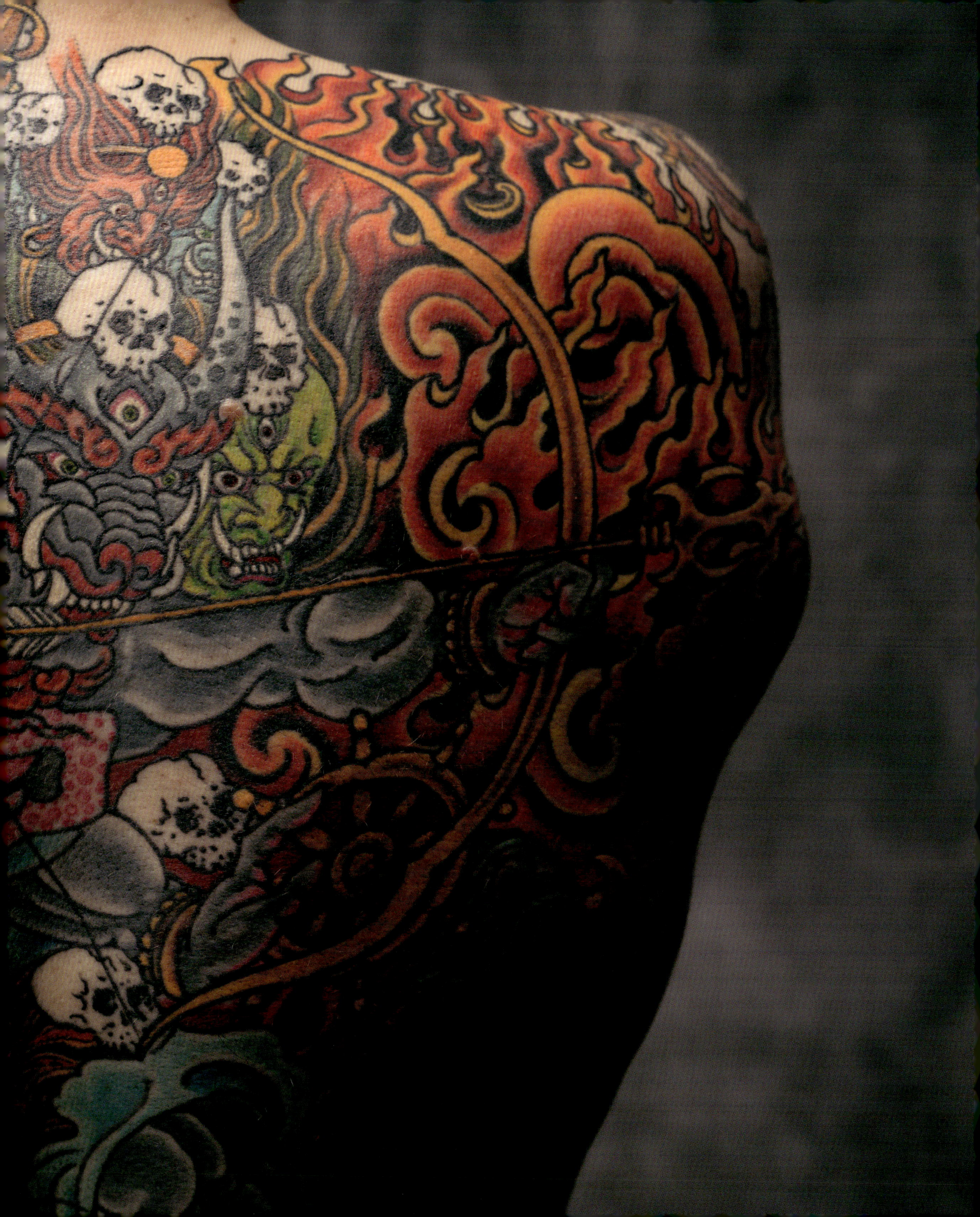

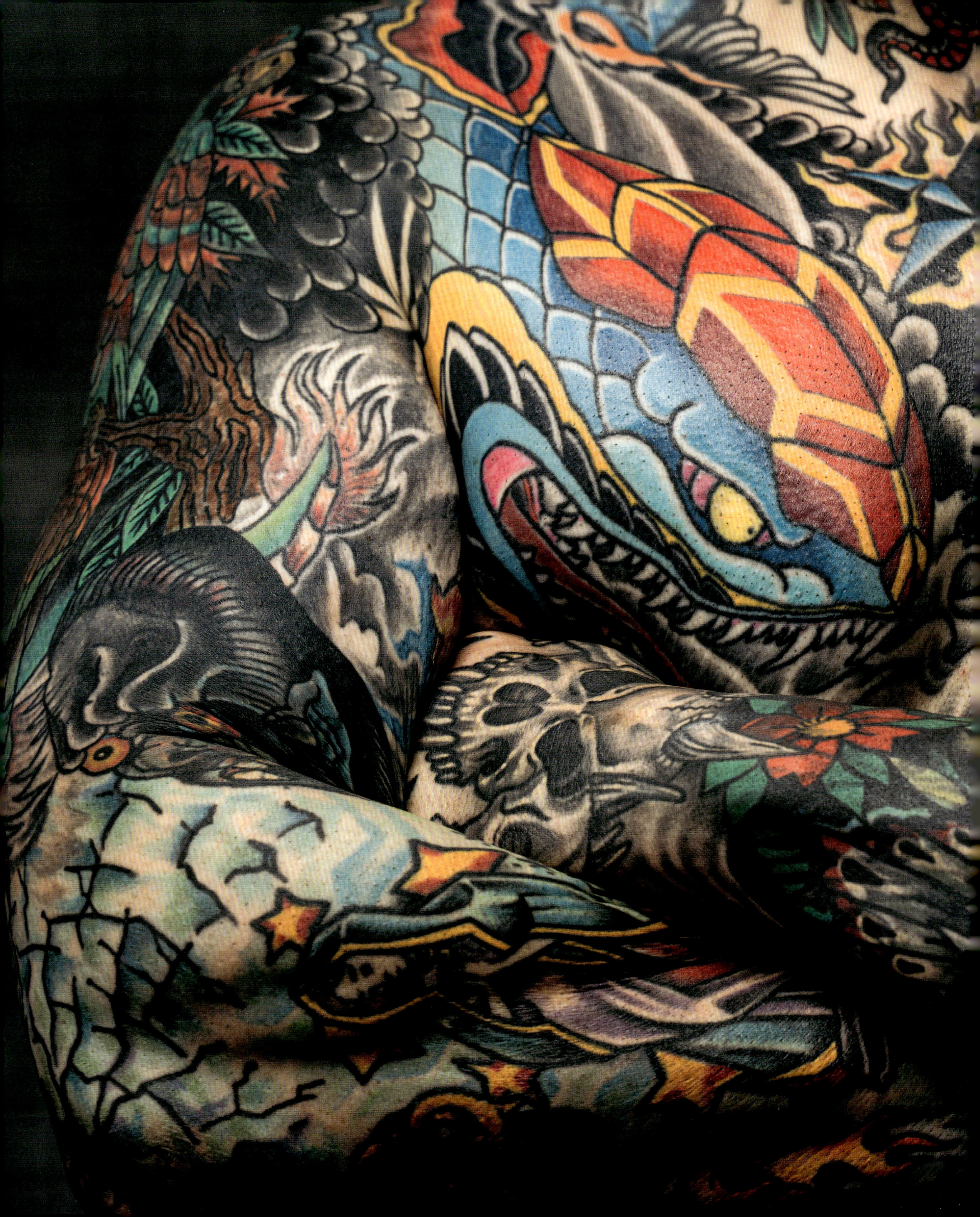

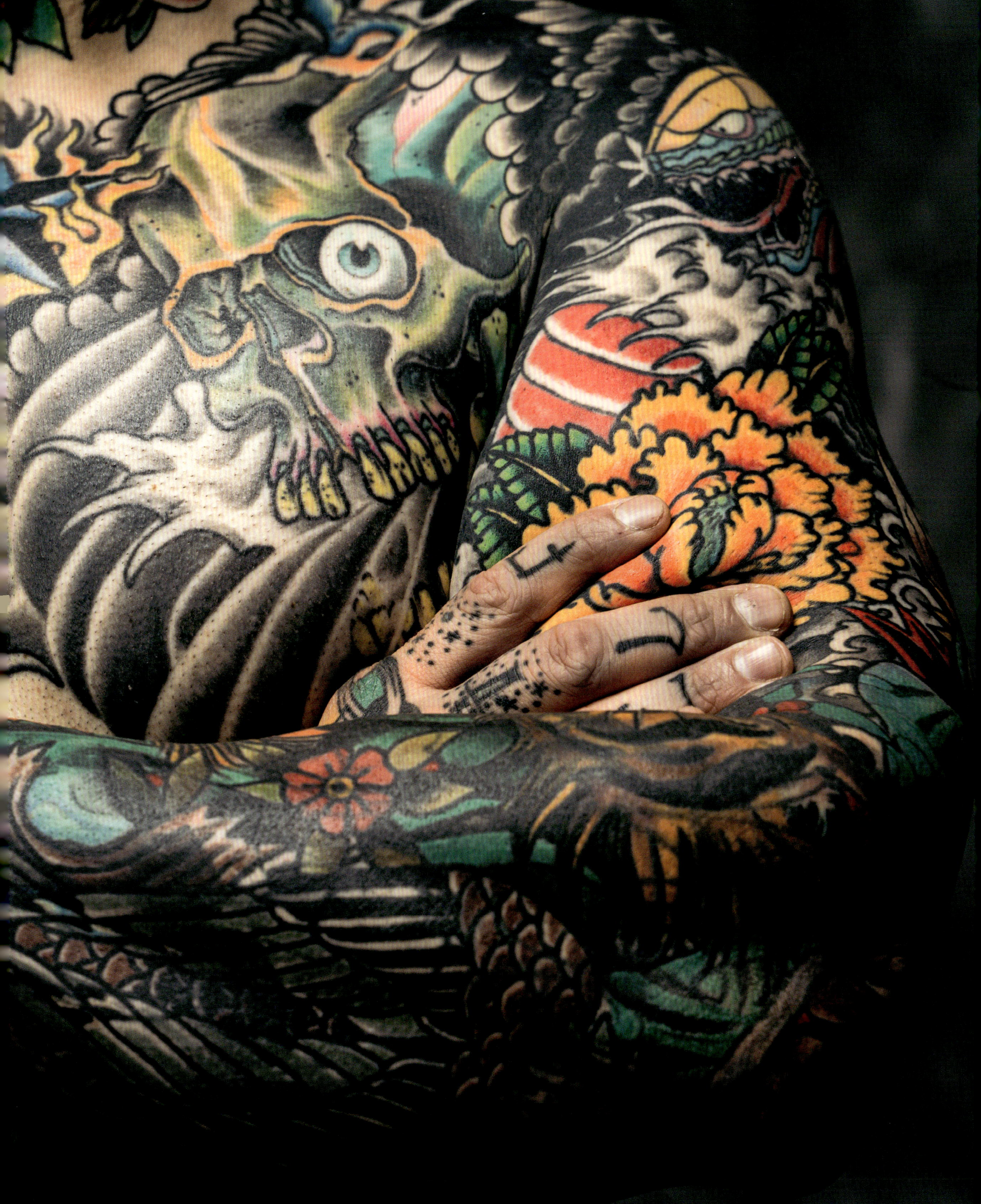

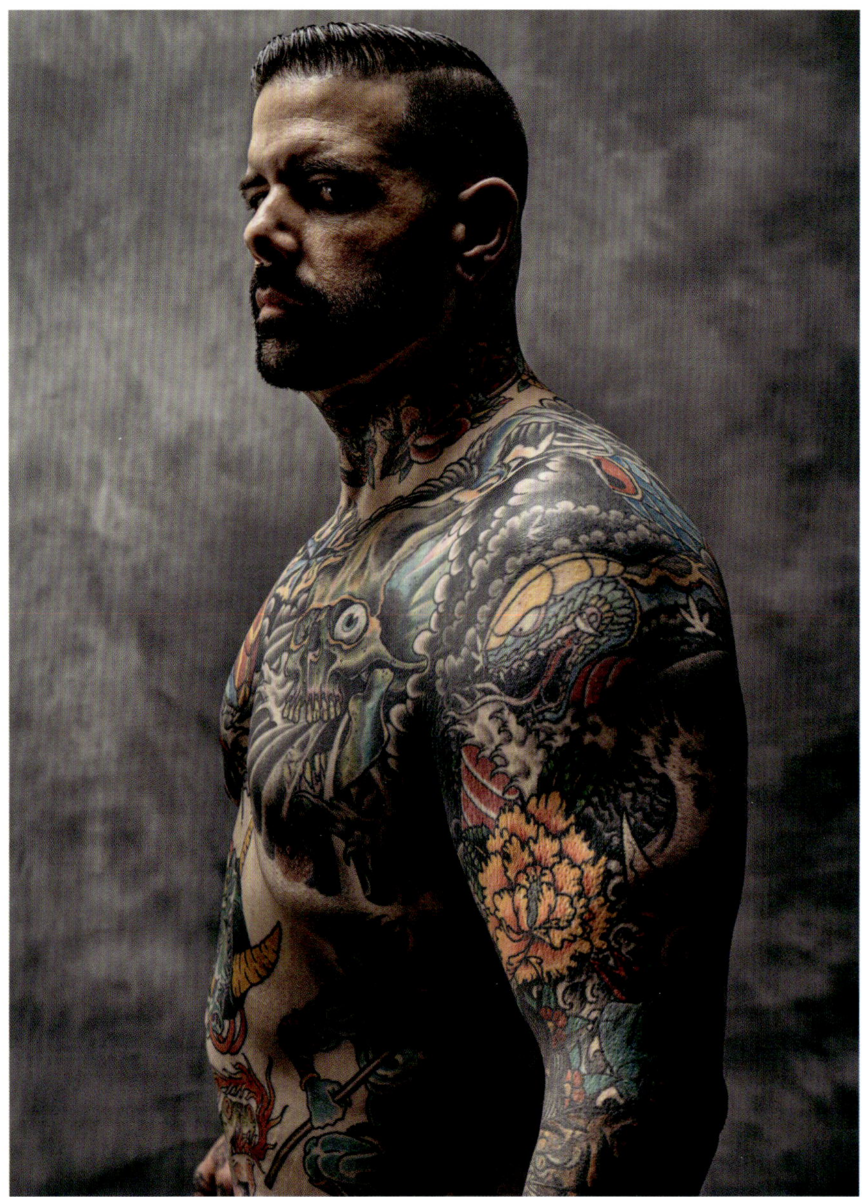

Pages 198–199: Tattooed by more than thirty artists, Rich DeCotis wears work from Oliver Pecker, Chris O'Donnell, Tim Lehi, and Tony Hundahl. His chest piece was tattooed by Chris Cautillo, his right bottom half sleeve, by Greg Christian, and upper right sleeve and full left sleeve, by Todd Noble.

Above: The Sacred Heart, compass, and roses on his neck were illustrated and tattooed by Chris Stuart, while the flower and snake on his throat are the work of Tony Hundahl.

Opposite: DeCotis' backpiece by Todd Noble, comprising a monkey head, tiger body, and snake for a tail, depicts the mythological creature Nue in Japanese folklore.

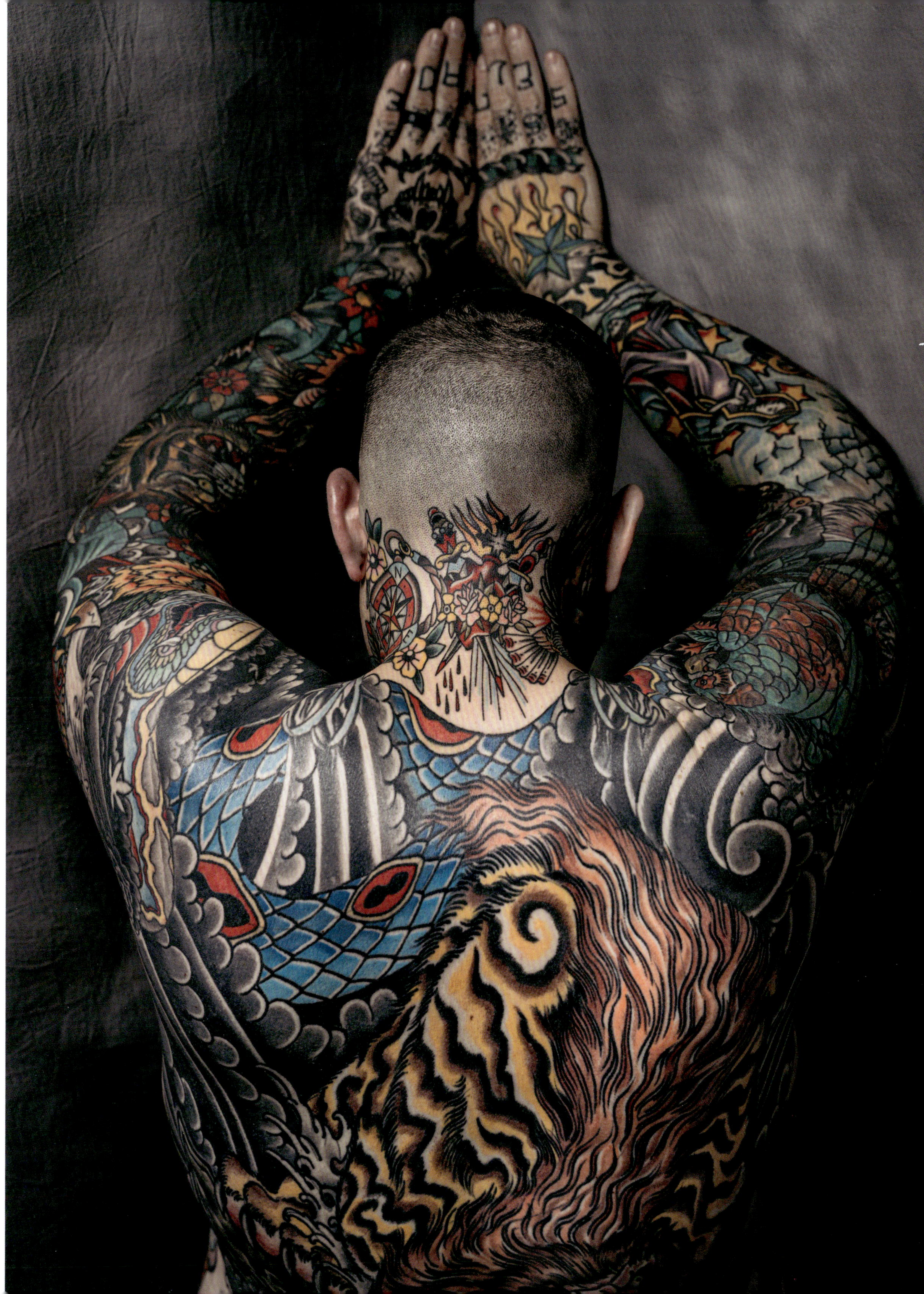

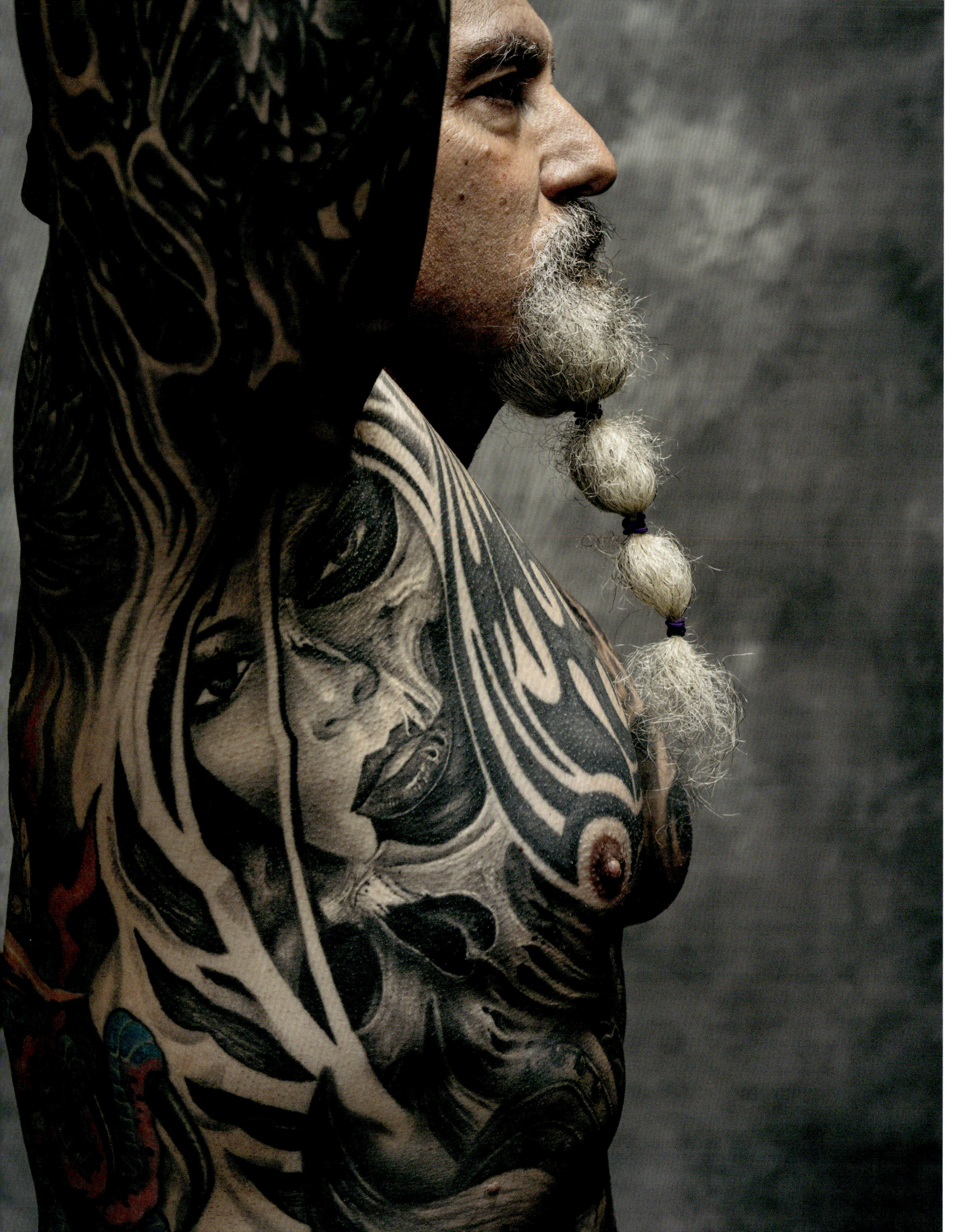

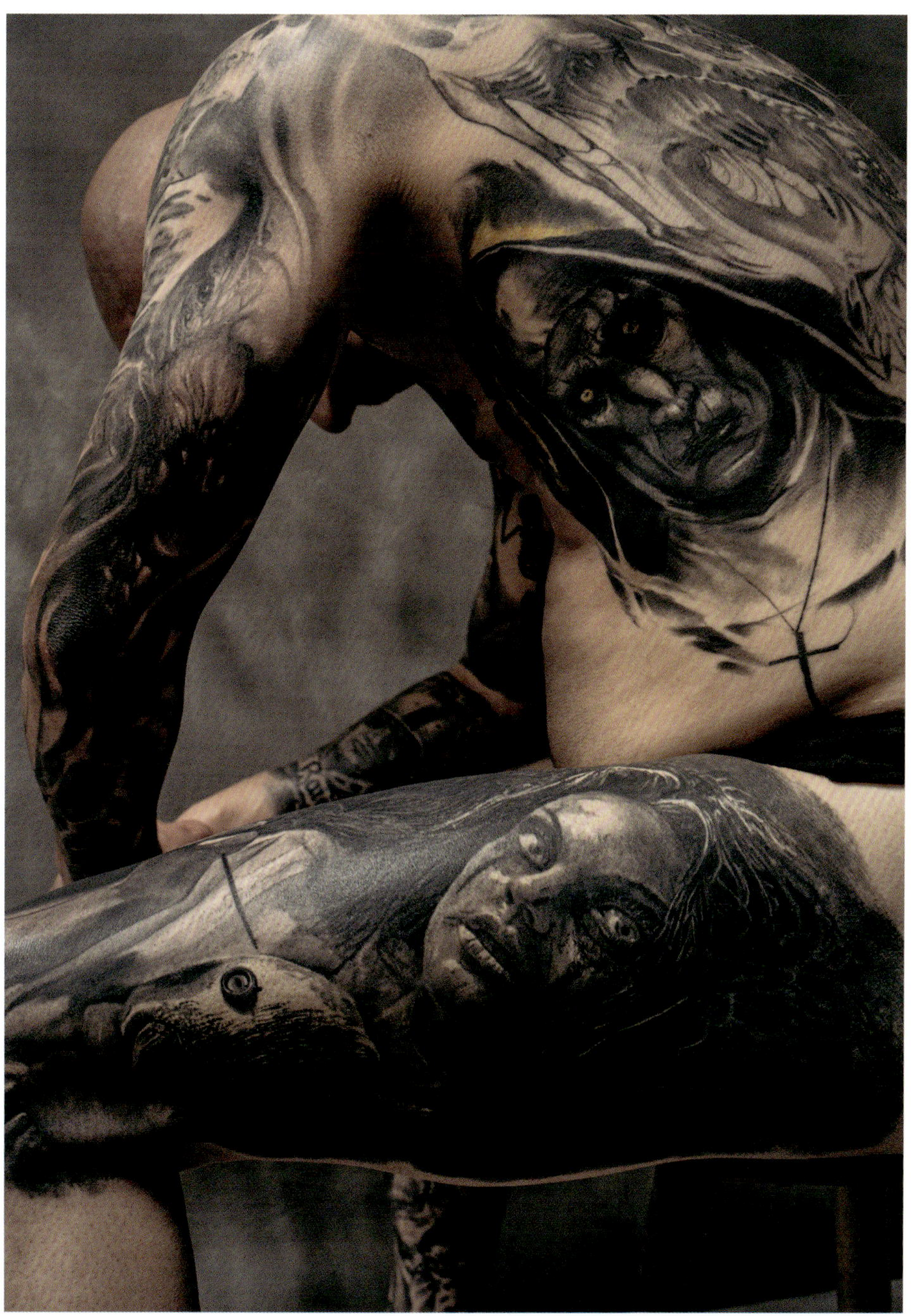

Opposite: After spending thirty years working for corporate America, Charles Venancio retired and then traveled the world to collect illustrations from artists including Bob Tyrrell, Carl Grace, and Steve Tefft.

Above: Tattoos greatly help ease the anxiety of Jason Braun, who wears realistic dark art from Luiz Lopes, Jordan Oterski, and Sandry Riffard. The voodoo girl on his thigh was done by Eliot Kohek.

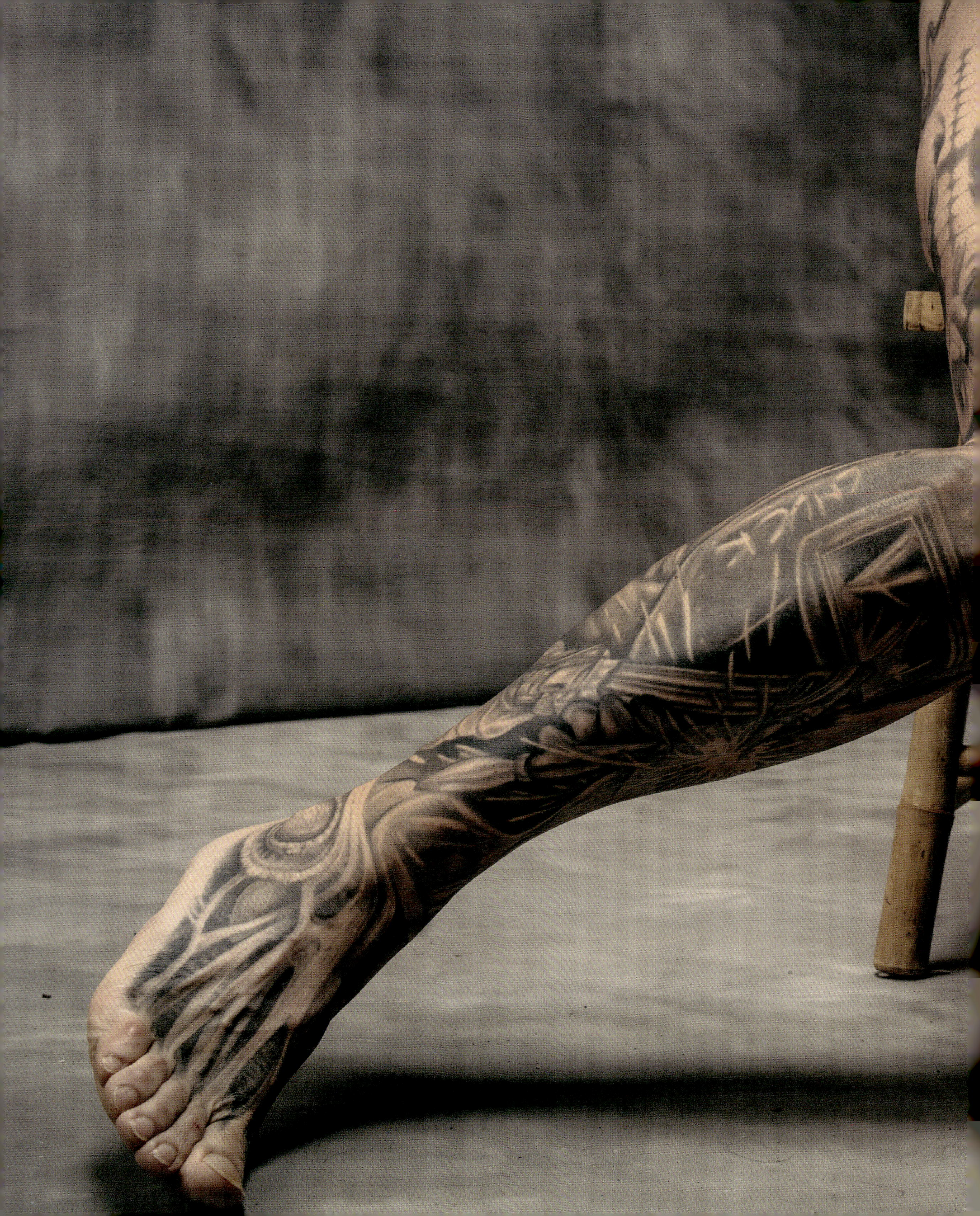

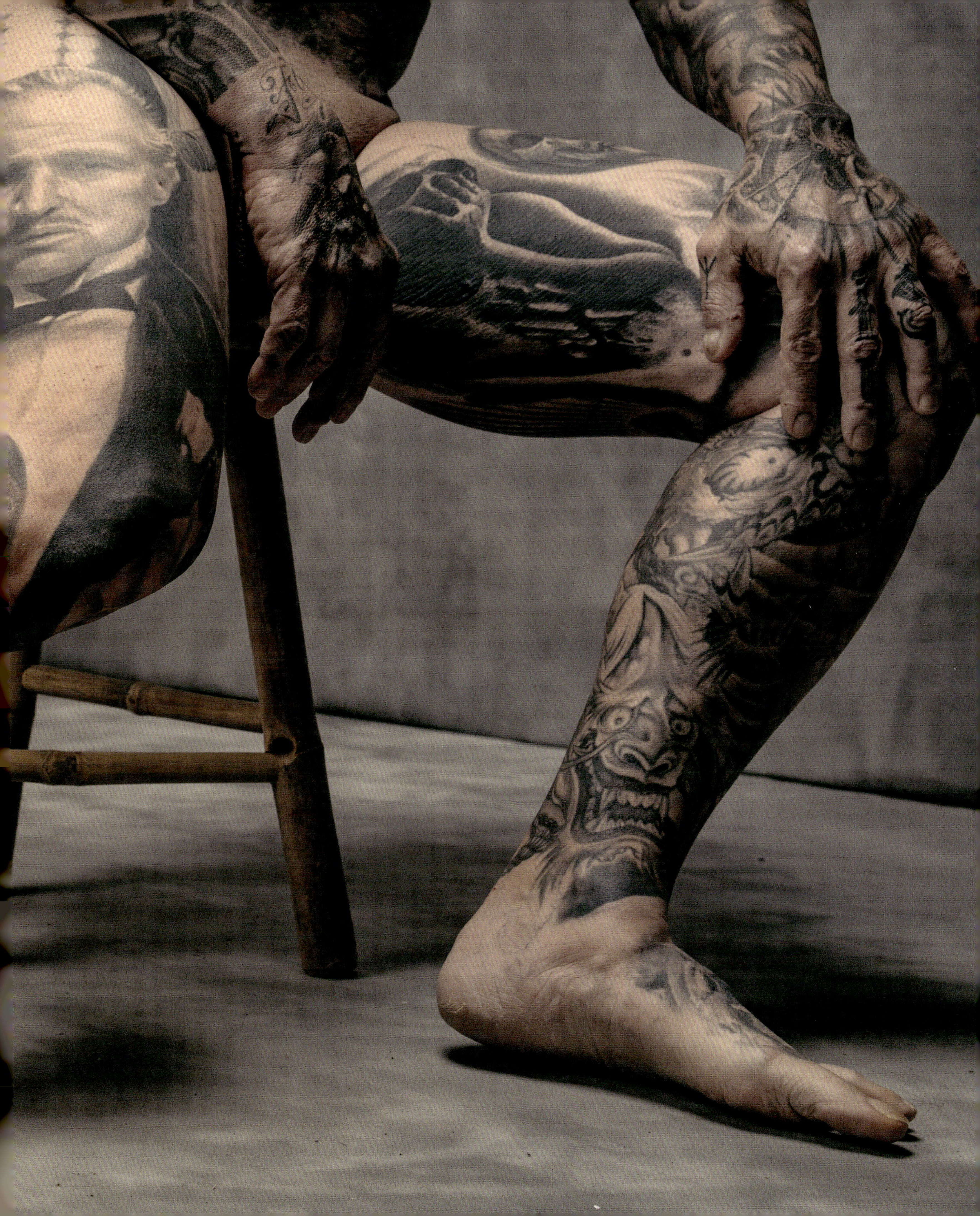

Pages 204–205: Venancio wears leg art from Shawn Barber, Tuyen Tran, Jessi Manchester, and Matt Clemmer, who is responsible for his Marlon Brando and Dirty Harry tattoos.

Opposite: Working on his second bodysuit after lasering off the work from his twenties, Ronald Vellucci is predominantly tattooed by Cris Kazantzis, whose work is on his neck, hands, and right arm.

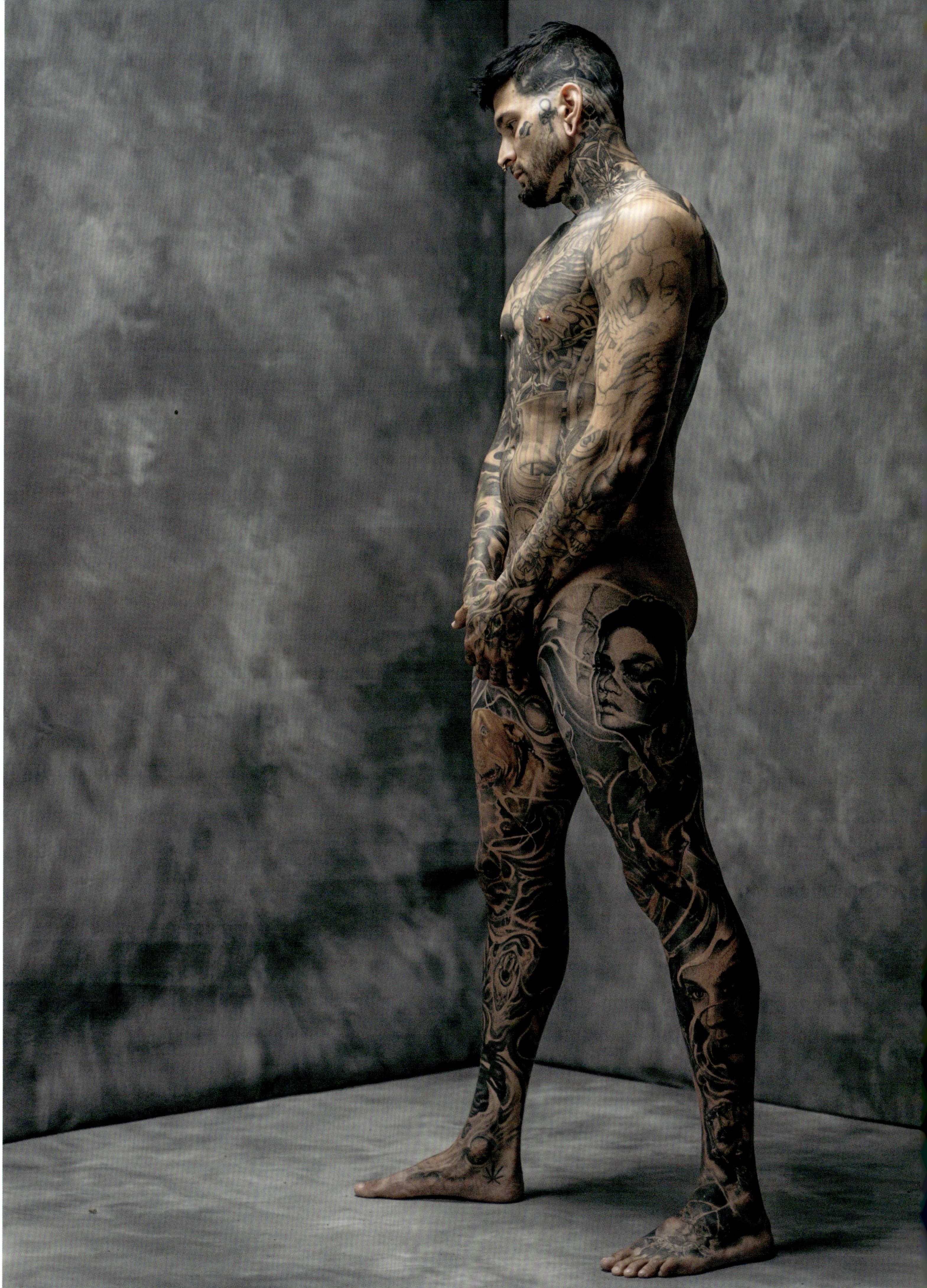

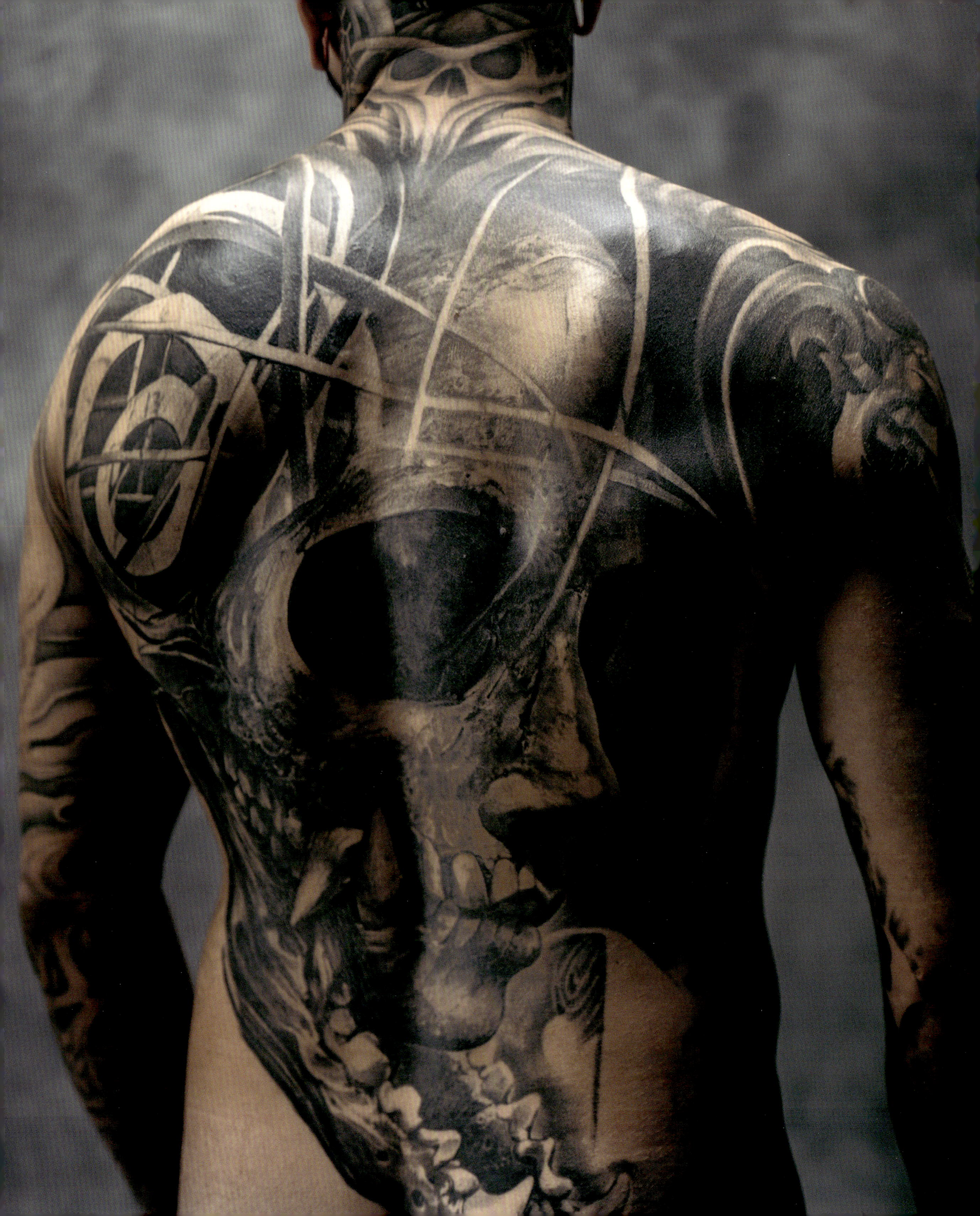

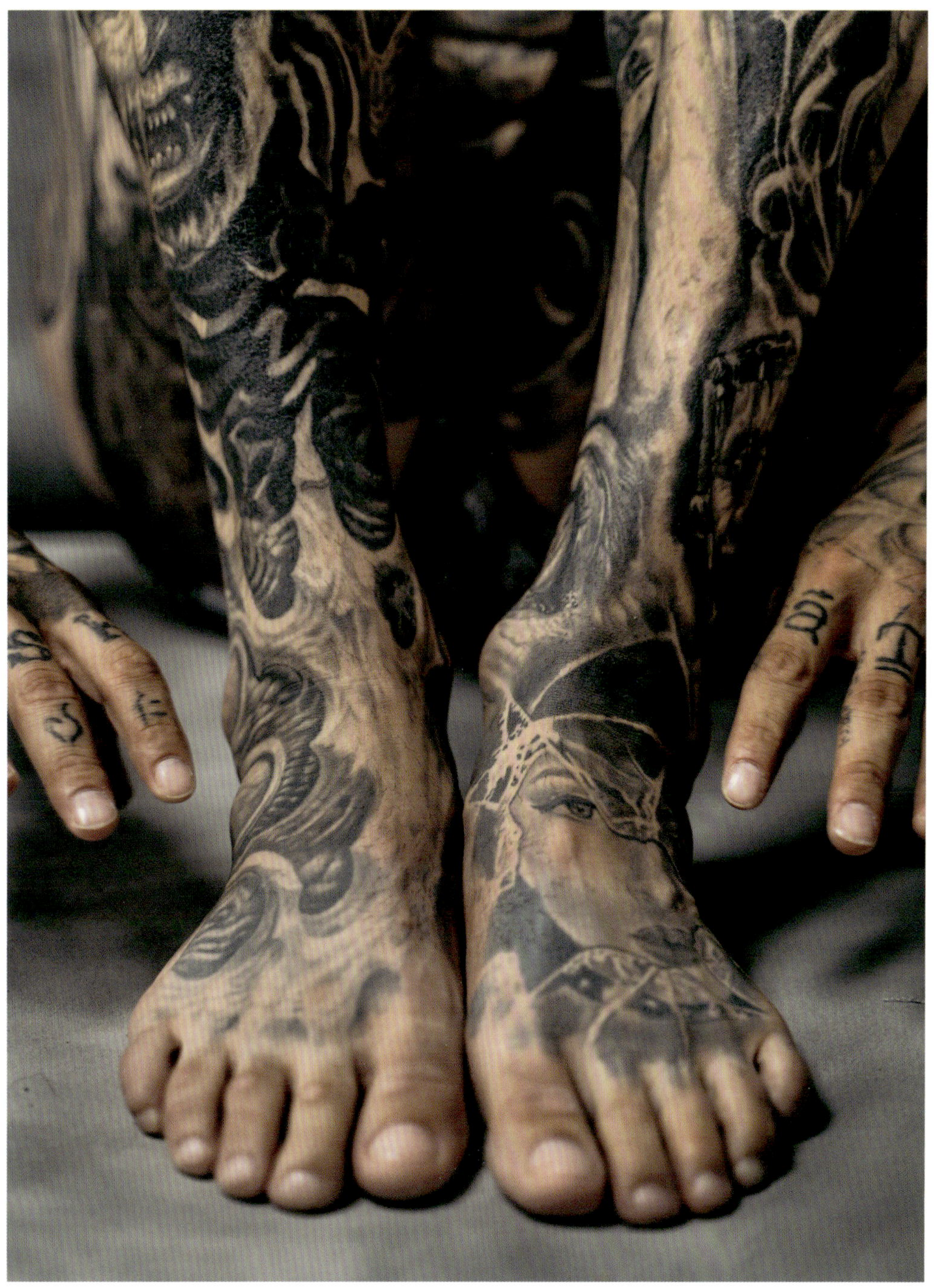

Opposite: Robby Latos illustrated Vellucci's back and also tattooed his left leg with Sean Foy and Bryan Merck.

Above: Vellucci's right leg was tattooed by Joe Matisa, Josh Ruff, and TeeJ Poole, while his left foot, of an ex's face behind shattered glass, was by Bryan Merck.

With a backpiece by Sergio “Bo” Gurule, much of Andre Hughes’ collection is of his family, including a portrait of his son by Gilbert Salas and of his grandmother by Fred Flores.

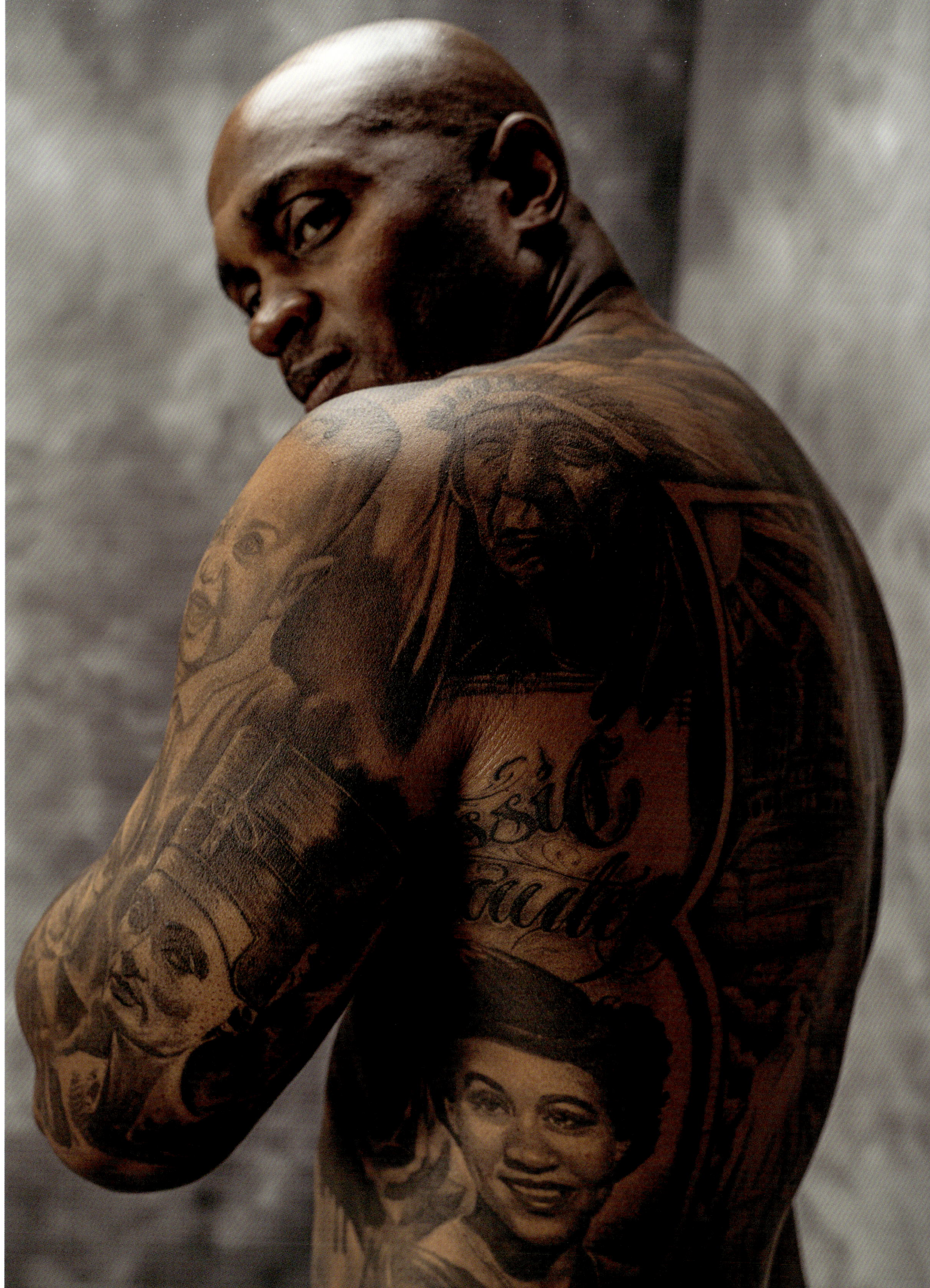

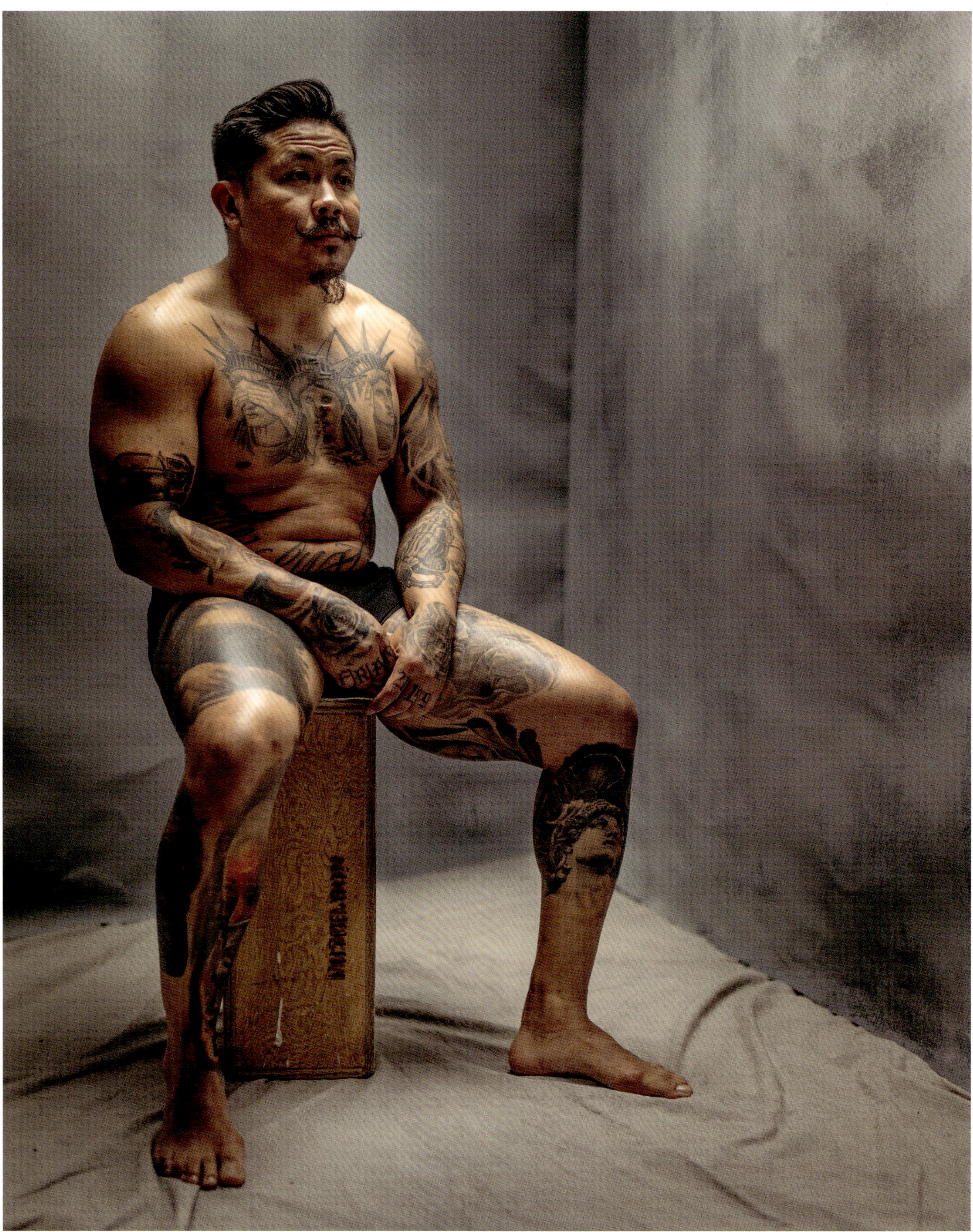

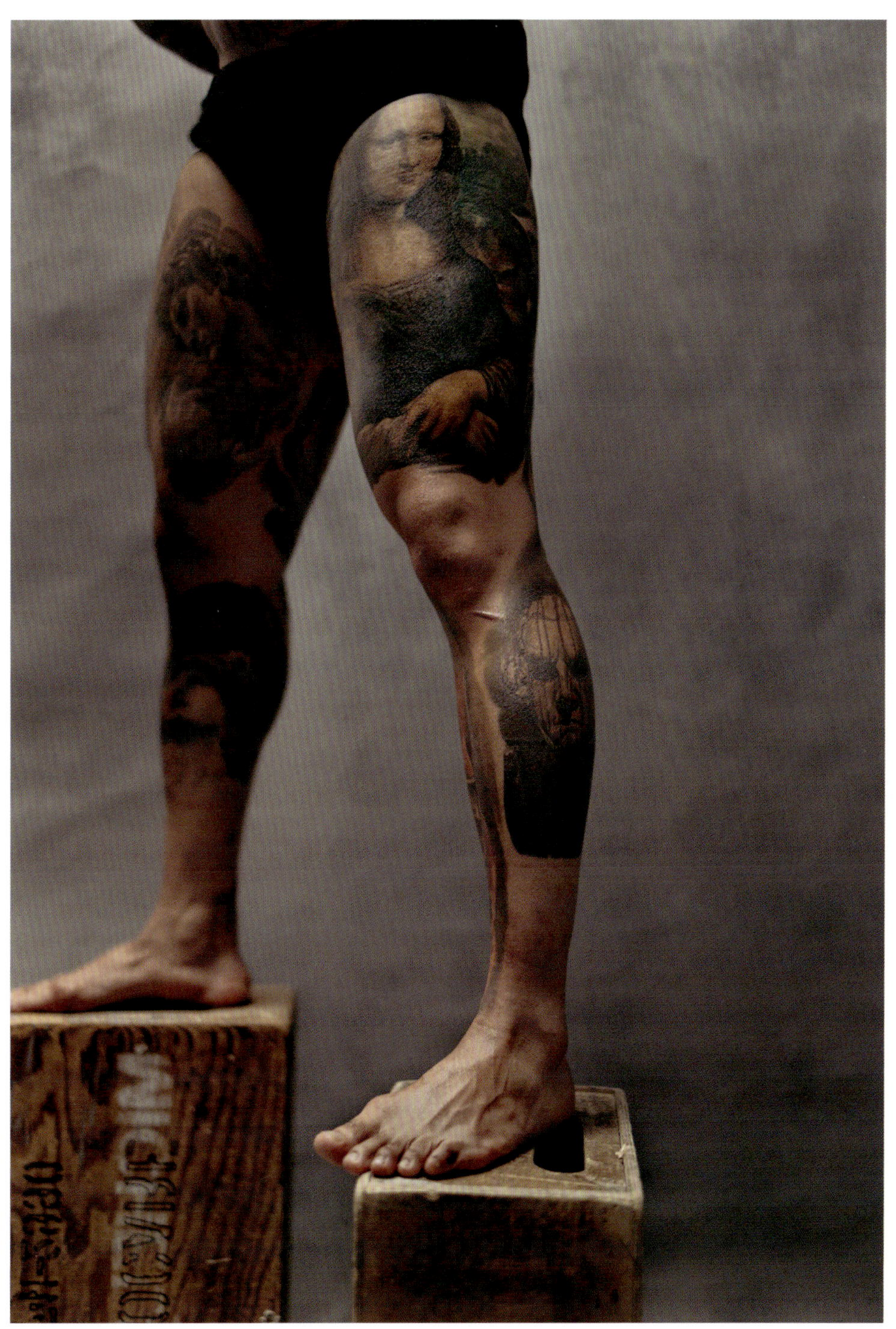

Opposite: Pat "Pat Tats" Buth's Lady Liberty chest piece by Abey Alvarez was inspired by the three wise monkeys in Hindu culture and represents an ideal society.

Above: Buth's tattoo collection also includes the Mona Lisa by Kyle Cotterman, Purge masks by Nikko Hurtado and Paul Acker, and a Medusa and Achilles statue by Alan Padilla.

New York funeral director and mortician Tara Pepitone wears a Japanese-inspired collection, mainly illustrated by Jay Sall.

Pages 216–217: "One story flows into the next," says Pepitone of her collection. "It's a calming vibe, and I wouldn't change a thing."

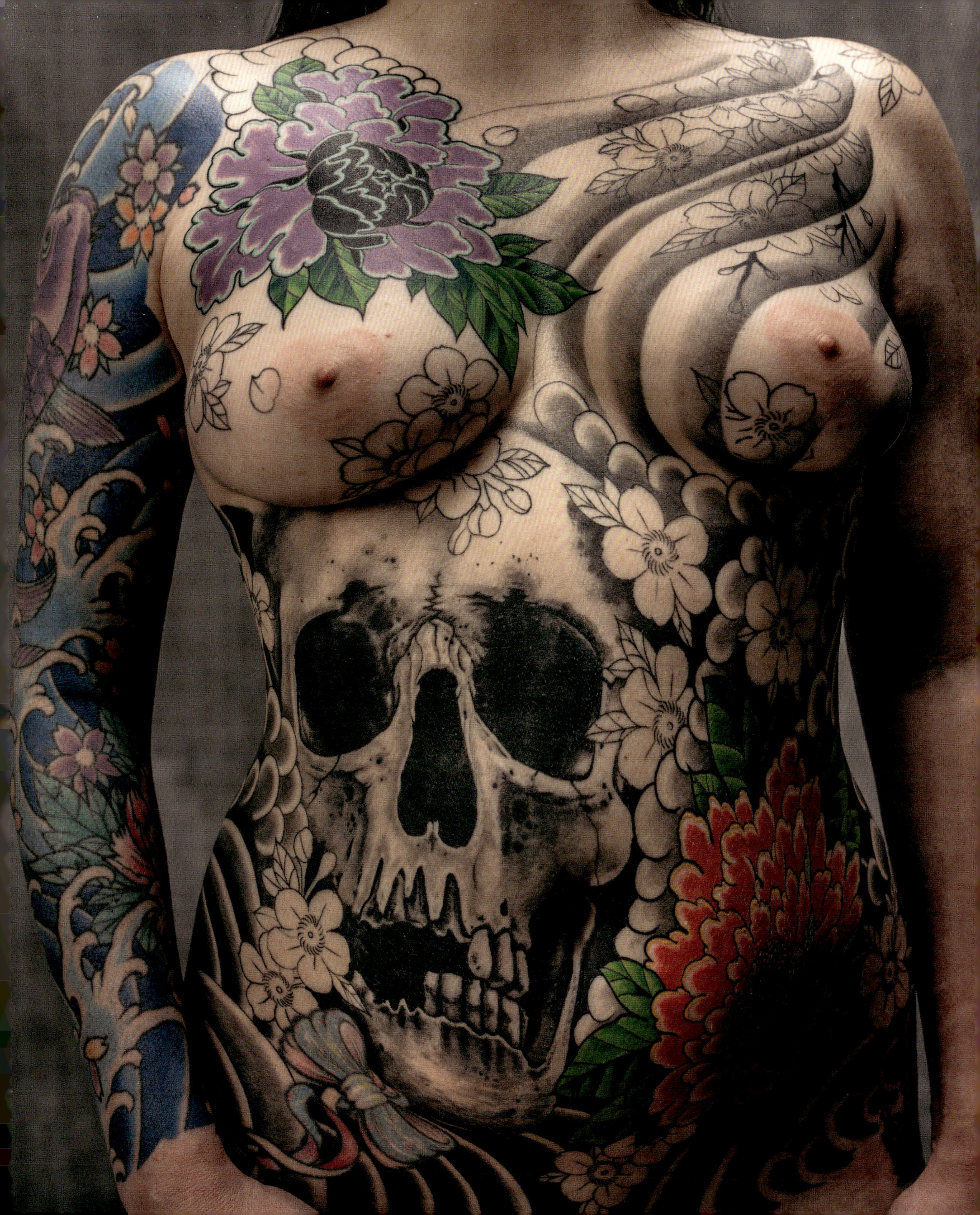

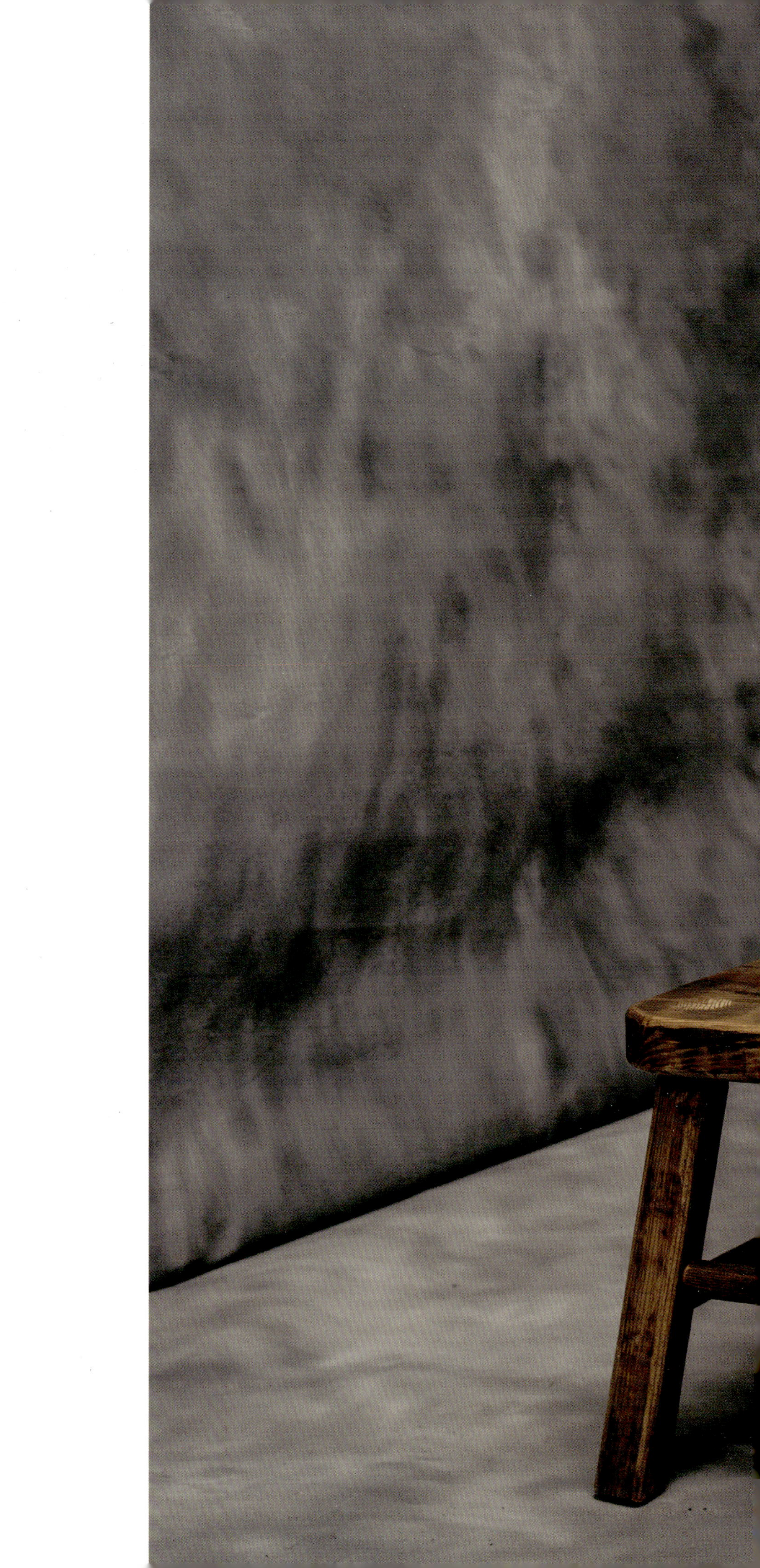

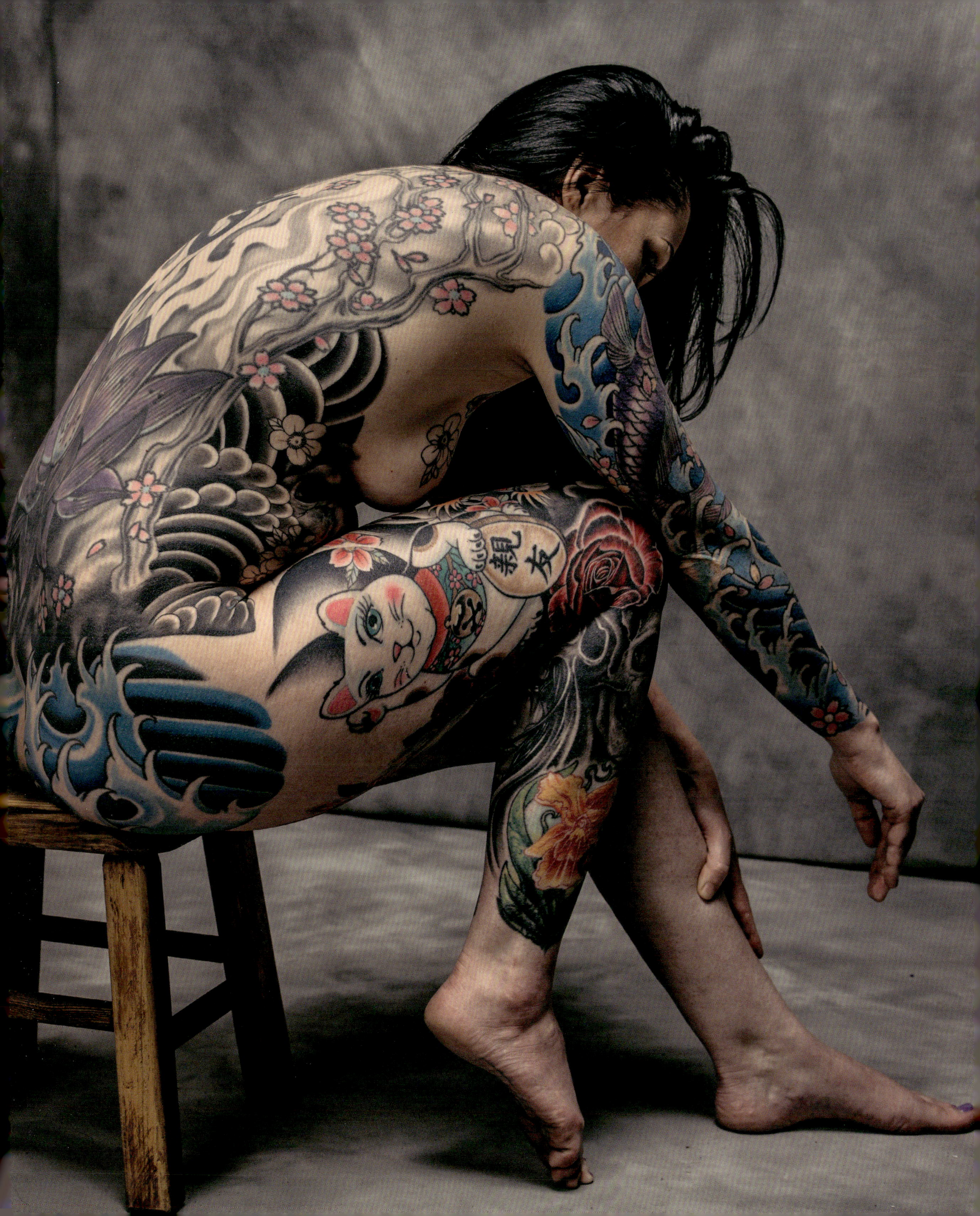
親友

Alicia Mecca's tattoo collection features soft and bold vintage-style blackwork with nature themes, illustrated by Ryan Ashley Malarkey, Courtenay Elliot Pierce, and Tyler Pawelzik.

Pages 220–221: Mecca wears the work of Nathan Ernce on her face, with her chest, neck, and right leg tattooed by Bob Lewis, and the back of her left thigh illustrated and tattooed by Courtenay Elliot Pierce.

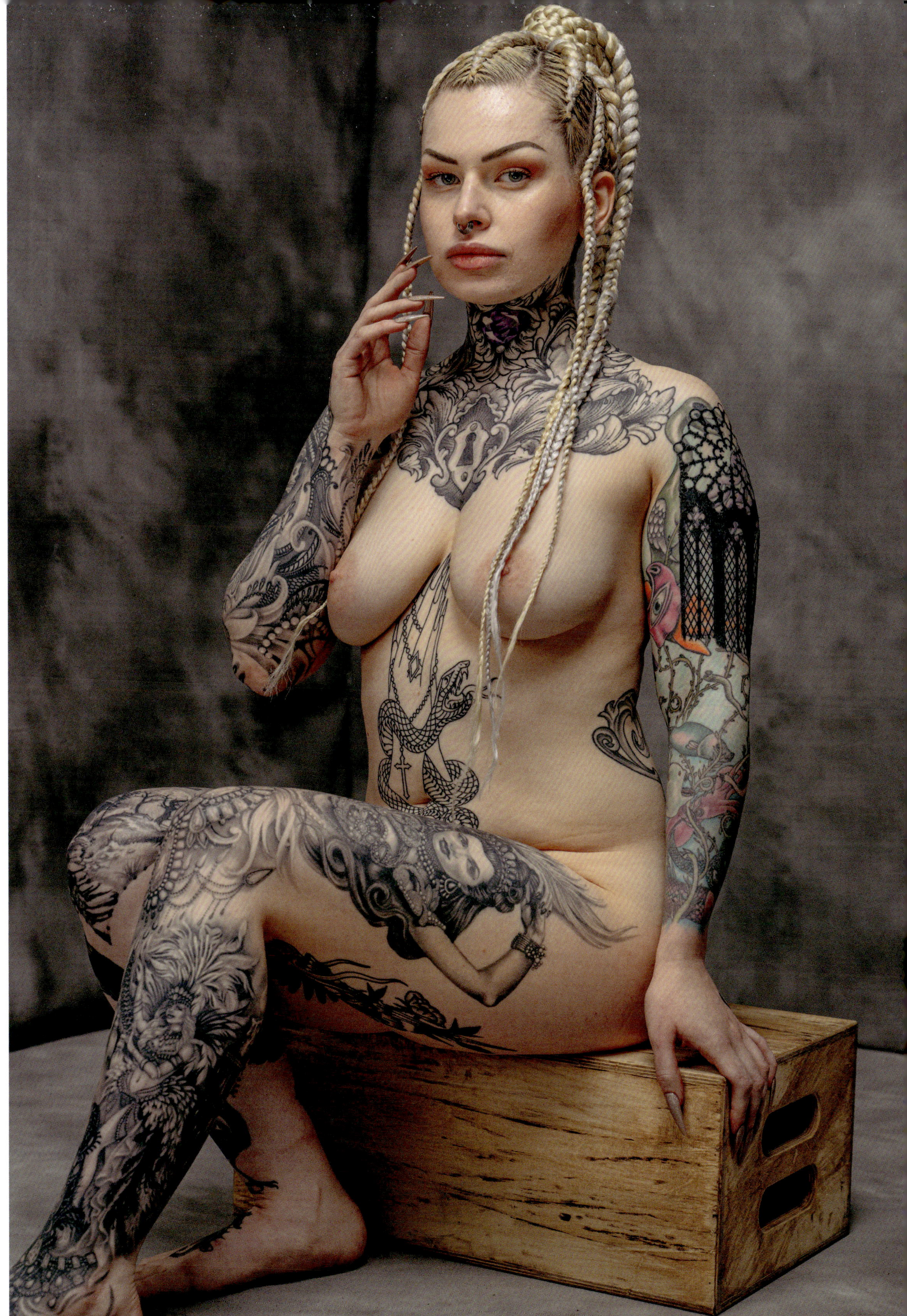

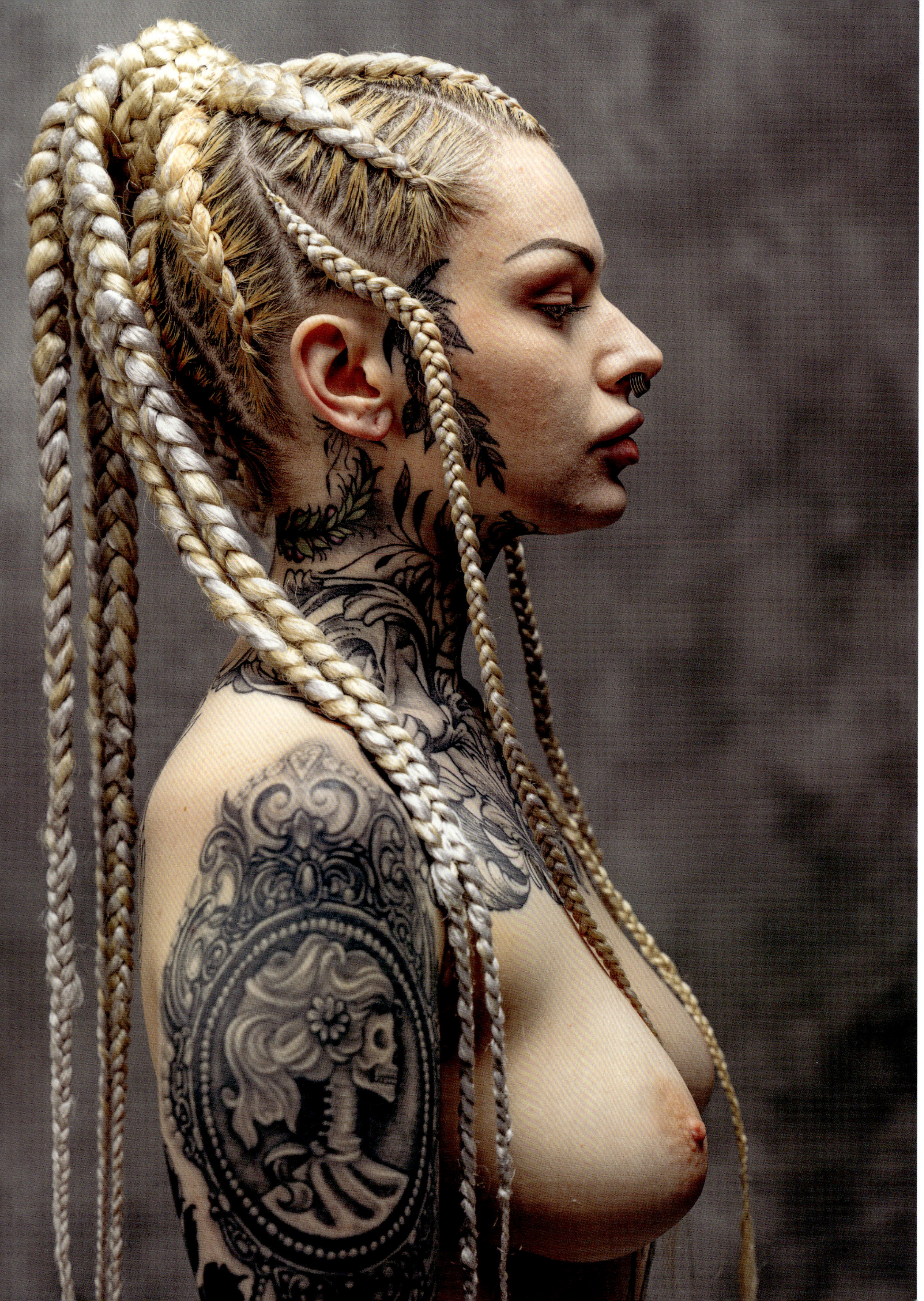

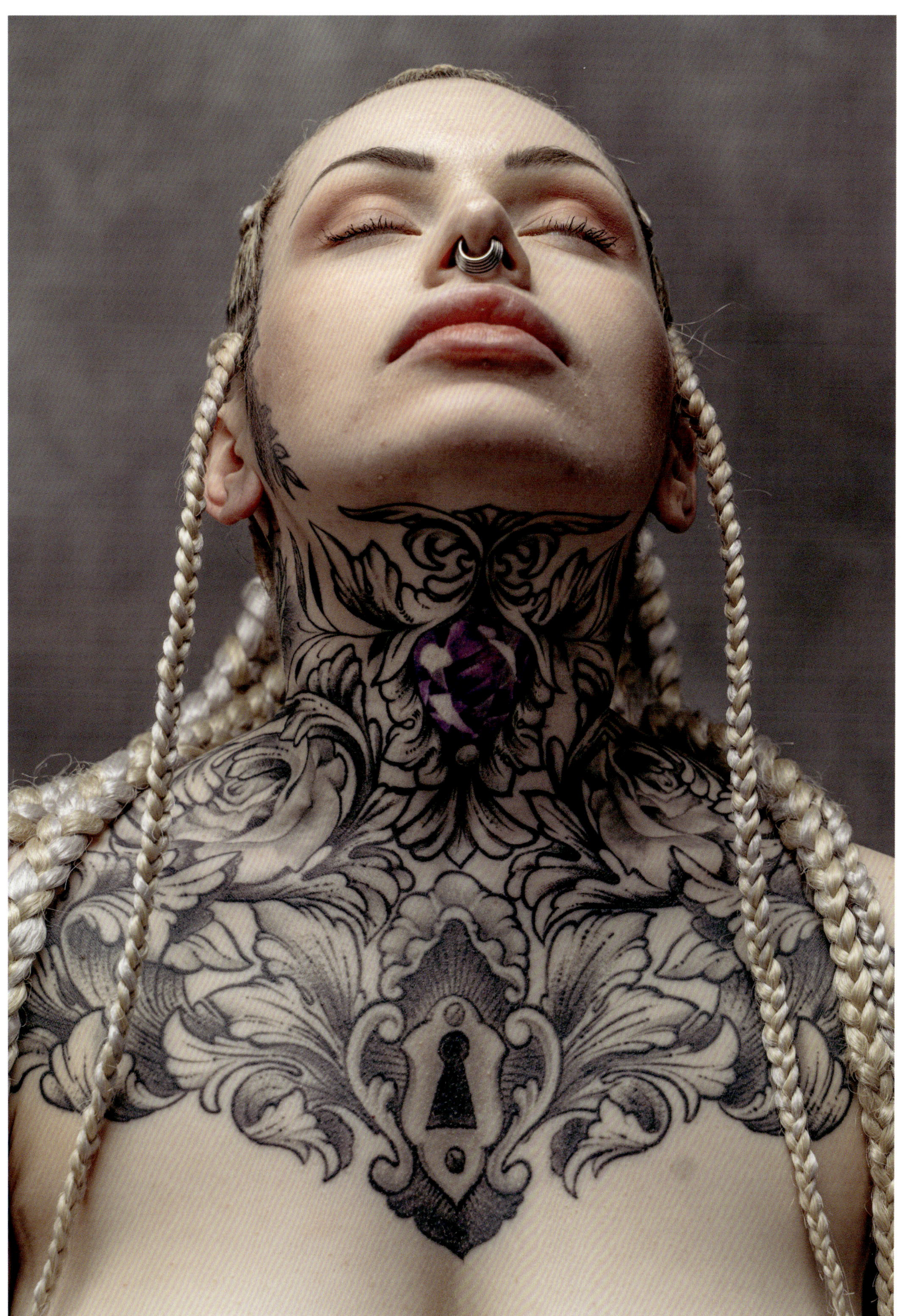

Many of BriAnna Wyble's tattoos were done by Tyler Pawelzik, owner and operator of Black Casket Tattoo, in Scranton, Pennsylvania.

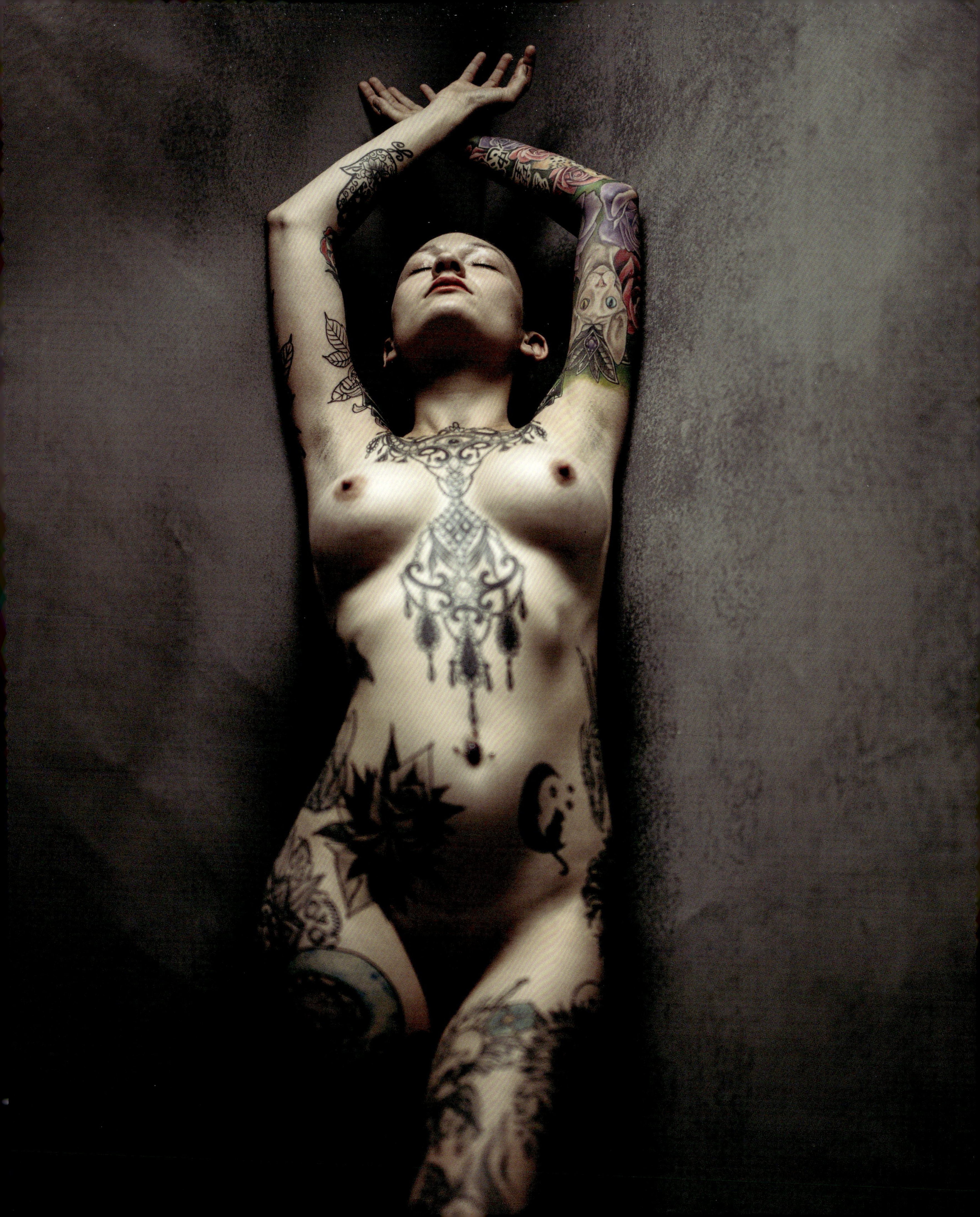

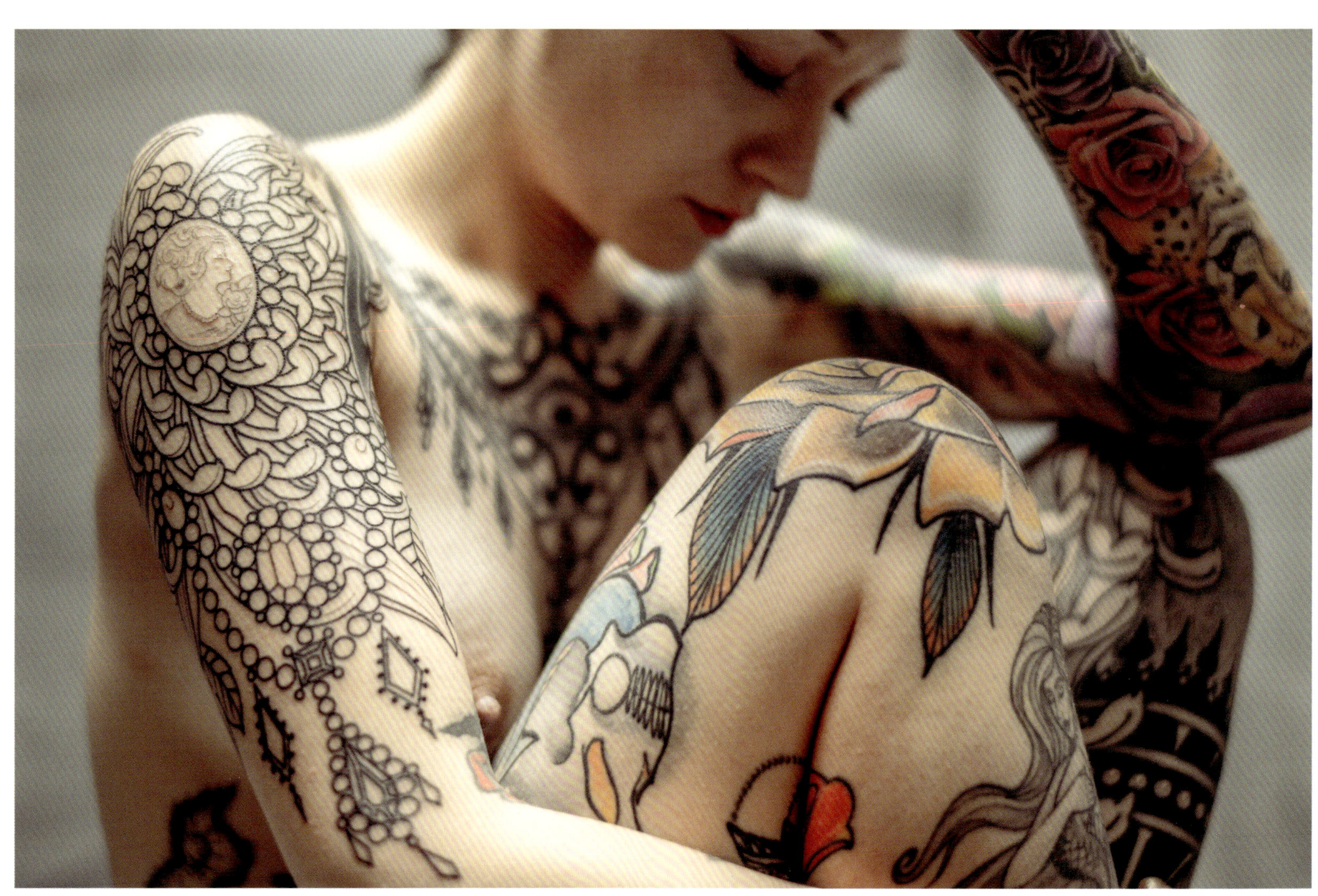

Pawelzik's work includes Wyble's decorative chest piece, leopard back, shin torch, and right-arm chrysanthemum.

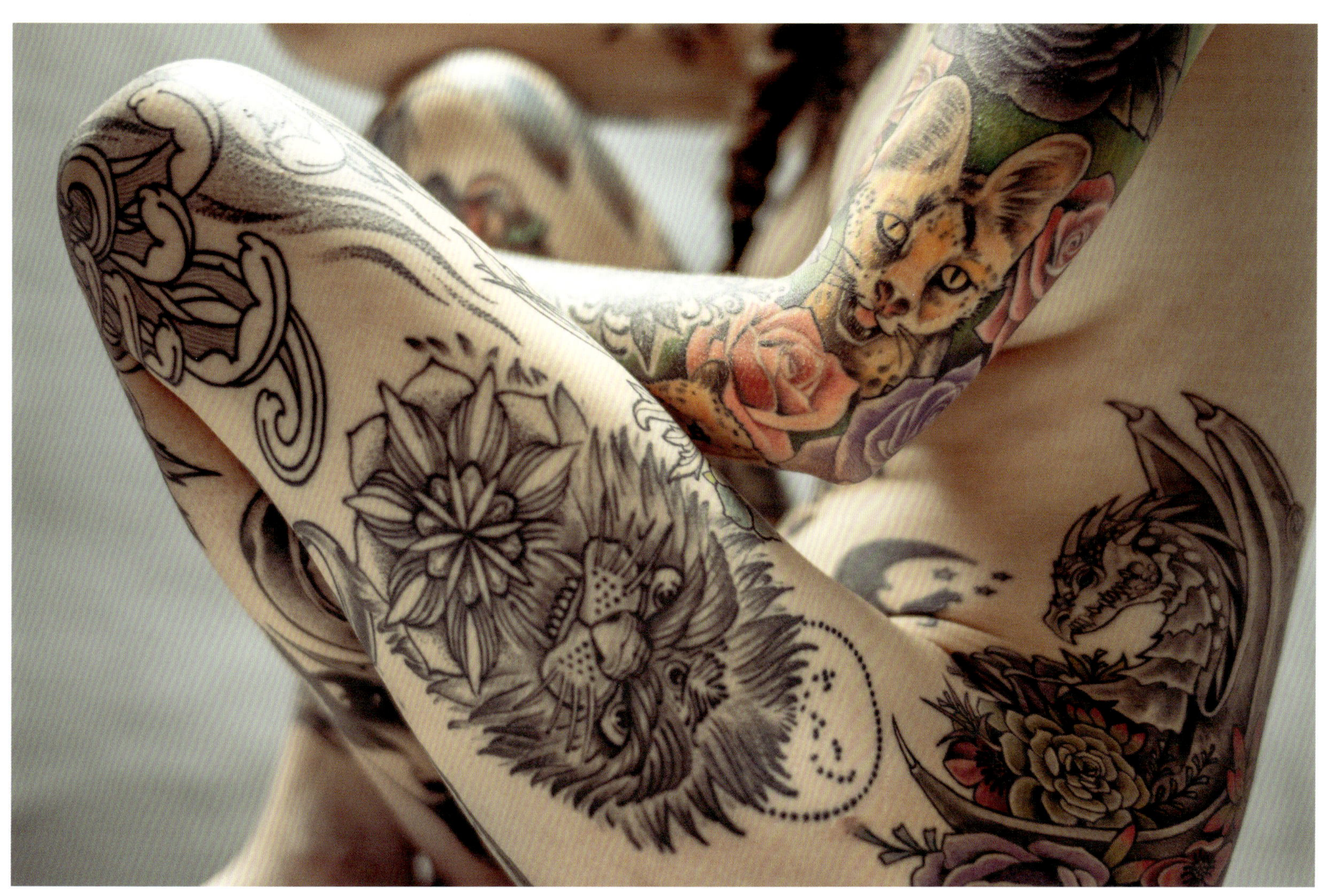

The mother of two's kitten sleeve on her left arm, dragon on her left hip, and mermaid piece with two babies were illustrated and tattooed by Arielle Rose Seltzer.

Professor Falcon tattooed Wyble's pinup peacock lady on her right inner thigh, and Ian Spong and John Kosco illustrated much of her legs and arms.

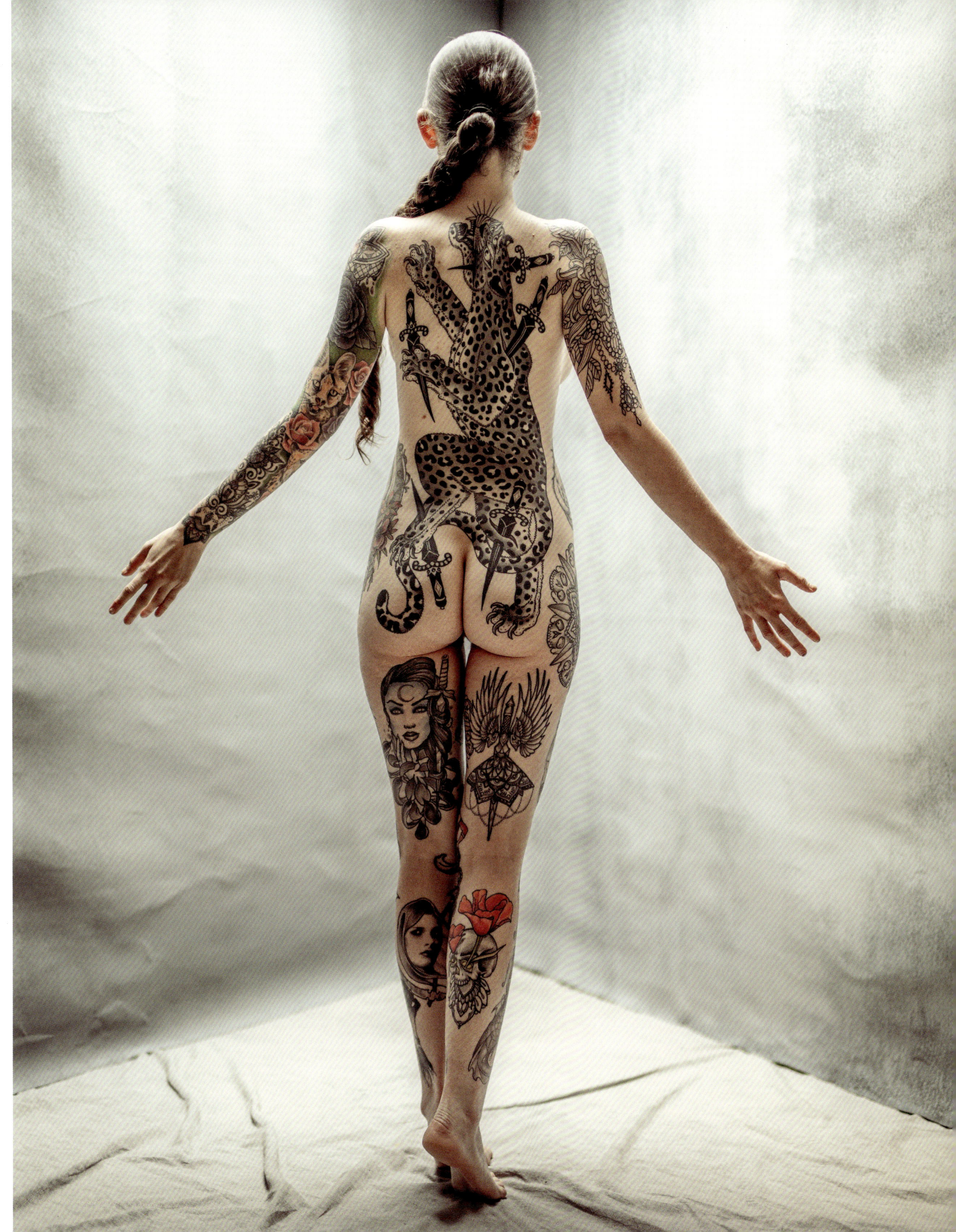

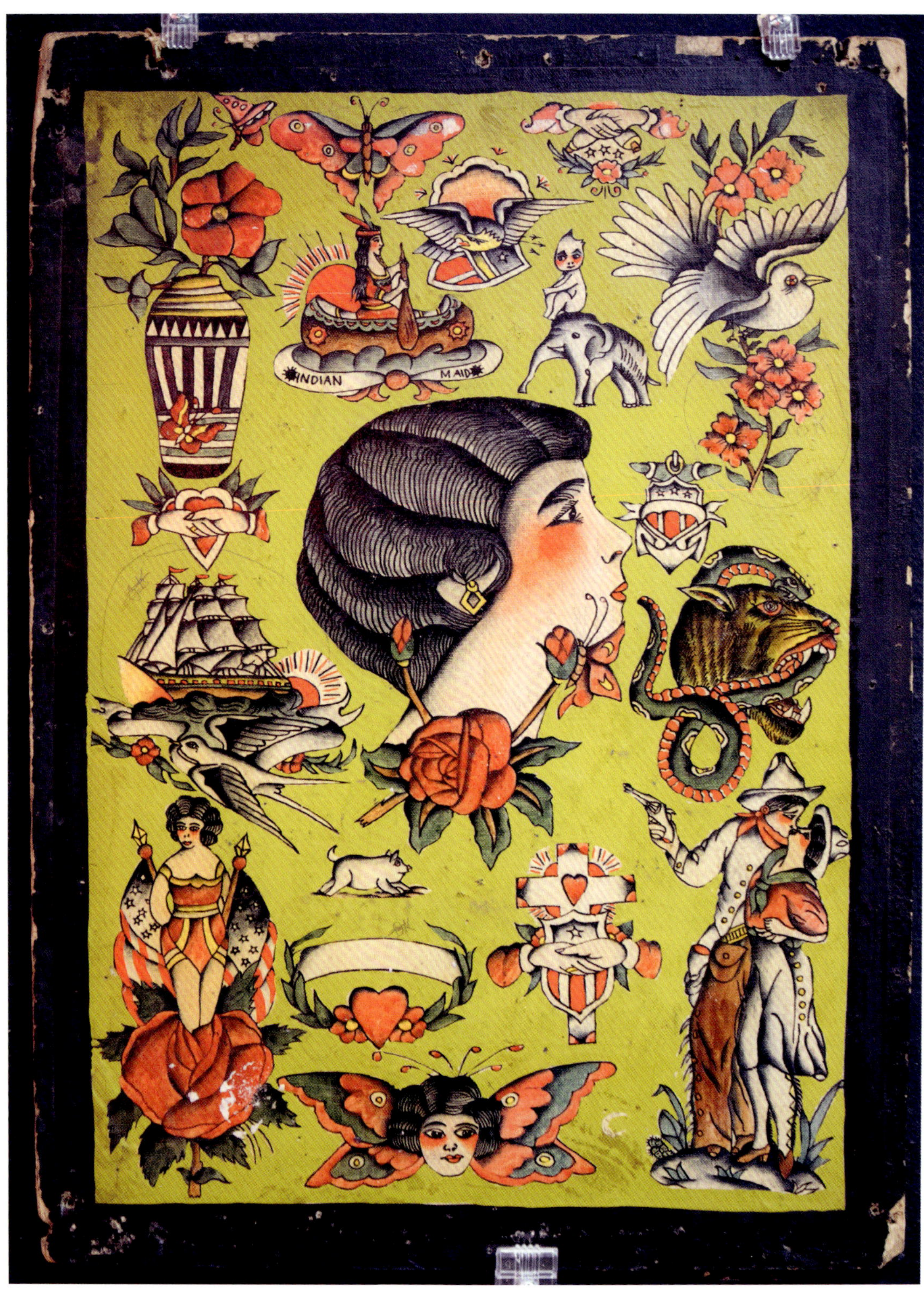

Painted tattoo flash by Charles "Red" Gibbons, early to mid-20th century.

RAY BRADBURY

EPILOGUE

It was almost midnight. The moon was high in the sky now. The Illustrated Man lay motionless. I had seen what there was to see. The stories were told; they were over and done.

There remained only that empty space upon the Illustrated Man's back, that area of jumbled colors and shapes.

Now, as I watched, the vague patch began to assemble itself, in slow dissolvings from one shape to another and still another. And at last a face formed itself there, a face that gazed out at me from the colored flesh, a face with a familiar nose and mouth, familiar eyes.

It was very hazy. I saw only enough of the Illustration to make me leap up. I stood there in the moonlight, afraid that the wind or the stars might move and wake the monstrous gallery at my feet. But he slept on, quietly.

The picture on his back showed the Illustrated Man himself, with his fingers about my neck, choking me to death. I didn't wait for it to become clear and sharp and a definite picture.

I ran down the road in the moonlight. I didn't look back. A small town lay ahead, dark and asleep. I knew that, long before morning, I would reach the town. . . .

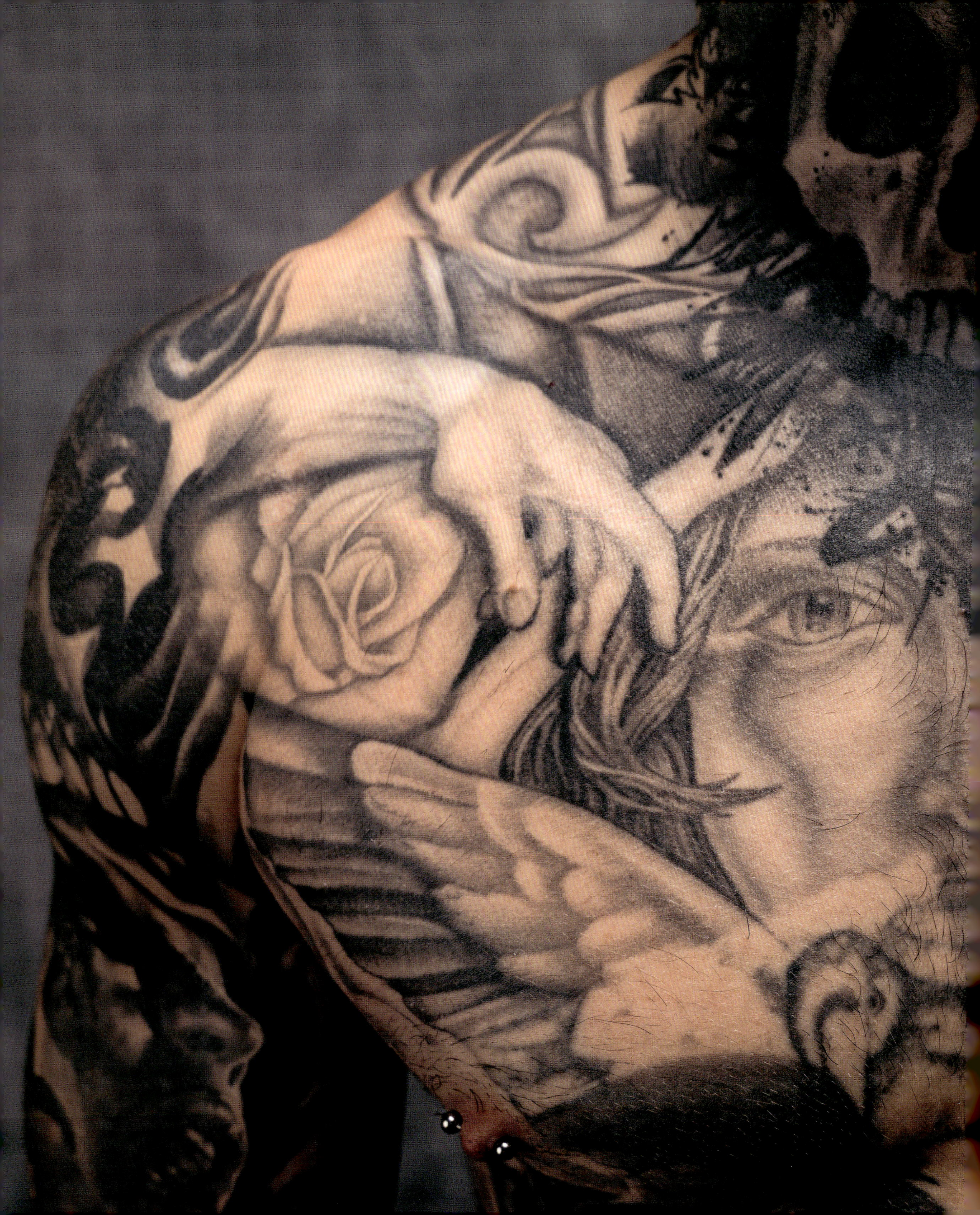

CONTRIBUTORS

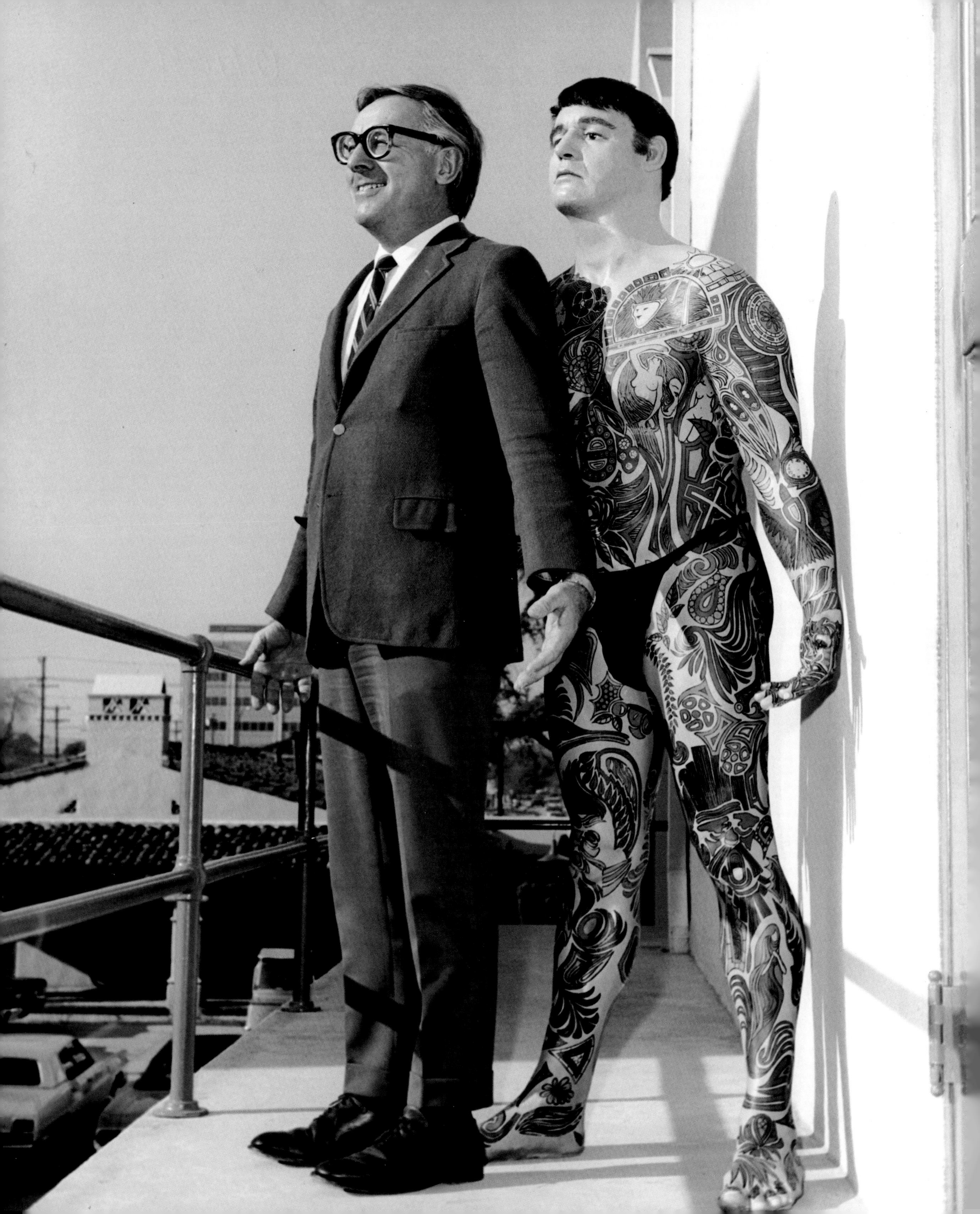

RAY BRADBURY

In a career that spanned more than seventy years, Ray Bradbury (1920–2012) inspired generations of readers in a wide variety of genres to dream, think, and create. A prolific author of more than four hundred published short stories and close to fifty books, as well as numerous poems, essays, plays, operas, teleplays, and screenplays, Bradbury is one of the most widely translated authors in the world and one of the most celebrated writers of our time. His enduring novels, novelized story cycles, and story collections include *The Martian Chronicles, The Illustrated Man, The Golden Apples of the Sun, Fahrenheit 451, The October Country, Dandelion Wine, A Medicine for Melancholy,* and *Something Wicked This Way Comes.* His stories received the O. Henry Prize for Short Fiction two consecutive years and continue to appear in hundreds of textbooks for new generations of readers.

The worlds of film and television have acknowledged Bradbury's mastery of storytelling as well. Numerous feature films have been based on his work, including *It Came from Outer Space, The Beast from 20,000 Fathoms, Fahrenheit 451, Something Wicked This Way Comes, The Wonderful Ice Cream Suit, A Sound of Thunder*, and *The Illustrated Man* starring Rod Steiger. He wrote for the theater, cinema, and TV, including the screenplay for John Huston's *Moby Dick* and the Academy Award–nominated 1962 animated short *Icarus Montgolfier Wright* based on his short story, and he won an Emmy for his screenplay for the TV movie *The Halloween Tree* in 1994 that was based on his novel.

The author also adapted sixty-five of his stories for the series *The Ray Bradbury Theater*, which garnered numerous awards for the production team. In addition, Bradbury's stories were adapted for the popular series *The Twilight Zone*, *Alfred Hitchcock Presents*, and *The Alfred Hitchcock Hour*.

Through his stories, books, and articles, Bradbury was one of the most prominent visionaries and inspirational figures of the Space Age. His dreams became the dreams of astronomers, astronauts, planetary scientists, and mainstream readers of all ages. The Apollo 15 crew named a crater on the Moon "Dandelion Crater" in 1971 after his 1957 novel, *Dandelion Wine*; an asteroid was designated "9766 Bradbury" when it was discovered in 1992; rocks on Mars were named "The Martian Chronicles" by the Spirit and Opportunity Mars rover scientific teams; a digital copy of *The Martian Chronicles* was aboard the Phoenix lander when it was sent to the high northern latitudes of Mars in 2007; and NASA named the Mars rover Curiosity's landing site "Bradbury Landing" in 2012. Though unofficial, popular lore has named one of the deepest chasms of Mars's "Grand Canyon," Valles Marineris, the "Bradbury Abyss."

Bradbury's numerous awards include the 2000 National Book Foundation Medal for Distinguished Contribution to American Letters, the 2004 National Medal of Arts presented by President George W. Bush, and the 2007 Pulitzer Prize Special Citation that recognized his "prolific and deeply influential" career.

Ray Bradbury's imagination emerged from his early life in small towns, having been born and raised in Waukegan, Illinois, and briefly living in Tucson, Arizona, during the height of the Great Depression. In 1934, the family moved west, landing in Los Angeles, where Bradbury attended high school and lived for the rest of his life. In 1947, he married Marguerite McClure, whom he met the year prior at a bookstore where she worked, and together they raised four daughters, who came to share their father's love of magic, movies, and imaginary worlds.

Page 232: Ray Bradbury poses with a plaster body used by the Warner Bros. makeup crew during the filming of *The Illustrated Man* starring Rod Steiger in 1968. Photo by Floyd McCarty / Warner Bros. Entertainment, Courtesy Albright Collection / The Center for Ray Bradbury Studies

Opposite: The author commissioned painter Louis Glanzman to do the cover art for the 1963 Bantam Pathfinder paperback edition of *The Illustrated Man*. Photo by Ray Hamilton

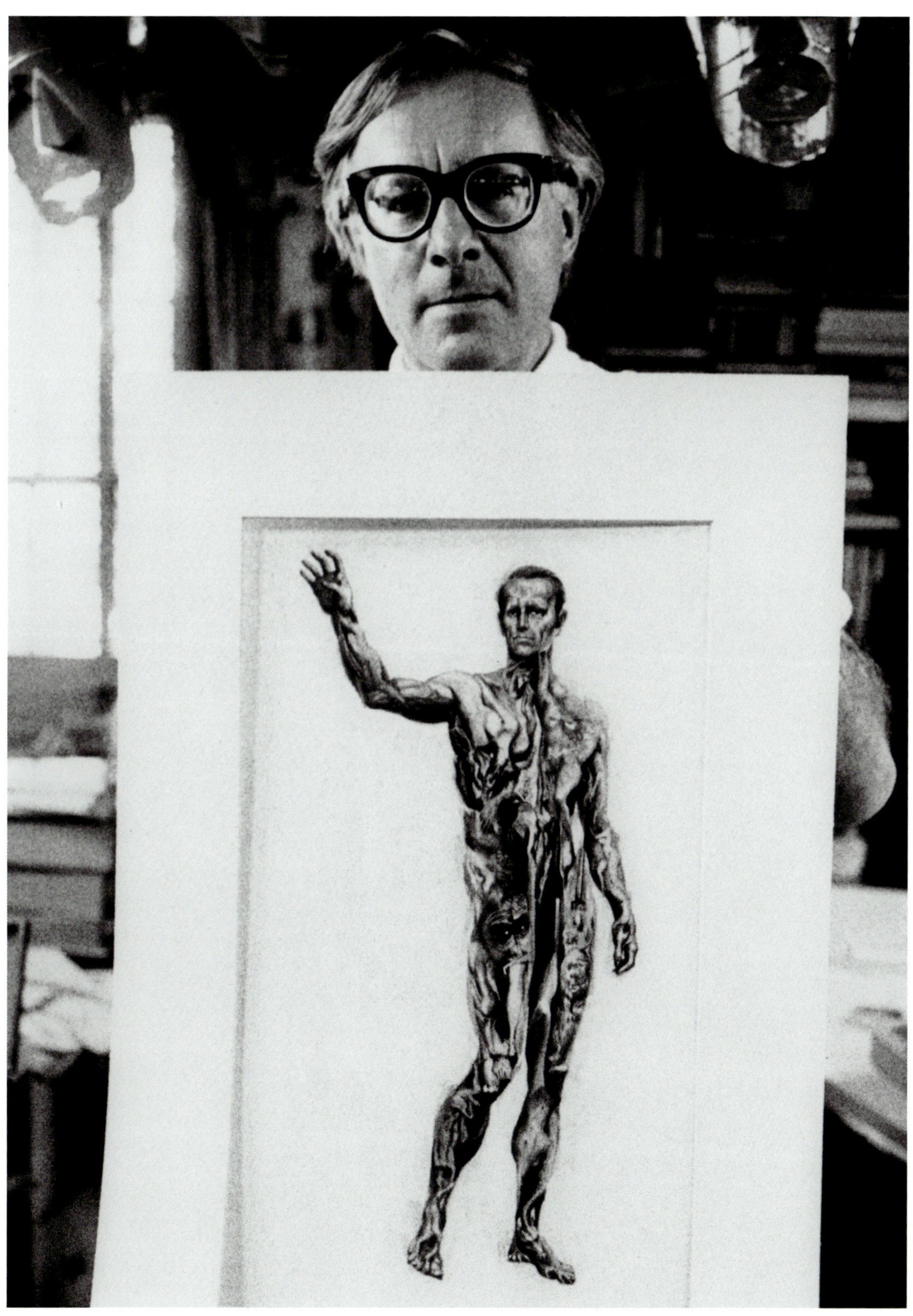

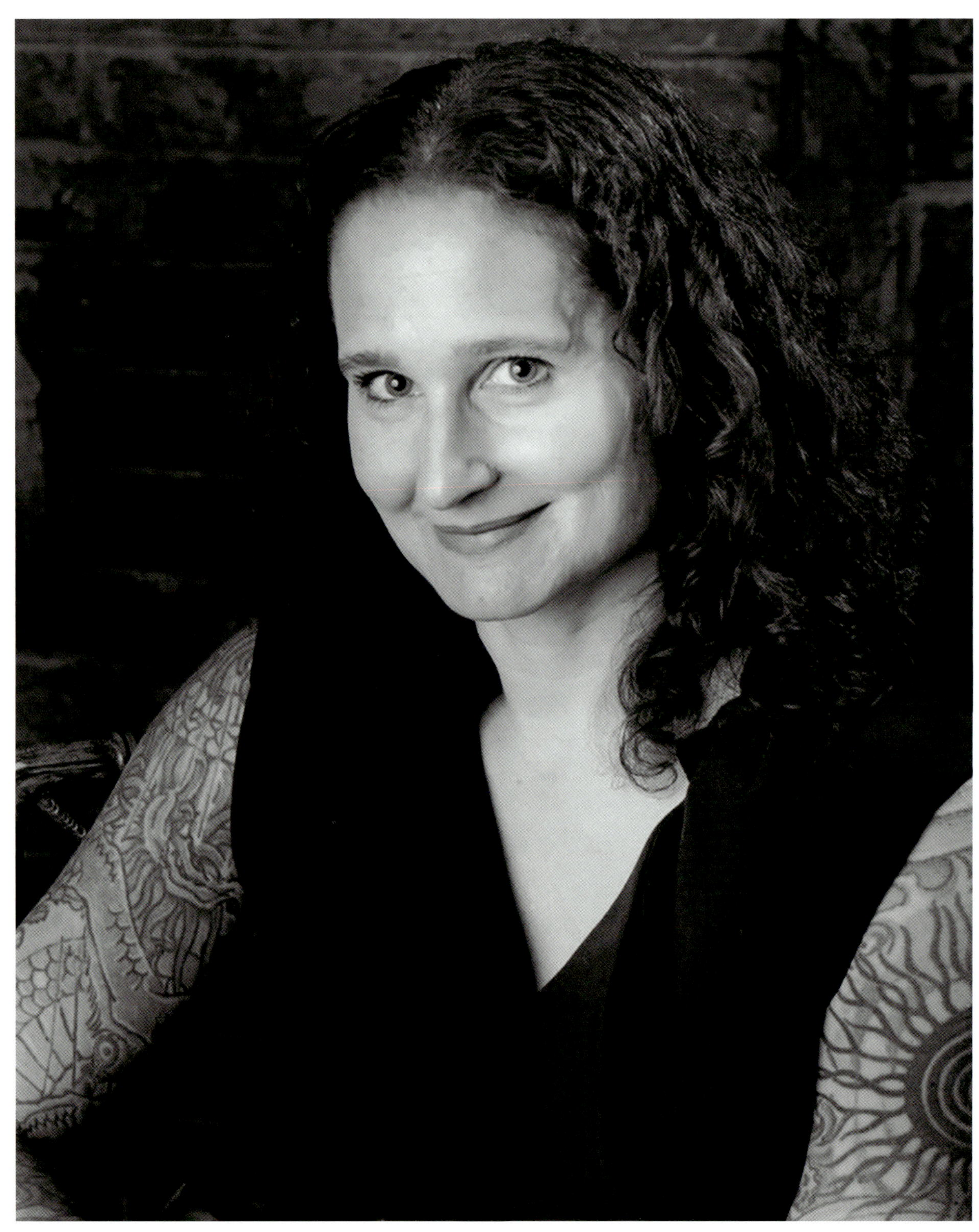

ANNA FELICITY FRIEDMAN

Interdisciplinary scholar Anna Felicity Friedman has been collecting tattoos and researching their history for nearly thirty years, starting in high school, when she wandered into the Peabody (now Peabody Essex) Museum's library seeking rare books that discussed sailor tattoos. She received her PhD from the University of Chicago in History of Culture with a dissertation on tattooing and writes widely about the subject, even launching the Center for Tattoo History and Culture, an educational and research foundation for academics, nontraditional scholars, and the general public.

Friedman's curatorial credits include the tattoo material in the 2009 Freaks and Flash exhibition at Intuit: The Center for Intuitive and Outsider Art, and her four-hundred-page definitive tome on the art practice, *The World Atlas of Tattoo* (Thames & Hudson and Yale University Press), which was released in 2015.

In addition to her passion for tattoos and body art, Friedman has spent considerable time lecturing and publishing on other topics. During her decade-long career as a college professor, she has taught at the University of Chicago and the Art Institute of Chicago in a variety of disciplines, including art history, liberal arts, social sciences, visual and critical studies, and performance art. Prior to teaching, she held curatorial roles at Chicago's Adler Planetarium, Museum of Contemporary Art, and the Field Museum. Recently Friedman returned to school to study data science, in part to advance tattoo-history research through digital humanities endeavors.

Sometimes she also plays bass in bands.

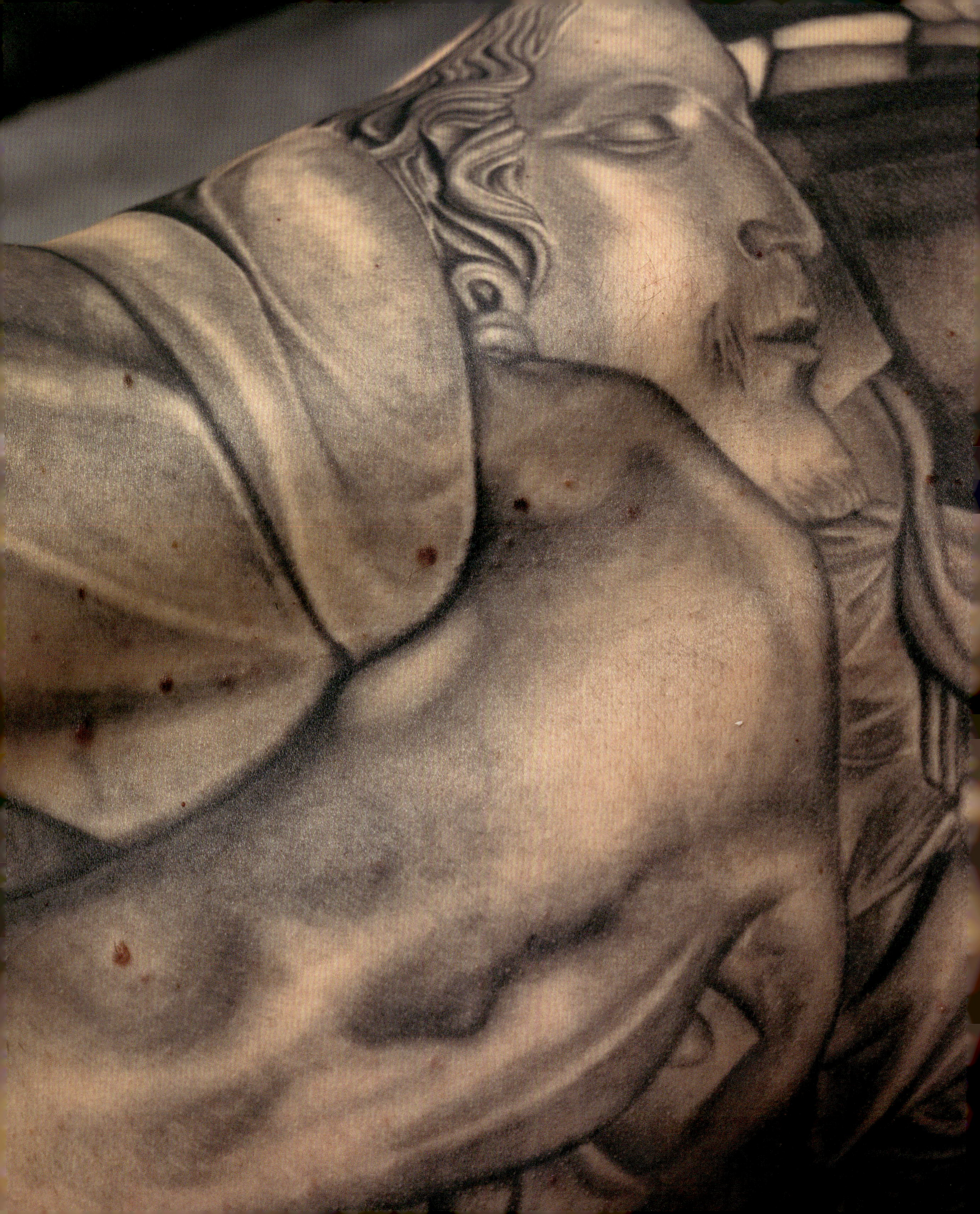

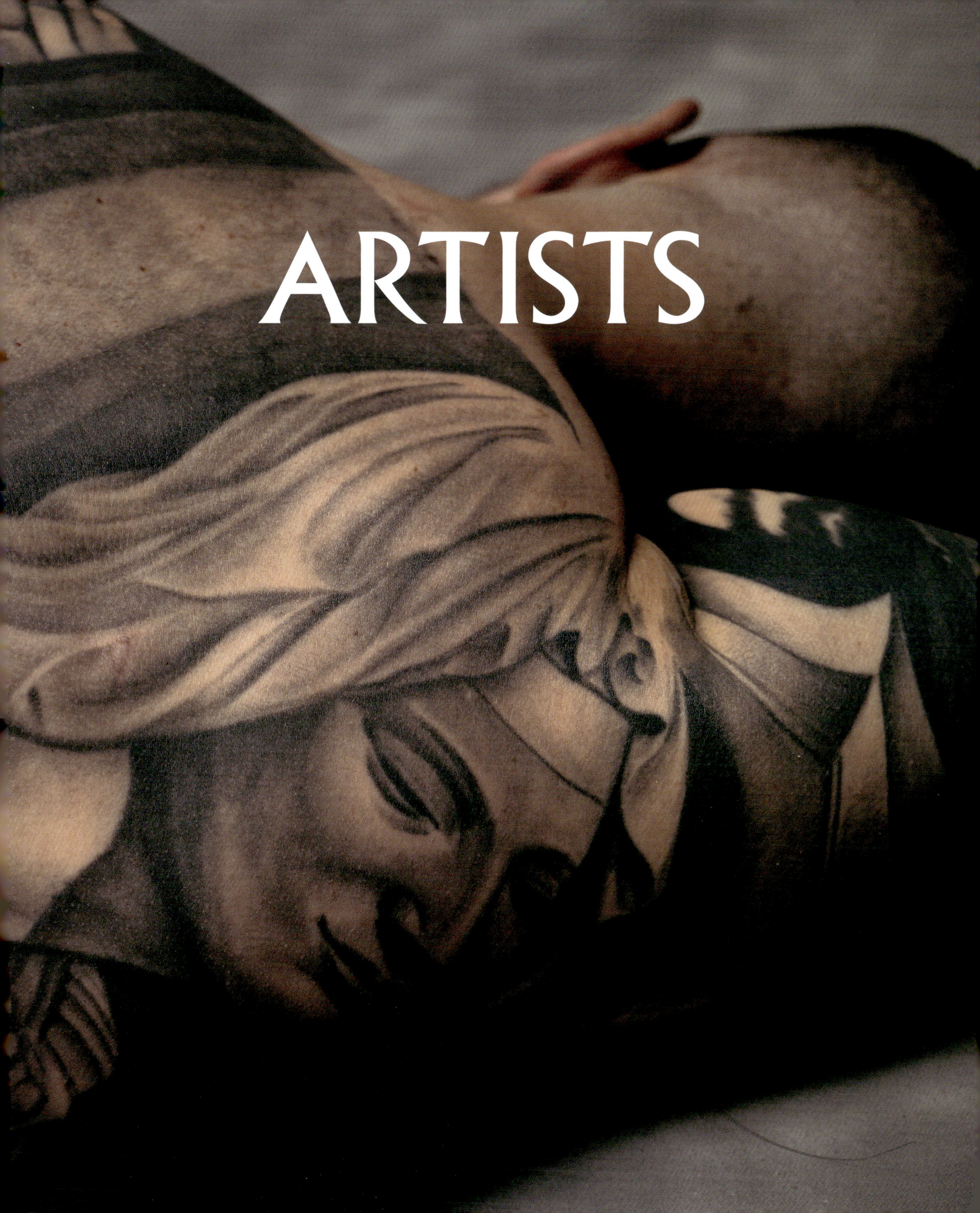

ARTISTS

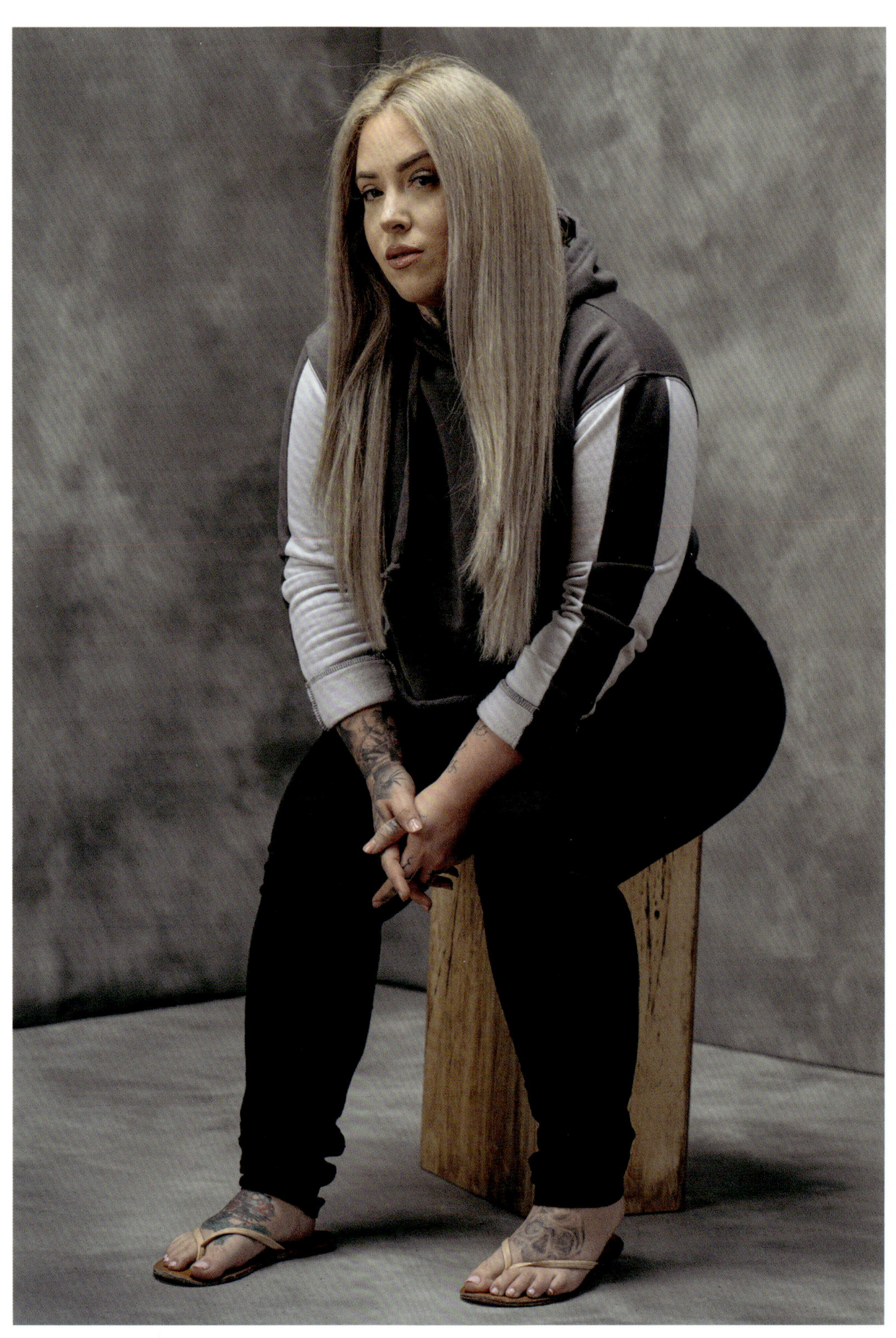

JESSA BIGELOW

Jessa Bigelow updates classic street-shop tattoos with a feminine touch. Her two signature types of imagery, while strikingly different, both focus on themes of the beautiful. She's developed her own take on the vintage lady-head tattoo, converting it from pinup eroticism to elegant timelessness. Rather than creating overtly sexual expressions on the faces of her women, she renders them as wistful, thoughtful. Roses and other flowers, more realistic than diagrammatic, romantically surround the visages. Strings of pearls and fronds of foliage add movement and breathe life into these characters.

Bigelow's other favored type of composition features geometric abstract flowers, rosettes, and mandalas. Sometimes she renders these more akin to engravings with crisp lines and clearly delineated shapes. Other times she employs dotwork and other shading techniques to soften some of the elements in the designs.

Bigelow's clear interest in classic mid-century flash motifs manifests in the smaller compositions she tends to ink. Compared to many other tattooers, she embraces working on individual, modest designs, understanding that size doesn't lessen psychological impact: "I'm in awe at the amount of confidence that even small tattoos can give people." A generalist, her portfolio reveals examples of tattoos in nearly every possible style: old school, black and grey, cartoon, calligraphy, watercolor, and blackwork. Regardless of genre, Bigelow appreciates the metamorphic impact her adornments have on customers: "I think a beautifully done, well-placed tattoo can completely transform a person and accentuate the fluidity and curvature of the body."

PAUL BOOTH

Father of the dark-surrealism genre of tattooing, Paul Booth exploded onto the 1990s New York tattoo scene offering a fresh take on black-and-grey style: haunting, morbid tattoos that pushed previous thematic boundaries of the art form into a sinister space. He innovated layered compositions by featuring webs of torn flesh that appear to offer glimpses of evils lurking beneath the skin. His morose themes have inspired countless other artists to create macabre designs.

At times merely gloomy or somber, much like the frightful imagery that wakes one up in the middle of the night, Booth's tattoos can range from dark clouds to terrifying demons. Gazing at many of his creations, a death-metal or hard-core-punk soundtrack pops into one's head. Angry eyes stare out from angular faces, pointed teeth are poised to devour anything that crosses their path, sharp claws appear to rip into skin, and swirls of murky ether leave one wondering what imagined awfulness they obscure. Although his tattoos may initially feel gruesome and ominous, they are also astonishingly beautiful in their impeccable draftsmanship that evokes Renaissance chiaroscuro.

Booth's early work tended to be brutally graphic, but his more recent tattoos exhibit a softer line quality that ties in to his regular endeavors with painting, settling into the skin with almost an aged-leather appearance. He appreciates that his tattoos probe the stygian depths of the soul and shape all who wear them: "Tattoo art is a transformative process, and I am grateful to play a role in that for my clients."

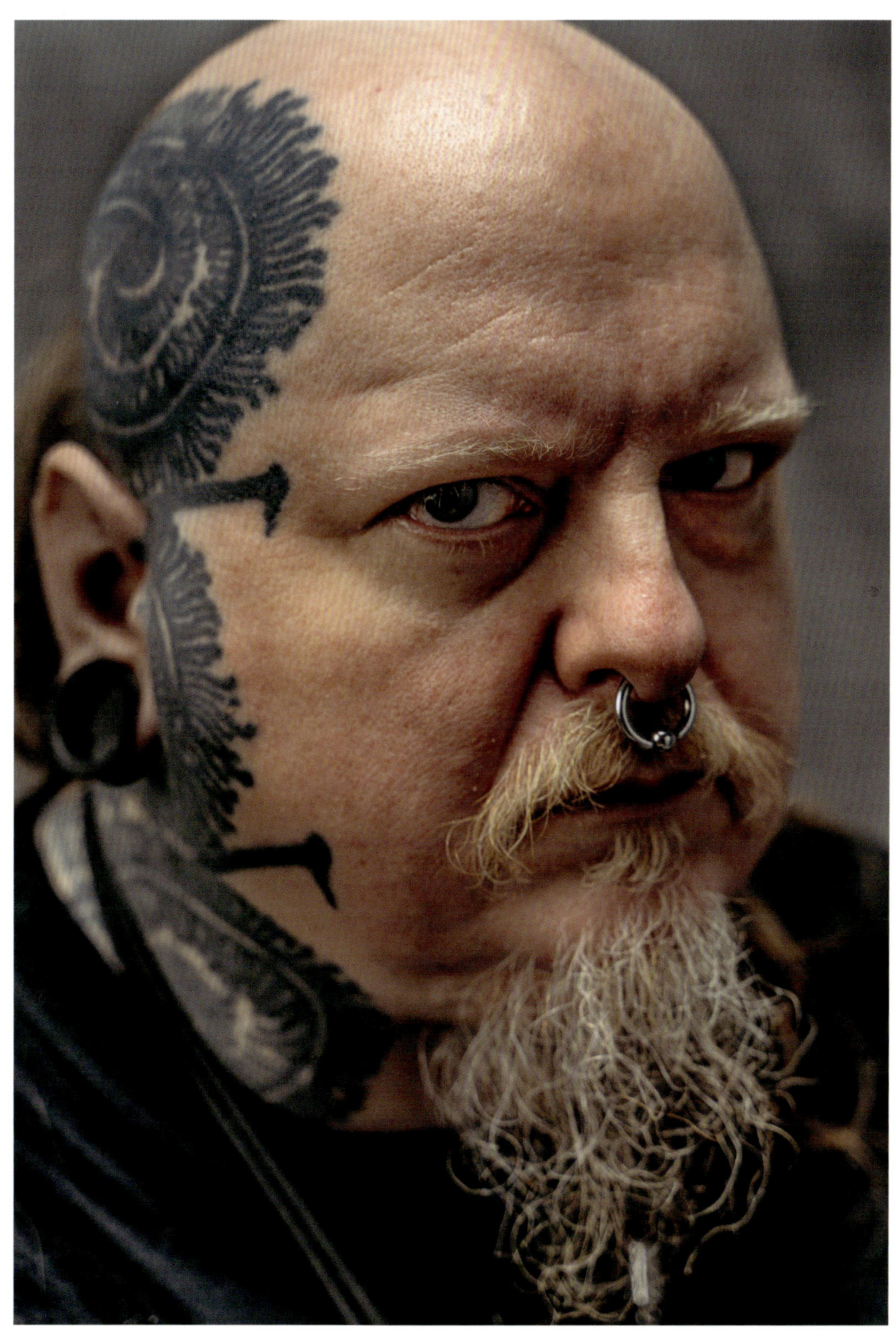

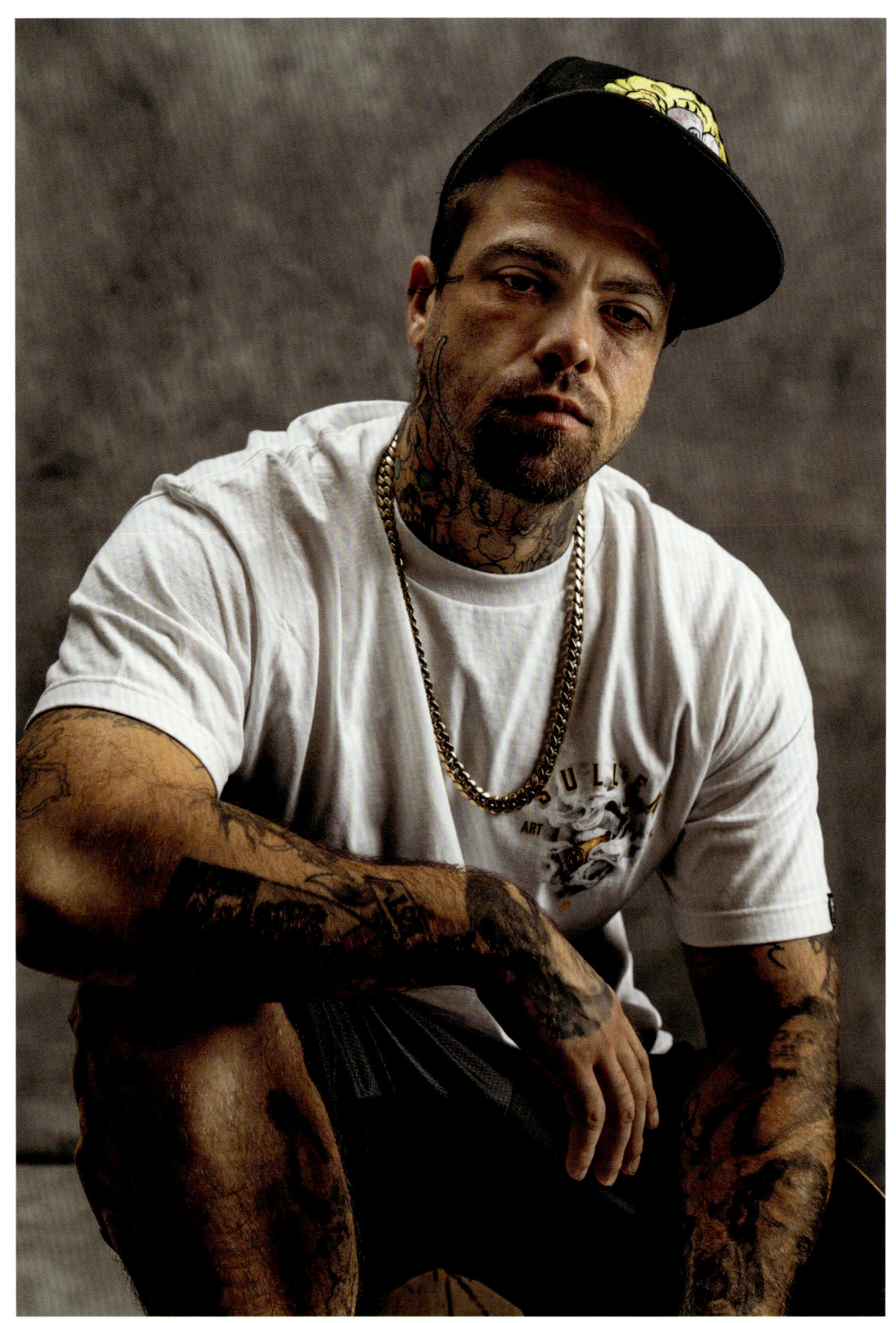
ART

STEVE BUTCHER

Hyperrealism defines Steve Butcher's exquisitely detailed tattoos of prominent personalities and iconic pop-culture moments. Looking through his portfolio is comparable to flipping through high-definition TV channels: a football player readies himself to tackle an opponent, an animal emerges from the jungle, an idol croons to a live rock concert crowd, a villain from a Hollywood movie prepares for battle.

People choose tattoos of their favorite actors, musicians, and sports stars to channel their talent, to internalize their power, and to vicariously experience their fame. Professional athletes, especially basketball players (Butcher also played and coached), might be his most requested tattoo. These figures exude mightiness, poised to jump or run off the skin. Droplets of sweat bead on their foreheads. Intense glares look for the ball in the distance.

Butcher's fine-art training in New Zealand, including evident knowledge about the evolution of realism and photorealism into hyperrealism, has made him remarkably skilled at using color to render flawless facsimiles of people, animals, and moments, whether the reference is a photograph or film still. His ability to render human skin so realistically in tattoos creates a fascinating interplay between a client's skin and the simulated one layered on top.

That Butcher relocated to Los Angeles makes sense given his clear love of how people and animals are channeled through media. Self-admittedly full of wanderlust, Butcher enjoys that his tattoos are in constant motion: "The most fulfilling part about my job is applying my art to people's skin and having them walk around the world showcasing it."

RYAN ASHLEY MALARKEY

Unabashedly ladylike, Ryan Ashley Malarkey's jewelry tattoos adorn bodies of all genders. Her eternal accessories seem purposefully timeless, not subject to the whims of fashion, an interesting counterpoint to her formal training at New York's Fashion Institute of Technology. Malarkey aims to preserve "tiny little ornate pieces of history left at thrift stores and forgotten about." She's taken an essentially black-and-grey style of tattooing and repurposed it to represent trompe l'oeil jewelry that appears to hover over the body's surface. Silver, pewter, and gold metalwork twines over skin. In feats of virtual lapidary, she styles vibrant amethysts, sapphires, rubies, and garnets into stunning arrangements that seem to dangle and dance.

Her intricate and often enormous work — cuffs, foot pieces, epaulettes, breastplates, and more — would be difficult to achieve with traditional metalwork, as they often spread across wide expanses of her clients' bodies, or hang from impossible locations. Her favorite design to ink, the wristlet tattoo, typifies this: "I love creating these exaggerated bracelet-type of tattoos that crawl from the hand up the wrist and create a beautifully flowing feminine silhouette." Sometimes Malarkey's creations incorporate a central image — a portrait or cameo — festooned with elaborate frames of filigree, chains, and precious gems. More recently, she has been expanding her repertoire while still incorporating her trademark accessories: animals and mythological creatures bejeweled with decorations, more abstract compositions of metalwork-like curvilinear forms, and sprays of flowers intermingled with brooches, pendants, and chains.

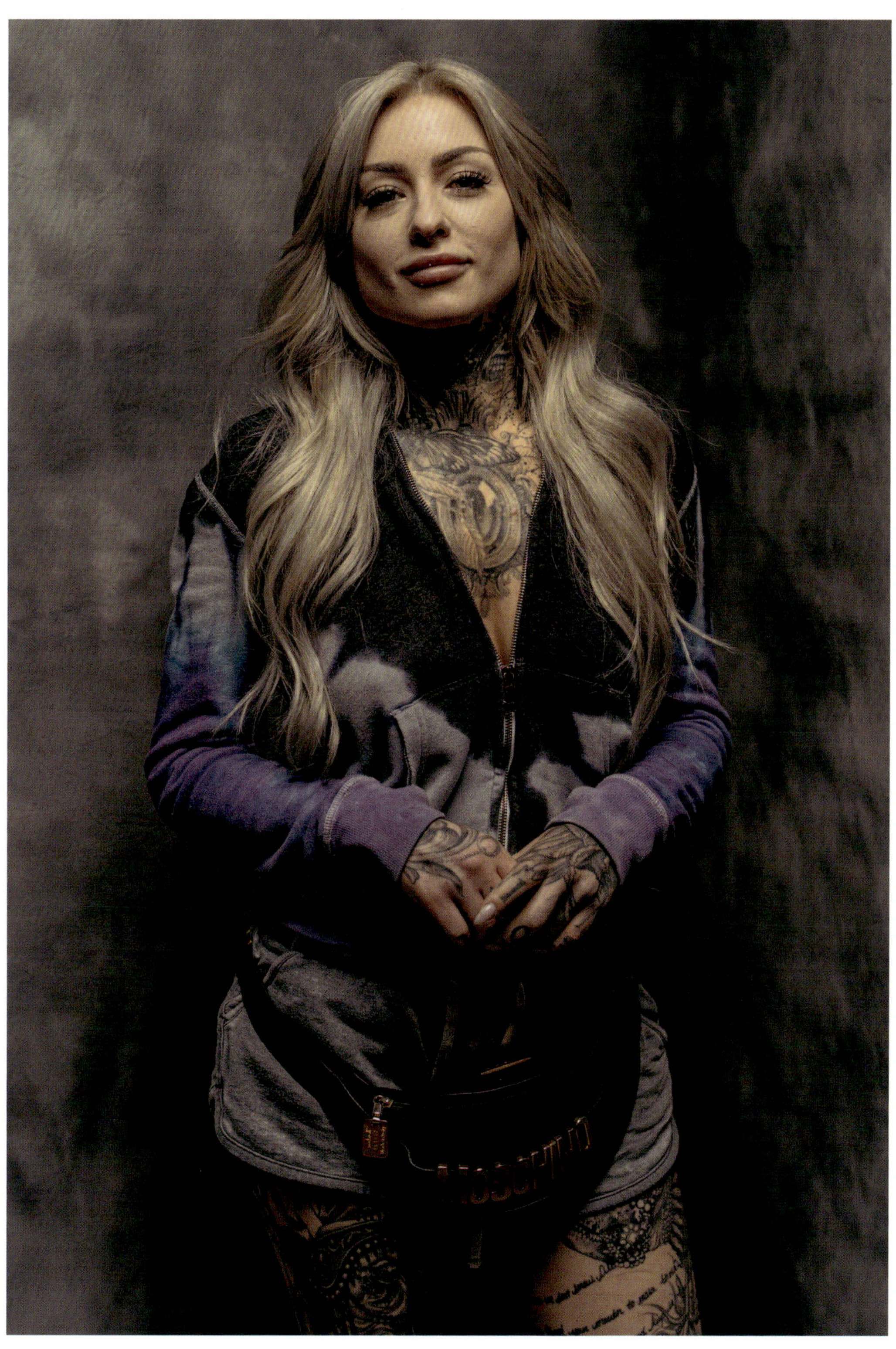

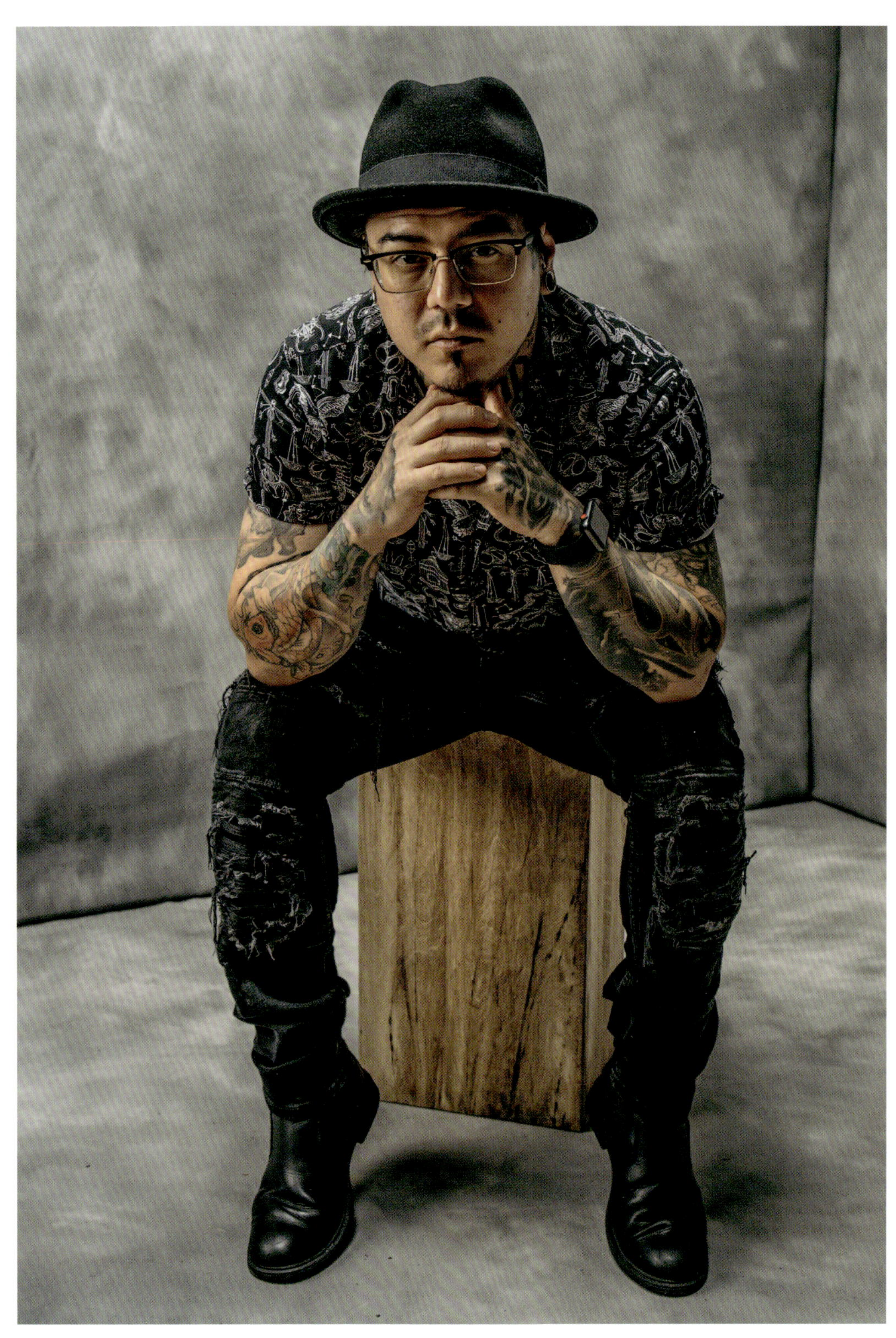

YOMICO MORENO

At first glance, Yomico Moreno's dreamy, realistic tattoos serve as a mirror of the world, but a closer look reveals painterly touches that blur the boundary between reality and fantasy, evoking faded snapshots that have been vibrantly retouched. His meticulous, large-scale tattoos are often tinged with the dark and macabre — sometimes the stuff of nightmares and other times that of vivid acid trips — that hearken to his roots in Venezuela's black-and-grey tattoo community and his mentorship by the venerable Paul Booth of the dark Surrealism tattoo movement.

Nature dominates many of Moreno's creations: writhing sea creatures churning the ocean and animals on the hunt appearing to jump from the skin out of jungles of vegetation. Other compositions reference his interest in Surrealism, though he also has done impressive portraits of loved ones or celebrities and scenes from popular media that showcase painstaking draftsmanship. Regardless of the subject matter, Moreno's interest in creating narratives comes through: "I like creating concepts that tell a story... that it is understood without... it being explained."

Moreno's commitment to both accurately rendering a vision and telling stories with tattoos manifests in his preferred placement for tattoos: the forearm, which doesn't tend to distort over time and is also easily displayed to others. "You can wake up and see your tattoo on your forearm, and it will be positive if you love it or negative if you hate it. This is why I think it is visually powerful."

ANDY PHO

Tattooing for only a few years, art school–trained Andy Pho has quickly developed a following for his meticulously drawn monochromatic tattoos that resemble pencil and charcoal drawings. The influence of his half-brother and mentor, Robert, a renowned industry veteran, is unmistakable: Both of their styles, although realistic, possess a dreamy quality, more soft and velvety than that of other artists working in the genre. The two met after their father's death and bonded over tattoos.

Of Cambodian descent, Andy wears a black-and-grey bodysuit of Angkorian elements that brother Robert tattooed, and Andy's own clients sometimes request similar Asian-fusion imagery. But more often his clients request living things — elegant lions, tigers, birds, flowers — to grace their bodies. "Weird and quirky" subjects comprise his favorite imagery to tattoo: jumbled bits of Las Vegas assembled into a sleeve, gruesome skulls costumed or mixed with arcana, and bits and pieces of maps and travel souvenirs are developed into one cohesive piece.

Andy considers tattoos to be more than just the visual material inked into skin: "Whether you just get it for fun, there's a deeper meaning behind it, or because you're just practice for your friend . . . the tattoos themselves, how and why you got it, speak about who you are more so than the imagery and words of the actual tattoos."

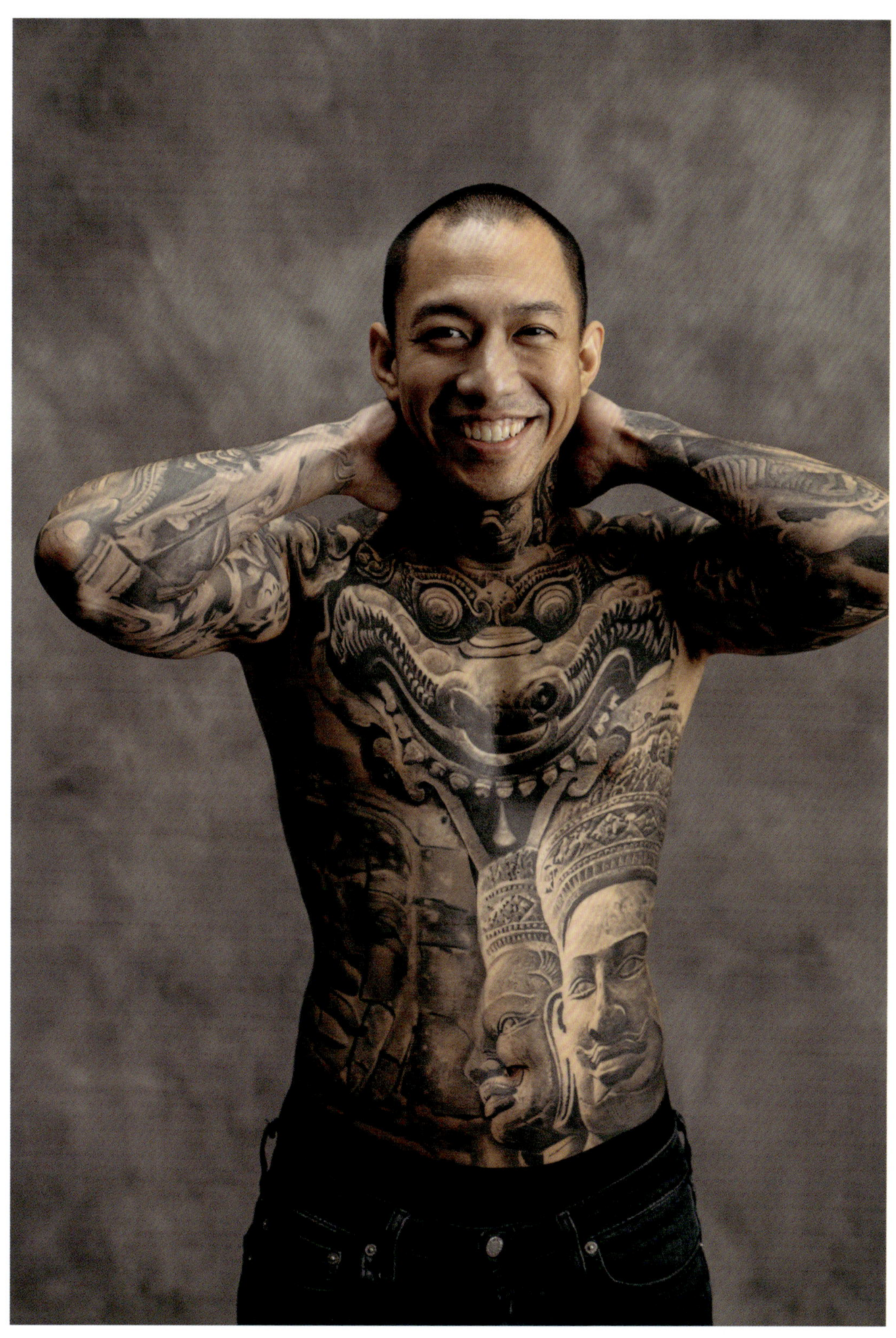

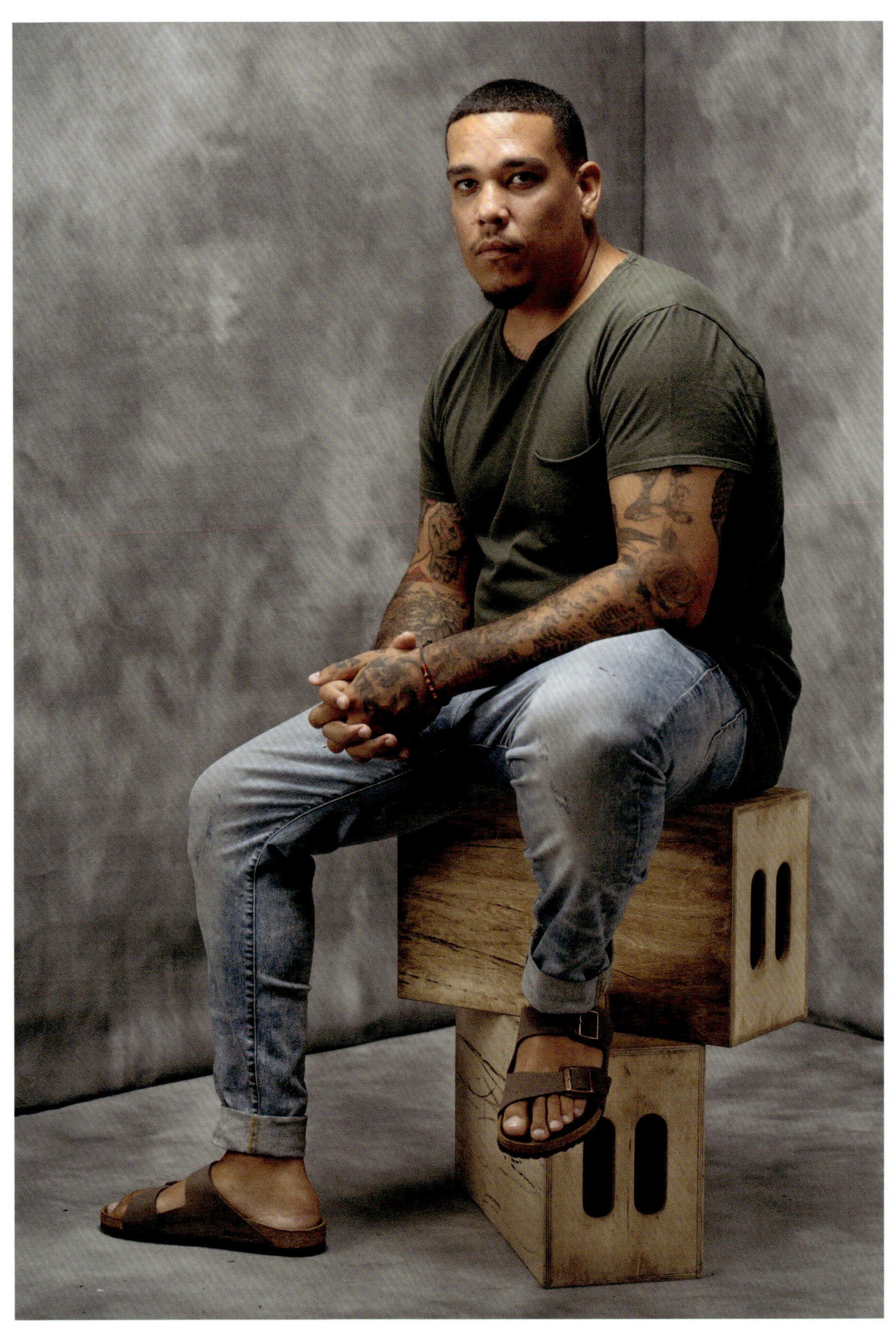

TEEJ POOLE

Like Southern Gothic novels come to life, TeeJ Poole's fastidious black-and-grey tattooing expresses grim emotion. The despair so often present in that literary genre is manifested in the faces of the somber characters the native North Carolinian inks. His work includes bent metal street signs placed over a woman's pierced visage, faces that seem to melt away as if made of wax, a giant eye reflecting storm clouds and lightning, and waves below a lighthouse forming into a menacing Neptune. A dark romanticism marks his less overtly warped creations: pouty women shrouded in darkness, cherished celebrities staring fiercely. Uncanny touches in many of his compositions deepen their complexity and craft cryptic tales that seem painful or even phantasmagorical: "I enjoy designing something that tells a story with no words, and something that can create an emotion with no sound." Occasional exceptions to his gritty portfolio offer a glimpse at tenderness: a smiling portrait, two animals touching noses, a pet memento.

His Southern background and recent inspirational travels to Spain and Ireland shape his visual take on a sinister magical realism that meshes with the grotesque present in so much European tattooing today. Even Poole's floral compositions seem funereal, while his wildlife appears as if caught in a hunter's night cam. That designs of decay and anguish could elate adds an appropriately ironic twist to what Poole desires most: "creating a smile on my client's face for a lifetime."

DUKE RILEY

Maritime blood runs through Duke Riley's body and heavily informs his tattoos, which resemble endearingly quirky scrimshaw. His coastal Massachusetts upbringing cultivated his interest in "the designs and motifs of various cultures… that came together working on ships," and led him to mix seafaring arts with elements from 17th-century maps, early American embroidery, and whittling. Stylized dolphin-like creatures lift their heads above water, waves appear as if carved and printed from wood-engraved blocks, and ornate cartouches frame miniature oceanic scenes.

An activist at heart, tattooing is one way Riley expresses his concerns about "the social, political, and environmental dilemmas of maritime communities, often using history as a lens to understand them." The ship itself, in his tattoos, serves as a metaphor for our global urban culture in which we are all sailors. And in one inked composition, a lobster is immortalized as if on a trophy plaque, presaging a future when the creature might be extinct from overfishing.

Cryptic tales are common in his portfolio. Four birds lift an island with a lighthouse by ropes, seeming to urgently need to transport it to somewhere crucial. Tiny houses float amid waves while an airplane surveils from above, leaving viewers wondering about the fate of their inhabitants. Riley waxes philosophical about how his craft is connected to nautical oral history, and how he treasures them both: "In those idle times, people would also share information and ideas and pass stories along. Working in a tattoo shop has this same element of storytelling."

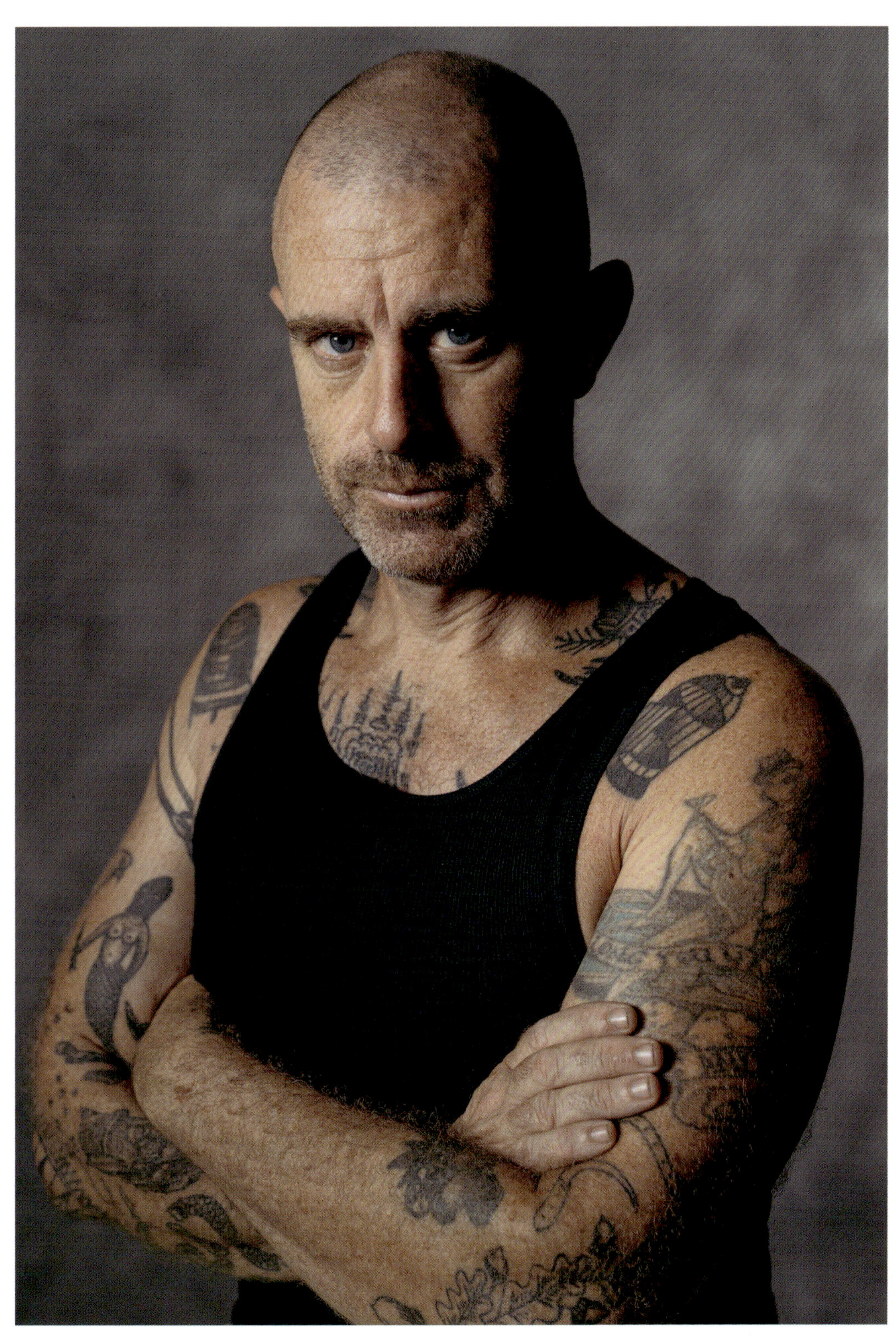

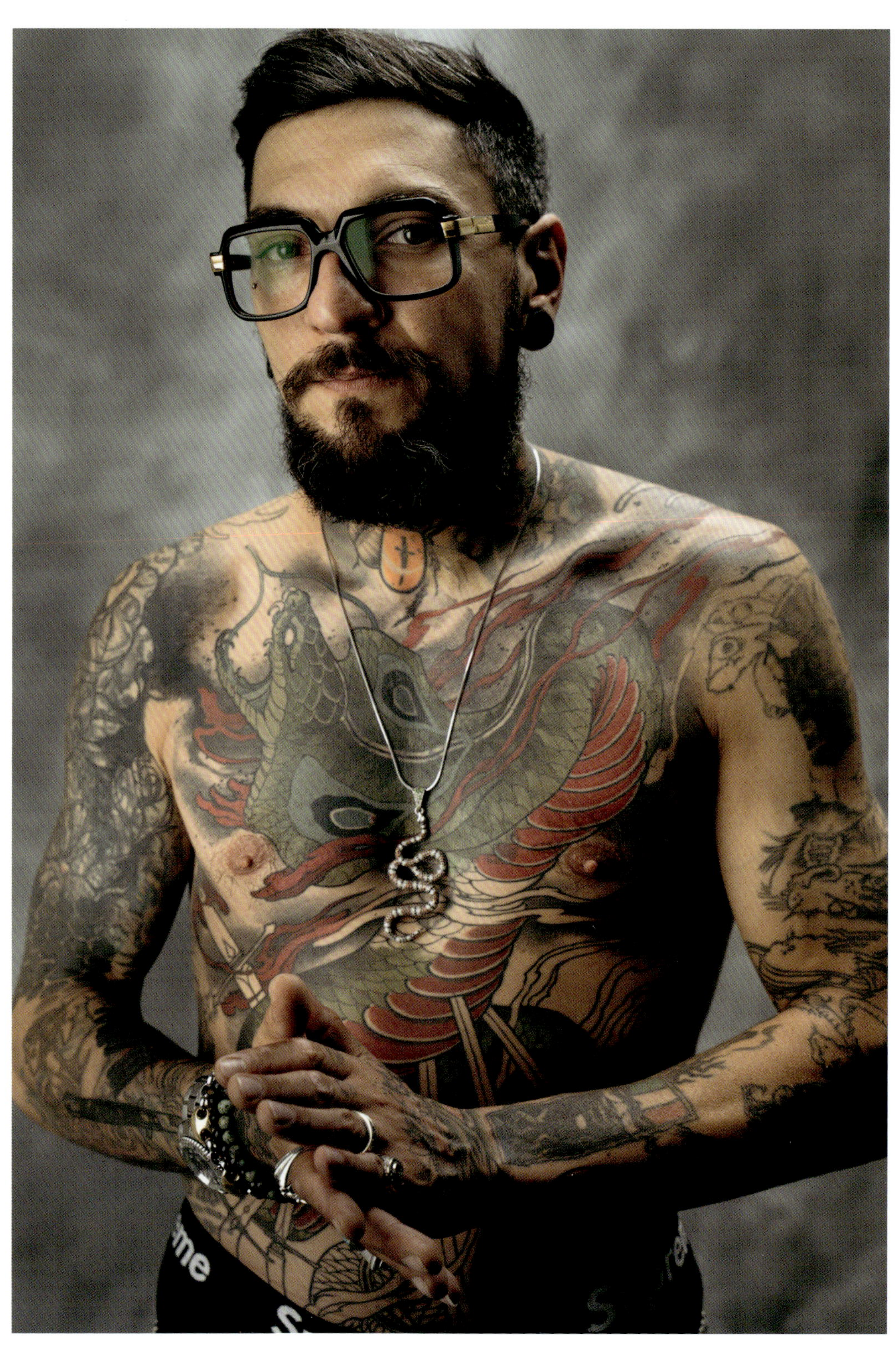

DJ TAMBE

Most elite tattooers focus on one particular style, but DJ Tambe, who says, "My mind thinks art, constantly," has become an expert in three. His original foray into tattooing, hand-poking peers as a high-school dropout, informs his skillful black-and-grey realism, while his adolescent years of perusing *Lowrider* magazine clearly inform this monochrome work. A somber tone and heavy shading characterize his portraits, and his nature and animal scenes, generally depicted during nocturnal hours, are moody as well.

Tambe's color work, on the other hand, exudes Technicolor emotion, often joyful and sometimes ferocious, venturing into surrealist territory and referencing his early interest in drawing both comics and graffiti. A tiger's paw juts out from an arm while its head twists back toward the shoulder, a giraffe with an oversized head licks a lollipop, a bull snorts clouds of pumpkin-like smoke out its nostrils. The vibrancy of his colored tattoos may be due in part to Tambe's upbringing in Las Vegas, a city awash in neon and over-saturated visual stimulation. Techniques such as foreshortening, distortion, and exaggerated poses also grant some of his tattoos a quirky air.

Asian-influenced themes comprise a third style for Tambe. Traditional motifs such as dragons, demons, and peonies merge with his signature style to create unique syntheses, a process he revels in: "[Tattooing] is a way to express yourself without having to say a word. It's a way to get what's inside my head out for others to see. Even when it's a client's idea that I'm designing, I try to stamp my style into every piece I do."

TATU BABY

One of only a few Latinas to join the elite ranks of tattooers in the world, self-taught Tatu Baby initially faced challenges breaking into the business as a teenager because of her age and gender, despite her clear artistic skills. Dedicated to her role as a visionary artistic conduit for her customers, she channels their stories into the tattoos she inks: "My favorite thing to do is to create meaningful custom tattoos for my clients. Most of the time, clients don't have a great imagination and tend to want tattoos that are in style, but I like to push their limits and design things specifically related to their story."

Although Tatu Baby does impressive black-and-grey portrait work and photo-realism, her iridescent color work is what makes her unique. The palette she employs reveals her Miami roots: vivid aquamarine, magenta, tangerine, lime, heliotrope, and more reference the city's architecture and flora. She also uses shading to create an eerie but striking effect. Skulls glow with blue light, amber faces exude deeper warmth, and chartreuse highlights hint at otherworldliness. One of her signature tattoos is her Technicolor makeover of La Calavera Catrina, the iconic Day of the Dead female skeleton so popular among black-and-grey enthusiasts. Through this reworking, she's shifted this icon from sultry-yet-sinister sexiness to vibrant power, no longer stuck in the realm of the dead but brought forth into the light. Tatu Baby's spirit is evident in all of her creations, and that's part of her attraction to the craft: "Each piece an artist tattoos carries a piece of that artist's soul in it."

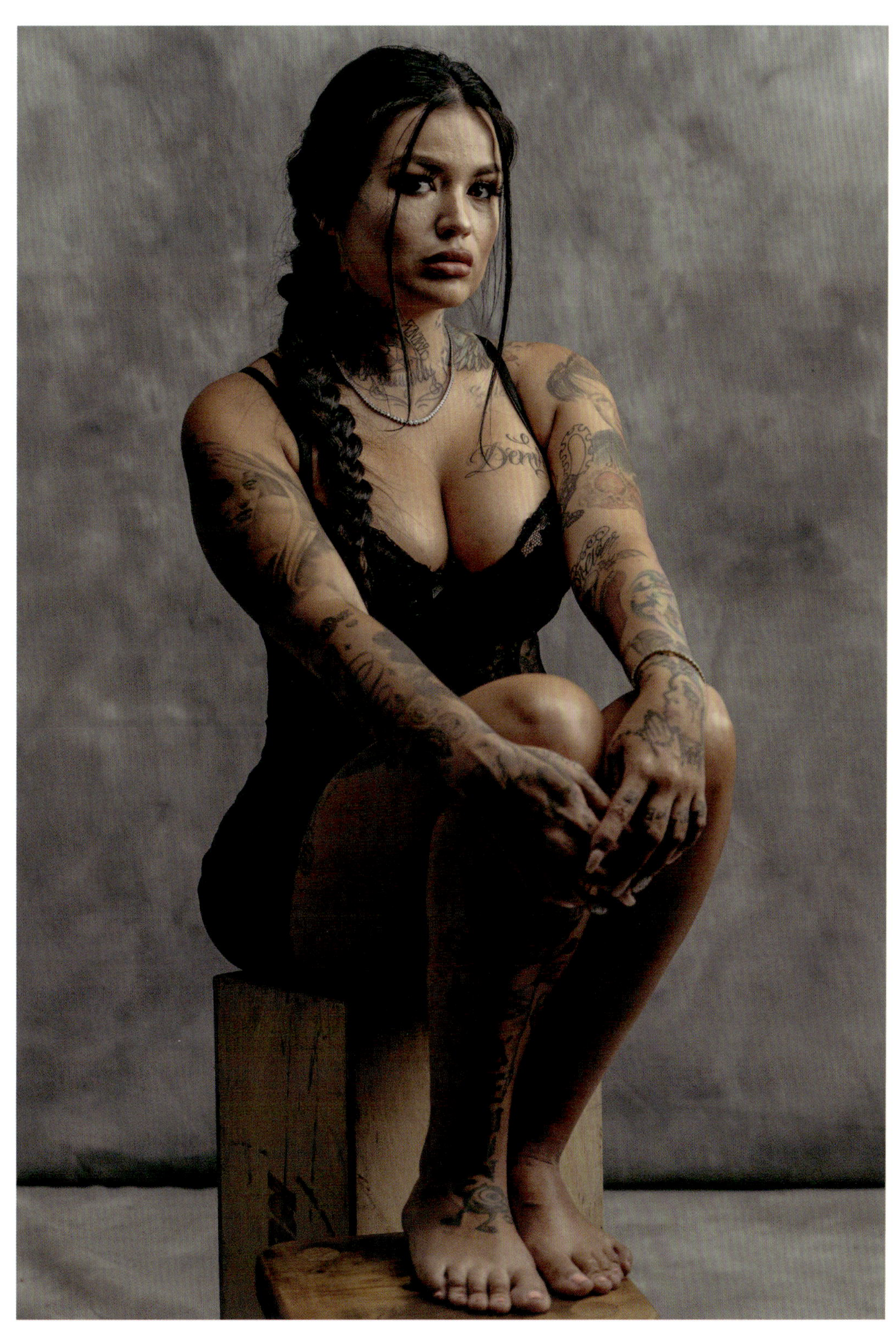

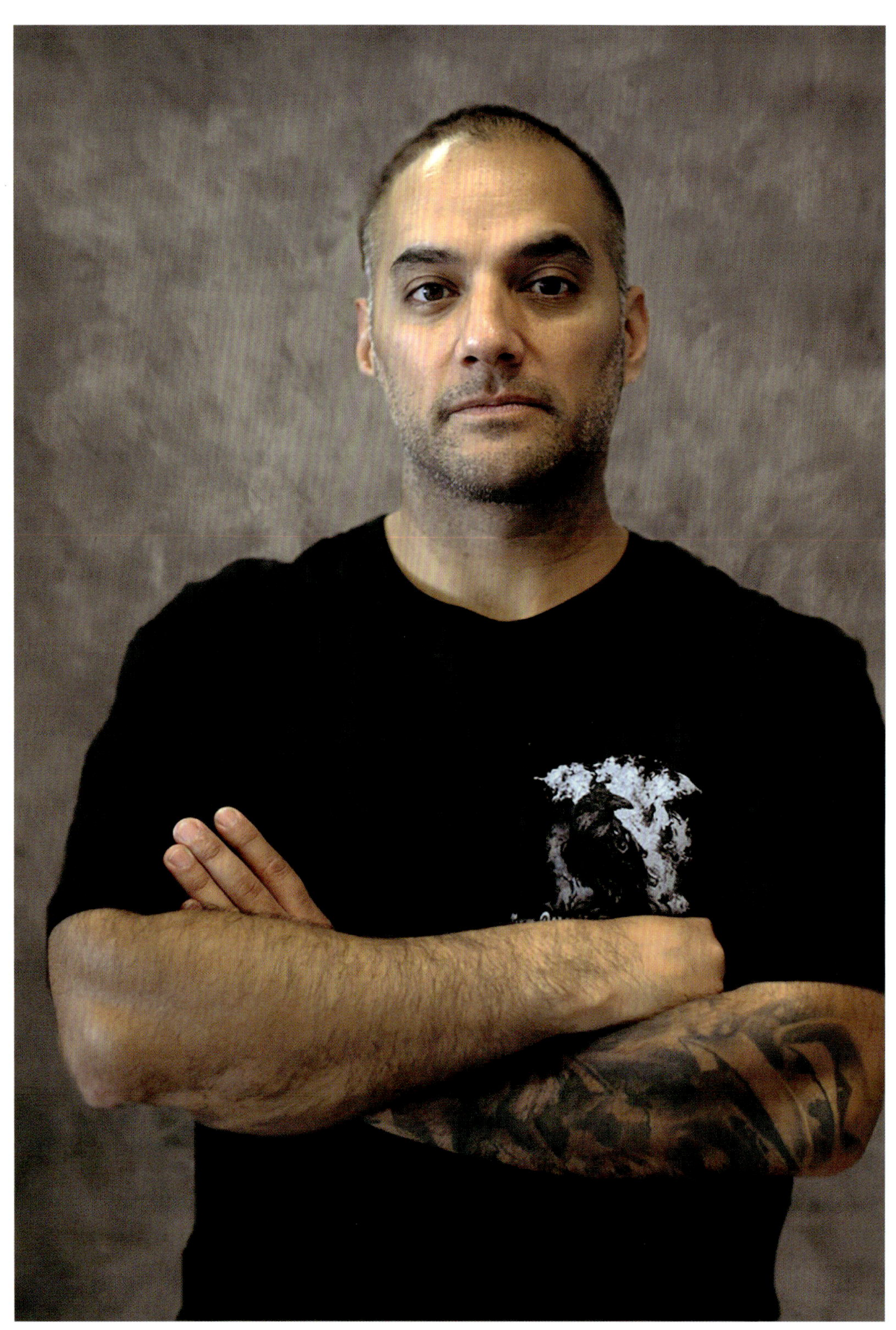

CARLOS TORRES

Baroque meets the 21st century in the elegant, breathtaking monochrome tattoos of Los Angeles native Carlos Torres. His gentle personality, rare in the tattoo world, shines through in his work. Largely absent from his oeuvre are the macabre, gruesome images that dominate the portfolios of so many black-and-grey artists. Instead, graceful bodies relax into skin, and mythical creatures prance. Describing himself as "a bit of a dreamer," Torres celebrates the gorgeous, noting, "I don't think you can go wrong with beautiful subject matter."

His work features few hard lines; details emerge from ethereal washes of tones of grey. Ornate flourishes like filigree or wispy clouds accent and overlay central motifs of fantasy or romance. A blindfolded woman, attired in the most delicate lace, plays an opulently carved wooden harp. A Viking maiden with intricately braided hair confronts a scaly Quetzalcoatl. A skeleton jester with an embroidered hat with bells pulls at spiderwebs with gnarled fingers.

Even when more somber or violent in tone, Torres' tattoos are infused with a tenderness that makes any hint of sadness seem eerily delightful. Extremely diligent in the research he does for custom tattoos, Torres maintains a library of source photography and has even had props made to use as reference. He enjoys painting from life in addition to tattooing, apparent in his masterpieces that appear to be created by brushes: "Backpieces are my favorite, because they are about as close as you can get to a traditional painting on canvas."

DMITRY TROSHIN

The methodically detailed tattoos of Dmitry Troshin conjure monochrome lithographs, pen-and-ink drawings, and mezzotints. An expert at rendering highlights and shadows, the Russian artist bestows a luminous quality on his tattoos, turning skin into a shiny surface. It's hard to believe he started his career as a self-taught artist, learning from videos and Internet research in his native Moscow. After settling into his current style, Troshin now tattoos only with his one preferred tool—a three-round liner, which achieves the effect of a fine-point pen. His particularness extends to preferences about where on the body he tattoos, as he feels the quality of the skin in certain places, specifically the forearm and chest, lends itself to his precise style: "It's like having 4K TV versus HD TV."

Troshin's imagery and subject matter vary widely, largely dictated by his customers' general desires that he then adapts: "The best way to work on a tattoo project for me is to get a story or idea from my client, and then have the freedom to think of a composition and overall feeling of the project." Portraits of loved ones mingle with celebrities. Gritty urban settings showcase flawlessly rendered automobiles and architecture. Religious scenes exalt the glory of the divine. Sinewy bodies flex each carefully sculpted, Michelangelo-like muscle. Anatomical, mechanical, and scientific drawings reinforce his interest in precision. Although conceptually dissimilar, Troshin's utterly masterful draftsmanship ties all of this diverse imagery together into an identifiable corpus of work.

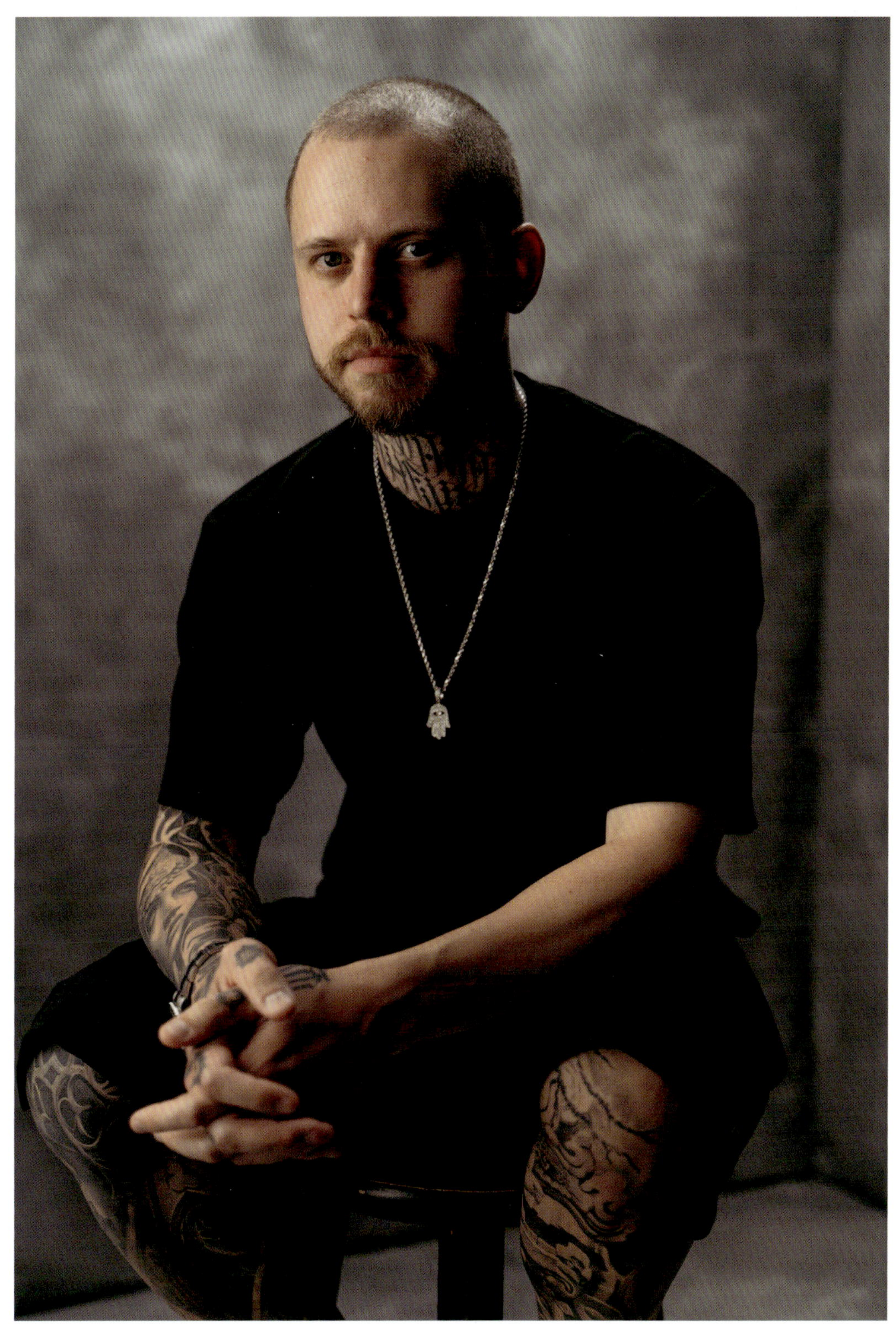

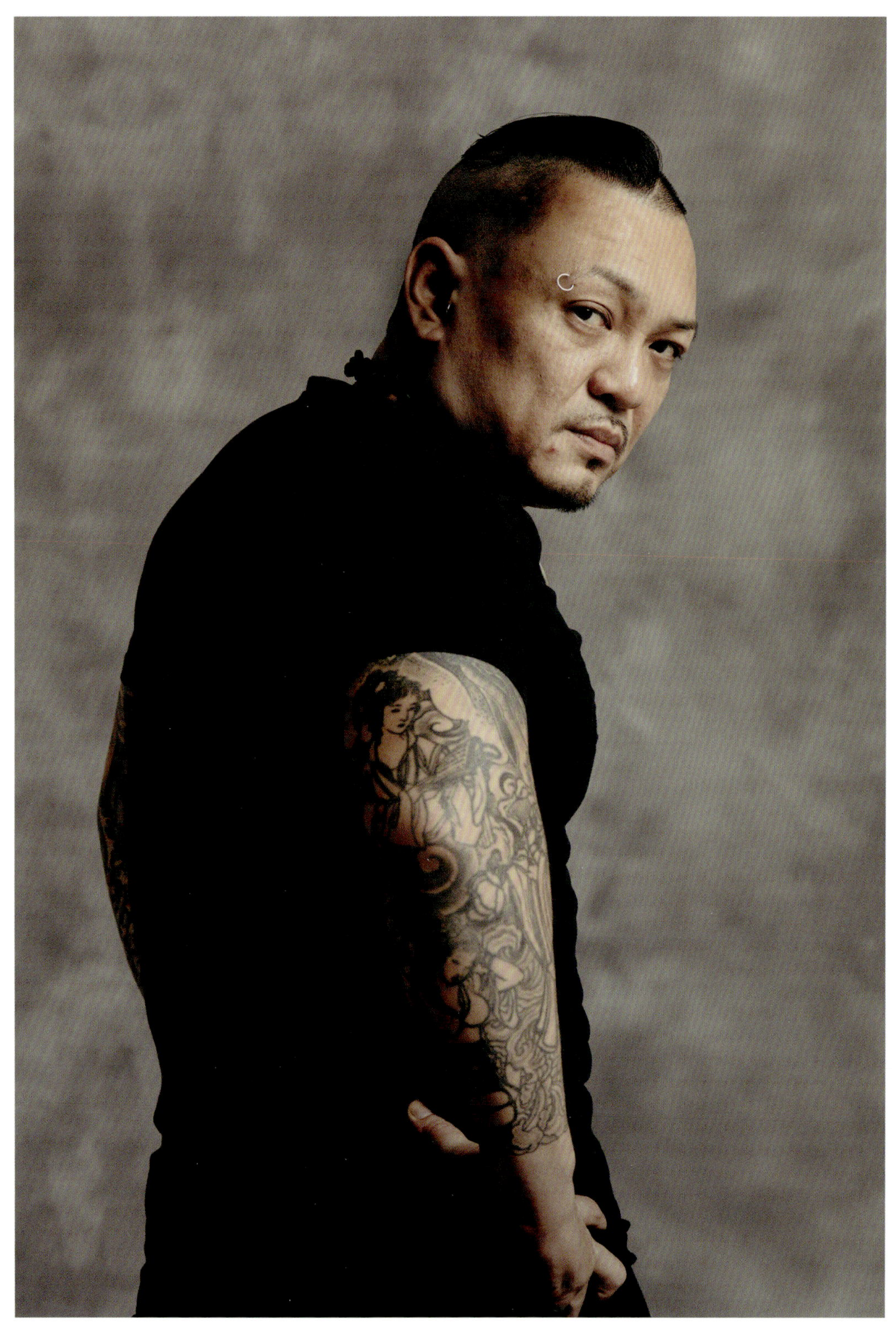

JESS YEN (HORIYEN)

Spanning multiple cultures, Jess Yen expertly inks New School realism–influenced oriental designs, traditional Japanese hand-tattooed *tebori*, and contemporary black and grey, as well as fusions of the genres. His alternate tattoo name, Horiyen, references the tradition of Japanese tattoo master-apprentice families where *horis* (master artists) pass down knowledge to others, who gain the right to use the honorific title. Committed to do the same, Yen has passed on his knowledge, through rigorous training, to the next generation of tattoo virtuosos to follow in his footsteps. For Yen, tattooing is more than just an image, it breathes the client's story to life: "When I use the needle and ink to create art on skin, the art becomes a living thing."

That he essentially speaks three different tattoo languages and fluidly switches among them makes sense given his origins in Taiwan, a cross-roads of cultures through its status as a historical base for Pacific maritime traders and its subjection to numerous colonial takeovers.

Yen's brilliance may be best appreciated in some of his full-body backpieces that intermingle his various styles. A vibrant Chinese dragon, straight out of a New Year's procession, dances across a back, glowing with supersaturated color, while the overall composition of the piece respects the traditional framework of a Japanese bodysuit. A samurai and the severed heads of his victims, instead of being rendered in the traditional stylized way that references Ukiyo-e prints, come to life in black-and-grey detail with fiercely emotional faces together amid floating coral-colored cherry blossoms, aesthetically true to the *tebori* tradition.

POPO ZHANG

That Popo Zhang studied oil painting in art school makes sense. His lustrous color photo-realism glows as if crafted with layers of paint, referencing Renaissance masters' glazing and scumbling to create depth and vitality in the image. At the same time, his black-and-grey work astounds with its near-perfect photographic mimicry. Sometimes he transforms the photos his clients bring him into optical illusions of sorts: adding three-dimensional touches that make the original source image appear to come alive on the skin, from a smiling starlet or a ferocious jungle animal to a cooing new baby or a menacing evil hero.

Portraits of loved ones and celebrities comprise the bulk of Zhang's recent work. Each face he tattoos is practically indistinguishable from the original except for the canvas on which the image lies — a skill that has garnered him numerous awards in the industry. Human faces are among the hardest images to replicate, but Zhang skillfully crafts his tattooed versions into special mementoes of affection and admiration. Born in China, he appreciates how his art can interact with the world, not be confined behind walls: "Most artists have an untouchable piece of work in a museum, but [my] clients display art in real life and show my work everywhere they go."

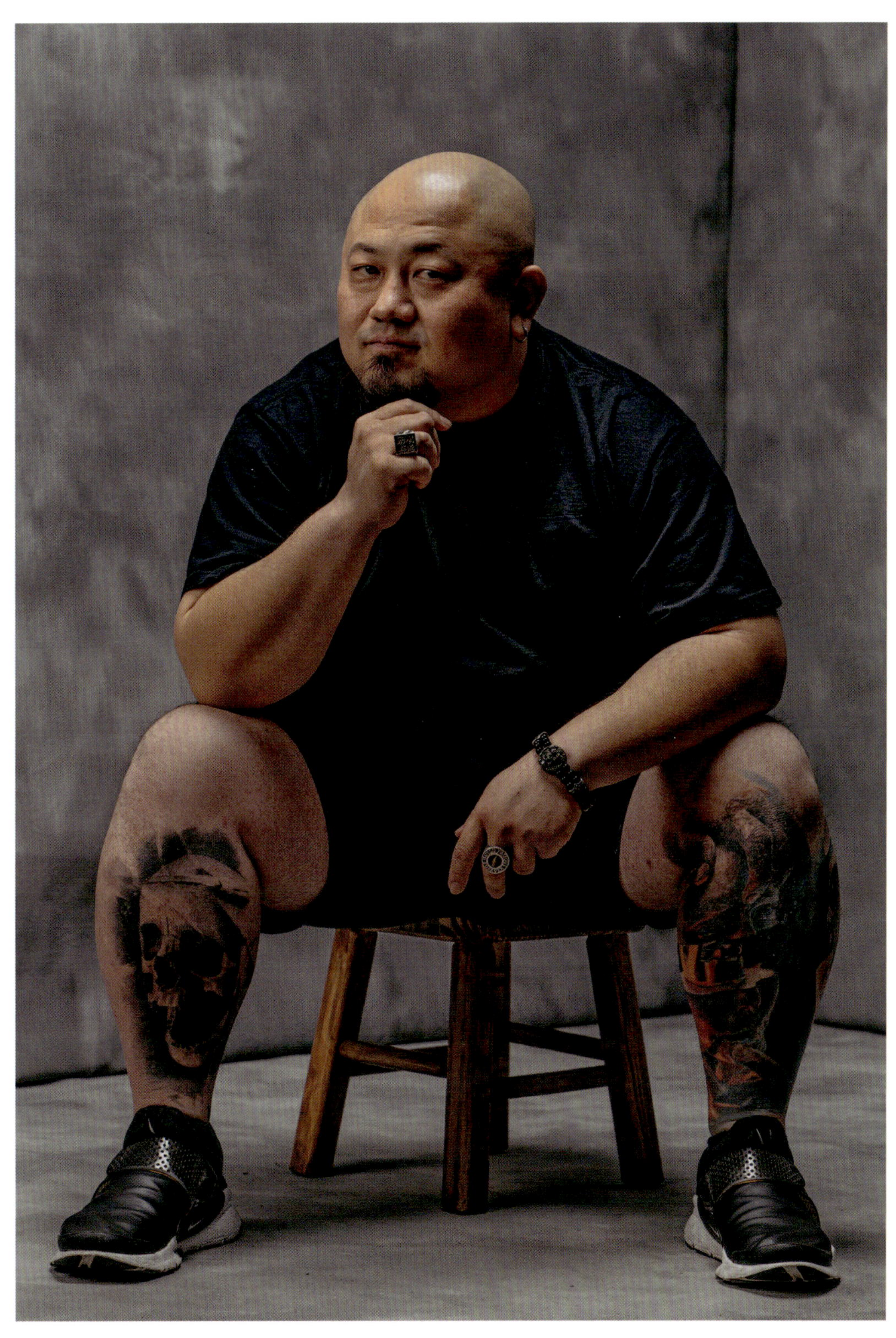

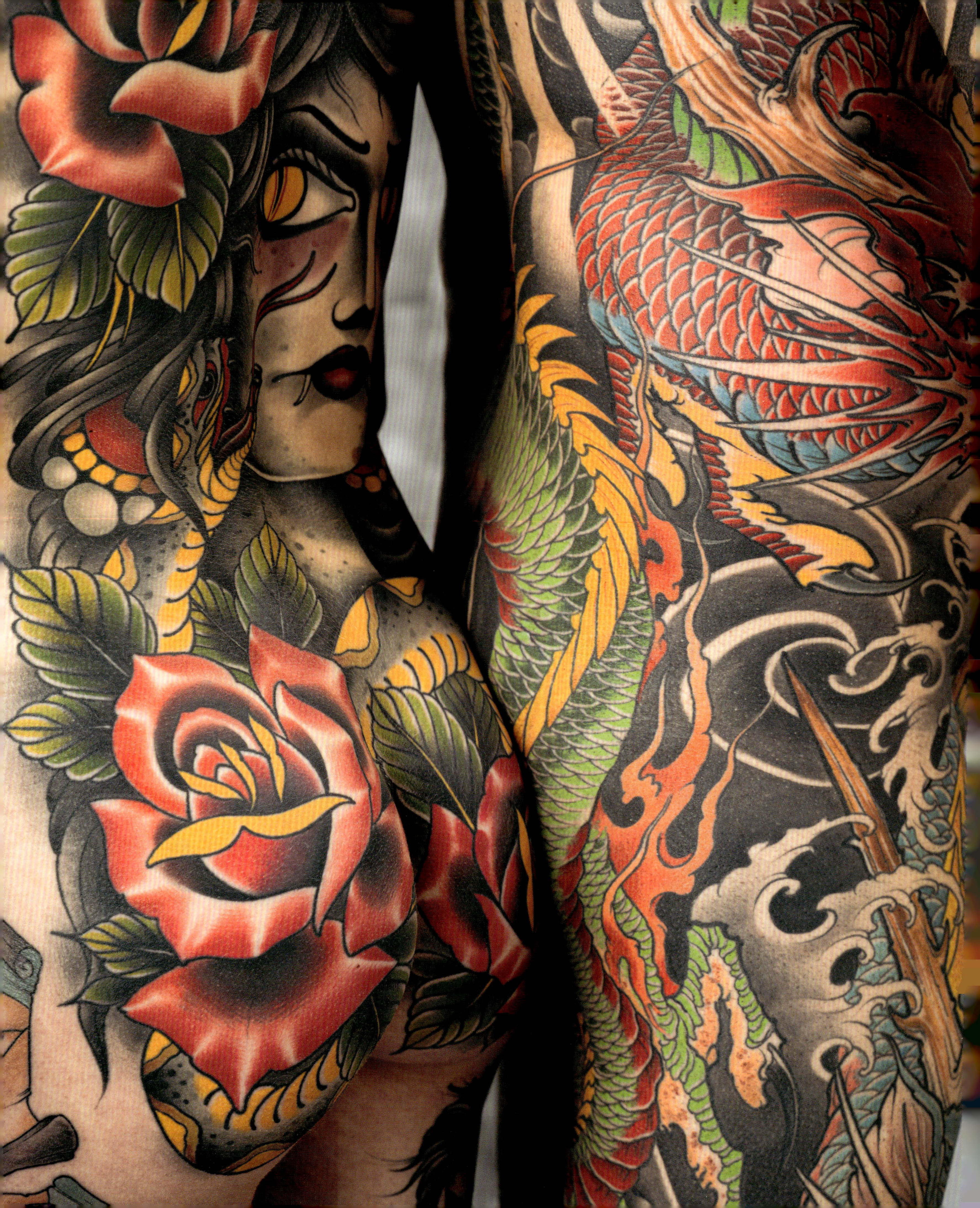

ACKNOWLEDGMENTS

The year 2020 would have marked Ray Bradbury's 100th birthday, and it is in his honor that this book is published. The seed of the idea came from the prologue of his classic short story collection *The Illustrated Man*, originally published in 1951 — followed a decade later by the solo tale, "The Illustrated Woman," published in *Playboy*. Bradbury's prologue describes his real-life encounter with a tattooed man from a carnival in Wisconsin: "'It keeps on going,' he said, guessing my thought. 'All of me is Illustrated. Look.'" With that one enticing gesture, generations of readers have been invited to look, too, and to marvel alongside him; some have even been inspired to render their own bodies as canvases.

This book could not have happened without the enthusiastic support of Bradbury's family: his daughters, Susan Nixon, Ramona Bradbury, Bettina Bradbury, and Alexandra A. Bradbury; and his eight grandchildren, especially Julia Handleman and Claire Handleman. Thanks as well to Michael Congdon, Cristina Concepcion, and Katie Grimm of Don Congdon Associates, Inc. for their help and guidance; Jon Eller, director of the Center for Ray Bradbury Studies, for being there for me 24/7 with his encyclopedic knowledge of all that is Ray Bradbury, along with his colleague Jason Aukerman; and the Bradbury Estate trustee James Sullivan and his colleagues Cheryl J. Carter and Ann L. Crane.

Inked magazine and its owner, Don Hellinger, proved to be invaluable partners in bringing Bradbury's indelible stories into the 21st century with photographs of today's tattoo devotees and artists. The *Inked* team is to be admired and thanked: Creative director Sami Hajar curated the collectors and artists included in this volume, poring through thousands of photographs to help make the selections, and managing editor Anastasia Adamakos conducted dozens of interviews and wrote the book's captions. It was a pleasure to personally work with photographer Peter Roessler, who captured an extraordinary number of subjects in record time with the assistance of Cassie Zhang and Aaron Nardi.

Much gratitude to the collectors and artists who allowed us to capture their passion for the art of tattooing, and to Anna Felicity Friedman for her lively writing and wholehearted embrace of this project. Thanks as well to Rafael Bekor at Lightbox Studios in Los Angeles and collector Dana Brunson, owner of Tattoo Designs by Dana, for graciously allowing us to photograph vintage tattoo relics and memorabilia in Cincinnati, Ohio.

My team has been with me all the way: Amy D. Kolsky and Collin McCarthy helped steer a steady course every step of the way. Henry Sanders hit another home run with his dynamic design. Thanks to Teena Apeles for copyediting, to Lainey Wolfe and Ginny Carroll at North Market Street Graphics for their production assistance, and to Nina Wiener for coming up with the title for the book, among many other ideas.

Last but not least, a big thank-you to Arthur Klebanoff and RosettaBooks for once again showing up, suited up and ready to play. There would be no book without Arthur.

— Lawrence Schiller, 2020

All Ray Bradbury stories reprinted by permission of Ray Bradbury Literary Works, LLC, and Don Congdon Associates, Inc. "The Illustrated Man" copyright © 1950 by Esquire, Inc., renewed 1977 by Ray Bradbury. "The Illustrated Woman" copyright © 1961 by HMH Publishing, renewed 1989 by Ray Bradbury. "Prologue" and "Epilogue" to *The Illustrated Man* copyright © 1951, renewed 1979 by Ray Bradbury.

Introduction and artist biographies copyright © 2020 Anna Felicity Friedman

Collector and artist photographs and compilation copyright © 2020 Wiener Schiller Productions, Inc.

Vintage tattoo photos courtesy Getty Images.

All other images are copyrighted © by their respective owners, who reserve all rights. In case of any inadvertent errors or omissions in credit, please e-mail contact@wsproductionsinc.com.

All rights reserved. No part of this book may be used or reproduced in any form or by any electronic or mechanical means, including information storage and retrieval systems, without permission in writing from the publisher.

For information, please contact RosettaBooks at production@rosettabooks.com, or by mail at 125 Park Avenue, 25th Floor, New York, NY 10017.

A Lawrence Schiller Book

Wiener Schiller Productions, Inc.
Lawrence Schiller, Principal
Henry Sanders, Art Direction & Design
Amy D. Kolsky, Editorial Coordination
Collin McCarthy, Production Coordination

RosettaBooks
Arthur Klebanoff, President & Publisher
Michelle Weyenberg, Marketing

Inked
Don Hellinger, Publisher
Sami Hajar, Curation
Peter Roessler, Photography
Anastasia Adamakos, Captions

First edition published 2020 by RosettaBooks in collaboration with Inked/Quadra Media, LLC, and Wiener Schiller Productions, Inc.

www.RosettaBooks.com

Printed in Italy by Graphicom Srl

Library of Congress Control Number: 2019949389
ISBN: 978-0-7953-5279-9
Artist's edition ISBN: 978-0-7953-5280-5

Pages 2–3: With a dragon backpiece by Tuyen Tran, executive Charles Venancio is proud to be a living reminder not to judge a book by its cover.

Pages 4–5: Sven Pfeiffer wears an *irezumi*-influenced backpiece by Troy Denning depicting the struggle between good and evil.

Pages 230–231: Ronald Vellucci's chest piece, illustrated and tattooed by Matt Jedlinski, represents the circle of life. His throat piece was a collaboration between Giannis "Sake" Karampetsos and Orge Kalodimas.

Pages 238–239: TeeJ Poole designed Brent Frodge's backpiece to represent a mother's love through life and after death using Michelangelo's Pietà statue in St. Peter's Basilica in Vatican City as reference.

Page 268: A variety of styles seamlessly weave together on Angel Mancini's canvas (left) by Devx Ruiz, Angel Reynosa, Matt Pardoners, Joey Ortega, Jadd McElroy, Omar Sanchez, and Lara Scotton. For Joseph Cucurillo (right), "tattoos, as with all the things I collect, reflect my appreciation of an artist's work and my desire to show it off."

Page 271 More than 150 artists have created Yallzee's bodysuit, including Lyle Tuttle, Freddy Negrete, Paul Booth, and Jess Yen.

Page 272 Jon Mesa gave artist Justin Hartman free rein for his backpiece, which was completed in seven sessions.

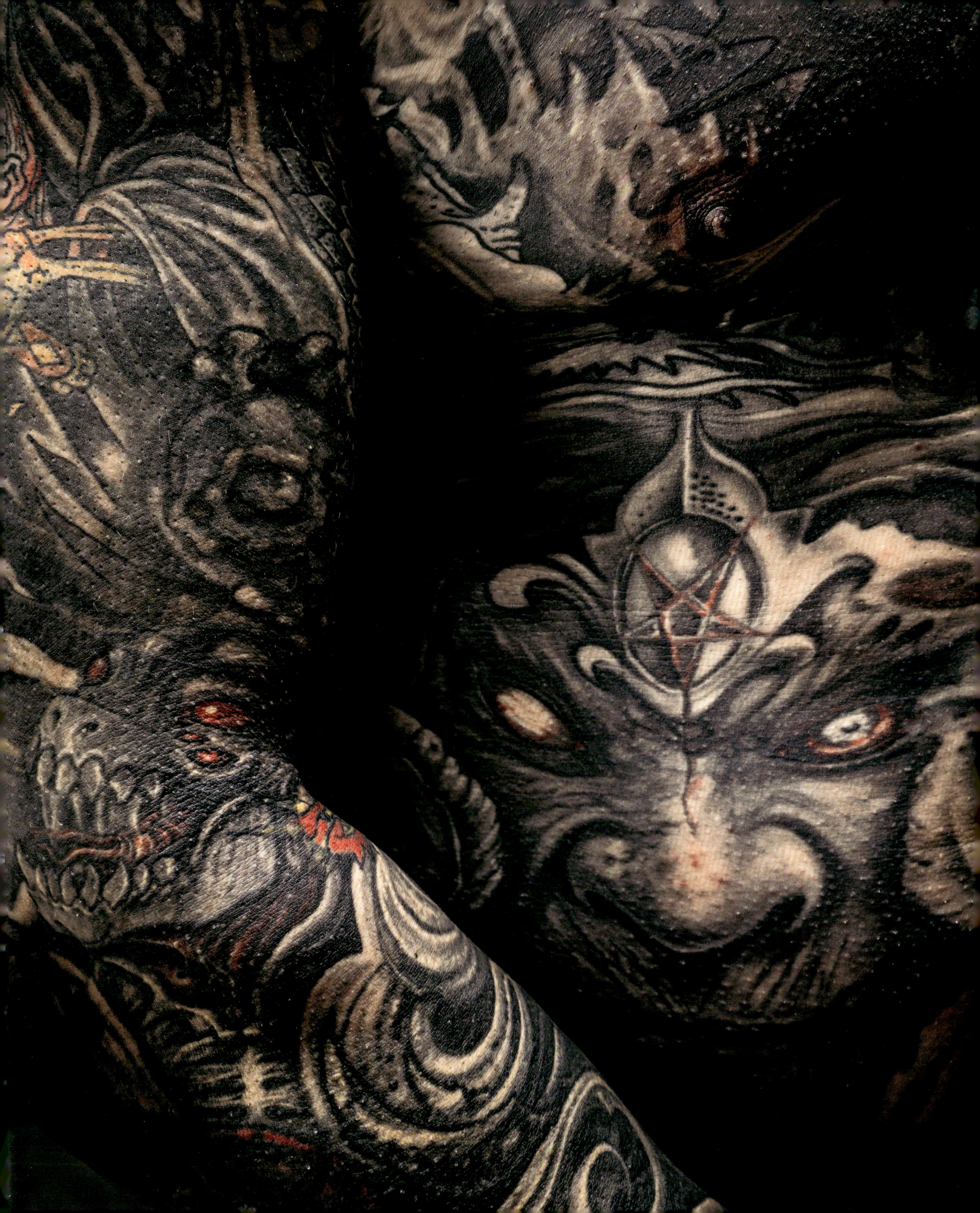

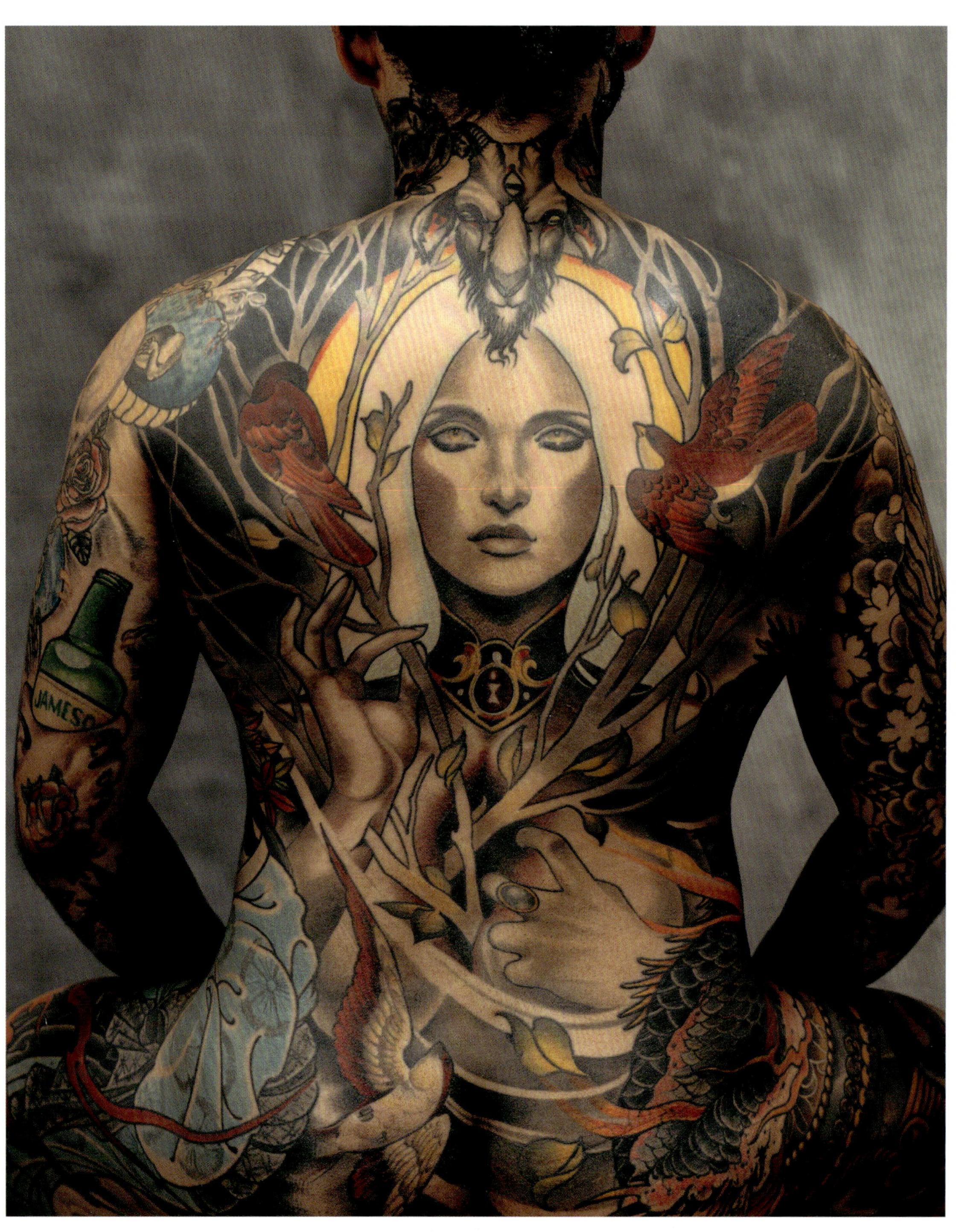
JAMESO